Teaching as an Act of Faith

TEACHING AS AN ACT OF FAITH

Theory and Practice
in Church-Related Higher Education

Edited with an Introduction and Conclusion by
ARLIN C. MIGLIAZZO

Fordham University Press
New York

Library of Congress Cataloging-in-Publication Data

Teaching as an act of faith : theory and practice in church-related higher education / edited with an introduction and conclusion by Arlin C. Migliazzo.
p. cm.
Includes bibliographical references and index.
ISBN 0-8232-2220-9 — ISBN 0-8232-2221-7 (pbk.)
1. Religion and sociology. 2. Sociology, Christian. 3. Teaching—Religious aspects—Christianity. 4. Church and education. I. Migliazzo, Arlin C., 1951– .
BL60.T43 2002
261.5'071'1—dc21   2002008237

Printed in the United States of America
03 04 05 06   5 4 3 2
First Edition

To Dr. Masakazu Iwata (1917–1998),
Christian scholar and gentle man;
my teacher, mentor, colleague, and friend.

CONTENTS

FOREWORD

In this book, Arlin Migliazzo and his several colleagues have collectively advanced the national conversation about the nature and the aims of church-related higher education to new levels of complexity and importance. More impressively still, they have made all of the essays, which consider serially the relationship between the Christian faith and higher learning from the vantage point of fourteen different academic disciplines, equally engaging and informative to all teacher-scholars, Christian and non-Christian alike, regardless of their fields of specialization. This is a rare achievement for an anthology.

Migliazzo's fine introductory essay, "An Odyssey of the Mind and Spirit," exemplifies what it recommends even as it provides both a framework and a model for the rest of the essays that follow it. After a brief personal narrative and a remarkably succinct historical and theoretical review of the dynamic relationship between faith and reason over the centuries, the essay moves directly to considerations of pedagogical practice. On the basis of a deeply informed survey of the hundreds of books that explore the connections and conflicts between Athens and Jerusalem from the ancient world to the present, Migliazzo rightly notes a troublesome absence in that vast literature. He remembers that when he was seeking guidance as a young teacher at a church-related college, he could find no work that provided "access to practical, tested pedagogical strategies for relating faith perspectives to teaching" in the several disciplines of the Academy. I am very glad to be able to assure the readers of *Teaching as an Act of Faith: Theory and Practice in Church-Related Higher Education* that Migliazzo's fourteen coauthors have now splendidly remedied that omission.

The book is very conveniently organized into four parts that coincide with the four major divisions of the Academy—the social sciences, the natural sciences, the fine arts, and the humanities—followed by a concluding essay in which Migliazzo explores the many and various thematic connections among these divisions and the several essays within each one of them. A reader might well begin by reading the essay that represents his or her own disciplinary interest, but it would be a grave mistake to stop there. For optimal learning about the theory and practice of church-related higher education, one must read the entire book. Indeed, this book demonstrates a truth that I have dimly grasped but never really understood until now: in order substantially to improve one's own pedagogy, one must learn from colleagues in several different disciplines, and one must come to understand one's own endeavors as a part of a larger whole whose complexities and diverse practices must constantly inform each of the parts.

Let me now follow the advice of the book and move from theoretical pronouncements to concrete experience. I am an historian by training. Had I only read Shirley Mullen's essay on history and therefore not read Mary Stewart Van Leeuwen's essay, "Scuttling the Schizophrenic Student Mind: On Teaching the Unity of Faith and Learning in Psychology," I would have missed a wonderful summary of the various Christian approaches to understanding the relationship between faith and learning. And had I omitted reading Robert Clark's essay, "Sociology and Faith: Inviting Students into the Conversation," I would not have benefited from an acute analysis of the many challenges—epistemological, economic, institutional, and personal—to the endeavor to integrate faith and learning within the boundaries of *any* discipline.

Had I confined myself to one or two of the essays in my division of the humanities, I would have missed many of the lovely motifs that cut across several of the essays. I would not have noticed and enjoyed, for example, the way in which the Reformed disposition to think in terms of a Christian worldview could work itself out pedagogically in such different disciplines as psychology and mathematics. The essayists typically begin with elaborate formulations of their own understandings of the relationship between Christian conviction and higher learning as those understandings have emerged from the Reformed or the Catholic or the Wesleyan or the Lutheran or the Anabaptist traditions. And they then proceed to show how these various inflections work themselves out in the classroom, in framing questions, designing exams, inventing assignments, and clarifying expectations. A reader who confines herself to one or two essays will miss this wonderfully enlightening medley.

Such a reader will also miss scores of very specific suggestions about how one might strengthen one's own teaching. Had I not read the entire book, I might have missed Charles Wilbur's many techniques for deploying the social teachings of the Catholic Church as a way of securing for his students a critical purchase on the constitutive assumptions of his own discipline of economics. And I might not have learned from the exceptionally fine-grained rhetorical distinctions in Lee Anne Chaney's essay, "A Careful Convergence: Integrating Biology and Faith in the Church-Related College." Chaney is remarkably effective in prompting all teachers to think about which questions and strategies are most appropriate for which students in which courses for what reasons. Her thinking about her various biology courses helped me think through my history courses in new ways.

Paired with George Marsden's *The Outrageous Idea of Christian Scholarship*, *Teaching as an Act of Faith* might be retitled *The Outrageous Idea of Christian Pedagogy*. And in one respect at least, the present book goes some distance toward answering one of the most frequent complaints directed to Marsden by his secular critics. A scholar's Christianity might indeed inform the logic of discovery, the process by which that scholar selects a subject and defines his original perspective on it. However, some complained against Marsden that a scholar's Christian convictions cannot have and should not have any bearing on the logic of justification, the process whereby the scholar defends her conclusions to the larger community of learning. Therefore, so the criticism went, Christianity is peripheral to higher learning after all.

This book answers that criticism by enlarging the academic imagination, by inviting all teacher-scholars, Christian and non-Christian alike, to ponder the ways in which religious and other non-academic commitments might well reshape and reconfigure the contours and the character of academic disciplines as these are most effectively transmitted to students. Harold Heie, for example, in his marvelous essay, "Developing a Christian Perspective on the Nature of Mathematics," does not appeal to Scripture to justify mathematical proofs. Nor does he argue that Christian conviction will lead to new breakthroughs in number theory. He does demonstrate convincingly, however, that Christian thought and practice can lead to fundamental reconceptions of how math is best taught at an introductory level, about the place of mathematics within general education, and about how to rethink basic questions about what every student needs to know about math.

Because *Teaching as an Act of Faith* is so resourceful about teaching, it can serve to open up and enliven conversations between Christian and secular teacher-scholars in a way that few other works about church-related higher education can. All good teacher-scholars care deeply about their teaching, and they are therefore eager to take good counsel and aid wherever they may find it. Precisely because the fourteen scholars who have written the essays in this book are reflecting upon connections between their faith and their own practices as teachers, practices that they for the most part share with their secular colleagues, they are unusually precise and thorough in helping *all* readers think through relationships between pedagogical ends and means, between a particular course or collection of students and the several strategies best pursued to advance learning within those specific contexts, and between a particular course or a particular discipline and the overall shape and purpose of higher learning.

This last set of connections is perhaps the most critical, since the book is finally about wholeness in education, a matter that should be as important to secularists as it is to religious people. It may be that, by virtue of both calling and conviction, Christians are especially concerned to keep the question of wholeness or integrity alive in the context of higher education. In his closing essay, Migliazzo writes about four different levels of integrity or integration as a way of reviewing the several preceding essays in the book. I will note only two senses here. First, as in Elizabeth Morelli's essay on "An Ignatian Approach to Teaching Philosophy," wholeness refers to "educating the whole person," intellectually, morally, and spiritually. But second, as Morelli also notes, "it takes an entire university to educate a student." We must, in other words, work constantly to insure that our colleges and universities really do provide something integral, an education that enables students to see life steadily and whole.

This may be finally the principal contribution that this volume has to make to the world of higher learning, namely, a set of very different glimpses into how we might make the education of the young integral once more. Cardinal Newman famously insisted that the university must provide a genuine circle of learning, arranged such that the various academic disciplines could correct, complete, complement, and comprehend one another. But Newman never explained just *how* this process of integration was to take place. He was quite thorough in his discussion of the aims, the ideals, and the arrangement of the university, but he was vague about the actual practice of integration. *Teaching as an Act of Faith*, being primarily about practice, begins to address this omission in Newman's work. Again and again, we are shown, not told, that the very need to locate one's own teaching of a subject or a discipline within a larger framework of calling, meaning, and commitment *forces* one to integrate, to make connections between one's own discipline and others, and to enable all students to deepen their disciplinary training by locating that education within transcendent horizons whose boundaries no one can fully know or comprehend. This task is finally the act of faith that is our teaching.

Mark R. Schwehn
Christ College
Valparaiso University
February 2002

ACKNOWLEDGMENTS

This book began sometime in the late 1980s as a list of names hastily scratched on a three-by-five card. At that time I had visions of editing a book of essays by Christian historians regarding how they brought their particular faith perspectives to bear in the teaching of history. That idea blurred, faded, and reappeared by the mid 1990s as my reflection on church-related higher education broadened and my teaching practice deepened. A generous grant in 1996 from the Lilly Endowment through the agency of the Lilly Fellows Program in Humanities and the Arts based at Valparaiso University set in motion a chain of events that ultimately made this volume possible. From that three-by-five card to this finished manuscript, through all the false starts and the apparent cul-de-sacs, my family has been a source of constant encouragement. Thank you Judi, Sara, and Nate.

But no matter how much encouragement I received, there would be no manuscript without the exceptional scholar-teachers whose labor with me in this project has proved to be one of the most enlightening and instructive experiences in my professional life. So it is to Charles Wilber, Mary Stewart Van Leeuwen, Ron Kirkemo, Robert Clark, Harold Heie, Lois Kieffaber, Lee Anne Chaney, John Steven Paul, Edward Knippers, Charlotte Kroeker, Elizabeth Morelli, Arlin Meyer, Shirley Mullen, and Mike Ingram that I owe a tremendous debt of gratitude. Their thoughtful essays graphically demonstrate just how profoundly pedagogical practice can be informed by vibrant faith perspectives.

Numerous associates at the institutions I have been privileged to serve as well as friends and supporters scattered across the country have been helpful at various junctures during the gestation, birth, and delivery of this anthology. Lanney Mayer, Kathy Lee, Ron Wells, Dale Soden, Frank Roberts, Joel Carpenter, Martin Bush, Robert Clark, and Albert J. Meyer, all in their own ways prodded, challenged, cajoled, and prompted me to pursue a more thoughtful and more ecumenical vision of the linkages between Christian faith and academic learning. Past and present colleagues from the Lilly Fellows Program in Humanities and the Arts at Valparaiso University and like-minded scholars have played an important role in my still unfolding comprehension of the dynamics of church-related higher education. Richard Hughes, Arne Selbyg, Pamela Jolicoeur, Les Steele, Mary Pat Seurkamp, Arlin Meyer, Mel Piehl, Elizabeth Morelli, Patrick Byrne, Greg Jones, Norval Kneten, Keith Egan, Paul Nisly, John Downey, Robert Wall, Mary Frances Malone, Bill Moncrief, James Peters, Leo Klein, Robert Brimlow, DeAne Lagerquist, Miriam Espinosa, Ron Ballard, F. Thomas Trotter, Mark Schwehn, and Roberta Bondi have contributed to this study through stimulating conversation, bibliographic assistance, and pointed questions.

Associates at Whitworth College, my home institution, have been more than generous with their time and assistance as this manuscript developed over the past five years. Corliss Slack, Dale Soden, Forrest Baird, Keith Wyma, and Alan Stanfield read and critiqued my introduction, and while it is stronger for their helpful comments, they can in no way be held responsible for lapses of logic or inaccuracies that remain. Jim Edwards facilitated my understanding of the Jewish educational program during the classical period, and Roger Mohrlang's expertise in the Greek language proved most helpful in the transliteration of Greek words. Hans Bynagle, director of the Harriet Cheney Cowles Memorial Library, and reference librarians Gail Fielding, Bob Lacerte, and Nancy Bunker greatly expedited my bibliographic research. Darrell Guder first gave me opportunities to explore the wider world of church-related higher education during his tenure as academic dean. His successor, the late Ken Shipps, and current dean, Tammy Reid, have been instrumental in creating possibilities for me to read and reflect more intentionally on the history and culture of Christian higher education. As she has so often, Barbara Brodrick provided invaluable assistance on occasions too numerous to recount here. Suffice it to say that she and Amanda Smith-Probst aided me substantially in a variety of ways with this project.

I also gratefully acknowledge permission from the editors of *Fides et Historia* and *Faculty Dialogue* for allowing me to reproduce sections from essays that appeared first in those journals. I also wish to thank the National Council of the Churches of Christ for permission to reproduce the biblical passages cited herein.

Finally, I wish to extend my appreciation to the Fordham University Press Editorial Board for believing in the significance of this anthology and its potential contribution to the ongoing reassessment of church-related higher education. Executive Editor Dr. Mary Beatrice Schulte, her staff, and associates, including my copyeditor, Sue O'Connor, have been gracious in shepherding the manuscript (and me!) through the complicated editorial process.

INTRODUCTION

An Odyssey of the Mind and Spirit

Arlin C. Migliazzo

THE SMALL, CHURCH-RELATED COLLEGE, perched on a scenic bluff overlooking the Columbia River in north central Oregon, offered me a tenure-track contract even before I defended the dissertation. My graduate professors congratulated me and wished me well in my first full-time faculty position. I recall more than one of them remarking what a coup it was to have a contract in hand before graduation, a throwback, they reminisced, to the heady days of the 1960s. I was just thankful to know a college wanted me—especially in the depressed academic marketplace of the early 1980s.

That first year out of graduate school left little time for reflection. Four preparations per quarter, added to my personal responsibilities as husband and father, kept me scrambling merely to stay one day ahead of my students. I also discovered in late summer that the college faced more serious financial difficulties than I had surmised during my interview. Consequently, even as I met my first-quarter classes, I began the search process all over. Fortunately I crossed the finish line in each course before my students and secured a more promising position at another church-related college in the Pacific Northwest.

Initially, life in my new academic home was only a little less frenetic. But by my third September, questions that had troubled me since that first year of teaching cried out for some redress, and for the first time, I had time and courage enough to face them. Should my teaching be any different at a Christian college than at my own research university or other public institution? If so, how? If not, why not? What impact do my personal faith commitments have upon my understanding of my discipline? Other disciplines? The nature and goals of higher education? My research program? My course projects, reading assignments, lecture topics, extracurricular involvement? As I grappled with these and other persistent questions, I reprised Tertullian's problematic query regarding the relationship between the realm of academic learning represented by Athens and the realm of Christian faith represented by Jerusalem. In so doing, I found myself less certain than he as to the prescriptive relationship between them, for I desired to know and understand that which I did not yet know or understand. And I believed that my quest for knowledge could and should intersect in significant ways with my quest for deeper spiritual insight. I just did not know how. I wandered somewhere between Athens and Jerusalem, but with no map to guide my steps.

As I pondered my course, I began to ask other questions that seem today as naive as they were sincere: What happened? Why does the Athens of secular learning appear so far removed from the Jerusalem of sacred learning? In mulling over these questions, it occurred to me that the distance resulted not from political decrees or institutional shibboleths, but from the competing epistemological bases of Western higher education—Greco-Roman critical rationalism and Jewish theistic authority.[1] Since both claim the path to true knowledge, one has episodically found itself foundering under the hegemonic influence of the other.

THE TWIN EPISTEMIC FOUNDATIONS OF WESTERN HIGHER EDUCATION

Once the Greeks began to question the efficacy of supernaturalism following the seventh century B.C.E., new answers to practi-

---

[1] The term *critical rationalism*, or any of its variants, delineates the acquisition of knowledge and the process of learning preeminently characterized by reliance on human reasoning abilities. Often called *empiricism*, it includes the processing of sense data, the sorting of information logically, and the development of organized systems of thought and action based upon these abilities. By *theistic authority*, I mean the Judeo-Christian epistemological position that accepts, as authoritative and prescriptive, knowledge communicated from God to hu-

cal as well as metaphysical questions had to materialize. And so they did, first with the school of philosophers based in Ionia at Miletus, then with thinkers from the western colonies of Magna Graecia. Generally these intellectuals concerned themselves extensively though not exclusively with cosmological and metaphysical speculation centered in their own rational abilities to make sense of the supposed natural order of the material universe. This deductive approach worked well for Thales (c. 640–c. 546), Anaximander (610–c. 547), Anaximenes (fl.546–525), Pythagoras (c. 550–c. 496), and Xenophanes (c. 570–c. 480), but it became obvious that none of them could agree on what comprised the truly real. The fifth-century standoff between Heraclitus of Ephesus (c. 535–c. 475) and Parmenides of Elea (c. 514–c. 440) typified the muddled state of speculative thinking. The cacophony of voices led to despair that there could be any agreement on absolutes upon which to base human knowledge. The impeccable, but ridiculous logic games of thinkers like Zeno (fl. c. 450) led the jaded Gorgias (c. 480–380) to note sarcastically that nothing exists; that if something did exist no one could know it; and that if one could know it, such knowledge could never be communicated to another. It was of course out of this speculative morass that Socrates (c. 470–399), Plato (427–346), and Aristotle (384–322) emerged, but not before a new band of intellectuals laid the foundations of formal education in the West.

The coterie of itinerant pedagogues known as Sophists emerged in the fifth century determined to set Greek learning on a new epistemological foundation. Seminal figures such as Protagoras of Abdera (c. 490–421), Hippias (fl. c. 450), Prodicus (fl.450–c. 410), and Gorgias came to be called "wise man or teacher *(sophistēs)* for they claimed to teach a kind of wisdom *(sophia)* or *aretē* that was political."[2] They dismissed speculative

---

mans through a host of mediating sources including Scripture, religious teachers, and members of the religious hierarchy. Such knowledge is acquired through educational programs emphasizing correct interpretation of sacred texts and the transmission of the already known to the next generation. Learning is focused preeminently on the mastery of a body of already extant knowledge entrusted by God to humans.

[2] Bruce A. Kimball, *Orators and Philosophers: A History of the Idea of Liberal Education* (New York: Teachers College Press, 1986), 17.

cosmological discussions out of hand and confined their inquiry to the natural world and the human role in it. They believed that through the systematic collection of facts and careful observation, they could posit both practical and theoretical conclusions regarding material reality. Sophists packaged their critical and rationalistic epistemology into distinct courses of study and marketed it to a Greek culture just emerging from the Persian Wars (490–449) and seeking practical but virtuous leadership for the new era.

While some uncertainty exists as to the exact content of the Sophists' curriculum, they carry the distinction of being the progenitors of formal liberal arts education in the West. This is not to imply that the Sophists sallied forth with one voice, educationally speaking, or that they were completely original, for there were private tutors and some formal instruction outside the regular setting of family life before they appeared. But the Sophists did offer the first comprehensive educational program in the West, and they spread it throughout Greece. Their curriculum and the epistemology that drove it became both a model and a foil for subsequent educational philosophies and programs.

The Roman Republic placed a tremendous premium upon the value of an informed and virtuous free citizenry and so adopted in large part the critical rationalism of the Sophists and other more prominent Hellenistic educational thinkers. After the intellectual revolution of the fifth and fourth centuries B.C.E., the Greco-Roman educational program focused primarily upon critical rationalistic inquiry. That the commitment to critical rationalism did not lead all scholars in the same direction is abundantly evident from even a cursory reading of Plato, Aristotle, or the Stoics. Yet the epistemological foundations for the variant philosophical and ethical systems competing for dominance in the Greco-Roman world (excluding the mystery religions) retained an allegiance to critical rationalism.

The Jewish people, however, maintained a different epistemological focus. For Judaism focused upon the Word. The Jewish synagogical tradition emphasized catechetical learning from a supernatural authority.[3] The authority itself remained unquestioned and provided the basis for a clearly articulated metaphysical sense of purpose and place.[4] From their recognition of purpose and place, the Jewish people proceeded to enact rules and regulations governing every aspect of life. So character for them also was an important component of education. The difference was that definitions of character for the Jews emanated not so much from what worked in the world of human affairs as from what God said worked in human affairs. It is no exaggeration to note that Jewish community life was predicated upon what God said community life should look like. Abundant evidence indicates that they did not always follow Yahweh's direction (as in the wilderness wanderings or the disregard of the Sabbatical and Jubilee years), but even so, they at least knew that ultimately they had not wronged each other so much as they had wronged their God. And unlike the rationalistically minded gentiles who surrounded them, they knew because of God's authority over them. It should be noted, however, that though they eschewed critical rationalism as an epistemological foundation for life and thought, successive generations of Jewish scholars increasingly utilized critical rationalism methodologically in the systematization of their faith.

In Palestine by the time of Christ, both Greco-Roman critical rationalism and Judaic theistic authority existed side by side but segregated in the educational programs of the conqueror and

---

[3] I am indebted to Arthur J. De Jong's *Reclaiming a Mission: New Directions for the Church-Related College* (Grand Rapids, Mich.: William B. Eerdmans Publishing Co., 1990) for calling this to my attention. For a more comprehensive discussion of Jewish educational patterns see E. P. Sanders, *Judaism: Practice and Belief, 63 B.C.E.–66 C.E.* (Philadelphia: Trinity Press International, 1992), especially chapter 10; Emil Shürer, "School and Synagogue," in *History of the Jewish People in the Age of Jesus Christ*, new English ed., vol. 2. Rev. and ed. by Geza Vermes, Fergus Millar, and Matthew Black. Literary ed., Pamela Vermes (Edinburgh: T & T Clark, 1979), 415–63; and George Foot Moore, *Judaism in the First Centuries of the Christian Era, The Age of Tannaim*, 3 vols. (Cambridge, Mass.: Harvard University Press, 1970), vol. 1, 29–47 and vol. 2, 3–15.

[4] Alexander Miller has noted that much the same educational outlook held sway in India as early as the sixth century before Christ in *Faith and Learning: Christian Faith and Higher Education in Twentieth Century America* (New York: Association Press, 1960), 35.

the conquered. As long as converts to the new Christian faith came from among Jews steeped in their indigenous cultural supernaturalism, the educational transition they had to make was minimal since Christianity matched Judaism in its unshakable belief in God's authority and mighty works in human history. Christians had just as strong a conviction in God's ability to contravene the laws of nature for divine purposes as did the Jews. Although certain Christian doctrines themselves caused tensions for these early believers, as the text of the Acts of the Apostles clearly documents, the metaphysical assumptions undergirding abstract doctrines and the strategies used to convey them do not seem to have been a cause of concern. The fact that Christian doctrine had a heavy practical component centered on bearing witness to Christ in this world through holy living also connected with the Jewish tradition.

As the Church expanded to include gentiles from the empire, however, educational matters soon joined theological ones as ongoing sources of contention. Owing to the initial outcast status of the Church and its millennial hope in the momentary return of Christ, early sources of irritation had more to do with class or ethnic privilege than the education accompanying such privilege. But by Tertullian's time (c. 160–c. 225 C.E.), it was not at all apparent that an active Christian intellectual life that included extra-biblical knowledge was desirable for the sincere believer. Yet, with Christ's return delayed, Christians had to make their way in the world while not becoming worldly. When Christianity moved from renegade to regnant status, further complications arose. In either situation the dilemmas were palpable, and they signaled the intellectual currents thoughtful Christians have had to navigate for the past twenty centuries.[5]

In the midst of a culture that in one way or another challenged the faith on nearly every front, the grand dilemma remained: how can one live fully as a Christian in an environment inhospitable to such an affirmation? The question was particularly vexing for the Christian intellectual because of the evident disparity between the epistemology used in "knowing the sacred" and

---

[5] H. Richard Niebuhr's classic *Christ and Culture* (New York: Harper & Row, 1951) still speaks effectively to these timeless issues.

that used in "knowing the secular" as well as the obvious imperatives exerted by religious knowledge upon secular knowledge and the interpretation of such knowledge. Christian scholars did their best to appropriate classical learning for the glory of God:

> When Greeks and Romans of education became Christian they used all the resources of those literatures (Greek and Latin) in their own thought and writing. The Greek Fathers in particular adopted more or less consistently the view that ancient philosophy and literature were in a way a foreshadowing of an avenue leading to Christian theology.[6]

Yet, for all the attempts at synergy, there remained for many Christian scholars a recurring hesitancy to claim too clear a connection between sacred and secular learning. Jerome put his classical education to good use as one of the leading patristic writers, but he feared that his admitted love of non-Christian literature would consign him to God's condemnation as a Ciceronian not a Christian. In an attempt to sanctify classical liberal arts learning, leaders in the early Church such as St. Justin Martyr (c. 100–c. 165) took comfort in apocryphal pagan and Jewish stories placing Plato in Egypt, where he supposedly received his philosophical insights directly from Hebrew scriptures or from the Egyptians by way of the Hebrews. St. Augustine (354–430) even cited this myth, though rather more circumspectly.[7] His *Confessions* also demonstrate a healthy ambivalence for aspects of his own classical study.[8] St. Gregory the Great (c. 540–604) refused to subject sacred texts to secular standards of excellence. He went so far as to censure literary-minded bishops for daring to utter the name of Jove. And while Christian parents seem to have had little compunction about sending their children to Roman schools for a classical education taught by non-Christian masters, a continuation of intensive study of pagan literature

---

[6] David Knowles, *The Evolution of Medieval Thought* (New York: Vintage Books, 1964), 66.

[7] Kimball, *Orators and Philosophers*, 40; Arthur F. Holmes, *All Truth is God's Truth* (Grand Rapids, Mich.: William B. Eerdmans Publishing Co., 1977), 14. Jerome apparently turned to monastic life as a way of escaping the temptations of classical studies. See Knowles, *Evolution of Medieval Thought*, 68.

[8] St. Augustine, *The Confessions of St. Augustine* (New York: Penguin Books, 1961; reprint, 1983).

into maturity was officially discouraged.[9] Both St. Benedict and St. Gregory had the benefit of a classical liberal arts education, which they later repudiated.[10]

On the other hand, even for those who disdained classical learning, accommodation occurred without wholesale acceptance. For all his railing against Athens, Tertullian's written corpus drew extensively on his classical legal training in logic and literary studies as well as his knowledge of Stoicism.[11] While St. Benedict's Rule ignores classical learning, nascent monastic culture in general found in the curriculum of the classical liberal arts one of three great sources of its genesis and evolution.[12] Perhaps even more significant was the tacit acceptance of critical rationalist method to ground much of the scholarship and learning of Christian intellectuals.

Clearly, the Christian intellectual community was not of one mind as to the proper relationship between the two epistemologies of learning, much less the fruits proceeding from a classical education. The Jewish people had always chosen theistic authority (albeit liberally infused with the Greco-Roman critical spirit as evidenced by rationalistic legalism). But as Christianity made inroads into the power elites of the Roman Empire, such abrupt fideism became less tenable. Still, Christian intellectuals exhibited more than a little queasiness at accepting the full educational program of the non-Christian classical world. And this ambivalence is precisely the problem that begged for resolution. It was the towering figure of St. Augustine, more than any other Christian thinker, who articulated a coherent melding of the critical rationalism of the classical liberal arts with the theistic authority of Judaism and Christianity. Boethius (c. 480–c. 524),

---

[9] James J. O'Donnell, *Cassiodorus* (Berkeley: University of California Press, 1979), 159; Knowles, *Evolution of Medieval Thought*, 66–67. The *Constitution of the Holy Apostles* explicitly warned Christians against reading non-Christian books. For its text see Kendig Brubaker Cully, *Basic Writings in Christian Education* (Philadelphia: The Westminster Press, 1960), 76–78.

[10] Norman Zacour, *An Introduction to Medieval Institutions* (New York: St. Martin's Press, 1969), 204, 207.

[11] Chester G. Starr, *A History of the Ancient World*, 2d ed. (New York: Oxford University Press, 1977), 618–19.

[12] Jean Leclerq, O.S.B., *The Love of Learning and the Desire for God: A Study of Monastic Culture* (New York: Fordham University Press, 1982; reprint, 1985), 22.

Cassiodorus (c. 484–c. 582), St. Isidore of Seville (570–636), Alcuin (735–804), Rabanus Maurus (c. 776–856), and Smaragdus (fl. c. 800–830) are perhaps some of the most noted Christian scholars in the centuries following the fall of the Western Empire. They labored diligently to actualize Augustine's syncretic vision, but they were not all of one mind, neither were they alone. The lives and work of later Christian thinkers such as St. Peter Damian (1007–1072) Lanfranc of Bec (1010–1089), Berengar of Tours (c.1010–1088), Abelard (1079–1142), St. Bonaventura (1221–1274), St. Thomas Aquinas (1225–1274), John Duns Scotus (1266–1308), and William of Ockham (c.1285–1349) demonstrated that Christian intellectuals early in the second millennium continued to appropriate critical rational method for their theological investigations. It is also apparent that all scholars did not agree on the proper relationship between what came to be called *philosophia saecularis* or *mundialis* (the worldly wisdom of the classical thinkers) and *philosophia spiritualis* or *divina* (Christian wisdom).[13] By the sixteenth century, critical rational inquiry began its inexorable move to epistemological centrality in the intellectual community of the modernizing West, which was clearly evident by the Enlightenment. By the latter nineteenth century in the premier institutions of higher learning, theistic authority might be tolerated, but the dominant ethos was that any truth apprehensible by humans could only by discerned via empirical means. It still might be worthwhile to visit Jerusalem, but for increasing numbers of scholars from the nineteenth century forward, Athens was the place of residence.

Christian educators and institutions were able to adapt to these conditions, at least in part, because of the historical precedent set by two theological traditions.[14] The Thomistic synthesis of Aristotle and Christianity and his conviction that God's hand was everywhere evident in the natural world paved the way for the self-confident optimism of Christian humanists, and by extension Roman Catholic higher education, in the modern period.

---

[13] Leclerq, *Love of Learning*, 100–02; Knowles, *Evolution of Medieval Thought*, 82.

[14] The cost of adaptation for Christian scholars, however, was the severe compartmentalization of knowledge born of faith commitments and knowledge born of professional affiliation.

Thomas Reid and his Scottish colleagues' unshakable belief that all truth was God's truth, and that all the creation demonstrated the fact, established a Christian apologetic that allowed scholars of faith to face the challenge of defending Christianity from the epistemological revolution spurred by the Enlightenment. In both cases, critical rationalism external to Christian orthodoxy was completely acceptable because inquiry based on its premises could only lead us closer to the Creator.

For the times in which they were born, these approaches to reclaim learning for those of faith were entirely valid and performed an incredibly important service for the advancement of Christian higher education. But the late modern era of the twentieth century exposed the weaknesses of both positions. The Thomistic theological apologetic was formulated in an age saturated with Christian faith. Reid's realism emerged when the foundations of faith had already been somewhat shaken but while the ethical and moral norms of Western society were still decidedly Christian. Both, however, were built upon an implicit assumption of the a priori existence of God. When even ethical and moral norms were called into question in the twentieth century, implicit assumptions had to be exposed as the only defense against the relentless attacks of modernists. As these prescriptions were laid bare, theistic authority could not stand up to the test of naturalistic scientific inquiry and was dismissed as epistemologically irrelevant. By the mid-twentieth century, triumphant critical rationalism, now thoroughly objectified via scientific naturalism, obscured if not obliterated the paths between the twin cities of our heritage.

By the end of the second third of the twentieth century church-related institutions faced an apparently insoluble dilemma—hold tightly to Christian presuppositions and suffer increasing intellectual marginality or attempt to find some common ground with the wider modernist academy and seek respectability by downplaying or eliminating any overt reference to theistic authority. There seemed no possible way to remain distinctly Christian and to achieve respect from the increasingly secularized academy at the same time, for modernist assumptions allowed only objective, empirical investigation as a valid epistemology.

By the end of the 1960s a significant number of church-related institutions had set a course toward modernist respectability. In assuaging their sense of academic inferiority and epistemological parochialism, church-related colleges made hiring decisions with more emphasis upon academic credentials than Christian commitment, greatly reduced or eliminated curricular and institutional connections to Christianity, and diluted the faith dimension of mission statements while accenting the hallmarks of the modernist academy—academic excellence, the open-ended search for truth, and the virtue of tolerance in all values and assumptions regarding truth so discovered.[15] Leaders of educational commissions of various church bodies tended to equate the Christian mission of their institutions with generic and culturally innocuous pronouncements shared by the wider academic community. The communication of such mission statements used much of the vocabulary of the modernist academy, while generally keeping implicit and nearly unexpressed any presuppositions rooted in theistic authority.[16] The only problem was that unless administrators, faculty, and students shared these implicit assumptions, the mission statements could often be met just as easily by a conscientious public or private nonreligious institution as one affiliated with a church body.[17]

---

[15] There are many examples of this phenomenon. For an overview of how this looked within Presbyterian colleges see, Bradley J. Longfield and George M. Marsden, "Presbyterian Colleges in the Twentieth Century," pp. 106–23 in George M. Marsden and Bradley J. Longfield, eds., *The Secularization of the Academy* (New York: Oxford University Press, 1992). In the 1970s my own institution muted its Christian mission by noting that the college was committed to the "theme of Jesus Christ." Just what this theme entailed baffled readers of the catalog.

[16] This strategy has resulted in what might be called implicit self-evidentialism. The term refers to the tendency on the part of many serving in church-related institutions to assume that we stand for a Christian distinctiveness by virtue of the fact that we are scholars serving in church-related institutions without any clear articulation of what that distinctiveness is or how it is integrally related to Christian faith or education. In demolishing any sort of objective foundationalism, postmodernists struck directly at the heart of this deep problem in our institutions and, from my perspective, have left us without valid claim to distinctiveness unless we choose to emphasize in explicit and concrete ways the Christian presuppositions animating our colleges and universities.

[17] Dr. F. Thomas Trotter, who began his term of service to the Board of Higher Education and Ministry of the United Methodist Church in 1973, ar-

Even as many church-related institutions severely compro-
mised their Christian distinctiveness in a drive to find legitimacy
in the modernist academy, they found themselves rocked by
postmodernist critiques of critical rationalism and all it had
wrought.[18] Once their lot had been cast with empirical objectivism, church-related colleges and universities found themselves
open to the same charges brought by postmodernism to the
academy in general. At the same time, many in their own midst,
thoroughly imbued with modernist presuppositions (and postmodern relativism when necessary), stridently resisted attempts
to strengthen what tenuous links to founding faith traditions
still existed. Burdened by these twin dilemmas, the reintroduc-
tion of once-abandoned linkages to Christian faith or denominational association at these institutions became next to
impossible.[19] The end result has been the accommodation of

---

gued that the distinctiveness of a United Methodist college or university came
from 1) a celebration of the intellectual love of God, 2) service as a prophetic
critic of society, and 3) an agent of education for those with otherwise limited
access. The 1967 "Land O' Lakes Statement," drafted by Roman Catholic educators and theologians, begins with two full paragraphs explaining the distinctiveness of a Catholic university. Mentioned in the first sentence of the first
paragraph is the "strong commitment to and concern for academic excellence." In the next sentence the necessity of institutional autonomy and academic freedom is noted. Only in the last nine words of the second paragraph
is there any reference to the importance of Roman Catholicism itself to the
distinctiveness of the Catholic university. Even then the only stipulation is that
at a Catholic university "Catholicism is perceptibly present and effectively operative." Just what this phrase entails is never spelled out clearly in the entire
document. See F. Thomas Trotter, "The Ministry of a Church-Related College,"
pp. 113–19, in Robert H. Conn, ed., *Loving God with One's Mind: Selected Writings by F. Thomas Trotter* (Nashville, Tenn.: The Board of Higher Education and
Ministry of the United Methodist Church, 1987), 116–17, and "Land O'Lakes
Statement: The Nature of the Contemporary Catholic University," 7–12, in
Alice Gallin, O.S.U., ed., *American Catholic Higher Education: Essential Documents, 1967–1990* (Notre Dame, Ind.: University of Notre Dame Press, 1992).

[18] For one of the best overviews of this process across various Christian faith
traditions, see Marsden and Longfield, eds., *The Secularization of the Academy.*

[19] I have been intrigued in my study of these phenomena by the observation
noted by many that, in the scramble of church-related colleges to attain some
semblance of respectability in the modernist academy, the first casualty was
deep connectedness to the founding denomination. The second was a more
ecumenical Christian ethos. In the postmodern era, the attempt to recapture
the sense of Christian distinctiveness at church-related institutions begins with
ecumenical dialogue in the hope that such dialogue will aid in reimagining
linkages to founding bodies of faith. Both the Lilly Fellows Program in Hu-

church-related higher education to wider intellectual and cultural norms.

Viewed in the long term, the problematic relationship between the original epistemological ground of Western higher education in critical rationalism and the imperatives of Christian faith centered in theistic authority has led us to this postmodern divide through nearly twenty-five hundred years of history. Betrayed by both on too many fronts, yet simultaneously obliged to them, those of us privileged to serve at church-related institutions wander, trying to find our way through.

In Search of Paths Between

As I began to understand how the life of the mind and the life of the spirit had become so antithetical to each other, I recognized the origin of my own epistemological ambivalence. That recognition allowed me to take my first steps forward. The journey became tremendously important to me, and yet I did not see my college discussing the concerns generated by it—at least not in my presence. The administration spoke of our commitment to Christianity and our relationship with the Presbyterian Church (U.S.A.) remained rock solid. Our campus had an active chapter of Amnesty International, weekly chapel, and regularly sponsored programs advocating justice and equity for oppressed populations at home and abroad. Still, it struck me that much of the business we were about, whether in the classroom or the student union, appeared ominously disconnected from the things we said we believed about sin, salvation, grace, humility, mercy, and service. As assistant professors are prone to do, I assumed my colleagues had long ago worked out appropriate linkages to these issues and were busily addressing them in their courses and research. I thought perhaps everyone else knew the connections and how they worked, and they were just waiting for me to stumble upon them so they might congratulate me for my ingenuity, as if I had passed some cabalistic initiation rite.

---

manities and the Arts and the Rhodes Consultation on the Future of the Church-Related College are prime examples of this latter tendency.

With such an elaborate theory to make sense of my experience, I demurred in speaking to other faculty members about such matters, fearful of appearing a simpleminded charlatan masquerading as a respectable up-and-coming academic. But gradually I realized that no conspiracy of silence existed. No grand discussion of these questions and the answers they engendered occurred between tenured professors and high-ranking administrators behind doors closed to me. This was no test of my mental or spiritual acumen. There was merely the assumption that the associations were obvious and understood. But I also discovered that most of my colleagues wandered about every bit as perplexed in their personal understanding of the relationship between the imperatives of faith and the commitment to academic learning as I did.

Once I grasped our collective ignorance on these matters, I knew that any links to be found between faith and learning would have to be forged in good postmodern fashion by me. This revelation came as something of an epiphany. I rejoiced that I was free to explore my own sense of the connections between my faith and my professional life. I did not to have to fit someone else's conception of a Christian professor—only my own. At the same time, I experienced a healthy dose of discouragement, for I found few guideposts and fewer travel guides. If there existed a route (or routes) to join my Greco-Roman intellectual curiosity to my life of faith centered in the Jerusalem event, it would be found after countless errant steps and false starts. And while I remained concerned about the philosophical and theoretical implications of the questions I asked of myself, my most pressing dilemmas had to do with what I taught and why I taught it the way I did. Dissatisfaction with my initial efforts in the classroom pushed me toward those relatively few Christian scholars who charted a course where I could find no path. Many of their insights, now as then, challenge my own search, stimulate my thinking, and crystallize my convictions.

As I reviewed the literature on church-related higher education,[20] it coalesced into three general categories that have re-

---

[20] In the following notes, it is my intent to acquaint the reader with a few of the more prominent recent studies in each category. For a more extensive listing of relevant sources, see the bibliography at end of the book.

mained relatively constant.[21] Sustained theoretical and philosophical inquiry surrounding Christian approaches to learning comprised the first category. Such studies can be either highly critical of or passionately committed to a Christian approach to higher education. In either case they serve to increase dialogue on pertinent strategic concerns and thereby advance the cause of church-related higher education in any of a number of its variant forms. Most often, studies in this vein are both critical and committed at the same time. Theoretical and philosophical inquiry has an extensive and ongoing bibliography in the recent past.[22] A second growing area of scholarly interest has

---

[21] It could be argued that a fourth line of inquiry exploring the nature and course of faith-based intellectual inquiry has also been opened. The Roman Catholic scholar Monsignor John Tracy Ellis might be seen as its progenitor, with more recent contributions made by other Christian scholars. This type of literature does not center on church-related higher education itself, although the significance of college and university educators is readily apparent. See John Tracy Ellis, *American Catholics and the Intellectual Life* (Chicago: The Heritage Foundation, Inc., 1956); Mark Noll, *The Scandal of the Evangelical Mind* (Grand Rapids, Mich.: William B. Eerdmans Publishing Co., 1994); George M. Marsden, *The Outrageous Idea of Christian Scholarship* (New York: Oxford University Press, 1997); James C. Turner, "Something To Be Reckoned With: The Evangelical Mind Awakens," *Commonweal* (January 15, 1999): 11–13; Anthony J. Diekema, *Academic Freedom and Christian Scholarship* (Grand Rapids, Mich.: William B. Eerdmans Publishing Co., 2000); Robert Sweetman, "Christian Scholarship: Two Reformed Perspectives," *Perspectives: A Journal of Reformed Thought* 16, no. 6 (June/July 2001): 14–19; Richard T. Hughes, *How Christian Faith Can Sustain the Life of the Mind* (Grand Rapids, Mich.: William B. Eerdmans Publishing Co., 2001); Andrea Sterk, ed., *Religion, Scholarship, and Higher Education: Perspectives, Models, and Future Prospects* (Notre Dame, Ind.: University of Notre Dame Press, 2002); and the theme issue "Christian Scholarship in the Twenty-First Century: Prospects and Projects," *Christian Scholar's Review* 30, no. 4 (summer 2001).

[22] Prime Roman Catholic contributors include Mary C. Boys, *Educating in Faith: Maps and Visions* (Kansas City, Mo.: Sheed & Ward, 1989); Bernard Lonergan, *Topics in Education: The Cincinnati Lectures of 1959 on the Philosophy of Education*, vol 10 in Robert M. Doran and Frederick E. Crowe, eds., *Collected Works of Bernard Lonergan* (Toronto: University of Toronto Press, 1993); Theodore M. Hesburgh, C.S.C., ed., *The Challenge and Promise of a Catholic University* (Notre Dame, Ind.: University of Notre Dame Press, 1994); Alice Gallin, O.S.U., ed., *American Catholic Higher Education, Essential Documents, 1967–1990* (Notre Dame, Ind.: University of Notre Dame Press, 1992). Recent Protestant volumes include Arthur F. Holmes, *The Idea of a Christian College*, rev. ed. (Grand Rapids, Mich.: William B. Eerdmans Publishing Co., 1987) and *Shaping Character: Moral Education in the Christian College* (Grand Rapids, Mich.: William B. Eerdmans Publishing Co., 1991); Harold Heie and David L. Wolfe, eds., *The Reality of*

been in the history of church-related higher education. Included under this rubric are specific institutional histories, general histories of the role of Christianity in the development of higher education, histories of particular church contributions to higher education, and the impact of culture upon church-related higher education. Usually this research is monographic in nature, but some excellent anthologies have also been produced.[23] A third fruitful line of recent inquiry has been the topical or case study. Often topical or case studies utilize a comparative approach. They can take a number of variant forms, but generally all offer some kind of analytic diagnosis of church-related higher education and conclude with a prognosis for the future. Volumes range from specific denominational studies to trans-denominational prescriptions. Also in this category are anthologies that concentrate on one institution or one issue of concern. They may

---

Christian Learning (Grand Rapids, Mich.: Christian University Press and William B. Eerdmans Publishing Co., 1987) and *Slogans or Distinctives: Reforming Christian Higher Education* (Lanham, Md.: University Press of America, 1993); Nicholas Wolterstorff, *Reason Within the Bounds of Religion* (Grand Rapids, Mich.: William B. Eerdmans Publishing Co., 1984); Mark Schwehn, *Exiles from Eden: Religion and the Academic Vocation in America* (New York: Oxford University Press, 1993); Stanley Hauerwas and John H. Westerhoff, eds., *Schooling Christians: "Holy Experiments" in American Education* (Grand Rapids, Mich.: William B. Eerdmans Publishing Co., 1992). See also the multiple volumes published by HarperCollins on various disciplines and the Christian faith in the *Through the Eyes of Faith* series.

[23] Major recent contributors to this genre include Joel A. Carpenter and Kenneth W. Shipps, eds., *Making Higher Education Christian: The History and Mission of Evangelical Colleges in America* (Grand Rapids, Mich.; Christian University Press and William B. Eerdmans Publishing Co., 1987); Philip Gleason, *Contending with Modernity: Catholic Higher Education in the Twentieth Century* (New York: Oxford University Press, 1995); George M. Marsden and Bradley J. Longfield, eds., *The Secularization of the Academy* (New York: Oxford University Press, 1992); George Marsden, *The Soul of the American University: From Protestant Establishment to Established Nonbelief* (New York: Oxford University Press, 1994); David J. O'Brien, *From the Heart of the American Church: Catholic Higher Education and American Culture* (Maryknoll, N.Y.: Orbis Books, 1994); Richard W. Solberg, *Lutheran Higher Education in North America* (Minneapolis: Augsburg Publishing House, 1985); William C. Ringenberg, *The Christian College: A History of Protestant Higher Education in America* (Grand Rapids, Mich.: Christian University Press and William B. Eerdmans Publishing Co., 1984); Douglas Sloan, *Faith and Knowledge: Mainline Protestantism and American Higher Education* (Louisville, Ky.: Westminster John Knox Press, 1994). The number of journal articles and institutional studies of individual colleges and universities is vast.

center on a particular denomination's explorations in higher education. They might also focus on how institutions in different Christian traditions do higher education. While topical and case studies have appeared periodically in the literature over the course of the past forty years, the current enthusiasm for this model of inquiry is reflected not only in a host of recent volumes but also in numerous ongoing national ecumenical dialogues on church-related higher education.[24] I have no doubt that my tripartite classification minimizes the considerable overlap between works in different categories. Nevertheless, it does reflect relatively fixed patterns of research in church-related higher education as I found them.

The more I read in the literature, the more encouraged I became that other scholars had given the questions with which I wrestled serious thought. However, the most urgent need in my own professional life at that point in my young career—access to practical, tested pedagogical strategies for relating faith perspectives to teaching in my discipline by recognized scholar-teachers—was absent from the literature.[25] Even today, nearly fifteen years after my search began, there exists no text dedicated to practical pedagogy that might serve as a resource for

---

[24] For a sense of the wide variety subsumed under this topical/case-study rubric see J. Patrick Murphy, C.M., *Visions and Values in Catholic Higher Education* (Kansas City, Mo.: Sheed & Ward, 1991); John P. Langan, S.J., *Catholic Universities in Church and Society: A Dialogue on* Ex Corde Ecclesiae (Washington, D.C.: Georgetown University Press, 1993); Richard T. Hughes and William B. Adrian, eds., *Models for Christian Higher Education: Strategies for Success in the Twenty-First Century* (Grand Rapids, Mich.: William B. Eerdmans Publishing Co., 1997); James Tunstead Burtchaell, C.S.C., *The Dying of the Light: The Disengagement of Colleges and Universities from Their Christian Churches* (Grand Rapids, Mich.: William B. Eerdmans Publishing Co., 1998); Merrimon Cuninggim, *Uneasy Partners: The College and the Church* (Nashville: Abingdon Press, 1994); Robert Benne, *Quality with Soul: How Six Premier Colleges and Universities Keep Faith with Their Religious Traditions* (Grand Rapids, Mich.: William B. Eerdmans Publishing Co., 2001). The Lilly Fellows Program in Humanities and the Arts and the Rhodes Consultation on the Future of Church-Related Colleges are but two of the numerous ecumenical dialogues currently in progress around the country.

[25] I might also add that at the numerous conferences I have attended, whether sponsored by the Presbyterian Church (U.S.A.), the Rhodes Consultation, the Council for Christian Colleges and Universities, the Lilly Fellows Program, or other such ecumenical gatherings, little if any time is spent upon practical pedagogical concerns.

faculty members taking up residence in a church-related college or university.[26]

From Theory to Practice

This present volume is offered as an initial foray into the neglected realm of teaching strategies for church-related higher education.[27] The plural, strategies, is intentional. Just as there can be no monolithic Christian view of education or economics or history or biology, it is impossible to speak of *"the* Christian strategy" of teaching these disciplines or others that are the just domain of higher education. There are instead Christian views and Christian strategies. Such pluralism energizes the enterprise of higher education because it is rooted in who we are as people of faith, with our heritage in the past and our vocation in the present age.

At least three strands contribute to Christian pluralism on these issues. First, the specific faith tradition of which we as individual scholars are a part provides the theological backdrop for the kinds of questions we ask and the context of the answers we find. And even if Wesleyan, Pentecostal/Holiness, Roman Catholic, Orthodox, Reformed, Episcopalian, Anabaptist, and Lutheran communicants ask similar questions, the answers they find will most likely be informed, at least in part, by the particular theological perspectives of their given tradition. The faith tradition serves as the matrix through which the personal faith experience of the individual might be interpreted. The second factor, personal faith experience, is a powerful interpreter in its

---

[26] As this volume goes to press, it should be noted that two very recent contributions to the literature on religiously based scholarly inquiry each contain a section on pedagogy. While theory still tends to predominate even in these studies, there are some instructive teaching strategies included. See Hughes, *How Christian Faith Can Sustain the Life of the Mind,* pp. 97–133, and Sterk, *Religion, Scholarship, and Higher Education,* pp. 161–229.

[27] This is not to imply that Christian faith assumptions are the only ones with pedagogical implications. Interfaith dialogue and scholarly writing on teaching and learning from religious traditions other than Christianity would be both fruitful and enlightening. For the sake of internal coherence, however, this book confines its inquiry to five of the major Christian traditions.

own right. Finally, the faith tradition of the institution at which one teaches can be a third influence upon one's sense of the interplay between faith and the scholarship of teaching and learning.

The accomplished teaching scholars who have contributed their expertise to this study will serve as guides, exploring potential pathways between Athens and Jerusalem for the reader. Each of them provides a map of sorts that can be of use to the reader regardless of Christian faith tradition or disciplinary expertise. Such is the beauty of a volume committed to pedagogical strategies—teaching methods, unlike theoretical or philosophical discourse, are unbound by theological or disciplinary walls. They can be adapted to suit the unique theological and disciplinary inclinations of the reader who desires to tread a path between the cities of our heritage. The strategies are also transferable with a minimum of effort to fit the particular institutional context of any church-related college or university. The essayists themselves mirror the breadth of God's large kingdom and reflect the vitality of Christian pedagogical pluralism.[28] The essays they have written for inclusion in this anthology are meant to be instructive, not definitive, of the particular faith tradition and discipline of each author. Representing fourteen of the most common disciplines taught in contemporary U.S. colleges and universities, these scholar-teachers have spent years honing their theological understanding and their teaching strategies at a wide variety of church-related colleges and universities.[29] The result has been their construction of seminal pathways between mind and spirit, teaching and faith, Athens and Jerusalem.

---

[28] It could be argued that this anthology provides only a limited Christian pluralism on the topic of pedagogy since no contributor or institution represents an Orthodox, Episcopalian, or Pentecostal perspective, for example. Neither are all academic disciplines included. While these are valid observations, the fact that this is an initial foray into an otherwise neglected field does not preclude the possibility of future studies highlighting different traditions and disciplines. Space constraints in this present work made further expansion both unwieldy and imprudent.

[29] Institutions represented by the contributors include those of Anabaptist, Lutheran, Reformed, Roman Catholic, and Wesleyan heritage. The contributors themselves teach and write out of these five traditions.

What these authors share is eminently practical, for this anthology is only secondarily about theoretical concerns. While it is true that method without theory is aimless, theory without practice is pointless. Theoretical discourse on church-related higher education, as instructive as it has been, has overshadowed its practical pedagogical implications in the literature. As a corrective to this oversight, readers will find here example after example of classroom-tested strategies the authors have found of particular merit in addressing the convergence between faith and the teaching of their courses. It will be apparent to the reader that although theoretical considerations play a supporting role in these essays, each author's practical teaching strategies proceed from thoughtfully consistent philosophical and theological presuppositions that provide the context from which the strategies emerge.[30]

What each author shares is also personal, passionate, and idiosyncratic—which of course is why they are considered masters in the art of teaching. Too often what little personal signature our writing (or thinking) had before we entered graduate school quickly evaporated altogether in some first-year seminar in our quest to become objective scholars under the watchful eyes of our mentors. Unfortunately, we caught the disease all too easily and continue to subject each other too often to blandly sterile professional scholarship. But in teaching—real, life-changing teaching—there is passion, there is engagement, there is relationship. The reader will find all of these characteristics of vital teaching in the essays that follow. The essayists do not stand apart from their subject. They connect deeply to it. As Parker Palmer reminds us,

> good teachers possess a capacity for connectedness. They are able to weave a complex web of connections among themselves, their subjects, and their students so that students can learn to weave a world for themselves. . . . The connections made by good teachers are held not in their methods but in their hearts—meaning *heart*

---

[30] For further reading on philosophical and theoretical bases for church-related higher education, see the bibliography at the end of each essay and at the end of the book.

in its ancient sense, as the place where intellect and emotion and spirit and will converge in the human self.[31]

Because the contributors to this anthology do not stand apart from but speak with integrity from within their experiences in the classroom, readers will be drawn to reimagine their own teaching in light of their personal disclosures. That is the power of teaching and of the strategies included in each essay. The personal is most powerful when it is shared with other practitioners so that they might touch it, taste it, and mold it to make it their own. At the same time, it must be noted that everything advocated here will not sit well with all readers. There are, unfortunately, limits to any attempt at ecumenicity. But this also is as it should be. For out of the midst of cognitive or theological dissonance may proceed new insight and pedagogical vitality gleaned from essays on disciplines far afield from one's own and from scholars with quite different theological assumptions.[32]

For example, the sacramental and activist nature of Roman

---

[31] Parker J. Palmer, *The Courage to Teach: Exploring the Inner Landscape of a Teacher's Life* (San Francisco: Jossey-Bass Inc., Publishers, 1998), 11.

[32] Some professors at church-related colleges and universities are more than chary of the type of direct linkage of Christian faith assumptions to the liberal arts disciplines apparent in the essays of this anthology. They contend that such connections detract from the supposed objectivity of the discipline—a cherished goal of the modernist academy. It is my firm conviction that this objection is rooting the schizophrenic nature of our own graduate training. Aside from those among us who are creative artists (whose graduate experience was replete with its own set of standards), most of us were continuously reminded of the goal of objectivity in our work. While postmodern critiques of objectivity have theoretically rendered the notion passé, dispassionate investigative empiricism still reigns regardless. We do know, however, that those who profess objectivity are often the least objective teachers and scholars. The late Carl Sagan's now infamous introduction to his phenomenally popular PBS series *Cosmos* is just one of the more flagrant examples of faith assumptions masquerading as empirical inquiry. The pedagogical methods we use may be value neutral, but the content and presuppositions underlying the application of those techniques are anything but objective. The most dangerous scholars are not those who examine values and encourage exploration of them with sensitivity and compassion in the classroom but those who use the concept of objectivity to propound their own philosophical or religious ideals surreptitiously—sneaking them in as it were under the guise of disinterested scholarly pursuits. We must overcome our misdirected preoccupation with objectivity, recognize the limitations of our pursuit of it, and accept the real place of faith and values issues in our classrooms and beyond them.

Catholic theology means that the thoughtful essays of Wilber and Morelli may initially speak more forcefully to Roman Catholic readers of the volume because of the readers' resonance with that approach to the life of faith and to higher education than perhaps the essays of Mennonite Kroeker or Calvinist Van Leeuwen. At the same time, certain Protestant readers looking primarily for affirmations of evangelical Protestant presuppositions might just as easily take issue with these latter essays. I am confident, however, that inquisitive readers will be motivated to adapt strategies to fit their own pedagogical needs from essays outside their particular theological heritage and even outside their discipline.

A Lutheran professor of rhetoric may balk at Southern Baptist Ingram's use of Scripture in the ethics course, but his strategy of dealing with ethical dilemmas in the field might spark that colleague to develop a unit on an ethic of communication centered in the great theological affirmations of the Luther's *Short Catechism.* By the same token, Professor Chaney's creative use of cartoons in her biology or scientific traditions courses to illustrate personal values, beliefs, and worldviews could be imported with just a modicum of effort by a Roman Catholic professor of medieval literature using period art.

This anthology is offered in just such a spirit of discovery. The reader will be invited to consider a wide variety of teaching strategies from disciplines as varied as physics, psychology, music, English, biology, and communications, and from five of the great theological traditions of historic Christianity. The intent is to demonstrate the myriad of possibilities available to inquiring practitioners interested in relating their faith to the teaching of their discipline in the classroom. Regardless of the theological or disciplinary proclivities of readers, they will find like-minded teachers here sharing from the breadth of their experience with the hope that together we might more effectively serve the colleges and universities of the church. Readers can take inspiration from the integrative strategies employed by these teacher-scholars, for methodology, like passion, is boundless, allowing fluid translation from one discipline to another as well as from one faith tradition to another.

More than a decade has passed since my first halting efforts at theological and professional synergy. The years since my initial explorations into faith and learning issues have brought some classroom successes and more than a few failures, plenty of errant steps and more false starts than I care to recall. I am thankful for the small triumphs and for the realization that paths exist, even if I personally have not yet made the complete journey between Athens and Jerusalem. At present I find myself exploring the in-between places—constructing my own path, if you will, to join the twin cities of my heritage, which at this point in my life is right where I need to be. Because of my belief that the stimulating effects of our individual efforts only grow more vital as we pool our wisdom, the essays that follow are offered not as *the* path between the cities of our destiny but rather as guideposts to encourage those who find themselves beholden to the legacies of both Athens and Jerusalem to step out and find their own way between them.

Part One
The Social Sciences

1

Teaching Economics While Keeping the Faith

Charles K. Wilber

I HAVE SPENT the past thirty-five years as a professor of economics. Over the course of my tenure at American University, in Washington, D.C. (1965–75) and the University of Notre Dame (1975–present), however, I became ever more disenchanted with the capacity of traditional economic theory to enable people to lead a good life. I found myself unable to accept the values embedded in economic theory, particularly the elevation of self-interest, the neglect of income distribution, and the attempts to export these values into studies of the family, the role of the state, and so on. Christian thought and biblical tradition make self-interest a central aspect of *fallen* human nature, which as believers we are bound to strive to counter with prayer, good works, and the cultivation of virtue. As a result, I started researching and writing on the nature of economics and the role of ethics in economic theory.

This work has led me to two important conclusions. First is the conviction that economic theory is not value-free as is so often claimed. Rather, it presupposes a set of value judgments upon which economic analysis is erected. Second is the realization that the economy itself requires that the self-interest of economic actors be morally constrained. My current research attempts to explore the role that ethics actually plays and should play in economic analysis and policy. My teaching has tried to make use of these insights.

Since economic theory is based on a set of assumptions that are problematic for Christians, this provides an opening for the teacher to encourage students to examine critically the dominant economic policies in the United States today from an avowedly Christian standpoint. Economists assume that people act out of self-interest and that this motivation enables us to predict the outcome of policies such as tax increases. Economists further assume that it is self-evidently good that people get what they want. I structure both my Introduction to Economics and Economics, Ethics, and Public Policy classes to get students to discuss this set of assumptions in light of what is demanded of us by the Gospel. The following essay will emphasize the topics in these two courses that are closely connected to issues of faith.

ECONOMISTS, VALUE JUDGMENTS, AND ECONOMIC THEORY

The first section of both courses deals with the role of values in economics. Many economists argue that while values might have a place in what is termed normative economics, they should be kept out of the everyday scientific business of the profession—the development and testing of falsifiable propositions, which is often referred to as positive economics. This separation, however, is problematic. Economists, as persons, necessarily work from a viewpoint that structures the questions asked and the methods, evidence, and answers deemed acceptable. If there is no objective access to the real world, an economist is forced to see that world through the lens of theory. Does that mean "facts" are theory laden? And value laden? What would this mean for economic theory? Ultimately, the question becomes "How does one do economics in a world where facts and values cannot be conveniently disentangled?"

In looking for an answer to this question, economics students find to their surprise that they have much to learn from Adam Smith. My lecture and the readings show that Smith's economic theory was closely related to his moral thought. For example, while Smith often used the metaphor of the watch in describing how the self-interested actions of individuals worked for the good of the whole, he saw the machine itself as the product of a beneficent God, which moreover depended on the virtues of individual actors to operate smoothly. Smith's *Theory of Moral*

Sentiments,[1] written before *The Wealth of Nations*,[2] offers a rich moral vision of society that contrasts with the thin gruel of "rational economic man." Smith argued that over the course of history, society advanced through successive stages, each requiring more advanced values than the previous stage. Smith became less sanguine about moral progress over the course of his life, but moral standards continued to play a crucial role in his work.

I point out to the class that since the work of Thomas Kuhn and other historians of science, it has been increasingly recognized that scientists cannot be neutral in matters of value. In an article I co-authored with Roland Hoksbergen,[3] we survey what others have had to say about value neutrality in economics, showing that there has been a lively debate on the subject in the years since 1970. One group argues that economists can successfully separate values from facts, which are perceived as "out there" in the world, by adhering to a positivist methodology. According to this group, a failure to maintain this distinction will lead to a disastrous slide into relativism. Critics of value neutrality, on the other hand, marshal a wide variety of arguments to make their case. It is argued, for example, that there is no access to objective reality except through the lens of a theory, and therefore, values shared by the community of economists color their judgment in determining just what the relevant "facts" are.

Hoksbergen and I come down on this side of the issue in the final part of our paper, in which we argue that neoclassical economists share a worldview—a notion of the good—that shapes their analysis of the economy. This worldview includes three main elements: (1) people are rational and self-interested; (2) the purpose of life is to pursue happiness as people define it; and,

---

[1] Adam Smith, *The Theory of Moral Sentiments* (1759), ed. by D. D. Raphael and A. L. Macfie. In vol. 1 of *The Glasgow Edition of the Works and Correspondence of Adam Smith*, general editors D. D. Raphael and Andrew Skinner (Oxford: Clarendon Press, 1976).

[2] Adam Smith, *An Inquiry into the Nature and Causes of the Wealth of Nations* (1776), ed. in two vols. by W. B. Todd. In vol. 2 of *The Glasgow Edition of the Works and Correspondence of Adam Smith*, general editors D. D. Raphael and Andrew Skinner (Oxford: Clarendon Press, 1976).

[3] Charles K. Wilber and Roland Hoksbergen, "Ethical Values and Economic Theory: A Survey," *Religious Studies Review* 12:314 (July/October 1986): 205–14.

(3) the ideal world is one in which people are free to compete to achieve their ends and in which market forces lead to optimal equilibrium outcomes. This is certainly a set of value judgments, in need of justification like any other; if these judgments indeed correctly characterize economics, they should be openly debated, rather than tacitly assumed.

The lectures and readings so far have emphasized how economists bring certain values to their interpretation of the facts, for example, by imposing a neoclassical template on the world they observe. I then have students read an article by Frank, Gilovich, and Regan that takes it a step further.[4] This article experimentally demonstrates that economists' values can affect the real world itself—and not just economists' interpretations of it. This happens when economists export values into the classroom by teaching the economic theory of rationality. The authors report an experiment in which they gave students a prisoner's situation, with actual cash at stake. In a regression model of the resulting data, with the decision to defect as the dependent variable, the variable of a major in economics was significantly positive; those who had studied economics the most were more likely to take the most self-interested action. If this kind of effect is common, then even clearly self-interested behavior may not constitute an independent verification of the theory of rational self-interest but instead may be a *product* of that theory. The lectures and readings in this section of the course thus provide students with several different approaches to the relationship between facts and values in economics. They demonstrate that the role in economics of ideals such as objectivity is unsettled. The debate is a longstanding one, and it continues.

How I present this material depends on the nature of class reactions. I believe the professor can plan class presentations only so far. Teachers must watch students' eyes for the Little Orphan Annie effect—blank eyes signaling boredom or incomprehension. My usual approach is to ask questions on the assigned readings to see if there is general understanding, provide

---

[4] Robert H. Frank, Thomas Gilovich, and Denis T. Regan, "Does Studying Economics Inhibit Cooperation?" *Journal of Economic Perspectives* 7, no. 2 (Spring 1993): 159–71.

mini-lectures where needed, and devise student participation projects such as debates and class presentations. Experience tells me that on some topics every class will need extra help, and on other topics most classes will understand the material with the readings and some simple lectures. On the issue of the permeation of values in economic theory, I usually designate a student to give a five-minute presentation on why economics is value-free and another student to critique that presentation. I usually require the first student to e-mail a one-page statement to all the students the day before class.

Rationality, Ethics, and the Behavior of Economic Agents

After teaching the fundamentals of microeconomics—scarcity, choice, opportunity cost, supply and demand—I then design a section in the introductory course discussing limitations of the microeconomic way of thinking. Basically, economic theory posits that wants are always greater than resources; therefore, scarcity is *the* economic problem. Since by assumption everyone wants to get the most for the least, the logic of the model follows. The extensions are particularly troubling—couples choose between a new car and a new baby; elected representatives act so as to maximize the possibility of re-election. Even altruistic behavior is seen as self-interested—people give money to charity because it makes them feel good or it brings them social approval. Christian self-sacrificing love has no role. I point out to the class that all evidence indicates that economic actors (consumers, workers, firms) act out of more than calculated self-interest. Thus the assumption of rationality used in economics may be insufficient in some cases and inappropriate in others. In fact, people's behavior is influenced by many things, including ethical norms. We discuss what impact this has upon the ability of economic theory to predict outcomes of economic actions. For example, given imperfect information, purely self-interested actors might be tempted into strategic behavior that results in sub-optimal outcomes. Morally constrained behavior might reduce that opportunism.

I argue that economists have several reasons to be concerned.

First, to the extent that economics is based on a faulty theory of human behavior, economics will be unable to predict and control. For example, how should government encourage people to behave in socially beneficial ways, say, to donate blood? If people are rational maximizers, government can best achieve its ends by providing a proper set of economic incentives for such behavior. But if economics misconceives the way people are motivated, such incentives might fail to work. In fact, there is some evidence that blood donations decline when a system of cash payments is introduced. How could this be?

It is not clear how to account for the decline in contributions. But one possible answer relates to a second, *generative,* role for economic theory. By this is meant its role in generating behavior as opposed to merely predicting or controlling it. Economics can play this role in several possible ways. First, as the reading by Frank, Gilovich, and Regan in the previous section of the course suggests, economics can become a sort of philosophy of life for those who study it, leading them to behave in economically rational ways. Second, and more appropriate for the blood-donation case, economically rational ways of behavior can be taught by exposure to social policies and practices that presuppose economic rationality. Thus, even those who initially behave according to social norms about giving blood may come to view blood donation as just another economic transaction, once they see people being paid for their donations. Thus, their non-economic motives are undercut by an economic policy based solely on self-interest. This topic frequently leads to some of the most spirited debate in the course.

I then point out that another reason to be skeptical regarding the assumption of economic rationality has to do with its normative role. In the previous section of the course, I noted that the practice of neoclassical economics, despite claims of a positive-normative distinction, commits one to certain moral beliefs. For example, when economics merely identifies and describes certain behaviors as rational, the label of rationality carries a positive connotation that may lead some to see such behavior as desirable or even morally good. Another normative role for the theory of economic rationality is as a benchmark of economic success. Economists measure the success of the economic system by its satisfaction of individual preferences, as opposed to some other measure such as reductions in infant mortality or the elimination of demeaning working conditions. In this benchmark role, the economic theory of rationality is normative because it dictates how policies and behaviors are to be judged.

Thus, I tell the class, there are a number of reasons why one should be concerned about whether the economic theory of rationality is a good one. How would one begin to determine the answer to that question? Certainly it is relevant to ask whether people actually behave according to the theory. One article we read in this section of the course does just that, using experimental evidence.[5] However, keeping in mind the generative role that theory potentially plays, one must also ask what the consequences are of adopting the neoclassical theory of value. In an article for this section, I suggest among other things that a society constructed on the basis of pure economic rationality might face overwhelming problems of moral hazard, resulting in a kind of crisis of the moral environment.[6]

Several themes are presented in this section on rationality, ethics, and the behavior of economic agents. One of the crucial issues is the empirical validity of the neoclassical theory. Another issue is the potential consequences of adopting the theory as society's operative theory of human nature. A third issue is the question of exactly *how* people might deviate from the rational model. If people are moral agents in addition to rational maximizers, how *do* they care about the world? For example, do they simply care about the utility of other agents, or do they obey certain moral strictures—like those against lying—regardless of their effect on others' happiness? What the readings so far make clear is that there is no one form of behavior, whether self-interested or moral, that is dictated by human nature. There is

---

[5] Robin M. Dawes and Richard H. Thaler, "Cooperation," *Journal of Economic Perspectives* 2, no. 3 (Summer 1988): 187–97.

[6] Charles K. Wilber, "Trust, Moral Hazards and Social Economics: Incentives and the Organization of Work," in *On the Condition of Labor and the Social Question One Hundred Years Later: Commemorating the 100th Anniversary of Rerum Novarum and the Fiftieth Anniversary of the Association for Social Economics* (Toronto Studies in Theology, vol. 69), eds. Thomas O. Nitsch, Joseph M. Phillips, Jr., and Edward L. Fitzsimmons (New York: The Edwin Mellen Press, 1994), 173–84.

abundant evidence for this. The question then becomes how the various aspects of human nature—economically rational and otherwise—can be elicited so as to create an efficient and just society. I next have them read "God and the Ghetto," by Glenn Lowry, [7] who argues that policymakers must recognize that creating incentives based solely on the assumption of rational self-interest is doomed to failure. Students should understand that a conception of virtuous living needs to be revived in the public debate over workable policies. More surprising to the students, coming from an economist, is Lowry's argument that virtuous living requires a spiritual motivation that is learned in the home and church.

I have used a variety of approaches with this material, from simple discussion sessions to requiring students to write a one-page statement on their motives for doing what they do. They turn the statements in to me, but I do not grade them. Instead I write comments that push them to be more critically self-aware of the choices they make. I then lead a class discussion peppered with leading questions such as "Do your parents pay you to take out the garbage? Why or why not?" and "If you found a wallet with one hundred dollars cash and identification, what would you do?" With these prompters in mind, I have them read the selections from Scripture noted below and Chapter IIA, "The Christian Vision of Life: Biblical Perspectives" from the United States Catholic Bishops' pastoral letter on the economy.[8]

We read the scriptural passages in class and use the commentary from the bishops' letter to guide class discussion. What emerges from this discussion is a realization that the strong emphasis in the Old Testament prophets calling for social justice and condemning excessive and irresponsible wealth should change our way of seeing the world. Central to the biblical view is that justice in a community is most directly tested by its treatment of the powerless in society—most often described as the widow, the orphan, the poor, and the stranger (non-Israelite).

---

[7] Glenn C. Lowry, "God and the Ghetto," *Wall Street Journal*, February 25, 1993.

[8] *Economic Justice for All: Pastoral Letter on Catholic Social Teaching and the U.S. Economy* (Washington, D.C.: National Conference of Catholic Bishops, 1986), 16–32.

The prophets continually call the king and the people back to commitment to justice for the powerless. They direct scathing attacks at the rich and powerful who "sell the righteous for silver, and the needy for a pair of sandals—they . . . trample the head of the poor into the dust of the earth, and push the afflicted out of the way" (Amos 2:6–7). Isaiah pronounces God's judgment on those "who have devoured the vineyard; the spoil of the poor is in your houses" (3:14). Jeremiah condemns the man "who builds his house by unrighteousness, and his upper rooms by injustice" (22:13). He praises King Josiah because "he judged the cause of the poor and needy." Jeremiah then adds the startling statement: "Is not this to know me? says the Lord" (22:16). He then adds, "Your eyes and heart are only on your dishonest gain" (22:17). Thus, doing of justice is equated with knowledge of the Lord. The practice of justice is constitutive of true belief. And the pursuit of self-interest is seen as a stumbling block to knowing and serving God.

If Jesus is, as Christians claim, Lord and the Son of God, then he is Lord of every aspect of our lives, including the economic one, and his teaching and example must have some relevance to economics as well. In fact, Jesus followed in the prophetic tradition, taking the side of those who are powerless or on the margin of his society, such as the tax collectors (Luke 15:1 ff.), the widow (Luke 7:11–17; Mark 12:41–44), the Samaritan (Luke 17:11–19), the sinful woman (Luke 7:36–50), and children (Mark 10:13–16). Jesus' description of the final judgment in Matthew 25 (31–46) should haunt us with its powerful message of what it means to be a Christian.

CATHOLIC SOCIAL THOUGHT AND ECONOMICS

To make the biblical message concrete and apply it to our time and place, the next section of the introductory course gives a brief review of theories of justice with a more extended discussion of Catholic social thought. The course on Economics, Ethics, and Public Policy does this in much greater detail. We use the bishops' pastoral letter, Pope John Paul II's encyclical *Centesimus*

Annus,[9] and various commentaries.[10] I begin by lecturing on the history of Catholic social thought. Since 1891, popes, individual bishops, and national conferences of bishops have spoken out on issues of economic justice through the issuance of encyclicals and pastoral letters. They have attempted to articulate a clearly Christian view on issues of economic ethics and justice. Because they tend to speak at a general level, there is room for disagreement, and thus rival interpretations flourish. Using the readings as the starting point, we then begin class discussion, which I guide to focus on the following issues.

Catholic social thought is rooted in a commitment to certain fundamental values—the belief in human dignity, the need for human freedom and participation, the importance of community, and the nature of the common good. These values are drawn from the belief that each person is called to be a co-creator with God, participating in the redemption of the world and the furthering of the Kingdom. This requires social and human development where the religious and temporal aspects of life are not separate and opposed to each other. As a result of these fundamental values, two principles permeate Catholic social thought. The first is a special concern for the poor and powerless that leads to a criticism of political and economic structures that oppress them. The second is a concern for certain human rights against the collectivist tendencies of the state and the neglect of the free market.

Ever since *Rerum Novarum* in 1891,[11] Catholic social thought has taught that both state socialism and free-market capitalism violate these principles. State socialism denies the right of private property, excites the envy of the poor against the rich leading to class struggle instead of cooperation, and violates the proper order of society by the state's usurping the role of indi-

---

[9] Pope John Paul II, *Centesimus Annus* (100 Years After) (Washington, D.C.: National Conference of Catholic Bishops, May 1, 1991).

[10] See Charles K. Wilber, "*Centesimus Annus*: 100 Years of Catholic Social Thought," *National Catholic Reporter* 27, no. 32 (June 7, 1991): 8, 10; Peter L. Berger, Richard John Neuhaus, and Michael Novak, "The Pope, Liberty, and Capitalism," *National Review*, Special Supplement (1991): 2–3, 8–9, 11–12.

[11] Pope Leo XIII, *Rerum Novarum* (On the Condition of Workers) (Washington, D.C.: National Conference of Catholic Bishops, May 15, 1891).

viduals and social groups.[12] Free-market capitalism denies the concept of the common good and the "social and public character of the right of property,"[13] including the principle of the universal destination of the earth's goods;[14] it also violates human dignity by treating labor merely as a commodity to be bought and sold in the marketplace.[15] Pope John Paul II summarizes the thrust of Catholic social thought when he notes that

> the individual today is often suffocated between two poles represented by the State and the marketplace. At times it seems as though he exists only as a producer and consumer of goods, or as an object of State administration. People lose sight of the fact that life in society has neither the market nor the State as its final purpose, since life itself has a unique value which the State and the market must serve.[16]

The concept of the common good in Catholic social thought emphasizes both the dignity of the human person and the essentially social nature of that dignity. Both civil and political liberties on the one hand and social and economic needs on the other are essential components of the common good. The common good is not the aggregate of the welfare of all individuals. Rather it is a set of social conditions, necessary for the realization of human dignity, that transcend the arena of private exchange and contract. Such conditions are essentially relational. To exist they must exist as shared. In short, individual persons have rights to those things necessary to realize their dignity as human beings. Catholic social thought argues further that as people pursue the common good, special concern must be given to the economy's impact on the poor and powerless because they are particularly vulnerable and needy.[17]

Pope John XXIII, in his encyclical *Pacem in Terris*,[18] set out in

---

[12] See *Rerum Novarum*, paras. 7–8; *Centesimus Annus*, paras. 13–14.

[13] Pope Pius XI, *Quadragesimo Anno* (On Reconstructing the Social Order) (Washington, D.C.: National Conference of Catholic Bishops, May 15, 1931), para. 46.

[14] See *Rerum Novarum*, para. 14; *Centesimus Annus*, para. 6.

[15] See *Rerum Novarum*, para. 31; *Quadragesimo Anno*, para. 83; *Centesimus Annus*, para. 33–35.

[16] *Centesimus Annus*, para. 49.

[17] *Centesimus Annus*, para. 11.

[18] Pope John XXIII, *Pacem en Terris* (Peace on Earth) (Washington, D.C.: National Conference of Catholic Bishops, May 15, 1963).

detail a full range of human rights that can only be realized and protected in solidarity with others. These rights include the civil and political rights to freedom of speech, worship, and assembly. He also includes a number of economic rights concerning human welfare. First among these are the rights to life, food, clothing, shelter, rest, medical care, and basic education. To ensure these rights, everyone has the right to earn a living. Each person also has a right to security in the event of illness, unemployment, or old age. The right to participate in the wider human community requires the right of employment, as well as the right to healthful working conditions, wages, and other benefits sufficient to support families at a level in keeping with human dignity.[19]

Catholic social thought repudiates the conventional wisdom that the level of unemployment, the degree of poverty, the quantity of environmental destruction, and other such outcomes should be left to the dictates of the market. Emphasis on the common good means that the community has an obligation to ensure the right of employment to all persons,[20] to help the disadvantaged overcome their poverty,[21] and to safeguard the environment.[22] Catholic thought views society as made up of a dense network of relationships among individuals, families, churches, neighborhood associations, business firms, labor unions, and different levels of government. Thus, every component of the social order has a role to play in ensuring basic human rights and the common good. In Catholic social thought this is expressed as the principle of subsidiarity.

> Just as it is gravely wrong to take from individuals what they can accomplish by their own initiative and industry and give it to the community, so also it is an injustice and at the same time a grave evil and disturbance of right order to assign to a greater and higher association what lesser and subordinate organizations can do. For every social activity ought of its very nature to furnish help *(subsidium)* to the members of the body social, and never destroy and absorb them.[23]

---

[19] *Pacem en Terris*, paras. 8–27; *Centesimus Annus*, paras. 8, 15.
[20] *Centesimus Annus*, para. 15.
[21] *Centesimus Annus*, paras. 19, 40.
[22] *Centesimus Annus*, para. 37.
[23] *Quadragesimo Anno*, para. 79; *Centesimus Annus*, para. 15.

This principle provides for a pluralism of social actors. Each constituent actor, from the individual person to the federal government, has obligations. More inclusive levels of authority should not usurp the authority of lower levels except when necessary. However, the principle works both ways. When individuals, families, or local communities are unable to solve problems that undermine the common good, the state governments are obligated to intervene, and if their resources and abilities are inadequate, then the federal government assumes the responsibility. This principle also extends into the international economy. As Pope John Paul II says, "this increasing internationalization of the economy ought to be accompanied by effective international agencies which will oversee and direct the economy to the common good, something that an individual State, even if it were the most powerful on earth, would not be in a position to do."[24]

In contrast to Catholic social thought, economic theory is rooted in an individualist conception of society. Society is seen as a collection of individuals that has chosen to associate for mutual benefit. The common good is simply the aggregate of the welfare of each individual. Individual liberty is the highest good, and if individuals are left free to pursue their self-interest, the result will be the maximum material welfare possible. Economic theory conceives of people as hedonists who want to maximize pleasure and minimize pain. It assumes that pleasure comes primarily from the consumption of goods and services. Pain comes primarily from work and from parting with income. Thus, given resource constraints, the goal of the economy should be to maximize the production of goods and services. In short, more is better.

The Catholic tradition rejects this materialist view of human welfare. In his 1967 encyclical, *Populorum Progressio*, Pope Paul VI wrote:

> Increased possession is not the ultimate goal of nations or of individuals. All growth is ambivalent. It is essential if man is to develop as a man, but in a way it imprisons man if he considers it the supreme good, and it restricts his vision. Then we see hearts harden and minds close, and men no longer gather together in

---

[24] *Centesimus Annus*, para. 58.

friendship but out of self-interest, which soon leads to opposi-
tions and disunity. The exclusive pursuit of possessions thus becomes an obstacle to individual fulfillment and to man's true
greatness. Both for nations and for individual men, avarice is the
most evident form of moral underdevelopment.[25]

On the twentieth anniversary (1987) of *Populorum Progressio*,
Pope John Paul II wrote in *Sollicitudo Rei Socialis*, "All of us experience first hand the sad effects of this blind submission to pure
consumerism: in the first place a crass materialism, and at the
same time a radical dissatisfaction because one quickly learns . . .
that the more one possesses the more one wants, while deeper
aspirations remain unsatisfied and perhaps even stifled."[26]

In his latest social encyclical, *Centesimus Annus*, Pope John
Paul II observes "It is not wrong to want to live better; what is
wrong is a style of life which is presumed to be better when it is
directed toward 'having' rather than 'being,' and which wants
to have more, not in order to be more but in order to spend life
in enjoyment as an end in itself."[27]

At this point to stimulate discussion, I use a vivid example
from an old Sears Christmas catalogue to demonstrate the usually implicit but pervasive process our economy uses to teach
people from an early age that true happiness comes from consumption. The catalogue advertises a new doll named Shopping
Sheryl. Sheryl comes equipped with a supermarket, which has a
rotating checkout counter, a ringing cash register, a motorized
checkout stand, shelves, a cart, and groceries. Sheryl is a vinyl
doll that picks things up with her magnetized right hand and
grasps with her left hand. We can visualize Sheryl in her supermarket, picking and grasping, picking and grasping. I pose the
question "Is this what God wants—that our children have Shopping Sheryl and learn early in life that the true purpose of life is
consumption?"

At the end of the introductory course we discuss the pros and

[25] Pope Paul VI, *Populorum Progressio* (On Promoting the Development of
Peoples) (Washington, D.C.: National Conference of Catholic Bishops, March
26, 1967), para. 19.

[26] Pope John Paul II, *Sollicitudo Rei Socialis* (On Social Concerns) (Washington,
D.C.: National Conference of Catholic Bishops, December 30, 1987), para. 28.

[27] *Centesimus Annus*, para. 36.

cons of alternative economic systems. We discuss that the thrust of Catholic social thought has been to repudiate both state socialism and free-market capitalism. What economic system does it endorse? Explicitly, none. As Pope John Paul II says, "The Church has no models to present" for the best economic system; that is for history to decide in each individual case.[28] However, implied in Catholic social thought is a preference for a regulated market economy that protects the poor, defends human rights, allows all to participate in social groups such as trade unions, and controls market failures such as environmental pollution. The degree of regulation is not a matter of principle but rather a case of prudential judgment in particular cases. We use these fundamental principles of Catholic social thought near the end of the introductory course to evaluate economic policies. The students are required to write a paper on some economic issue (welfare reform, for example) and to do both an economic analysis and an ethical analysis. They do not have to use Catholic social thought, but whatever ethical analysis they use must be justified.

PEDAGOGY, FAITH, AND ECONOMICS

I believe that *how* the course is run is as important as its content. Students learn values from the process of learning. I strive for student participation, problem solving, and experiential learning as integral to a Christian approach to teaching economics. The paper projects are particularly crafted to meet these objectives. In my upper-division course on economics and ethics, students write three papers of approximately six to eight pages. The introductory students do versions of the first two papers but not the final paper, since volunteer work is not part of this course. This is because of the class size and the amount of material that must be covered. Students are encouraged to contact me—in person, by office telephone, or by e-mail—to discuss their paper topics. The first paper utilizes *Uncle Sam's Budget Balancer,* a computer program and database that students can

---

[28] *Centesimus Annus,* para. 43.

download from my web page. This program makes it easy for students to try their hand at balancing the federal budget. They can modify the president's current fiscal year budget with over three hundred options researched and documented by the Congressional Budget Office. Options for spending and revenue changes are described, including the pros and cons of implementing each one. The program also contains educational information on the budget process.

The subsequent paper must provide the student's economic *and ethical* rationale for the way he or she balanced the federal budget. They must provide their reasoning for each rationale and for each category of expenditure and taxation. In addition, students need to articulate an overarching rationale for their approach to the budgeting process itself. This project may be done in concert with like-minded colleagues. If pursued as a group project, the paper will be more detailed and therefore proportionately longer than an individual paper. The group must meet to make joint decisions, but the parts are independently written. This topic is not as exciting to the students as it once was because the budget is no longer front-page news, but it still drives home the difficulty of choosing what programs to cut and by what criteria they should be cut. Students are encouraged to discuss explicitly if and how matters of personal religious faith guide their decisions.

The second paper concerns a question regarding welfare reform or some other policy approved by me. This is a two-part paper. The first part articulates the question being asked and presents the way in which the question will be investigated and answered. For example, the question could be asked, what are the economic and ethical costs of moving mothers off of welfare and onto a payroll in the state of Wisconsin? To generate answers to this question, others need to be considered. What are the economic costs? (Job training, day care.) What are the ethical costs? (Loss of income, loss of medical care, impact on children of no parent at home.) How will the answers be found? In the newspaper? In government studies? In reports from other sources? Are there data upon which personal interpretations might be based? A one-page proposal that specifies the question being asked and how it will be answered must be submitted for approval one month before the due date. The second part of the paper consists of a summary of the results of student research.

The third paper asks students to reflect upon their semester field experience. In my Economics and Ethics class, each student contributes eight hours of voluntary labor to an organization devoted to working for justice, such as the Holy Family Catholic Worker House, South Bend Homeless Center, or St. Augustine's Soup Kitchen. Detailed information on the entire range of volunteer opportunities is provided at the beginning of the semester by staff from the Center for Social Concerns on campus. I ask the students to prepare a six- to eight-page paper reflecting on this service experience and tying it to the readings in the course.

I believe that both of my courses are successful in stimulating students to think about how economics and ethics are inextricably mixed in both theory and policy. They are also successful in demonstrating to students the need for understanding how their faith does shape and should shape their responses to economic issues.

Selected Bibliography

Unfortunately there are limited works dealing with the role of faith in economics. My inspiration has come mainly from the documents of Catholic social thought, many of which are listed in the footnotes. Beyond that, a major source has been the *Bulletin* of the Association of Christian Economists (Gordon College, Wenham, Mass. 01984). The following are books that I have read and found useful.

Beckman, David M. *Where Faith and Economics Meet: A Christian Critique.* Minneapolis: Augsburg Publishing House, 1981.
Budde, Michael. *The Two Churches: Catholicism and Capitalism in the World System.* Durham, N.C.: Duke University Press, 1992.
Clouse, Robert G., ed. *Wealth and Poverty: Four Christian Views of Economics.* Downers Grove, Ill.: InterVarsity Press, 1984.
Dorr, Donal. *Option for the Poor: A Hundred Years of Vatican Social*

Teaching. Dublin: Gill and Macmillan, and Maryknoll, N.Y.: Orbis Books, 1983.

Gannon, Thomas M., S.J., ed. *The Catholic Challenge to the American Economy: Reflections on the U. S. Bishops' Pastoral Letter on Catholic Social Teaching and the U. S. Economy*. New York: Macmillan Publishing Co., 1987.

Goudzwaard, Bob, and Harry de Lange. *Beyond Poverty and Affluence: Toward an Economy of Care With a Twelve-Step Program for Economic Recovery*. Grand Rapids, Mich.: William B. Eerdmans Publishing Co., 1995.

Haas, Richard C. *We All Have a Share: A Catholic Vision of Prosperity Through Productivity*. Chicago: ACTA Publications, 1995.

Halteman, James. *The Clashing Worlds of Economics and Faith*. Scottdale, Penn.: Herald Press, 1995.

Hay, Donald A. *Economics Today: A Christian Critique*. Grand Rapids, Mich.: William B. Eerdmans Publishing Co., 1989.

Hollenbach, David. *Claims in Conflict: Retrieving and Renewing the Catholic Human Rights Tradition*. New York: Paulist Press, 1979.

Johnson, Luke T. *Sharing Possessions: Mandate and Symbol of Faith*. Philadelphia: Fortress Press, 1981.

Lutz, Charles P., ed. *God, Goods, and the Common Good: Eleven Perspectives on Economic Justice in Dialog with the Roman Catholic Bishops' Pastoral Letter*. Minneapolis: Augsburg Publishing House, 1987.

McKee, Arnold F. *Economics and the Christian Mind: Elements of a Christian Approach to the Economy and Economic Science*. New York: Vantage, 1987.

Milbank, John. *Theology and Social Theory: Beyond Secular Reason*. Cambridge, Mass.: Blackwell, 1991.

Mitchell, John J. *Critical Voices in American Catholic Economic Thought*. New York: Paulist Press, 1989.

Novak, Michael. *The Catholic Ethic and the Spirit of Capitalism*. New York: The Free Press, 1993.

Tamari, Meir. *With All Your Possessions: Jewish Ethics and Economic Life*. New York: The Free Press, 1987.

Tawney, R. H. *Religion and the Rise of Capitalism*. New York: Harcourt, Brace & World, 1926.

Zweig, Michael. *Religion and Economic Justice*. Philadelphia: Temple University Press, 1991.

2

Scuttling the Schizophrenic Student Mind: On Teaching the Unity of Faith and Learning in Psychology

Mary Stewart Van Leeuwen

ALTHOUGH IT NOW HAS a more technical meaning in the mental health lexicon, the original Greek meaning of the word *schizophrenic* was *split mind*. It is my contention that Christian college students come to the study of psychology with profoundly split minds, due to their exposure to modern and postmodern thought patterns and the Church's accommodation to both. From a Calvinist perspective, the psychology professor needs to identify, challenge, and overcome this cognitive dualism while introducing students to the intriguing range of topics that comprise psychology—the empirical, theoretical, and applied study of the mind and behavior.

My goal is for students to view the content and methods of psychology from a coherent Christian worldview. What is a worldview? It is a set of pre-philosophical, pre-empirical faith assumptions held by every human being in answer to questions such as, What is the nature of the universe? What is the nature of human beings? What is humankind's basic problem? What is the solution to this problem? And how, if at all, can humans obtain reliable knowledge? In more popular terms, the questions that a worldview answers for each person are, Where am I? Who am I? What's wrong with me? What's the remedy? and How can I know anything at all?[1]

---

[1] For a more detailed discussion of worldviews, Christian and otherwise, see for example Leslie Stevenson, *Seven Theories of Human Nature* (New York: Ox-

Getting students to think worldviewishly about psychology involves a certain amount of scuttling, a nineteenth-century nautical term meaning "to cut a hole in the deck of a ship for the purpose of saving her cargo." The "cargo of intent" that most Christian students bring to the study of psychology is basically sound. If they were not committed to loving and serving God and neighbor, if they were not prepared to expose their minds to the process of Christian formation, then they would hardly take on the financial burden of attending a Christian college rather than the local state university. But the actual cargo inside their heads is unstable: bits and pieces of Christian belief slide to and fro alongside modern and, increasingly, postmodern assumptions. To rearrange and stabilize what is valid, while separating out what is questionable, some mental surgery is required. That the process should be undertaken carefully, compassionately, and with good humor goes without saying. But this does not preclude challenging and reshaping students' assumptions so that they can begin to deal with the complexities of psychology as *Christian students*—not just as *students* who happen to be *Christian*.[2] In this essay, I analyze the pedagogical process of challenging and reshaping. I offer a selective and by no means finished account of a Calvinist approach to pedagogy developed over three decades of teaching both in public and Christian institutions of higher education.

JUMBLED CARGO: THE CONTEMPORARY STUDENT MIND

Most students bring to the psychology classroom a contradictory combination of modern belief in the separation of facts from values and postmodern belief in the impossibility of knowing *any* facts and the relativity of *all* values. To begin with, students have learned from natural and social science to treat facts and values as logically quite distinct. In this perspective, facts are totally

---

ford University Press, 1974); James Sire, *The Universe Next Door: A Basic Worldview Catalogue*, 3d ed. (Downers Grove, Ill.: InterVarsity Press, 1997) and Brian J. Walsh and J. Richard Middleton, *The Transforming Vision: Shaping a Christian World View* (Downers Grove, Ill.: InterVarsity Press, 1984).

    [2] See Walsh and Middleton, *The Transforming Vision*, especially chapters 6–9.

objective, but values—including those arising from religious conviction—are totally subjective. Facts are said to be "intersubjectively verifiable" (they can be agreed upon by impartial observers) whereas values are idiosyncratic. Facts can be verified or falsified by observation, but values are arbitrary and thus cannot be tested empirically. Finally, beliefs about facts can be judged rational or irrational but values, being faith- or emotion-based, are simply nonrational. In this view, writes philosopher Stephen Evans, "the world consists of brute facts, and values are only introduced when a subject turns up who has a personal preference."[3]

Christian students have usually assimilated one of two responses to the claim that facts are quite distinct from values. Fundamentalists have been rightly suspicious of rationalist attempts to sideline religious authority as a source of truth. But rather than argue that truth comes in forms other than what can be affirmed by scientific rationality, many chose to rationalize and scientize the Bible, reducing it to a list of historically and scientifically literal propositions. Ironically, while claiming to fight godless science, fundamentalists let this same rationalist science dictate a limited definition of truth that they then proceeded to impose on Scripture.[4] For much of the twentieth century, students in this tradition did not find their way to Christian liberal arts colleges at all. Instead they formed separatist enclaves in Bible colleges, where Scripture was treated as the only needed textbook for understanding history, psychology, geology, and so on. We might call this the "Biblical positivist" approach to relating faith and learning.

Evangelical and mainline church students have generally absorbed a different but more common strategy. Rather than turning the Bible into a scientific fact book, they have simply accepted the modern distinction between facts and values and have been encouraged in this dualism by many church-related colleges. On this account, the college classroom is the place to learn the reputedly neutral facts and techniques of psychology,

---

[3] C. Stephen Evans, *Wisdom and Humanness in Psychology: Prospects for a Christian Approach* (Grand Rapids, Mich.: Baker Book House, 1989), 107.

[4] George M. Marsden, *Fundamentalism and American Culture* (New York: Oxford University Press, 1980).

biology, engineering, and so on. Outside the classroom, with the help of extracurricular resources (the college chapel program, service-learning opportunities, campus Christian groups), students learn the spiritual content of the faith and how this can be an inspiration for evangelism, personal character development, and public service. From this perspective, a Christian psychologist is simply a good psychologist—a well-trained professional who does not mistreat students, overcharge clients, or fabricate data when doing research, and who also tithes professional and personal resources to advance the goals of the Church. We might call this the "add God and stir" approach to relating faith and learning.

At the opposite extreme to both these responses are the postmodernist assumptions to which young people are now routinely exposed. What passes for impartial truth, according to the postmodern critique, is only a local narrative or mythic base that forms the ideological glue holding a community together. This includes the myth of finding universal truth through scientific rationality, which, from the postmodern perspective, is as much a product of its time and place as any other elitist construction of reality. The postmodern critic thus attacks modern epistemology at the very point where it claims superiority—namely, its observational impartiality and its democratic inclusivity of all persons as both objects and subjects of research.

Although students come to college knowing little about academic discourse on postmodernism, the appeal of its popularized form is undeniable. In deconstructing the image of the rational, autonomous knower, postmodernism supports a radically social view of the self. This is understandably attractive to young people for whom the myth of rugged individualism—leading as often to loneliness as it does to fame and fortune—has lost much of its appeal. Moreover, the postmodern privileging of local over universal narratives supports a pluralist view of society, and students often confuse support for social justice and multiculturalism with a commitment to cultural and moral relativism. Indeed, it is not unusual for students to believe that unconditional tolerance of *every* worldview and lifestyle is required by the Christian imperative to love one's neighbor. We might call this the "judge not" approach to relating faith and learning.

The Unity of Faith and Learning in Psychology:
A Calvinist View

How does a professor of Calvinist convictions address this mix of fundamentalist, modern, and postmodern sensibilities in the psychology classroom? It is common for Christian academics to speak of the challenge of *integrating* faith and learning, but I prefer to speak of the *unity* of faith and learning, for reasons that I now need to explain.[5]

Christians in the Calvinist tradition have been among the strongest critics of modernity, even though they have also affirmed science as one way of exploring God's creation. Well before the advent of postmodernism, Calvinists working in the tradition of Abraham Kuyper resisted the dichotomy between facts and values. They insisted that *all* living and learning is filtered through a prior set of faith-based convictions, if not to Christian theism then to naturalism, Marxism, nihilism, or some other worldview from the marketplace of ideas.[6] Against modernism and with the postmodern critique, these Kuyperian Calvinists asserted that there is no such thing as "immaculate perception" or a "view from nowhere" when doing scholarship of any sort. All scholarship proceeds from the pre-empirical, faith-based foundation of the scholar's worldview.

Calvinists have not denied that propositional truths are present in Scripture, but have viewed these truths through a wider, redemptive-historical lens. Seen through this lens, the Bible is a cumulative, God-directed narrative whose successive acts (creation, fall, redemption, and future hope) comprise a continuing cosmic drama in which all persons, consciously or otherwise, are players. Thus, against the postmodern claim that worldviews

---

[5] See also Mary Stewart Van Leeuwen, "Five Uneasy Questions, or: Will Success Spoil Christian Psychologists?" *Journal of Psychology and Christianity* 15, no. 2 (1996): 150–60.

[6] See in particular Abraham Kuyper, *Lectures on Calvinism: The Stone Foundation Lectures of 1898* (Grand Rapids, Mich.: William B. Eerdmans Publishing Co., 1970) and, for more contemporary analyses, Walsh and Middleton, *The Transforming Vision*, and Albert Wolters, *Creation Regained: Biblical Basics for a Reformational World View* (Grand Rapids, Mich.: William B. Eerdmans Publishing Co., 1985), and James Bratt, ed., *Abraham Kuyper: A Centennial Reader* (Grand Rapids, Mich.: William B. Eerdmans Publishing Co., 1998).

(including Christian ones) are merely human social constructions, Calvinists have insisted that something deeper is at
work—namely, the *worshiping* impulse, which is an irreducible
aspect of human creatureliness. All human thought patterns will
be guided by a worldview that reflects allegiance to the one true
God or else (inevitably) to some substitute idol. So it was naive
of modern thinkers to believe that religious convictions could be
relegated to private life, away from public and neutral rationality. For from the Calvinist perspective, *all* of life is religiously
motivated, and as a result all human beings are characters in
search of an author. If they do not yield to the true Author of the
cosmic drama, they will certainly succumb to worship of one or
more aspects of the creation—such as science, politics, art, or
personal power and pleasure—things that are God's good gifts
in their rightful place but that when substituted for God get
turned into idols. "It is simple to make an idol," writes Reformed theologian Lewis Smedes. "Just slice one piece of created
reality off from the whole and expect miracles from it."[7]

The significance of all this for teaching should now be clear.
We cannot separate the study of psychology from the faith convictions of its practitioners, then decide how to integrate the
two, because all scholarship is filtered through a prior faith allegiance, notwithstanding clichés about the neutrality of psychological investigation. *All* persons reason within the bounds of
religion. The trick is to get students to grasp this in a way that
also invites them to respect and enjoy psychology as a legitimate
(albeit limited and fallible) source of knowledge about people.
How, in other words, do we teach students a hermeneutics of
both trust and suspicion toward psychology?

I have found that a good place to start is with the Bible itself
and specifically with passages that point to the Calvinist doctrines of antithesis and common grace. For example, the apostle
John's first letter, and particularly 1 John 4 on "testing the spirits" seems to draw a sharp antithesis between believers' "spirit
of truth" and unbelievers' "spirit of error." It does not seem to
be issuing much of an invitation to learn from non-Christian

---

[7] Lewis Smedes, *Sex for Christians* (Grand Rapids, Mich.: William B. Eerdmans Publishing Co., 1976), 26.

sources; indeed, John seems to be anticipating Tertullian's famous rhetorical question of the third century: "What has Athens to do with Jerusalem?" But compare this with an Old Testament passage such as Ezra 1, which records the end of the Babylonian captivity and God's use of the pagan King Cyrus to get the Jews back to Jerusalem. Here is one of many indications that God can get work done through whomever God pleases. Thus as we study psychology, common grace—the affirmation that God's truth does not come solely through those who confess God—needs to be kept in tension with John's antithesis between being "of the world" and "of God."

The paradox I want students to grasp from the very first day is this. On the one hand, through Scripture and the Holy Spirit, Christians have insights into the ultimate origin, structure, and purpose of human life. Thus the Bible, while not a psychology textbook in the usual sense, provides us with certain background assumptions or "control beliefs"[8] by which Christians can both shape and judge psychological theory and research. These include belief in human freedom, constrained but not overwhelmed by biological embodiment, and belief in moral accountability as well as human sociability and altruism: humans are not naturally good and unselfish, but neither are they mere utility-maximizers. It also includes a confidence that what we share in terms of human cognition, personality, and purpose is more significant than the variables of ethnicity, class, or gender, and more than just the outcome of evolutionary adaptation. Such control beliefs constitute the framework of the disciplinary house we are trying to build. We must use available materials and our intelligence to add the siding, the floors, the wiring, and so on, and as God's accountable stewards, we have considerable freedom in doing so. But to have a house that will endure, we must work within the God-ordained limits of the framework. For many issues in psychology, the Bible provides such a framework.

On the other hand, the cultural mandate and God's sustaining

---

[8] See Nicholas Wolterstorff, *Reason Within the Bounds of Religion*, 2d ed., (Grand Rapids, Mich.: William B. Eerdmans Publishing Co., 1984) for an elaboration of this term.

common grace are not limited to believers, and pervasive depravity (another durable Calvinist doctrine) is not limited to unbelievers. That is why Kuyper could wryly observe, with regard to both intellectual and ethical issues, that "the world often does better than expected and the church worse."[9] Truth—also in psychology—is thus a gift of God, whoever its human mediators happen to be. The perpetual challenge, of course, is to recognize it when we see it—to separate wheat from chaff in the work of believers and unbelievers alike.

What specific pedagogical techniques can be used to reinforce these concepts? I use two—a reading and a writing assignment. The reading is Stanton Jones's "Relating the Christian Faith to Psychology,"[10] which discusses four ways of defining this relationship—"Christian Anti-Integrators," "Scientific Anti-Integrators," "Limiters of Science," and "Christianizers of Science." The test of their understanding comes in the form of a four-page letter-essay assignment.[11] In it, students are to imagine receiving two letters in the same week from two high school friends, Chris (who has chosen to go to a Bible college) and Jamie (who has chosen to go to a state university). Each friend wants to know (but for quite different reasons) why our student has chosen to go to a Christian liberal arts college. Chris (a "Christian anti-integrator) is convinced that no Christian needs to study anything but the Bible, and Jamie (as a "scientific anti-integrator") holds to the modernist conviction that the Bible is an outdated, subjective set of myths that should be replaced with faith in so-called objective science. The student must write a letter challenging each friend's position, in a way that gives credit where due but shows the limitations of that view and argues for the writer's decision to study psychology in a liberal arts context rather than either a Bible college or a state university.

This is a challenging assignment for a class mostly made up of freshmen, and I do not require it until several hours of lectur-

---

[9] Quoted in G. C. Berkhouwer, *Man: The Image of God* (Grand Rapids, Mich.: William B. Eerdmans Publishing Co., 1962), 186.

[10] In Stanton L. Jones, ed. *Psychology and the Christian Faith: An Introductory Reader* (Grand Rapids, Mich.: Baker Book House, 1986), 15–33.

[11] My thanks to Daryl Stephenson of Houghton College for the idea behind this assignment, which I have been using for over a decade.

ing and discussion of the relevant concepts have taken place. There are students who do not get it even then: rather than mounting a coherent argument, they write a testimony of their own faith to reassure Chris of their orthodoxy or an evangelistic tract to Jamie with the goal of making a convert. But many are able to advance a convincing case for studying psychology within a Christian worldview, while acknowledging the working of common grace in non-Christian scholarship.

Teaching the Unity of Faith and Learning in Specific Areas of Psychology

Research Methods

The mixed legacy of wheat and chaff in psychology is obvious from the very beginning, when texts introduce students to the accepted research methods of the discipline. One of the first films I have my introductory students watch is a video titled *Methodology: The Psychologist and the Experiment*.[12] Though ethical standards for research are tighter now than when this film was made, it is still common for social psychologists to deceive participants as to the true purpose of an experiment, and students view a rerun of one such study. In the discussion that follows, I am concerned that students focus not just on the deception as such (though that is important, because if social scientists can lie for a good cause, that has a powerful role-modeling effect on the rest of society) but on the implicit anthropology and epistemology that underlie it. No one recalls ever having had to lie to frogs or iron filings in other experimental settings, so why do psychologists lie to their human research participants?

Most students can figure out that this is done to get a spontaneous response to the independent variable, thus avoiding the guinea-pig effect that would come from knowing the true actual experimental hypothesis. In effect, experimenters are using deception to make an end run around human reflexivity (the capacity to use acquired knowledge to act in unprecedented

---

[12] Source: CRM Films, 1–800–421–0833.

ways). But if self-conscious reflexivity is such a powerful human capacity, why do social psychologists keep trying to neutralize it, rather than studying it directly and carefully as an important feature of personhood?

The answer seems to lie in their commitment to methodological determinism—to viewing humans simply as larger rats or slower computers—and to organizing psychology around the thesis of the unity of science. This thesis holds that there is only one method that all genuine sciences employ, consisting of the search for causal, deterministic explanations that are empirically testable.[13] For psychologists committed to methodological determinism and to the unity of science, if there are features of personhood that cannot be studied using methods borrowed from the natural sciences, then these simply will not be studied at all. Students need to understand that the choice to do research in this way is not itself based on impartial research. It rests on a faith-based allegiance to scientism—the belief that the scientific method, as traditionally understood, is the best way to study all aspects of reality and that psychologists should therefore accommodate this method and the determinist working assumptions that underlie it.

Learning

Methodological determinism often degenerates into metaphysical determinism in psychology, as is evident in the thoroughgoing materialism of evolutionary psychology and in the strong program of artificial intelligence research.[14] But students in introductory psychology may best grasp the weaknesses of metaphysical determinism by taking a look at the rise and fall of behaviorism as psychology's ruling paradigm, and particularly at the eccentric figure of B. F. Skinner. Here we are helped by historical film footage of Skinner in his Harvard laboratory.[15]

---

[13] For a further discussion of these issues, see C. Stephen Evans, *Preserving the Person: A Look at the Human Sciences* (Downers Grove, Ill.: InterVarsity Press, 1977).

[14] For a discussion of the latter, see Mary Stewart Van Leeuwen, *The Person in Psychology: A Contemporary Christian Appraisal* (Grand Rapids, Mich.: William B. Eerdmans Publishing Co., 1985), especially chapter 8.

[15] "Learning and Behavior." Source: Carousel Film and Video, 260 Fifth Avenue, New York, N.Y. 10001.

From one point of view, the claim that behavior is shaped by the rewards and punishments that follow it is neither startling nor unbiblical. As embodied beings connected downward to the rest of creation as well as upward to God whose image they reflect, humans are inevitably affected by their environments. This is so much the case that the Bible issues strong warnings to rulers, teachers, and parents about abusing their power by making conditions miserable for those under their authority. Moreover, it is easy to demonstrate the effectiveness of well-designed schedules of reinforcement in promoting certain kinds of learning and the effectiveness of behavioral therapy techniques in overcoming certain undesirable habits and phobias. But in the case of Skinner, what should have been advanced as one way of learning with limited application to human beings became a full-blown, faith-based worldview masquerading as well-attested science.

Skinner's metaphysical behaviorism is vividly displayed both in the 1963 film and in his 1948 utopian novel *Walden Two*. In both he held that humans were so completely shaped by their learning histories that free will could only be described as illusory. Instead, a complete account of humans could be achieved by studying only their external behavior, mental processes being at best epiphenomena of completely material brain and body processes. Upper-level psychology students often find it instructive to read and compare *Walden Two* to C. S. Lewis's novel *That Hideous Strength*, also published in the late 1940s but as a cautionary tale about the dangers of the very kind of scientific utopia Skinner was promoting.[16] To profit from this, they need to analyze each novel worldviewishly—that is, as a pair of competing morality plays trying to answer (in very different ways) those ultimate worldview questions, Who are we? Where are we? What's wrong with us? What's the solution? And how can we know anything?

Introductory students have enough to do to discern some of the contradictions inherent in Skinner's worldview, contradic-

---

[16] B. F. Skinner, *Walden Two* (New York: MacMillan Publishing Co., 1948; reissued 1974); C. S. Lewis, *That Hideous Strength* (London: John Lane the Bodley Head, 1946; reissued MacMillan Publishing Co., 1965).

tions they will later revisit in other determinist theories, like evolutionary psychology or the strong version of artificial
intelligence. At one point in the film documentary, Skinner suggests that humans should accept that they, no less than molecules of gas, are environmentally controlled. Yet he also suggests
we should use this knowledge "to raise [ourselves] to new
heights of kindness, intelligence, and happiness."[17] How, we
might ask, can totally determined organisms transcend their environmental determinism to take charge of an environment that
has totally determined them? And if everything, including our
morals, is environmentally determined, on what basis can anyone's (including Skinner's) injunctions about what we should do
be taken as binding? Presumably his concern to raise himself to
new heights of happiness is no less the product of his learning
history than a Christian's concern for the saving of souls.

Students thus come to understand that in the world of metaphysical behaviorism, there is no way to rank-order values. In
such a world, the end result is often that might alone makes
right. Ironically, given its very different epistemological starting
point, the same is true of the world of postmodernism. If all
values are socially constructed, on what grounds can anyone cry
foul if one group's values (whatever they are) end up being the
dominant ones? Discussions of this sort expose the non-neutral-
ity of behavioral science and the importance of critically assessing it according to Christian control beliefs.

Perception

Perception can be most entertaining and fascinating to teach.
The complexities of selective attention, depth perception, visual
illusions, and the interaction of culture with all of these allow
for some fine demonstrations and discussions in the classroom.
Ironically, given psychology's more common embrace of objectivism, it is also perceptual theory and research that most graphically challenge the cliché that seeing is believing. Much of the
research on visual illusions seems to point to the opposite conclusion, namely that believing is seeing. In other words, "normal

---

[17] As interviewed in the film "Learning and Behavior," A.A.A.S. Films, 1963.

everyday perceptions are not objective selections of reality but rather imaginative constructions—fictions—based more on the stored past than on the present."[18] This subjectivist tradition in perceptual research appeals to the postmodern side of some students.

On the other hand, much evidence exists that even with only limited, two-dimensional, upside-down retinal images at our disposal, we manage to survive quite handily. Somehow, with the help of binocular vision and various gradually learned depth cues (size, overlap, linear perspective, and so on) human beings manage to construct a visual map of their environment that enables them to navigate most of the time without accident. But in most psychology textbooks, this adaptationist tradition of research points students toward the biologically reductionist conclusion that our perceptual capacities have evolved as well as they have due to random genetic mutations that happened to comport well with the survival demands of the environment over time. Students need to understand that this is a position no less morally and teleologically vacuous than that of postmodernism or Skinner's behaviorism. It is a point that takes some specific lecturing to get across. Students need to realize that, on the Darwinist account, there is nothing progressive about evolution: it simply is the result of environmental adaptation—which means that after a nuclear holocaust, the fittest (perhaps the only) survivors might be cockroaches. Again, there is nothing in this that helps us to transcend existential meaninglessness or, at best, a might-makes-right worldview.

But long before Darwin, the medieval theologians had a doctrine of fitness more in keeping with the biblical drama. They reasoned that God would not have placed humans on earth with the task of unfolding and subduing it without giving them the potential perceptual, cognitive, and social skills needed to get the job done. Thus our perceptual capacities are at most secondarily the result of genetic adaptation: they are first and foremost given to us as tools to carry out the Calvinist cultural mandate "to glorify God and enjoy Him forever." Bert Hodges of Gordon

---

[18] R. L. Gregory, *Eye and Brain: The Psychology of Seeing* (New York: McGraw-Hill, 1972), 176.

34 MARY STEWART VAN LEEUWEN

College has wrestled thoughtfully with the twin truths of perception (seeing is believing and believing is seeing), drawing on
Christian control beliefs, on a third tradition in perceptual research (James Gibson's ecological approach[19]), and on the work
of philosopher of science Michael Polanyi.[20]

Hodges's article "Perception, Relativity and Knowing and
Doing the Truth" is a challenge for beginning psychology students but worth the effort. It is a fine example of doing psychology on the foundation of a Christian worldview, showing
students that they need be neither objectivists nor relativists to
be competent perceivers, scientists, or followers of God. He first
exposes the reader to intriguing examples of the apparent relativity of perception and of some of its actual ecological depend-
ability. He finally concludes that God has created us with
enough stability of perception for us to carry out our mandate
as stewards of the earth but with enough uncertainty to keep
us seeking after ever clearer truth. On this account, all human
knowledge—perceptual, religious, or scientific—is limited and
relative, in the sense that none of us can jump off our own shadows and get a totally decontextualized point of view. That is
why multiple perspectives and cooperative learning are part of
the pursuit of truth.

Moreover, the conduct of science is unavoidably value laden,
affected by everything from economic conditions to religious
convictions. True objectivity consists not in denying these influences but in stating our theoretical assumptions with clarity and
rigor and showing how they lead to imaginative and testable
hypotheses. In addition, we often know more than we can tell,
which is why scientific, perceptual, and religious knowledge are
all advanced by active praxis—in the laboratory for the scientist,
in the physical world for the perceiver, and in engagement with
worship and with other people for the Christian. Science, per-

[19] Bert H. Hodges, "Perception, Relativity, and Knowing and Doing the
Truth," in Stanton L. Jones, ed. *Psychology and the Christian Faith: An Introductory Reader* (Grand Rapids Mich.: Baker Book House, 1986), 51–77; James Gibson, *The Ecological Approach to Visual Perception* (Boston: Houghton Mifflin Co.,
1979).

[20] Michael Polanyi, *Personal Knowledge: Towards a Post-Critical Philosophy* (Chicago: University of Chicago Press, 1962).

ception, and Christian living all require what Saint Augustine called "faith seeking understanding." All three require that we commit ourselves to learning from a prior tradition, or paradigm, to be able to develop that tradition in new and surprising ways. As Lesslie Newbigin puts it, "The holding of [a scientific] theory is an act of faith in the rationality of the cosmos. The justification—if one may put it so—is by faith; only afterward, as a spin-off, does one find that it is also justified because it works. The analogy with Christian faith hardly needs to be pointed out."[21]

Values show up even in the labels chosen for psychological concepts. Just ask students whether they would rather be labeled "socially conformist" or "socially sensitive"; whether Nicaraguan *contras* should have been called "terrorists" or "freedom fighters;" whether the increasing rate of divorce should be interpreted as "the decline of the family" or "an increase in personal autonomy." After a few such exercises, students begin to understand that very same behavior is often interpreted in very different ways, depending on the social scientist's theoretical orientation—one that precedes research but that ought to be fine-tuned in the course of that research as well.

Psychotherapy

From their introduction to learning and perception, students begin to realize that the chief tension in psychology's epistemology is between objectivism and relativism, and they begin to discern with the help of Christian control beliefs that there is a third way. As they move from academic to applied psychology, they are confronted with another tension, this time anthropological. If academic psychology's bias has been to regard humans in strictly causal, material terms, much of counseling psychology does just the opposite. Heavily dependent on humanistic and existentialist thought, psychotherapy as originally developed by people like Carl Rogers, Abraham Maslow, and Albert Ellis sees human beings as essentially free, good, and capable of

---

[21] Lesslie Newbigin, *The Gospel in a Pluralist Society* (Grand Rapids, Mich.: William B. Eerdmans Publishing Co., 1989), 46.

great creativity and self-actualization once they have thrown off the shackles of societal restraint. If psychological epistemology lurches between positivism and skepticism, psychological anthropology lurches between reductionism and self-deification.[22]

From a combination of readings, lectures, and film discussions,[23] students begin to understand that humanistic psychologists' high view of persons is actually parasitic on their culture's Christian past, for the very notion of individual personhood began with the early Church's efforts to express the nature of God and the Trinity. Having clarified the personhood and freedom of God (in contrast to the Greek notion of ontological necessity, to which even God was said to be bound), the church fathers also came to assert the dignity and freedom of persons made in God's image. It is hardly insignificant that Carl Rogers, the architect of client-centered therapy, came from a very strict and legalistic Christian family. His therapy consequently embodies (albeit in secularized form) the kind of grace and loving acceptance that the Bible says God extends to all people who are willing to ask for it.

But it is one thing to deal with clients in an empathic and accepting manner, which has certainly been shown to be the single best predictor of positive therapeutic outcomes. It is quite another to *reduce* therapy to the processes of facilitation and affirmation, on the assumption that once the client feels safe to express all feelings candidly these feelings will be infallible guides to action. Such a stance reflects the dubious saying that it does not matter what you believe or feel, as long as it is sincere. Here too Christian control beliefs need to be critically applied, and in the context of class discussions, even students tending towards postmodern relativism begin to see how. The process of therapeutic affirmation is not enough, because not all goals,

---

[22] See Evans, *Wisdom and Humanness in Psychology* and Van Leeuwen, *The Person in Psychology* for further discussion of these tensions. See also Stanton L. Jones, "A Constructive Relationship for Religion With the Science and Profession of Psychology: Perhaps the Boldest Model Yet," *American Psychologist* 48 (1994): 184–99.

[23] There is a well-known series of video-reconfigured films showing three therapy pioneers (Carl Rogers, Fritz Perls, and Albert Ellis) working with the same client: "Three Approaches to Psychotherapy," Psychological and Educational Films, 3334 East Coast Highway, Suite 252, Corona Del Mar, Cal. 92625.

behaviors, and feelings are equally trustworthy, even when freely and sincerely chosen.

Processes like clarifying, accepting, and encouraging are good, because all persons are due dignity and respect as bearers of God's image. But these processes are not enough to guarantee personal and interpersonal health. Perhaps if humans had not fallen into sin, then they *would* be able to rely on what Rogers called "organismic valuing processes" to lead them to good decisions and actions. But due to sin and human finitude, we are easily self-deceived into assuming that whatever we want to do will always benefit both ourselves and others. Moreover, just as there is no such thing as immaculate perception in academic psychology, so too there is no such thing as completely nondirective therapy in applied psychology. When watching historical footage of Carl Rogers and other humanistic psychologists working with clients, students often note that selective affirmation and social reinforcement are being given to the extent that the client moves in the direction of the therapist's preferred worldview. There is no doubt that all therapy should begin nondirectively—otherwise how would the therapist ever get to know the range and depths of the client's concerns? But at some point the therapist's worldview will inevitably be engaged, and it is better that this should be done honestly than denied in pursuit of an unobtainable (and ultimately unhelpful) neutrality.

Even some non-Christian psychologists have pursued the humanistic paradigm long enough to become disenchanted with it. Their writings are a salutary corrective to prior excesses, and a witness to the working of common grace. A recent example is the perceptive book *Soul Searching,* by William Doherty, head of the marriage and family counseling program at the University of Minnesota.[24] In it he argues that therapists need to develop

---

[24] William J. Doherty, *Soul Searching: Why Psychotherapy Must Promote Moral Responsibility* (New York: Basic Books, 1995). For expanded Christian analyses of humanistic and other therapies, see Paul Vitz, *Psychology as Religion: The Cult of Self-Worship,* 2d ed. (Grand Rapids Mich.: William B. Eerdmans Publishing Co., 1994); Don S. Browning, *Religious Thought and the Modern Psychologies* (Philadelphia: Fortress Press, 1987); Robert C. Roberts, *Taking the Word to Heart: Self and Others in an Age of Therapies* (Grand Rapids, Mich.: William B. Eerdmans Publishing Co., 1993); and Robert C. Roberts and Mark R. Talbot, eds., *Limning the Psyche: Explorations in Christian Psychology* (Grand Rapids, Mich.: William B. Eerdmans Publishing Co., 1997).

virtues such as commitment, justice, truthfulness, and community-mindedness in their clients, and to implement the virtues of caring, courage, and prudence in their own practices. This is a long way from Carl Rogers and goes some way (as Doherty himself freely admits) towards a recovery of classical Christian virtue ethics.

CONCLUSION

"Like the scientist," writes Lesslie Newbigin, "the Christian believer has to learn to indwell the tradition. Its models and concepts are things which he does not simply examine from the perspective of another set of models, but have to become the models through which he understands the world."[25] This summarizes my aim as teacher of psychology—to help students see that faith and reason are not two separate ways of knowing but that both interact in the pursuit of truth, whether in psychology, theology, or the process of everyday living. In all these pursuits, by God's grace, humans unfold the riches of God's creation and purposes whether they give God the glory or try to keep it for themselves. And in all of them, chaff is mixed with the wheat, for humans are finite and fallen creatures and continue to see through a glass darkly.

My aim is to teach not merely the content areas of psychology, fascinating though these continue to be, but to challenge the split between facts and values that most students as children of modernity take for granted. In addition, I wish to address the postmodern despair of attaining any truth at all, which is the message that students are absorbing in the current cultural milieu. By inviting students to indwell the biblical drama as characters who have found the Author and have begun to discern that Author's purposes, I hope to provide them with what John Calvin called the "spectacles" of faith. With their vision thus clarified and their minds more unified, my hope is that, at the end of an introductory semester of psychology, they are on their way

---

[25] Newbigin, *The Gospel in a Pluralist Society*, 49.

to becoming Christian students—not just students who happen to be Christian.

Selected Bibliography

Browning, Don. *Religious Thought and the Modern Psychologies.* Philadelphia: Fortress Press, 1987.

Evans, C. Stephen. *Preserving the Person: A Look at the Human Sciences.* Downers Grove, Ill.: InterVarsity Press, 1977.

———. *Wisdom and Humanness in Psychology: Prospects for a Christian Approach.* Grand Rapids, Mich.: Baker Book House, 1989.

Jones, Stanton L. "A Constructive Relationship for Religion with the Science and Profession of Psychology: Perhaps the Boldest Model Yet." *American Psychologist* 42 (1994): 184–99.

———, ed. *Psychology and the Christian Faith.* Grand Rapids, Mich.: Baker Book House, 1986). Note especially the introductory chapter by Jones and the chapters on perception by Hodges and on the self by Evans.

——— and Richard Butman. *Modern Psychotherapies: A Comprehensive Christian Appraisal.* Downers Grove, Ill.: InterVarsity Press, 1991.

The Journal of Psychology and Christianity, Theme Issue on "Integration Revisited." 15, no. 2 (summer 1996).

Middleton, J. Richard and Brian J. Walsh. *Truth Is Stranger Than It Used to Be: Biblical Faith in a Postmodern Age.* Downers Grove, Ill.: InterVarsity Press, 1995.

Myers, David G. and Malcolm A. Jeeves. *Psychology Through the Eyes of Faith.* San Francisco: HarperCollins, 1987.

Newbigin, Lesslie. *The Gospel in a Pluralist Society.* Grand Rapids, Mich.: William B. Eerdmans Publishing Co., 1989.

Roberts, Robert C.. *Taking the Word to Heart: Self and Others in an Age of Therapies.* Grand Rapids, Mich.: William B. Eerdmans Publishing Co., 1993.

——— and Mark R. Talbot, eds. *Limning the Psyche: Explorations in Christian Psychology.* Grand Rapids, Mich.: William B. Eerdmans Publishing Co., 1997.

Sire, James. *The Universe Next Door: A Basic World View Catalogue*, 3d edition. Downers Grove, Ill.: InterVarsity Press, 1997.

Van Leeuwen, Mary Stewart. *Gender and Grace: Love, Work and Parenting in a Changing World*. Downers Grove, Ill.: InterVarsity Press, 1990.

———. *The Person in Psychology: A Contemporary Christian Appraisal*. Grand Rapids, Mich.: William B. Eerdmans Publishing Co., 1985.

Vitz, Paul C. *Psychology as Religion: The Cult of Self-Worship*, 2d edition. Grand Rapids, Mich.: William B. Eerdmans Publishing Co., 1994.

Walsh, Brian J. and J. Richard Middleton. *The Transforming Vision: Shaping a Christian World View*. Downers Grove, Ill.: InterVarsity Press, 1984.

Wolters, Albert. *Creation Regained: Biblical Basics for a Reformational World View*. Grand Rapids, Mich.: William B. Eerdmans Publishing Co, 1985.

Wolterstorff, Nicholas. *Reason Within the Bounds of Religion*, 2d edition. Grand Rapids, Mich.: William B. Eerdmans Publishing Co., 1984.

3

At the Lectern Between Jerusalem and Sarajevo: A Christian Approach to Teaching Political Science

Ron Kirkemo

A Personal Context

THE SEARCH FOR LINKAGES between our faith and our learning, in particular our theological world of love, hope, and grace and our political world of power, pride, cooperation, and destruction, or between Jerusalem and Sarajevo, is a continuing quest. On one hand, to compartmentalize or separate the classroom lectern and its academic scholarship from the chapel podium and its Christian message is a dereliction. On the other hand, I fear the other approach of seeking a tight integration, for those who claim they know what constitutes a Christian policy for welfare reform or nuclear strategy or tax policy have far too often merely baptized their self-interest in the waters of shallow hermeneutics. A third approach to link Christianity and political science uses political science methodologies to study behavior and attitudes of Christians in politics. There is value in that approach, but I find it too narrow. My fourth approach is both more cautious and more ambitious. I prefer to work with models rather than absolutes and certainties, building models of both theology and political science and testing them against each other, finding persuasive linkages, research topics, and a Christian political perspective.

I have the good fortune to teach at an evangelical Christian college, sponsored by the Church of the Nazarene, in which eighty percent of the students are born again and in which there is denominational diversity—only twenty-seven percent of the student body is Nazarene. Given these contexts of my professional life, the goals of my career are what I call Liberal Arts Plus Two.[1] The plus-two factors are my role in building a vibrant department and in shaping career choices. I also work to promote the three transitions students face in college. The first is the transition into college—making it past homesickness or the culture shock of college academics. Having made the transition into college, the danger is that students will mistake campus life for college. Students need to transition into the major. This transition enables them to see themselves as political science majors, not just college students, and to define the goal of college not as a diploma but as attaining entry to their chosen career or admission to the law school or graduate school they want. A departmental affiliation changes their self-definition and their commitment to study so that professors can shape students' attitudes and perspectives. Students can then focus on the depths of the major, build a community of scholars and friends, and count on involvement and responsibility.[2] The senior year should be a transition into career-mindedness. My role as a professor of political science is to help students define themselves and, in the absence of a calling to the pastorate or mission field, to find a career path of Christian value in public service.

---

[1] Liberal arts education is more than just curricular breadth and should influence students to adopt intrinsic values such as openness and personal creativity. For teachers, liberal education is more than passing on content to students; for students, it is more than acquiring the necessary knowledge for a good job after college. The opposite of indoctrination, liberal arts education seeks intellectual coherence but avoids dogma by a commitment to humane values and moral reflection. Liberal arts education enables people to transcend the parochialisms of their time, place, and station. The place of political science in the liberal arts is described in John C. Wahlke, "Liberal Learning and the Political Science Major: A Report to the Profession," *PS: Political Science & Politics* (March 1991): 48–60 and Douglas C. Bennett, "Political Science Within the Liberal Arts: Toward Renewal of Our Commitment," *PS: Political Science & Politics* (June 1991): 201–4.

[2] A commitment to this transition has been justly criticized for being too exclusivistic for a liberal arts campus, for failing to understand the social needs of students, and for generating elitist attitudes. These are potential attitudinal dynamics, and I oppose them when I see them arise.

My Wesleyan tradition affects my basic assumptions about Scripture, grace, and epistemology, and so impacts how I teach political science. Methodism arose seeking a middle way between the Roman Catholic emphasis on tradition and holiness and the Reformed Protestant emphasis on Scripture and justification by faith. Wesleyans find the Reformed doctrine of *sola Scriptura* too independent and too vulnerable to a literalistic and authoritarian hermeneutic, too much the equivalent of Mao's Little Red Book—an ideological tract cut off from evidence and experience. The Bible is made personal and dynamic by the leading of the Holy Spirit, and Scripture must be handled with sophistication and subject to biblical study with the methods of higher criticism. Using the Bible this way allows me to deal honestly with issues like the Canaanite genocide. Yet I must remain mindful of the risk that some literalist pastors will take offense and claim the professor is abandoning the Bible and shaking the faith of young students.[3] Like Jacob, anyone who has gone through such a struggle and manages to come out exonerated still also comes out with a permanent limp in his or her professional life.

Wesleyans are strong Trinitarians and believe not only in creation and redemption, but also in holiness—that is, an existential Christian life lived in the power of the spirit of Christ, the risen Lord. Christ through grace is in the world as well as in our individual lives. That grace is available to all if they will choose it and is transformational for both individuals and society. Grace seeks to awaken our individual souls and draw us to a life with a spiritual sense and a personal relationship with the triune God. Grace also humanizes people and society by enabling people to act morally—by affirming human dignity and moral choices and inspiring service and hope. Hence Wesleyans believe in both personal righteousness and social reform to achieve justice.

---

[3] As one example, where the public response is only a partial reflection of a wider and deeper non-public assault on a professor, see Richard Taylor's attack on C. W. Cowles who questioned God's role in the Canaanite genocide. C. W. Cowles, "Canaanite Genocide and the God of Love," *The Preacher's Magazine* (December/January/February 1995–96): 44–49, and Richard Taylor, "A Personal Letter," *The Preacher's Magazine* (December/January/February 1996–97): 44–46.

Wesleyans also believe grace influences our thinking. But while the followers of Abraham Kuyper believe sin so distorts thinking that a coherent Christian worldview must be developed in opposition to an assumed coherent secular worldview, Wesleyans do not make such clear, diametrically opposed categories.[4] Grace pervades the continuing creational processes of this world, so we must recognize a totality of experience. We affirm a fact-value holism rather than disjunction, so thinking should always be normative and hallowed. Rather than Kuyper's forced bipolar categories, we accept the fact of differences. Thinking is embedded not only in a moral community but also in a personal and historical matrix of behavior, habits, and expectations. Wesleyans are therefore reluctant to draw conclusions too early or too tightly. Rather than drawing up a worldview, they are more willing to leave space for individual differences, which in turn reinforces the grace of human dignity.

From this perspective, it is not scandalous that there is no tight intellectual integration of faith and learning. Structures of reality are too dynamic and the rate of our new scientific and social discoveries and understandings too rapid to claim much finality. Wesleyans see ambiguity and tension in efforts to understand the two realms and so are comfortable with differing viewpoints and efforts at reconciliation rather than with the certainties of integration.

I teach at Point Loma Nazarene University. The Nazarene Church is part of the holiness wing of Protestantism that emphasizes personal experience and life in the Spirit and has more concern with personal sin and right living than with social sin and justice. Thus, one Nazarene writer could assert that the way to world peace is for Christians to be nice to their neighbors and coworkers.[5] Obviously, there is no link between world peace and

---

[4] For a summary description of Kuyper's bipolar model and Emil Brunner's concentric circle model of sin and thinking see Stephen K. Moroney, "How Sin Affects Scholarship: A New Model," *Christian Scholar's Review* 28, no. 3 (spring 1999): 432–51. As an alternative to these two static models, I build on the work of Nancey Murphy and George F. R. Ellis, *On The Moral Nature of the Universe: Theology, Cosmology, and Ethics* (Minneapolis: Fortress Press, 1996), particularly pages 64–87 and 204–5.

[5] See, for example, Morris Chalfant, "On Earth, Peace" *Herald of Holiness* (December 1990): 2–3.

being nice at work or school! Part of my task, then, is to help students see that prayer for world hunger or two-week mission trips to Brazil or Armenia or Kenya to hold puppet shows and vacation Bible schools are not going to do anything for world peace. I try to demonstrate the need for action, for programs, and for careers in public service.

Working then, as an evangelical Wesleyan Christian who teaches political science, I apply certain guiding principles to my pedagogical praxis. First, if students are going to handle political science in a sophisticated way, they also need to handle their ideas of Christianity in a sophisticated way. That means moving beyond the God-talk of undefined terms—sin, human nature, total depravity, common grace, and "God in control of history."[6] If such terms are not defined, operationalized, and tested, they run the risk of becoming either self-contained mental constructs unrelated to reality or merely ideological lenses placed over the subject matter of our field, which relegates teaching to indoctrination. Invoking such words as *sin* or *love* or *sovereignty* like mantras to justify realism or pacifism or mandates or delegations is not enough. I do try to deal with these terms, but since freshmen are far too sensitive or suspicious of any such efforts, I do so in my upper-division classes.

Second, I make tolerance a prime virtue in my classes. For the past decade, most students have had political views different from mine. I expect them to give mine a fair hearing. I in turn give them respect as people with different views, and views that need to be heard and respected by me. Sometimes students change; other times we learn from each other, kid each other about our beliefs, and have great discussions. Still, it may not be enough, and some students have looked elsewhere for a major. I had a student tell me he was changing his major to Communication Studies because he did not want to think about his beliefs; he just wanted to learn how to express them better. I did not try to stop him.

Third, I have a basic three-part developmental strategy. The

---

[6] All these terms, undefined, are found in Dean C. Curry's effort to lay out a "Biblical starting point" in *A World Without Tyranny* (Westchester, Ill.: Crossway Books, 1990), 64–66, 83.

Christian views of politics that students bring to college are fairly unsophisticated but are strongly held. The task that all liberal arts professors face in all fields is how to open up students' views and broaden them through reflection and testing, and how to lead students to find their own coherent, creative, and moral views. When I was a freshman at Humboldt State University my political science professor, Dr. Ross Y. Koen, told us that we were like medieval fortresses, whose windows were narrow slits, wide enough to shoot arrows out but too narrow to let arrows in. His job, he said, was to knock holes in those walls and make wider windows. If that was true of political views in a state university, it is even truer in a Christian college today. So at the first stage, I try to open up students' views by discussing scriptural hermeneutics and the diversity of alternative Christian views. I work to show them how a Christian view is a construct from various ideas and how different ideas are put together into a creative and coherent reconciliation. At the second stage, I move to more focused efforts in upper-division classes to challenge students to link their Christian values and certain policy issues. I do not try to tell them the correct view, but I use class assignments like simulations and problem-solving guides to provide some testing of their views. At the third stage, in some of my courses I seek to cross intellectual boundaries in a scholarly way. Here we confront the issue of how to conceptualize theology and social science, and we construct some epistemological grounds for building theological and social scientific models that can interact with each other. I try to define and operationalize key theological concepts so we can discuss them in a manner that is not foreign to a social science mentality.

Fourth, I place a strong emphasis on experience, for politics cannot be adequately taught from a textbook alone; its reality should be experienced. Our majors are required to take one semester's study off-campus at a national capital in what we call our Capitals Program. We use various programs, but they all must be entirely political science classes and have an internship. Typically students use the Council for Christian Colleges and Universities' American Studies Program, American University's

Washington Semester Program and World Capitals Program, and Drew University's United Nations Semester. Additionally, I build simulations into many of my courses, for they force students to make moral decisions in the context of lobbying and bargaining or in the context of crisis and pressure. They demonstrate that moral insight arises from reason and experience as well as from Scripture and tradition.

Fifth, in my personal approach to teaching, I seek remembrance and find grace. Too often I have heard various church leaders say students will not remember what we say in class; they only remember that we knew their name or talked to them while walking to chapel or exhibited pastoral attitudes. I resent and reject that view. Only those who do not aspire to greatness in academics hold such a view. If it is true of us, we need to change our teaching style drastically or find another job. I seek to make my courses memorable, with significant insights, with concepts that begin to define the boundaries of student perspectives, with practical insights that they will carry with them, with topics that embody the stakes and importance of the field, and with materials that will inspire new ideas about careers.

I also find grace. I was not called to be a professor the way my son was called to be a preacher. I grew up loving politics and wanted to be like one of my college professors. I earned my degrees in the field and was warmly welcomed at Point Loma. I read and think about politics, and I struggle with issues of principle, providence, and action in places like Sarajevo—much more than I do in Sunday school classes and Sunday worship services. As I develop new courses, these issues get raised in new contexts. As I struggle to understand and work out lectures, teaching becomes an act of worship and means of grace to me—and hopefully to my students.

From these elements of my personal context, I seek to link the world of Christian faith and the world of political science using a variety of strategies. The following courses and accompanying teaching strategies embrace most of the above contextual elements and reflect my attempts at building bridges between the norms of Jerusalem and the reality of the twice-infamous Sarajevo.

Introduction to Political Science

Most freshmen come to college without understanding the nature of a liberal arts college. Many students (and many parents) expect that their views of religion and government will be confirmed, not challenged or broadened. Some see college as a continuation of high school (only harder) and Sunday school ("Why isn't the required freshman religion class more devotional?" or, "I did so well in Bible quizzing, why am I getting such a bad grade in this Bible class?"). One of my primary goals in this class is to describe the liberal arts, affirming that we are open-minded not narrow-minded, cosmopolitan not parochial, and that we deal in moral reflection rather than indoctrination and promote creativity rather than dogma. What this class is about, I tell them, is broadening their views—their political views and their religious views. I construct my class as a survey of the basic fields of political science, and I try to use texts that deal explicitly with the normative element of politics and government. I always use supplementary texts and try to include at least one that raises moral issues. One of the best that I used was Stephen B. Oates's *Let the Trumpet Sound: The Life of Martin Luther King, Jr.,* until it was sold to another publisher and tripled in price. Another unbeatable supplement is Andrew Young's spiritual autobiography, *A Way Out of No Way,* which is a marvelous book for raising issues of God's direction in life and for addressing political principles. Currently I am using Gary Haugen's *Good News about Injustice.* Haugen describes his experiences as director of the UN team investigating genocide in Rwanda and offers helpful insights on why the evil of injustice exists and what Christians can and ought to do.[7]

I want students to understand that there are no easy answers, that a perspective is shaped by many different sources, and that many different perspectives have valuable insights. So, in addition to the texts, I reprint and bind as a supplementary reader a

---

[7] Stephen B. Oates, *Let the Trumpet Sound: The Life of Martin Luther King, Jr.* (New York: New American Library, A Mentor Book, 1982); Andrew Young, *A Way Out Of No Way* (Nashville, Tenn.: Thomas Nelson Publishers, 1994); and Gary A. Haugen, *Good News About Injustice* (Downers Grove, Ill.: InterVarsity Press, 1999).

series of materials, some of which I use to raise religious issues. I usually use Michael Cromartie's interview with Tony Campolo, Charles Colson, and Ralph Reed in an article entitled "One Lord, One Faith, One Voice?"[8] For the past several years I have used pages sixteen to thirty-nine of Oates' *Let the Trumpet Sound* (copyright permission must be obtained). Those pages describe King in college and seminary as he worked through the ideas of Marx, Nietzsche, Ghandi, Niebuhr, and other theorists. He held to some and discarded others, constructing, in the process, his own coherent Christian approach to social and political issues.

I wrote one of the documents in the reader to explain the differences between a devotional use of Scripture, commentaries on Scripture, and scholarly analysis of Scripture. It describes various hermeneutical approaches, gives a quick survey of basic parts of Scripture and lays out six religious traditions—realism, liberalism, pacifism, personalism, transformation, and apocalyptics—and shows how they flow from particular sections of Scripture. I usually get one of three responses to this article. Some dislike it because they find it disconcerting to approach the Bible in a non-devotional way. Others find it very enlightening, and they appreciate examples of new ways of looking at Scripture. And, as always, there is a third group, who simply do not care. But the discussion helps students rise beyond a simplistic use of Scripture and think about the sources from which they derive their assumptions about religion and politics.

The contemporary nature of political science makes it easy to use articles from newspapers and popular magazines to enliven the text and discussions, so I use them to supplement text and lecture material. Elections spawn numerous articles, and I will use one or more for material on candidates and their strategies. The 1992 election generated many articles about the new role of the Christian Right in the Republican Party, and I continue to use several of those to raise the issues of Christian agendas and appropriate strategy.[9] While I prefer this political aspect of polit-

---

[8] Michael Cromartie, "One Lord, One Faith, One Voice?" *Christianity Today* (October 7, 1996): 35–43.

[9] Kim A. Lawton, "The New Face(s) of the Religious Right," *Christianity Today* (July 20, 1992): 42–45; Laurence I. Barrett, "Pulpit Politics," *Time* (August 31, 1992): 34–35; Kim A. Lawton, "Estranged Bedfellows," *Christianity Today*

ical science, there are several fine empirical studies that could be used in a teaching strategy that emphasize a more scientific approach.[10] I also take this opportunity when discussing the Religious Right in politics to introduce students to the perspective of the professional literature with book reviews of recent literature on the Religious Right in the *APSA Review*.[11]

I use Aaron Wildavsky's 1989 John Gaus Lecture entitled "What Is Permissible So That This People May Survive?: Joseph the Administrator."[12] It is a wonderful discussion of the Joseph story in the Bible. It discusses how Joseph, as an advisor to the prince, suggested that pharaoh take the livestock, then the land, and then independence of the people of Egypt in exchange for food. Ultimately his advice brought him to an exalted position in Egypt but left that country worse off than it was before he came. In this one story, I can illustrate a way to use Scripture to show the impact of personal ambition and to demonstrate the need to factor consequences into discussions of the morality of policies.

Simulations allow students to solidify their recognition of interest groups, coalition building, and the self-interest of one's own religious views. They assume the role of lobbyists attempting to persuade parents, constituents, pastors, administrators, and trustees regarding the issue of dancing on campus. Just prior to this simulation, we discuss lobbying strategies, and they familiarize themselves with a computer program used by the Christian Coalition called In-House Lobbyist.[13] This program

(August 17, 1992): 40–41; and Jim Wallis, "Can Politics be Moral?" *Sojourners* (November 1993): 10–11.

[10] See, for example, Robert Booth Fowler and Allen D. Hertzke, *Religion and Politics in America: Faith, Culture, and Strategic Choices* (Boulder, Col.: Westview Press, 1995); Lyman Kellstedt, John C. Green, James L. Guth, and Corwin Smidt, "It's the Culture, Stupid! 1992 and Our Political Future," *First Things* (April 1994): 28–33; and Albert J. Menendez, *Evangelicals at the Ballot Box* (Amherst, Mass.: Prometheus Books, 1996).

[11] See the following issues of the *American Political Science Review*: (September 1992): 79–80; (June 1993): 491–93; (June 1997): 467; and (September, 1997): 752.

[12] Aaron Wildavsky, "What Is Permissible So That This People May Survive?: Joseph the Administrator," *PS: Political Science and Politics* (December 1989): 779–87.

[13] The program is available at www.virtualsoftware.com/Prodpage.cfm/ 1994.

graphically depicts how an organization can track members of Congress on issues, rate them by organizations, and identify them by key factors in order to develop targets and build coalitions. The versatility of In-House Lobbyist would also make it a useful tool in government and legislative classes.

In the section of the course on decision making, I run a simulation of the Cuban Missile Crisis to test the rational, organizational, and bureaucratic theories of policy making. Though most of the documents relating to that crisis are now found in several books, I purchased microfiche of Kennedy's White House files and the recordings of the Ex Com discussions during the crisis from the Kennedy Library. I use those materials and others to set up the simulation and assess the group dynamics of the discussions. As in any simulation, the students read some materials about the crisis, and I provide summary biographical materials on the participants. I call attention to Robert Kennedy's concern with the moral issues of the crisis, and I create three fictitious pastors with different views. I select one pastor to be a special advisor to the president and to participate in the Ex Com to represent one or another Christian view of politics and so raise even more directly the moral issues and test what happens to that view during the discussions. The other two pastors who represent two other Christian views of politics become a control group who pronounce their views through the public media without having the responsibility to make decisions about the crisis. Simulations are always successful because students want to participate in class and they learn existentially. As two students wrote on their evaluations, "Issues such as the Cuban Missile Crisis are much more complex than I thought. Up until then, 'I had the answer to everything,' politically speaking." Another wrote, "I learned first of all how to work together with a group of people that had conflicting ideas. We still got things done, but we all realized that maybe it wasn't the way we planned. I also learned how to compromise what I want for the better of another."

World Politics

Any political science field (and therefore the college class that addresses it) is, at a minimum, a body of content, described and defined for students by a textbook. But a liberal arts education is more than mastering bodies of content. As part of their transition from being first-year college students to being political science majors, students should be drawn into the intellectual excitement of debates at the heart and on the frontiers of the field. In one class or another, students should find an issue that moves them, arouses an emotional commitment, and perhaps leads them to career opportunities. Ultimately, students should find a home—an intellectual home where they feel connected to the issues and stimulated by the debates in at least one of the fields of the major. A field like world politics deals with deeply moving issues that involve threats to human life and humane values. In my world politics courses, therefore, I provide opportunities to structure Christian perspectives into the class, which I do through biographical readings and through a problem-solving exercise.

Biographies are versatile tools for class. I use thirteen readings from a book that is, much to my dismay, out of print—Joseph Kruzel and James Rosenau's *Journeys Through World Politics*.[14] It is a collection of intellectual autobiographies by eminent scholars of international politics. I obtained reprint permission and bind the essays as a required text. Though it is a graduate-level book, I use it to introduce students to world politics as an intellectual home—to what Joseph Nye in his chapter calls the "invisible college of scholarship," and to the role of foundations, mentors, and research agendas. Like the pages noted above in the Oates book, these biographies are very helpful for students to understand the concept of an intellectual journey. It takes them two or three chapters before they really engage the material. But when and if they do, they understand better how ideas are developed, how family background influences intellectual perspectives, and how professional careers work. The broader or professional academic world becomes real, and for some students that world becomes their own.

Several of the writers come from Christian backgrounds and

---

[14] Joseph Kruzel and James N. Rosenau, eds., *Journeys Through World Politics: Autobiographical Reflections of Thirty-four Academic Travelers* (Lexington, Mass.: Lexington Books, 1989).

remain Christians, and I find this faith dimension especially instructive for my students. Margaret Hermann writes about learning politics from watching her pastor-father deal with church boards; Bruce Russett about his consulting role to the National Conference of Catholic Bishops as the conference composed a pastoral letter on nuclear strategy; William T. R. Fox about why he moved beyond his Quaker "war-as-pathological-behavior" background; and Richard A. Falk about what he sees as his intellectual marginality and its role in developing his world-order perspective. In defense of the rather sharp tone in his essay, J. David Singer writes about the moral responsibility of all who choose to work in the field of world politics. Our issues, he writes, are not like arguments about Shakespearean authorship or architectural gracefulness. "Those of us who have chosen to teach, consult, research, and write in the world politics field have an extraordinary responsibility," he explains.

> Between the day that these lines are written and the book appears in print, untold human lives will be snuffed out by famine, terrorism, insurgency and war somewhere in the global village. . . . These are not trivial matters and it is not trivial how we study them, teach about them, write and speak about them—or keep silent about them.[15]

Jerusalem must relate to Sarajevo. One student wrote in his evaluation of the book that the reading of Singer "really spoke to my inner self about my responsibility as a Christian."

Additionally, I structure Christian perspectives into the class by taking a problem-solving approach to such issues as conflict resolution, internal war, refugees, human rights, population growth, environmental decay, and international capital flows, trade, and development. Students read widely on the World Wide Web in such official sources as the annual reports relating to human rights and refugees from the Web site of the UN High Commissioner for Refugees, called Refworld, the annual reports of the World Bank, the World Food Program, and the World Health Organization, the annual *Human Development Report* from the United Nations Development Program, and documents from

---

[15] J. David Singer, "The Making of a Peace Researcher," in Kruzel and Rosenau, *ibid.*, 228.

the UN and African human rights Web sites. Then I distribute a problem-solving guide, which lists the steps necessary for effective decision making.[16]

Twice during this section of the class, students must fill out the guide in relation to an issue of their choice. This exercise serves several purposes. I use it in several of my lectures to model how to think in such a framework. Students learn to engage World Wide Web material more deeply. Issues become more personal, and I hope to snare the interest of one or more students in one of the issue areas. Students have to make their Christian values explicit in the values clarification section and assess how those are congruent with, or in conflict with, national values and global governance values. On an issue like refugees, for example, most students see their Christian values clearly but divide on the national values—should the nation seek to help the refugees, or should it keep that money at home for its own people? On an issue like the environment, students split between a traditional value of subduing the earth and the more earth-friendly value of stewardship. The class discussions that result from the students' presentation of their perspectives become a further exercise in relating Christian values to the realities of politics. The exercise also provides the opportunity for students to face the philosophical implications of adherence to a deontological or consequentialist approach to political morality and ethics.

A problem-solving approach can also inspire student interest in a career path. When we discuss diplomatic tools we explore various NGOs and other members of the international donor community and their programs. Students enter a new world (to them) of secular and Christian international service agencies like Africare, CARE, Church World Service, Doctors without Borders, International Rescue Committee, Oxfam America, Refu-

---

[16] These steps include (1) nature and scope of the problem, (2) values clarification, (3) proximate and underlying causes, (4) policy options, (5) diplomatic tools, (6) evaluation, and (7) decision. The values clarification section is subdivided into Christian values, national values, and global governance values. The diplomatic tools section is divided into persuasion, coercion, relief, and development options.

gees International, World Relief, and World Vision.[17] They read summaries of the work of these agencies on the World Wide Web. I explain their interconnections, such as the fact that it takes five to six agencies doing specialized tasks to make a refugee camp both functional and humane. By describing the activities of prominent members of this community, I hope to interest some students in potential careers (or at least internships) with such organizations.

THE TOPIC OF WAR

War is an issue that intrudes into all world politics courses in one way or another. I treat it as a policy challenge in my U.S. Foreign Policy class and as a research topic in my Modern Study of War class. Each raises different issues for Christian pedagogy. My basic normative approach to the foreign policy course has been to reject the crusader mentality that can invade policy issues and to advocate a principled pragmatism. It is difficult to use supplemental books to present Christian perspectives, since they are rarely published and do not stay long in print. Currently, a very fine book with a conservative orientation is Mark Amstutz's *International Ethics*.[18] Similarly, while students read many articles for this class, their sources are academic journals, which, with the exception of *Ethics and International Affairs* from the Carnegie Council on Ethics and International Affairs, do not deal explicitly with moral issues.

Given the complexity of the issues, I do not try to invoke or advocate a distinctively Christian approach to war in particular or foreign policy in general in this class. Instead, I have generally identified Christian values with policies that resolve conflict, promote humane values and democratic processes, and minimize a moralized policy. I have discovered that emphasizing

---

[17] Home pages for most of these organizations can be found at www.charity .org.

[18] Mark R. Amstutz, *International Ethics: Concepts, Theories, and Cases in Global Politics* (New York: Rowman & Littlefield Publishers, Inc, 1999).

moral dilemmas is a good strategy for me. I make those dilemmas real to students by having them read a portion of Dean
Rusk's memoirs, and then an article about the split between
Rusk and his son. A similar father-son disagreement was published in the American Scientific Affiliation's journal. Jack
Swearengen, whose career included work in advanced weapons
systems development, and his son Alan Swearengen, an antiwar
campus activist, wrote the article.[19] Representing a policy dilemma through conflict between a parent and young adult is a
teaching strategy that captures the imagination of students.

The primary war issue during most of my teaching career has
been nuclear weapons. My graduate school years were strongly
influenced by the civilian strategists who brought greater rational control to nuclear strategy.[20] I could not accept pacifism and
came to believe that the most Christian approach to war was to
support a rational strategic policy that would maximize deterrence and minimize damage if the policy failed, while supporting arms control to strengthen crisis management. Despite the
shaking of my faith in the rationality of leaders by our experience in Vietnam, I continue to see no better alternative. Therefore, in my class, I lay out the issues and basic Christian
positions in lectures and advocate strategic deterrence without
extended deterrence.[21]

The fall of the Soviet Union removed nuclear weapons as a

---

[19] Dean Rusk, *As I Saw It* (New York: W. W. Norton & Co., 1990); Tom Ma-
thews, "The Rusk Family War—And Peace," *Newsweek* (June 18, 1990): 54–55;
Jack C. Swearengen and Alan P. Swearengen, "Comparative Analysis of the
Nuclear Weapons Debate: Campus and Developer Perspectives," *Perspectives
on Science and Christian Faith*, 42:2 (June 1990): 75–85.

[20] The story of this process is best told by Fred Kaplan, *The Wizards of Arma-
geddon* (New York: Simon and Schuster, 1983), who builds the story around the
career of Bernard Brodie. No moral discussion of the nuclear issue is complete
without Freeman Dyson's *Weapons and Hope* (New York: Harper & Row, 1984).

[21] I built upon this perspective in my book *Between the Eagle and the Dove* and
in a conference paper in which I argue that a holiness perspective does not
require an absolutist ethic that rejects a policy of nuclear deterrence. A holiness
perspective, however, does suggest certain principles that ought to set boundaries on a deterrence policy. See Ronald Kirkemo, *Between the Eagle and the
Dove: The Christian and American Foreign Policy* (Downers Grove, Ill.: InterVarsity Press, 1976) and "A Holiness Perspective on Nuclear Deterrence," unpublished paper presented at the Calvin College Conference on Evangelicals and
American Foreign Policy, 1988.

central issue of foreign policy and moral concern. Conflicts that blur the distinction between internal and external war are now extensive across the globe. These wars of extensive tragedy, as well as the continuing use of war as an instrument of coercion and expansion, have again made the issues of military policy and intervention the subjects of moral debate. The Persian Gulf War, the NATO military campaign against Serbia over Kosovo, and the ongoing war against terrorism have provided current focal points for explaining U.S. military policy and Christian perspectives and for conducting a simulation. Other U.S. interventions, such as in Somalia and Haiti, as well as decisions against intervention, such as in Liberia and Rwanda, are useful vehicles for dealing with moral issues of military intervention and war and provide excellent simulation opportunities.

My Modern Study of War course brings students to the scientific study of war by utilizing computer data sets and SPSS (Statistical Package for Social Sciences) for research into questions of war. Students complete certain exercises, and a small research project using the Jack Levy *Great Power Wars 1495–1815* and the J. David Singer and Melvin Small *Correlates of War Project: International War Data, 1816–1992* data sets.[22] One of the texts I use, which thankfully is now back in print, is *The Scientific Study of Peace and War*. It is a fine reader, and it also has a learning package designed to teach students how to apply principles of the scientific method to the study of war. I also use John A. Vasquez's *The War Puzzle* and an anthology of J. David Singer's articles as core texts.[23]

Since this course is built around social science methodology, I use it as an opportunity to introduce students to the fear of some Christians that such value-neutral methodologies will arbitrarily exclude religious and theological considerations or produce a

---

[22] These data sets and many others are available from the Inter-University Consortium for Political and Social Research (ICPSR) at the University of Michigan. They are free for institutions that are members of the ICPSR or may be rented for a two-year period for a small fee.

[23] John A. Vasquez and Marie T. Henehan, eds., *The Scientific Study of Peace and War*, (New York: Lexington Books, 1992); John A. Vasquez, *The War Puzzle*, (New York: Cambridge University Press, 1993); J. David Singer, *Models, Methods, and Progress in World Politics: A Peace Research Odyssey* (Boulder, Col.: Westview Press, 1990).

closed system of general laws that define causes and processes, thereby creating a state-university-style secular class. While this may be a real issue in other behavioral disciplines, it is less problematic here, for it is a misunderstanding of what we do in political science. We deal in correlations and probabilities, not closed systems, and our research agendas and process of hypothesis formulation are normative. I selected the text by Singer, a leader in the use of quantifiable data, because several of his chapters deal explicitly with the normative dimensions of his work, which I share.

Rebuilding Devastated States

This course represents my effort to push the boundaries of our curriculum to one of the newest areas of world politics, that of failed or devastated states. A devastated state is a reflection of human freedom, for usually it has been torn apart by racial/ethnic/religious hatred. Unable to win a civil war, rebels make civilian populations and the state infrastructure their targets, aiming for a collapse of the central government. By the time a cease-fire is established, whether in Mozambique, Liberia, Rwanda, Sudan, Tajikistan, or El Salvador, the state's social, economic, and political elements have been devastated. Thousands of teenagers and young adults who have only known war throughout their lives remain armed with modern weapons, while intimate exposure to brutality and displacement leave thousands of others psychologically scarred. The course is a political science course, but it serves as such a unique vehicle for serious work with theological concepts and theological ethics that I take the opportunity it affords to construct exercises that systematically bring together the realms of theology and political science. Because it deals with the stark issues of hatred, tragedy, and death, easy answers about sovereignty or love or control of history will not suffice.

Students study current policies and processes to demobilize the warriors, return the refugees, democratize the political system with reconciliation elections, and rebuild the social and economic infrastructures. I also concentrate upon efforts to create mechanisms for psychosocial healing, rehumanizing adversaries, and monitoring human rights. Unavoidably, the course is suffused with a general Christian sensitivity. I make an early effort to engage the emotions of my students with regard to these complex issues. I have found videos, articles, and Web sites particularly helpful. With this background data, I then take the class to a local church in an immigrant community of San Diego to meet refugees from the Sudan. We speak with some of the people about the conditions in their homeland to reinforce the enormity of the devastation and to give a human face to the text material.

Stuart Kaufman has described the process of "spiraling to ethnic war."[24] Can the reverse, a positive spiral toward trust, moderation, and a sense of shared community, be created? To define rebuilding, I work with a set of ten functional categories.[25] This is a political topic, but its roots are also psychological and spiritual. Here we deal in some depth with the social psychology of hate and the existence of two paths that result from bereavement—the path of anger and revenge or that of adjustment and reconciliation. I work with definitions of sin and depravity and grace to explore in depth how God through grace can move in these devastated states to rehumanize and heal. Then students can decide if there is any hope for rebuilding such a society and reconciling people.

Lincoln Bloomfield and Allen Moulton's CASCON (Computer Aided Study of Conflict) is a program for understanding and preventing conflict. They identify 3 stages and 154 potential factors that can operate in a conflict setting. They code the factors according to degree of influence in moving a dispute toward or away from conflict.[26] Since I regularly use CASCON in my World Politics class, students have worked with it before they get to

---

[24] Stuart Kaufman, "Spiraling to Ethnic War," *International Security*, 21:2 (Fall 1996): 108–38.

[25] These ten include rebuilding security, providing sustenance, reconstructing infrastructure and governance mechanisms, establishing policies of well being, dealing with bereavement, rebuilding trust, revaluing people, reconstructing a moral sense, and creating civil involvement and discourse.

[26] Lincoln P. Bloomfield and Allen Moulton, *Managing International Conflict: A Teaching Tool Using CASCON* (New York: St. Martin's Press, 1997). This is an updated Windows version of an earlier edition.

this upper-division class. My class applies their methodology to the study of mechanisms of psychosocial healing. Student teams choose a currently devastated state and then work to identify activities and programs within each functional category that can move that society away from animosity or toward reconciliation. The students then rank the factors by degree of influence.

Can we see God's immanence at work through grace in some of these processes? Here I turn to a model of grace. As political scientists, we cannot deal with the unpredictability of divine action as a variable, so I confine my definition of grace to that continuing pull on the human spirit that stimulates the remnants of the image of God. Grace is the love that God radiates to humanity, calling us to God's world of love—love of God and love of others. It is available to all people and is not static but dynamic. Creation and history are not closed but have degrees of dynamism and openness. People can resist grace or open up to it. If grace does work in these ways, we can postulate five levels of love toward others—from its absence through parity to other preference and finally to self-denial. [27] If programs of rebuilding can act as means of grace and lead people to a point of social relations even higher than parity, it can create sufficient movement toward reconciliation that there may be hope for some success in rebuilding a devastated society.

When the students and I review and analyze the governmental and non-governmental organization (NGO) programs working in a nation like Rwanda or Mozambique or the Sudan, we also consider whether those programs could be means of grace. Can the two interact? That is, do these programs serve as mechanisms that would stir the transcendence of the human spirit in ways that could build a new sense of common humanity and human dignity, lay a foundation for a return to moral choice, and transform fear and despair into hope? Posing this question helps us know what to look for and what data to seek in order to measure progress.[28] In psychological terms, the people who

---

[27] See Garth L. Hallett, *Christian Neighbor Love: An Assessment of Six Rival Versions* (Washington, D.C.: Georgetown University Press, 1989).

[28] This kind of attitudinal survey data is not found in the resources of the ICPSR or in United Nations documents like the *Human Development Reports*. Until serious surveys that probe these kinds of attitudinal change are con-

have lived through this kind of experience have enormous rela-
tional-development defects. The capacity to trust, to see beyond
one's own hurt, to become part of a community, must be transformed at a deeper level than is possible through functionalist
activities and education. The attainment of true personhood and
the ability to create and at a mere minimum, to express sociability, will require both developmental and therapeutic or restorative processes. If grace can be observed in the transformational
processes inherently built into the functioning of the human
psyche, then we can find a link between theology and psychology that could help us better understand the dynamics of openness and help us find appropriate political strategies of
reconciliation.[29] As the students work on their projects, they also
assess the capacity of each activity and program to be a means
of grace and promote the dynamics of openness. As they find
programs that could act as healing mechanisms and therapeutic
or restorative processes, they discover linkages among political
policies, psychology, and theology, and they develop a working
theological perspective on politics.

One key element in the class is the study of mechanisms for
reconciliation. How can a society get past what was done?
Should the society seek retributive justice by punishing the los-
ers through a war crimes tribunal as in Bosnia and Rwanda,
or should it seek restorative justice, confession, and forgiveness
through a truth and reconciliation commission as in Chile and
South Africa? I introduce the topic with two articles from the
World Press Review,[30] and use Web sites related to the tribunals

---

ducted in those countries, this is the only data available. Three sources with
some helpful materials are the Journal of Humanitarian Assistance at www.jha.ac/
and Accord at www.c-r.org/accord/index.html.

[29] I have been greatly helped in integrating psychology into my class by my
colleague G. Michael Leffel. See his "From 'Barely' to 'Fully' Personal: On
the Therapeutic Action of Prevenient Grace Within the Personality," in Maxine
Walker, ed., Grace in the Academic Community, (San Diego: Point Loma Press,
1996): 115–31.

[30] There are several articles under the cover story title of "Can Justice Be
Done?" in World Press Review (June 1996): 6–10 and under the cover story title
of "Healing Nations" in World Press Review (February 1997): 6–12. See also the
articles available online through www.wits.ac.za/csvr/ of the Centre for the
Study of Violence and Reconciliation.

and the South African Commission. I repeat Walter Brueggemann's statement from his study of David and Saul: "In David's
action, it is clear that forgiveness is not simply a religious matter
of grace, or a human matter of gentleness and intimacy. Forgiveness is a daring political act that can reorient political conflict."[31]
Then I turn to arguments from Donald Shriver's *An Ethic for
Enemies*, Mark Amstutz's critical review of that book, and the
work of Duke Divinity School's L. Gregory Jones to explore the
concept of national forgiveness.[32] I end the course by calling attention to the need for someone like Ghandi, Martin Luther
King, Jr., or Nelson Mandela to emerge in these societies—
someone who understands and can model the processing of
pain into moral transformation. Within societies of vicious politics, Christians should be people who try to find a way to process
the universal power of pain and persecution into a rebirth of
hope and a broadening of the moral imagination of society.[33]

In the Wake of 9/11/01

Many expected that the apparent moral clarity of Cold War for-
eign-policy issues would be lost in the twenty-first century
moral dilemmas of internal war and failed states such as Somalia and Rwanda. The attack on the World Trade Center and Pentagon changed that. I suspect that we in political science have
difficulty maintaining whatever detached intellectual culture
normally surrounded our teaching. The attack and the U.S. "war
on terrorism" (whatever it ultimately turns out to be) raise to

---

[31] Walter Brueggemann, *Power, Providence and Personality* (Louisville, Ky.:
Westminster/John Knox Press, 1990), 55.

[32] Donald W. Shriver, Jr., *An Ethic for Enemies: Forgiveness in Politics* (New
York: Oxford University Press, 1995); Mark Amstutz, "After the Death
Squads," *Books and Culture* (July/August 1997): 25–27; L. Gregory Jones, *Em-
bodying Forgiveness* (Grand Rapids, Mich.: William B. Eerdmans Publishing Co.,
1997) and "How Much Truth Can We Take?" *Christianity Today* (February 9,
1998): 19–24. Despite critics like Amstutz, forgiveness studies is an emerging
field of study. See Thomas Trzyna, "The Social Construction of Forgiveness,"
Christian Scholar's Review 26, no. 2 (winter 1997): 226–41, and Scott Heller,
"Emerging Field of Forgiveness Studies Explores How We Let Go of Grudges,"
The Chronicle of Higher Education (July 17, 1998): A18–A20.

[33] See Walter Brueggemann, *Hope within History* (Atlanta: John Knox Press,
1987), 49–87, especially 84–87.

new importance the role of those behind the lectern in political science seeking to relate issues of war and peace to the Christian faith.

What can we do to help students understand Christian concerns about this murderous attack on civilians and U.S. international leadership, the U.S. retaliation and war on terrorism, and the effort to build a viable peace? In my introductory class, I have students voice their perspectives of a Christian posture toward the events and the war, and then I ask them to write out their questions. Their concerns go to the heart of the issues. Several express concern about the moral acceptability of retaliation (the principle of returning evil for evil), and about whether there is a distinction between killing and murder. Other students want answers to questions about the relevance and effectiveness of such central Christian principles as forgiveness and loving our enemies. Others ask, "To what extent should I separate political thinking from religion?" and "How can we love and forgive killers of three thousand people?" Some students ask about leaving judgment up to God and resting in an assumed divine plan for world history. Occasionally a student may assume that this attack was a punishment for the moral decay of the U.S. or wonder how it could have positive effects on religion.

Most of my efforts are built on my existing teaching strategies. Since a primary goal in this class is to help students rise above their home and home-church backgrounds and broaden their views, my preliminary concern is to open up to them the diversity of opinion within the Christian community. I discuss with them the Lutheran, Calvinist, Catholic, Wesleyan, and Mennonite traditions. I replace my usual document on Scripture and war with a one-page summary and then use denominational statements about the attacks and the U.S. response—the pastoral letter to The Lutheran Church–Missouri Synod, the reaffirmation of its 1973 committee statement on war by the synod of the Christian Reformed Church in America, the pastoral letter of the United Methodist Church, and the pastoral message of the U.S. Catholic Bishops—which I printed off from the denominational Web sites.

I use Psalm 137 to discuss the revenge emotions of the exiles who hoped for infanticide—that someone will seize Babylonian infants and "dash them against the rock" (v. 9). I urge the students not to adopt a dual morality or to accept the infanticide (collateral damage) that would come with an indiscriminate retaliation. I refer to Ecclesiastes and its notion that there is a time for war and time for peace and introduce them to the Clausewitzian principle that a military strategy should not destroy the foundations for building a peace. I argue that Christians live in a series of interconnected circles of morality—personal, social, national, and international. Rather than joining the national chorus of "United We Stand" and "God Bless America," I argue that the Church (universal) should base its reaction on a higher circle of universal morality such as the Nuremberg principles regarding crimes against humanity, which principles reflect (and promote) the work of grace in affirming human dignity and moral values. As Christians, we should have hope that God's loving moral activities in the world will prevail. I endeavor to sum all that up in the suggestion that one Christian response is to insist that we should fight smart (avoid civilian attacks and a holy-war mentality) and fight right (for universal values).

Since the attack, I have replaced the usual class simulation of the Cuban Missile Crisis with a simulation done by Johns Hopkins University in June of 2001 called "Dark Winter."[34] It is a simulation of a bioterrorist attack utilizing smallpox. I had to modify it for use in a classroom, but the Hopkins material provides good information on the disease, its spread as an epidemic, and the policy decisions and choices that have to be made by the National Security Council. The Hopkins simulation primarily explores domestic issues and does not deal with a resort to force, so I add an intelligence briefing that identifies the source of the attack, and I then enumerate five general U.S. response options and the multiple options within each one. Student teams have to choose, write out the expected consequences of their choices, and explore how the denominational statements seemed relevant or irrelevant to their deliberations and decisions, and explain why.

My U.S. Foreign Policy class offers a superb opportunity to

---

[34] The simulation can be found at www.hopkins-biodefense.org/ , the Web site for the Johns Hopkins Center for Civilian Biodefense Strategies.

deal with these issues in more depth. I repeat the exercise with "Dark Winter," with some additional changes. First, I add a new section on religion in world affairs and the moral issues of dealing with extremists and with a "mad Caesar" (which did not exist in the rationalism of nuclear deterrence theory). Then I have the class read and discuss both Carl Bernstein articles in the *Washington Post* called "Ten Days in September" (which provide an inside account of President Bush and his inner circle's decision making in the days after the attack) and the statement Pope John Paul II read on the ecumenical Day of Prayer for World Peace on January 24, 2002, "No Peace Without Justice, No Justice Without Forgiveness."[35] With that background, the students do a two-day smallpox simulation. One day focuses on the domestic issues (for example, vaccine shortages, overwhelmed hospitals, states prohibiting travel, priority of medical care to military). Ethical issues pervade the political/legal decisions. The second day focuses on military reprisals. I supply an outline of the State Department's seven national interests and strategic goals, with space for the students to define the goals they found in the denominational statements and how those goals could be operationalized into national strategy. I also provide a spreadsheet listing five response options and sub-options, with space to identify projected deaths, impact on the international system, and congruence with moral principles/goals. Then we identify and explore the ethical and moral issues of what transpired as a result of the simulation.

To update the generational conflict I traditionally use in this class, I appropriate materials from Bill Moyers's NOW broadcast on PBS called *A Widow's Plea*.[36] Amber Amundson's husband was killed in the attack on the Pentagon, and she published a plea that the nation not resort to violence, a stance strongly at odds with that of her father-in-law.

The attack on the U.S. also raises moral issues relating to international political theory and the role of the U.S. as world hegemon. I use long-cycle theoretical analysis to model how the

---

[35] The document may be found at www.vatican.va/phome-en.htm the Vatican home page. Go to the Prayer for Peace site and then to the documents of January 1, 2002.

[36] At www.pbs.org the video is available.

struggle for power, according to realist theory, is relevant at the beginning and ending of long cycles when nations are competing for dominance. I then model the relevance of liberal internationalism and global governance theory during the long cycle when the hegemon defines and defends the moral values of the international system. What is appropriate policy for a hegemon? Is the West in decline as Huntington argues, and is this attack a part of the effort to bring down the hegemon? If so, does that cast moral issues in a different light?

The terrorist simulation and hegemon model are vehicles that allow the professor behind the lectern to go beyond description and engage in moral reasoning. Are moral values deontological or consequentialist? What are a nation's responsibilities toward global public goods and the common interest? What are the comparative moral dilemmas of a minimalist foreign policy, as reflected in Larry Eagleburger's views during the 1992 Balkans crisis, a conservative or liberal responsibility policy or a multilateral constraint policy advocated by George Weigel, Lea Brilmayer, and Robert McNamara, and a maximalist policy reflected in President Bush's war on world terrorism and the "axis of evil?"[37] There is no single right answer, and the Dark Winter exercise reflects a wide range of student opinion. Our goal is to sharpen the students' analytical power as they seek their own answers, especially with regard to the inner circle's strategic and tactical concerns. This level of analysis takes sustained dialogue beyond the simulation exercise. But, as J. David Singer reminds us, these are not just academic questions or approaches to personal purity. These are questions of the highest order—the issues of war and human dignity, the interplay between personal belief, public duty, political advantage, and professional ethics, and the construction of policies that could be means of grace. These are high-order questions also because political science and

---

[37] On Eagleburger see David Halberstam, *War in a Time of Peace* (New York: Scribner, 2001), 133–42; George Weigel, *Idealism Without Illusions* (Grand Rapids, Mich.: William B. Eerdmans Publishing Co., 1994), chapters 5, 9–13; Lea Brilmayer, *American Hegemony: Political Morality in a One-Superpower World* (New Haven: Yale University Press, 1994), chapters 1, 6, 8, and pages 217–24; and Robert S. McNamara and James G. Blight, *Wilson's Ghost* (New York: Public Affairs, 2001), 132–50.

international politics are action majors leading to careers in realms of potential public significance.

A final word. The 9/11 attacks and my engagement of students in simulating and evaluating the U.S. response have clarified a principle of my teaching and commitment to a Liberal Arts Plus Two orientation. Many faculty have teaching loads built around teaching freshman general education courses. They work hard at those courses and do wonderfully well, seeking to impart basic content and perspectives that will broaden student thinking. But their teaching tends to be an end in itself, and their life-shaping impact on students is marginal, for the individual students are less important than the class. Freshmen students are completing requirements and will pass through those classes to spend the next three years focused on a series of courses and curricular tracks in other majors. In my case, our major has no required general education course, so we spend most of our time with our own students and their developing career goals. That means, for me, teaching is not an end in itself. A major is not merely a series of prescribed and elective courses leading to a diploma. The students are the end! Entry into a career of service is the goal. The courses and the lectures are a means to shape students for careers of public significance and so must be cutting edge rather than generic. That implies much greater responsibility for insuring our courses have a strong moral/theological element and a praxis orientation. Also, my basic orientation to students should be professional (not in the medical or legal sense of being detached but in the sense of inspiring and holding students to high expectations and standards) rather than pastoral, to try to help each student mature into a serious major and inspire each one to embrace a career of public service and significance. That is a ministry of grace worthy of one's preoccupation, absorption, and personal best.

Conclusion

Political science and a Christian perspective are constructed realities, both of which try to define and understand human phenomena that intersect and interact. Through careful attention to distinctly Christian approaches to the teaching of political science, we can assist our students in achieving the goals of a Christian liberal arts institution of higher learning and the political science goals of defining the normative values and means to shape policy that will make politics more noble and bring the world into greater openness to grace.

SELECTED BIBLIOGRAPHY

Efforts to teach and think biblically and theologically about political science require assistance. The APSA has a section on Religion & Politics, which publishes a newsletter and organizes panels at the annual conference. It has four hundred members, both believers and non-believers. A group of believers created the Christians in Political Science organization, which publishes a newsletter and holds biennial national conferences. While there are hundreds of research centers of varying academic quality and integrity relating to politics,[38] there are only a few such centers with academic quality that deal directly with moral or Christian perspectives on political science and public policy. Among the most valuable are

1) The Carnegie Council on Ethics and International Affairs in New York.
2) The Center for Public Justice in Washington, D.C.
3) The Dawson Institute of Church-State Studies at Baylor University.
4) The Ethics and Public Policy Center in Washington, D.C.
5) The Henry Institute for the Study of Christianity and Politics based at Calvin College.

The following bibliography contains a representative short list of sources I have found instructive. It does not include those works listed in the body or footnotes.

Cromartie, Michael, ed. *Caesar's Coin: Christians and the Limits of Government*. Grand Rapids, Mich.: William B. Eerdmans Publishing Co., 1996.

---

[38] To explore these centers, institutes, and think tanks, www.lib.umich.edu/govdocs/psthink.html is a useful Web site.

Dunn, Charles W., ed. *Religion in American Politics.* Washington, D.C.: CQ Press, 1989.

Gremillion, Joseph. *The Gospel of Peace and Justice: Catholic Social Teaching Since Pope John.* Maryknoll, N.Y.: Orbis Books, 1976.

Hertzke, Allen. *Representing God in Washington: The Role of Religious Lobbies in the American Polity.* Knoxville, Tenn.: University of Tennessee Press, 1988.

Jelen, Ted G. *The Political World of the Clergy.* New York: Praeger, 1993.

Mott, Stephen Charles. *A Christian Perspective on Political Thought.* London: Oxford University Press, 1996.

Nardin, Terry, ed. *The Ethics of War and Peace: Religious and Secular Perspectives.* Princeton, N.J.: Princeton University Press. 1996.

Neuhaus, Richard John. *The Naked Public Square.* Grand Rapids, Mich.: William B. Eerdmans Publishing Co., 1984.

Ramsey, Paul. *War and the Christian Conscience.* Durham, N.C.: Duke University Press, 1961.

Smidt, Corwin. *In God We Trust?* Grand Rapids, Mich.: Baker Academic Press, 2001.

Weigel, George. *Tranquilitas Ordinis.* New York: Oxford University Press, 1987.

Yoder, John Howard. *The Politics of Jesus.* Grand Rapids, Mich.: William B. Eerdmans Publishing Co., 1972.

4

Sociology and Faith: Inviting Students into the Conversation

Robert A. Clark

An Invitation to Professional Wholeness

In the mid 1970s, with a fresh Ph.D. in hand, I started teaching at a church-related college where the integration of faith and disciplines was expected and encouraged. Integration was intriguing yet mysterious to me. Graduate school had been no help at all. My graduate training had attempted to separate facts and values and to convince me of the unique significance of sociology for explaining and changing the social world. I was prepared to teach the best sociology I knew, but when I did that, my students complained that it was not enough. My colleagues were engaged in "Christian scholarship" and were excited about incorporating it into their teaching. I was attracted by their passion and the substance of their work but confused by the whole notion of "Christian scholarship" and ill prepared to take it into the classroom.

Over time the meaning and value of integration became clearer to me. I have come to think of the word *integrity* when considering integration. It connotes connection and wholeness as opposed to fragmentation and inconsistency. So, instead of our understandings of Christian faith and sociology being unconnected or in an incoherent relationship, integration involves finding connections, coherence, or points of commonality between them. There are many views of this "substantive integration" and many forms it can take, but at base they all include meaningful interaction between the ideas of faith and the substance of sociology.[1] Integration thus involves a mutually enriching conversation between sociology and the principles, theories, assumptions, and purposes of faith. Through this conversation each can inform, complement, and challenge the other. I will also refer to the ways faith should influence how we teach, how we relate to students, and how we structure courses and classrooms as "process integration."[2]

I have found the integration of faith and sociology to be a compelling and fascinating mission, but it brings challenges for which those new to the integrative task will need to be prepared. For one thing, the synthesis of sociology and faith is unusually problematic. As with most disciplines, sociology is influenced by the broader academic culture that is, at best, indifferent to faith and often hostile to it. But sociology also seems to have a particular antipathy toward faith. As a relatively recent academic discipline, sociology is a product of the Enlightenment and bears the marks of this heritage.[3] For example, sociology developed on the basis of naturalism, the assumption that all that is (or all that matters) is the material world that we can see and measure.[4] Accordingly, we explain any social pattern X only in terms of other natural forces within the closed causal system; there is no room for gods or devils in this one-dimensional understanding of reality. Naturalism is pervasive in sociology and

---

[1] See Ronald Burwell, "On Sleeping With an Elephant: The Uneasy Alliance Between Christian Faith and Sociology," *Christian Scholar's Review* 10, no. 3 (Fall 1981): 195–203; David A. Fraser and Tony Campolo, *Sociology Through the Eyes of Faith* (San Francisco: HarperCollins, 1992); William Hasker, "Faith-Learning Integration: An Overview," *Christian Scholar's Review* 21, no. 3 (March 1992): 234–48; David Lyon, "The Idea of a Christian Sociology: Some Historical Precedents and Current Concerns," *Sociological Analysis* 44, no. 3 (1983): 227–42; Richard Perkins, "Values, Alienation, and Christian Sociology," *Christian Scholar's Review* 15, no. 1 (1985): 8–27; and David L. Wolfe, "The Line of Demarcation Between Integration and Pseudo-Integration," in Harold Heie and David L. Wolfe, eds., *The Reality of Christian Learning: Strategies for Faith-Discipline Integration* (Grand Rapids, Mich.: William B. Eerdmans Publishing Co., 1987), 3–11.

[2] The work of Christian author and sociologist Parker Palmer, especially his *To Know As We Are Known: A Spirituality of Education* (San Francisco: Harper & Row, 1983) is very helpful on this understanding of integration.

[3] Fraser and Campolo, *Sociology Through Eyes of Faith*, 27–100.

[4] On naturalism see Phillip E. Johnson, *Reason in the Balance: The Case Against Naturalism in Science, Law, & Education* (Downers Grove, Ill.: InterVarsity Press, 1995).

constitutes a formidable barrier to the desire for and practice of integration.

Sociology often appears to be a competitor with faith in interpreting the human scene. It has been said that the more the objects of concern for an academic discipline and faith overlap, the more the two are potential rivals. If a scholar studies spider mites or quadratic equations there will be fewer points of contact and tension with faith than if one studies human life and social problems. It is not surprising that people of faith have looked with suspicion on sociology and its secular interpretations of the human story. It is also not surprising that sociologists typically have a disaffection for religious views of social life and are less likely than other academics to be persons of faith.[5] Given this great potential for competing interpretations, it can be a daunting task to bring faith and sociology together. Remember, though, that this overlap of subject matter means that the potential for a mutually enriching conversation between faith and sociology is also greater.

The easy thing for Christian professional sociologists to do is to become "disciplinary deists." Though we believe in God and may act faithfully in much of life, in our academic work we act as if God were irrelevant. As sociologists we describe and explain the social world and its problems solely in human categories, building a "sociology from below" that simply ignores God. So as we engage in the daily tasks of teaching, we must be very deliberate about doing integrative work. It requires consistent, intentional effort to overcome the many incentives and pressures to keep our faith sealed off from our academic work. Identifying specific integrative goals and finding support among colleagues will help counter the prevailing practices of the academic world.

Another challenge involves the time it takes to incorporate integrative materials into our courses. Many of us at church-related colleges have heavy teaching loads along with extensive advising and committee work. We are expected to improve our

---

[5] Fraser and Campolo, *Sociology Through Eyes of Faith*, 22–24; James A. Mathisen, "The Origins of Sociology: Why No Christian Influence?" *Christian Scholar's Review* 19, no. 1 (September 1989): 49–65.

teaching continually and to keep up with new pedagogical developments. Our integrative work adds time—the time to obtain and study integrative materials and incorporate them into our courses. To teach about divorce, for example, we not only need to be current on the relevant sociological literature, but we also need a grasp of various Christian views, Biblical texts, and ethical reasoning.

The dilemma, then, is that you either push yourself to do it all, or you leave something out in order to incorporate integrative materials into your courses. It may be difficult to give up reading some sociology journals to study Christian social thought. You may miss going to an ASA meeting because you used your limited travel money to go to a conference on faith and learning. You may fear that as you introduce readings on Christian perspectives to your students, you will need to omit some of the sociological material being taught at the university.

I think this quandary is one of the most important practical issues we face in relation to integration. We all struggle with this dilemma and resolve it in different ways. Some maintain their identities as professional sociologists and feel that time and effort spent in integrative activity would displace their sociological training. If they remain at the church-related colleges, they either endure frustrated sociological aspirations or they neglect their integrative responsibilities to pursue mainstream sociology. Others continually strive to balance these commitments, and while they may not become influential contributors to the discipline, they do their best to nourish their sociological competence and contribute in regional associations or local research projects.

My approach to this dilemma is to regard teaching at a church-related college as a special calling. There are thousands of sociologists in universities who teach mainstream sociology and have the facilities, funding, and time to do sophisticated research. Some of those sociologists are Christians, but given their narrow specializations and the requirements for promotion, tenure, and funding in secular universities, their ability to do integrative work is very limited. By contrast, those of us at church-related colleges have the privilege and responsibility to view our discipline through eyes of faith. Why should we struggle to imitate what thousands of others are doing when we have the unique facilities, funding, and opportunity to accomplish an alternative task? We can be the scholars that the Christian community turns to for thoughtful faith perspectives on society and social issues. We can teach our students in ways that will empower them to approach graduate school, the professions, and life in community as citizens of an alternative Kingdom.

My integrative efforts may mean that my students will not get quite as much sociology as they might at the university. But there is an important upside to this trade-off. It seems to me that through our study of ethics, epistemology, philosophy of science, and theology, my students and I become better sociologists and more critical, imaginative thinkers. We can enjoy the richness of interacting with sociology in light of a broader range of knowledge. And we can participate more effectively in the larger conversations of the intellectual and civic realms. So as you wrestle with this dilemma, my hope is that you will come to see doing integrative work not as a sacrifice but as a worthy calling.

Note that the nature of an academic institution strongly conditions both the extent and form of classroom integration. The mission of the institution, administrative support, denominational tradition, and the strength and diversity of faith commitments among faculty and students are significant contextual elements. Some Christians in sociology will have abundant resources and support for integrative classroom work while others will experience indifference or even resistance to their efforts.[6] I will be

---

[6] Sociologists who feel isolated from Christian scholarship on their campuses can seek support from their Christian colleagues in other institutions. Work by Christian scholars in related disciplines such as anthropology, psychology, and history can be very instructive. Workshops on integration are a helpful resource. Faculty can join the community of Christian scholars by reading such periodicals as *Christian Scholar's Review* or *Books & Culture*. The broader community of Christian sociologists is also available. The Christian Sociological Society (www.christiansociology.com) promotes fellowship, networking, and support among Christian sociologists. They publish "The Christian Sociologist" newsletter, host an email discussion group, and meet informally in conjunction with the annual ASA meetings. A related organization, the Association of Christians Teaching Sociology (ACTS), is more focused on teaching and offers an annotated bibliography and position papers. ACTS (www.actsoc.org) holds an annual meeting with presentations on sociology and faith and time for exchanging ideas on classroom applications.

sharing integrative strategies and resources that have worked for me within the context of my tradition and the institutions in which I have taught. My hope is that sociologists new to the integrative task or those who want to develop further their classroom integration strategies will find some helpful resources here that can be adapted to their traditions and institutional settings.

An Invitation to a Pedagogy of Wholeness

Integrative work should be approached as a process of inviting students into an ongoing conversation. Rather than transferring an established body of integrative knowledge to students, focus on engaging them as participants. Your thoughtful questions can provoke them to enter the dialogue. You can prepare them with background resources—students need to know who is in the conversation and where the conversation has already gone if they are to be effective participants. But the emphasis should be on attracting students to an open-ended conversation in which they can make discoveries and contributions, perhaps taking the conversation in exciting new directions.

To accomplish this you will need to vary your teaching strategies to fit your students. Some students are enthusiastic about integrative issues and always want more, while others are skeptical and always want less. With the skeptics you need to be especially winsome and subtle, watching for teachable moments. Clearly finesse will be required in managing your classrooms such that both enthusiasts and skeptics can be drawn into the conversation.

As I see it there are three areas of common concern for sociology and faith that lend themselves to integrative activity in the classroom. The first is social ontology. Both sociology and faith make claims about and operate on assumptions regarding social reality and the causes of human behavior. Both deal with questions about human nature, the nature of relationships, communities, social history, and social problems. A second area of common concern is epistemology. Sociologists and people of faith make claims about how we know what we know about social life. What counts as legitimate knowledge of the social?

What are the relative merits of religious and social scientific epistemologies? How do social conditions affect what we know in faith and in sociology? The final area of common concern is social ethics. How should we live our lives together? Sociology and faith operate in terms of explicit or implicit visions of healthy persons, relationships, and communities. In light of these visions, we critique social practices and talk about what ought to be done. From the standpoint of faith and of sociology, what is good and bad in our life together? What is our hope? I want to get students involved in finding relationships between faith and sociology in these areas of common interest, connecting their sociological knowledge of proximates with their beliefs about ultimates in meaningful ways. The teaching strategies I use proceed from the four goals for classroom integration I seek to achieve.

Cultivating Student Expertise

My first goal is to help students develop the knowledge base needed for fruitful integrative work. Some students want to jump in right away with Christian views on everything. You will want to nurture that motivation but also convince students that they need the tools to do a good job of relating faith and sociology. Specifically, students need to grow in their knowledge of sociology, the Bible, and Christian social teachings. Students cannot develop a good Christian position on capital punishment or postmodernism without solid grounding in the relevant sociological data and theory.

Your students will also need some knowledge about the philosophical context of sociology. In varying degrees in the introductory course and in social theory, I expose students to the philosophical bases of sociology and to such concepts as paradigm, worldview, and metasociology. They need to recognize that there are contestable assumptions underlying sociological thought and that alternative assumptions can produce alternative sociologies.[7] I use Durkheim's social theory of religion to

---

[7] For a range of views on this subject, consult Fraser and Campolo, *Sociology Through Eyes of Faith*; S. D. Gaede, *Where Gods May Dwell* (Grand Rapids, Mich.: Zondervan Publishing House, 1985); David Lyon, *Sociology and the Human*

demonstrate the operation of naturalistic assumptions in sociology and the way they can shape "findings" in research. Theory students can be asked to identify the assumptions about human nature and society made by Marx and Weber in their portrayals of social history and the future. Students in small groups can compare the assumptions and predictions that sociobiologists, behaviorists, and symbolic interactionists would make regarding sexuality or mate selection. I often use a reaction paper assignment in courses in which students read a supplementary text. The assignment requires them to use half of the paper summarizing the text and the other half reacting to the work. They are asked to identify and respond to the author's assumptions and the ways those assumptions may have influenced the text. Becoming aware of the importance of assumptions in sociological work is valuable because it helps my students become critical thinkers, even about sociology itself. I want them to be able to interact critically with their texts, not just accept sociology as a given. Awareness of the assumptive bases of sociology also gives my students a sense of permission to begin thinking about the relationship between their faith assumptions and sociology.

If sociology students at church-related colleges want to participate in the integrative conversation, they need to be familiar with the biblical story and appropriate ways to interpret and use the Bible. Such knowledge is crucial if one is to create or assess the adequacy of integrative work. I have found that I cannot go very far with students who are unfamiliar with the Bible, or who use their shallow knowledge to assert glibly that the Bible says "judge not" or "wives must obey their husbands." At times I must provide more. If I want to use the story of Daniel to illustrate the difference between sin and deviance, I must summarize the story of Daniel. For the most part, however, I need to rely upon and make connections with what students have learned in their theology and religion courses and what they bring from their religious traditions.

To do effective integrative work, students also need to have an

Image (Downers Grove, Ill.: InterVarsity Press, 1983); John Milbank, *Theology & Social Theory: Beyond Secular Reason* (Oxford, U.K.: Blackwell Publishers, 1990); and Richard Perkins, *Looking Both Ways: Exploring the Interface Between Christianity and Sociology* (Grand Rapids, Mich.: Baker Book House, 1987).

understanding of Christian social thought. There are many good sources describing elements of a Christian worldview and Christian views of human nature and personhood from a range of Christian traditions.[8] I find that personal accounts and vivid case studies are more effective in helping students comprehend these abstract issues. For example, theologian Langdon Gilkey's compelling account of his time in a Japanese prisoner-of-war camp during World War II provides an arena in which Christian and non-Christian assumptions about personhood, sociality, greed, and reason are played out against each other.[9] Such accounts come off as less didactic and will trigger less resistance among students who are unenthusiastic about Christianity. Similarly, a field trip to a nearby Hutterian Brethren community provides a teachable moment to discuss how the Anabaptist tradition and its vision of radical Christian discipleship translates into community life.[10]

In the introductory course, I expose students to small doses of material on diverse Christian stances toward society (the "Christ and culture" issue), Christian teachings regarding wealth and poverty, affluence, ecology, and Christian social responsibility.[11]

---

[8] On a Christian worldview, see, for example, Arthur F. Holmes, *Contours of a World View* (Grand Rapids, Mich.: William B. Eerdmans Publishing Co., 1983); James W. Sire, *The Universe Next Door: A Basic Worldview Catalog*, 3d ed. (Downers Grove, Ill.: InterVarsity Press, 1997); and Brian J. Walsh and J. Richard Middleton, *The Transforming Vision: Shaping a Christian World View* (Downers Grove, Ill.: InterVarsity Press, 1984). For Christian views on human nature, see Ray S. Anderson, *On Being Human: Essays in Theological Anthropology* (Grand Rapids, Mich.: William B. Eerdmans Publishing Co., 1982); C. Stephen Evans, *Preserving the Person: A Look at the Human Sciences* (Downers Grove, Ill.: InterVarsity Press, 1977); and Lyon, *Sociology and the Human Image.*

[9] Langdon Gilkey, *Shantung Compound* (New York: Harper & Row, 1966).

[10] Videos and readings about Amish or Hutterite life can substitute for such a trip. Students especially enjoy Christian sociologist Donald B. Kraybill's *The Riddle of Amish Culture* (Baltimore: The Johns Hopkins University Press, 1989). The Bruderhof Web site (www.bruderhof.org) with its thoughtful *Plough Online* magazine is also very interesting.

[11] Regarding Christ and culture, see Fraser and Campolo, *Sociology Through Eyes of Faith*, chap. 13; Donald B. Kraybill, *The Upside-Down Kingdom* (Scottdale, Pa.: Herald Press, 1990); H. Richard Niebuhr, *Christ and Culture* (New York: Harper & Row, 1951). For a sampling of materials on wealth, poverty, and affluence, see Rodney Clapp, ed., *The Consuming Passion* (Downers Grove, Ill.: InterVarsity Press, 1998); Jacques Ellul, *Money & Power* (Downers Grove, Ill.:

In my course on deviance, students learn of Christian teachings on the nature of sin, conformity to social standards, state enforcement of moral norms, criminal justice, and particular forms of deviance. For example, they participate in panels and debates on capital punishment and legalized gambling that present competing Christian and non-Christian moral arguments about these practices.

Students in my marriage and family courses learn about a range of Christian teachings on the meaning and purpose of marriage, cohabitation, sex outside of marriage, gender roles in marriage, and divorce and remarriage.[12] Again, a debate format on cohabitation or a text presenting different Christian views on divorce makes the material more attractive to students, especially when they are religiously and behaviorally diverse.[13] Similarly, in my marriage class, students select one of four point-of-view texts (Christian and non-Christian) and respond to it in a reaction paper.

Building a knowledge base in sociology and faith will produce more fruitful integrative work as students develop. This is a collaborative task; just as you are not giving students all the sociology they will get, so you do not need to give them all the biblical and Christian thought they will need. It may be helpful to find out from your colleagues in religion what sorts of biblical

---

InterVarsity Press, 1984); Paul Hanley Furfey, *Love and the Urban Ghetto* (Maryknoll, N.Y.: Orbis Books, 1978); Ronald J. Sider, *Rich Christians in an Age of Hunger: A Biblical Study*, 20th anniversary ed. (Dallas: Hope Publishing, 1997); Tom Sine, *Live It Up! How to Create a Life You Can Love* (Scottdale, Pa.: Herald Press, 1993). For a Christian sociological view of ecology, see Tony Campolo, *How to Rescue the Earth Without Worshipping Nature* (Nashville, Tenn.: Thomas Nelson, 1992). On Christian social responsibility, see Tony Campolo, *Wake Up America!* (San Francisco: HarperCollins, 1991); Charles P. DeSanto, Zondra G. Lindblade, and Margaret M. Poloma, eds., *Christian Perspectives on Social Problems* (Indianapolis: Wesley Press, 1992); Fraser and Campolo, *Sociology Through the Eyes of Faith*, chaps. 15 and 16; David O. Moberg, *The Great Reversal: Evangelism and Social Concern*, revised ed. (Philadelphia: J.B. Lippincott, 1977); Tom Sine, *Wild Hope* (Dallas: Word Publishing, 1991).

[12] A good source on family issues is Jack O. Balswick and Judith K. Balswick, *The Family: A Christian Perspective on the Contemporary Home*, 2d ed. (Grand Rapids, Mich.: Baker Book House, 1999).

[13] For example, see H. Wayne House, ed., *Divorce and Remarriage: Four Christian Views* (Downers Grove, Ill.: InterVarsity Press, 1990).

and theological material they give students at each level, especially in required courses, so that you can build upon and reinforce their contributions to the integrative task.

Before I move to my second goal, let me emphasize some matters of process integration. As we try to help students integrate their faith with their sociology, our aim is to draw them into the conversation. This means that we will try to get students to connect personally with the material and not just see it as detached information being imposed on them. I think it helps students to become more engaged with this material if we have personal relationships with them and are willing to reveal our commitments and struggles in the classroom. Students can then see that we care about our faith deeply and do not view it merely as a body of information to be taught or something in a separate compartment of our experience. Our teaching can encourage students to identify and clarify their own commitments in these areas. For example, I asked students to write a response to Gilkey's *Shantung Compound* in terms of what in his account reinforced or challenged their views of human nature. This encouraged them to enter into the material and identify their own views. Stopping in the middle of a lecture and giving students two minutes to do freewriting on what they are thinking about the material right then can help students plug into the material. Participating in debates, going on field trips, encountering vivid speakers or case studies, or writing reaction papers all get students to explore their own worldview and values.

If we want students to enter the conversation as participants, we also need to respect their integrity, whatever their religious commitments. When I present a lecture on a Christian view of the meaning and purpose of marriage, for example, I try to make it clear that students do not need to agree with the material but they do need to understand it. Similarly, when I assign Daniel Van Ness's Christian treatment of criminal justice issues, which includes lengthy examinations of biblical texts, I give students a study sheet with the following note:

> The goal with this book is to understand, think about, and evaluate a perspective. You do not need to be a Christian to understand and write about this perspective any more than you need to be a

Marxist to understand and answer questions about the Marxist perspective. Similarly, you may find great value in some of Van Ness's proposals and insights even if you do not share his larger perspective. So read and think![14]

Respecting the integrity of students means that I do not force them to speak as Christians. While at a college where all the students claimed to be Christians, I felt free to ask students on an exam or assignment to respond to an idea or reading "as a Christian." On other kinds of campuses, that would be quite inappropriate. I sometimes offer students a choice of exam questions or writing assignments that allows those who are eager to work with Christian themes to do so while allowing other students another option. I may ask students to show that they understand the material, or ask them to "compare the Christian perspective presented in class with the views in X's article," or ask them to respond in terms of their own values. Students should feel free to disagree with the Christian viewpoints we present, and we should respect them enough to listen to their honest responses.

This is made easier if we offer a variety of views that allows more students points of entry into the conversation. Rather than presenting *"the* Christian perspective," I frame a lecture as "my best understanding of Christian thought on this" or a reading as *"a* Christian perspective" on the topic. When I draw on a Catholic or a Mennonite scholar, I give credit to that tradition, allowing a wider range of students to connect with the material and feel invited into the conversation.

Connecting Sociology and Faith

My second goal for classroom integration is to help students make connections between sociology and faith. If students are to join the conversation, they need to see how integration is done, and they need practice in doing it. I want them to see the implications of sociology for faith and of faith for sociology. I want them to explore the parallels and useful partnerships be-

---

[14] Daniel Van Ness, *Crime and Its Victims* (Downers Grove, Ill.: InterVarsity Press, 1986).

tween sociology and faith. I want them to grapple with the tensions, contradictions, and mysteries found in the interface between sociology and faith. And I want them to consider how Christian assumptions might inform and renew sociology. Much of what I have done in terms of making these connections has been in the introductory course and in social theory.

I often begin by helping students personally experience the areas of tension between sociology and faith so that the need to find points of contact becomes subjectively real to them. I ask students in groups to develop explanations from a Christian point of view for why there is so much violence among young people in the United States. They come up with a variety of answers having to do with sin, spiritual emptiness, separation from God, and so forth. Later I have them address the same question but in terms of the sociology they have been studying. They now account for youthful violence in strikingly different terms, stressing peer groups, drugs, family breakdown, racism, and so forth. Which is it? I call it the problem of two vocabularies; when students think in terms of faith they use different phrases and explanatory categories than they do when they think sociologically. Faith and sociology thus seem to present competing explanations of human behavior; the easy thing to do is keep them in separate compartments or affirm one and abandon the other.

Once students experience this dissonance, strategies regarding how and why we might bring these apparently competing visions together become salient. I encourage students to think about why sociology would be worth studying for Christians, using motivation as a point of connection. They might want to study sociology because it provides helpful descriptions and understandings of social life for the Christian community.[15] For ex-

---

[15] See Raymond G. DeVries, " 'But I Want to Help People!' Notes on the Need for a Sociological Imagination," pp. 15–27, and Richard Perkins, "Why Study Sociology?," pp. 197–207, both in Michael R. Leming, Raymond G. DeVries, and Brendan Furnish, eds., *The Sociological Perspective: A Value-Committed Introduction* (Grand Rapids, Mich.: Zondervan Publishing House, 1989). David Martin's *Reflections on Sociology and Theology* (New York: Oxford University Press, 1997) is a good example of applications of sociology to ecclesiology. Students should be made aware that many denominations and religious organizations use sociologists to do research or to design and evaluate programs. Also, many

ample, I use Christian sociologist Michael Emerson's recent work, which presents statements by Christian leaders claiming that the best strategy to overcome racial tensions in this country is for Christians to engage in racial reconciliation in our personal relationships with members of other races.[16] Most students agree. I then conduct a survey to determine how many of the students had relationships with persons of another race among their close friends, in their classrooms, neighborhoods, youth groups, or workplaces when they were in high school. (By this time, students had read about Massey and Denton's work documenting the extent of racial segregation in U.S. cities.[17]) Building on their study and Emerson's analysis, students easily see that until there are structural changes to increase the proximity and similarity of the races, a strategy of interpersonal racial reconciliation on its own will be ineffective. They then recognize that sociological analysis can be a helpful way to achieve their Christian goals.

I also try to show students how understanding the social context of biblical passages can give us richer interpretations of the texts. For example, sociological knowledge of extended family and kinship systems in pastoral and horticultural societies and the place of kinless persons and orphans in them not only helps us make sense of some Old Testament practices but also provides very powerful understandings of the many passages referring to our being adopted into God's family as full heirs with Christ.[18]

We can move on to other ways of relating sociology and faith,

---

seminaries have sociologists (such as Jack Balswick at Fuller Theological Seminary), social workers, and anthropologists on their faculty to make use of their unique skills and perspectives.

[16] Michael Emerson, "Why Racial Reconciliation Alone Cannot End Racial Strife," *Christian Scholar's Review* 28, no. 1 (fall 1998): 58–70.

[17] Douglas S. Massey and Nancy A. Denton, *American Apartheid: Segregation and the Making of the Underclass* (Cambridge, Mass.: Harvard University Press, 1993).

[18] For examples of applications to Biblical studies and theology, see Robin Gill, ed., *Theology and Sociology: A Reader* (London: Cassell, 1996). The work of Catholic theologian Gregory Baum demonstrates how sociology can inform theological discourse. See his *Religion and Alienation: A Theological Reading of Sociology* (New York: Paulist Press, 1975) and *Theology and Society* (New York: Paulist Press, 1987).

exploring points of commonality and complementarity between them. We see that both sociology and faith insist that we are social beings. We see that sociology explores the nature and consequences of our sociality and the fact of our broken sociality. Students can explore basic sociological concepts, such as alienation or power, and apply or refashion them within a Christian framework. For example, my introductory students read an article that reflects on the sociological concept of culture from a Christian perspective.[19] It generates great discussions about relativism, ethnocentrism, truth, tolerance, missions, multiculturalism, and postmodernism. My chief goal with this article, however, is to give students a model of the fruitful conversation between faith and sociology, which can produce better comprehension of such things as culture, relativism, and truth.

Similarly, my introductory students work with the concept of social problems. After distinguishing between social problems as individual deviance versus structural conditions, I ask students to write down a list of sins. They typically mention immoral acts deliberately engaged in by individuals. We then explore the idea of structural evil, which parallels the concept of structural social problems.[20] The class considers the implications of this enlarged view of sin, including a comparison of Christian ministries such as Compassion International (individual charity) and Bread for the World (structural change). Through this comparative analysis, students see that sociology can provide insights that illuminate our faith and practice. We go on to sketch a Christian sociological approach to social problems, building on such concepts as idolatry to weave together the roles human sinfulness and social forces play in producing social problems.[21]

---

[19] Robert A. Clark, "Thinking About Culture: Theirs and Ours," in Leming, DeVries, and Furnish, *The Sociological Perspective*, 61. For additional literature in this area, see Robert A. Clark and S. D. Gaede, "Knowing Together: Reflections on a Holistic Sociology of Knowledge," in Heie and Wolfe, *The Reality of Christian Learning*, 55 and Charles E. Garrison, *Two Different Worlds: Christian Absolutes and the Relativism of Social Science* (Newark, N.J.: University of Delaware Press, 1988).

[20] For discussion of structural evil see Moberg, *The Great Reversal*; Stephen Charles Mott, *Biblical Ethics and Social Change* (New York: Oxford University Press, 1982); and Sider, *Rich Christians in an Age of Hunger*.

[21] See Jack O. Balswick and J. Kenneth Morland, *Social Problems: A Christian Understanding & Response* (Grand Rapids, Mich.: Baker Book House, 1990);

Similar linkages between sin and social forces can be made in explaining deviance. Christian assumptions can be used in shaping how we think about deviant persons, in assessing theories of deviance, and in making connections between sin and deviance.[22]

When I taught the social theory course, I found it to be a natural place to help students make conceptual connections between faith and sociology. They examined the relations between values and sociology and discovered the philosophical assumptions embedded within competing theoretical paradigms. This process made it easier for students to see the logic of faith-learning integration because they came to recognize the importance of contestable, nonempirical assumptions in sociological theory. We also explored what alternative Christian assumptions about persons, society, and social history might look like and used them in assessing and comparing sociological theories and paradigms. Social theory was something of a capstone experience for our majors, and I concluded it with a take-home exam on integration. In preparation for the exam, I assigned several articles by Christian sociologists and lectured on some of the tension points between faith and sociology and some of the common strategies for linking them. The exam (in more elaborate form) asked students to reflect on three issues in light of their learning in the course:

1. Should sociological and Christian thought be integrated? Why or why not? Which way of relating sociology and faith do you prefer, and why?
2. What do you see as the major ways sociological thought contradicts or challenges Christian faith? Pick one of these and discuss how you deal with this challenge.
3. What value do you see in sociological thought and method for the person of faith? How can sociology be helpful to the faith community in its thinking and practice?

Gaede, *Where Gods May Dwell*; and J. A. Walter, *Sacred Cows: Exploring Contemporary Idolatry* (Grand Rapids, Mich.: Zondervan Publishing House, 1979).

[22] For example, see Zondra G. Lindblade, "Christians and Deviance/Christians as Deviants," in Leming, DeVries, and Furnish, *The Sociological Perspective*, 169.

This exam was used in a course offered at a church-related college where it was assumed that all the students were Christians. But even on that campus a student once came to me and indicated that he was rather distant from the faith at that point and could not answer the questions with integrity. I honored his disclosure and with his help adapted the exam to be more appropriate for him. The revised version still asked him to show that he understood the issues involved in faith-learning integration, but we altered the exam to allow him to explore his worldview and its relationship with sociology. If I were to use this exam in a more religiously diverse setting, I would offer question choices that allow students to reflect on issues of values and sociological theory that are not specifically Christian.

Contemplating Social Ethics

My third goal for blending sociological and Christian perspectives in the classroom involves social ethics. In this form of integration, students bring together sociological data and analysis with their religious values to make reasoned value judgments. We do not need well-educated technocrats—the "best and the brightest"—whose highly trained skills are unconstrained by ethical values. Nor do we need narrow moralists who are uninformed about the state of the social world and the likely consequences of their decisions. We do need graduates who in their lives as family members, neighbors, workers, citizens, and community leaders can take positions informed both by their sociology and their Christian values.

Several tasks must be addressed so that our students can take well-grounded ethical stands. They need to become aware of their own developing values, beliefs, and commitments. They need to become aware of the ethical claims associated with their religious, social, and political commitments. Students should also learn through sociology the means to achieve their social goals, the consequences of different courses of action, and the dynamics and dilemmas of devising and implementing social policies.

Students need to learn the processes of ethical reasoning, primarily accomplished through courses in ethics. Faculty should at least be familiar with the major forms of ethical reasoning (for example, virtue ethics and consequential ethics) and with issues surrounding ethical relativism. Students should learn in their theology/religion courses how to derive moral principles and standards appropriately from the Bible. We should have enough hermeneutical savvy to redirect students who use Scripture to reinforce what they already believe or who treat localized, time-specific teachings in the Bible as generalized moral standards. Finally, students should practice taking and defending ethical positions.

There are a variety of teaching strategies I use to accomplish these tasks. I occasionally model defending a position by spelling out and justifying where I stand on an issue as a Christian sociologist. Through lectures in the marriage course, I compare several Christian viewpoints on the roles of women and men in family life, and I identify authors and organizations associated with different views (for example, Concerned Women of America, Christians for Biblical Equality). I then follow this set of lectures with an examination question that asks students to justify their preferred role arrangement and to demonstrate their awareness of the sociological trade-offs associated with it. This process gets them to clarify their views and articulate an argument.

In the introductory course, I lecture on some of the challenges facing modern societies. I begin by having students write a response to the following question: "What is your vision of the good life you hope to live in the future? Imagine that you are now forty-five years old and you have been successful and are living what you consider to be the good life. What does your good life look like?" Since their view of the good life is rather like a rudder that steers the course of their life, this is an important question for students to consider. Immediately after they write their response, I ask them to reflect on their vision of the good life. What place did material affluence have in it? What place was given to relationships, citizenship, faith, and service? They also complete a survey asking them in what kind of home and community they would like to live. Their responses to the essay question and survey become a baseline, so that as we consider issues from affluence and urban problems to ecology and family life, they may begin to see some of the consequences of their views and be motivated to clarify and revise them. As I complete each segment of the lecture series, I ask them: "What will you do? Will you reproduce the present with your choices, or will you follow an alternate path?" I regularly refer to Christian organizations, books, and periodicals that offer them thoughtful alternatives.[23]

Small group tasks and role-playing can prompt students to clarify their thinking. These strategies also provide them practice in taking positions on complex topics. In the introductory course, I present a scenario about "Sophie," a homeless mother, and ask small groups to discuss why there are so many Sophies and what should be done about all the Sophies in our society. After the groups present their thinking, which tends to focus on Sophie's imagined inadequacies, we explore sociological data and analysis on homelessness and alternative policies and Christian approaches to the issue. By that point, many students have refined and enlarged their thinking on homelessness.

Readings can be used to lay out alternative viewpoints and provide examples of how to make an argument. In the marriage course, I assign differing Christian and sociological readings on cohabitation and later ask students on an exam to take an informed position on the issue "in light of their values and the sociological data." Daniel Van Ness in deviance and Jack Balswick and his colleagues in family and social problems, for example, do an admirable job of showing how to derive principles from the Bible that are then blended with sociological analysis.[24] The reaction papers described previously ask students to take a position in response to texts that argue a point of view. I also try to assign articles that will introduce students to periodicals such as *Sojourners* or *First Things* that regularly offer arguments on social issues from various Christian perspectives.

I particularly like student panels and debates as a vehicle for presenting alternative ethical positions and giving students

---

[23] For example, Evangelicals for Social Action (www.esa-online.org), the Sojourners community (www.sojourners.com), or Catholic social justice teachings (www.justpeace.org).

[24] Van Ness, *Crime and Its Victims*; Balswick and Balswick, *The Family*; Balswick and Morland, *Social Problems*.

practice in taking positions that combine their values and sociology. In my deviant behavior course, students research Christian organizations that are active in criminal justice issues, such as Prison Fellowship and the Mennonite Central Committee.[25] Students then present the mission and policies of each organization and indicate how individuals can get involved. Debates, whether on cohabitation or legalized gambling, expose students to a variety of coherent viewpoints and give them practice in taking and evaluating ethical positions in terms of sociology, biblical texts, and Christian principles. The variety of viewpoints involved reaches a broader range of students and helps avoid the perception that we are "cramming Christianity down their throats."

If we are to be successful in working with a variety of viewpoints, we need to make our classrooms safe spaces for diversity. In each of the colleges where I have taught, students have developed a "party line" that dominated classroom discussions. However, I knew from student journals and private conversations that many in the class held different views but did not feel free to express them. Though the content of the "party line" differed from institution to institution, the problem remained the same. In our role as referees and in the way we handle diverse views, we can help create an atmosphere of trust. As Christian scholars we need to embody the principle that progress toward the truth requires both commitment and humility. We recognize that even our best understandings are incomplete and flawed. So we need to listen with care to other views and to our critics. If discourse is to be educative, we need to address each other with graceful respect and give generous constructions to our opponent's views. We can share with students our own uncertainties and show them how and why our thinking has changed. Students may then feel more willing to express unpopular views or try out unconventional ideas they may be considering. Such trust is more likely if students and faculty have preestablished relationships as a learning community.

If we are successful with this ethical integration, students will

---

[25] See www.prisonfellowship.org, www.justicefellowship.org and www.mcc.org.

be enabled to evaluate social life and to judge what is in light of what ought to be. They will be more capable of making reasoned value judgments about personal choices and social issues. And they will be more able to imagine alternative ways of living outside the bounds of the given order.

Encouraging Reflective Action

My fourth and final integrative goal for teaching is to encourage students to engage in reflective action, often called praxis. Praxis involves bringing together knowing and doing, thinking and acting in an organic relationship.[26] Knowing and thinking are not ends in themselves. Knowing is for doing and theory is for practice. Similarly, doing leads to knowing and action informs our theorizing. So praxis involves a cycle wherein our understandings of truth are expressed in actions which, in turn, test and refine our understandings. Integration in the classroom cannot merely be an intellectual exercise that brings together the cognitive components of faith with sociological thought. Integration must weave together our living with our faith and learning.

Our department provides volunteer opportunities for students to act on their care for others through community service and to express their social-ethical views by engaging in social action. To complete the cycle, service and social action stimulate curiosity and reflection, encouraging them to refine their sociological knowledge, evaluate their motivations, and review their faith.

We address this goal primarily through internships, service learning, and study/service tours. Most of our students participate in an internship and many enroll in service learning courses. While students act out their sociological knowledge and faith commitments in internships or service learning courses, we ask them to reflect on their actions through journals, papers, and conferences with faculty. One of my students who felt called by her faith to work with troubled young people did an internship

---

[26] See Robert A. Clark, "Praxis Makes Perfect: Beyond Conceptual Integration in Sociology." Paper read at the annual meeting of the Association of Christians Teaching Sociology, Eastern College, St. Davids, Pa., 1983; and Perkins, Looking Both Ways, 153.

at a juvenile detention center. In the middle of her internship, she came to a simple but important insight: "I have been surprised by how much you need to know to do this right and make a difference in kids' lives," she said. What else but that experience could have gotten her to that insight? From then on, coursework had new meaning for her.

My colleague, Professor Don Liebert, uses a unique praxis approach in his social research course in which students conduct a group research project. Don's tradition is to have students do research for a group in the community that could not afford to hire a research team. The students work with that community group to develop the project, gather data, and ultimately supply a report of their findings to the community group. In recent years his students have, for example, done research for a group of black pastors and studied fear of crime in a low-income neighborhood. This assignment embodies the praxis approach by translating the students' sociological skills and faith motivations into service activities that stimulate their sociological imaginations.

Many of our students participate in a Central American study/service program cosponsored by our department. Students spend five months in Central America engaged in service activities, course work, and a month of living and working with families in remote villages. Their Christian convictions and preparatory course work launch them into the tour. Their service activities and their day-to-day life in Central America test their sociology, challenge them to learn more, and enlarge their faith. It is truly a life-changing experience for these students that colors their thinking and faith.

So I commend to you these four goals for integrative teaching. Help students develop the knowledge base in sociology, biblical literature, and church teachings requisite for fruitful integrative work. Enable students to make connections between sociology and faith. Give students practice in taking social-ethical positions that blend sociology and faith. Encourage students in praxis—actions that express and enrich an informed heart. As you do so, you will honor your special calling, thereby inviting students to see creation in light of the Creator. And with God's grace, as you relate sociology to the Center that unites all truth,

your teaching will help overcome fragmentation with wholeness.

Selected Bibliography

Berger, Peter L. *The Sacred Canopy: Elements of a Sociological Theory of Religion.* New York: Doubleday, 1967.
————. *A Rumor of Angels: Modern Society and the Rediscovery of
the Supernatural.* New York: Doubleday, 1969.
DeSanto, Charles P., Calvin Redekop, and William L. Smith-
Hinds, eds. *A Reader in Sociology: Christian Perspectives.* Scott-
dale, Pa.: Herald Press, 1980.
DeSanto, Charles P., Zondra G. Lindblade, and Margaret M. Po-
loma, eds. *Christian Perspectives on Social Problems.* Indianapo-
lis: Wesley Press, 1992.
Greek, Cecil. *The Religious Roots of American Sociology.* New York:
Garland Publishing, 1992.
Grunlan, Stephen A. and Milton Reimer, eds. *Christian Perspec-
tives on Sociology.* Grand Rapids, Mich.: Zondervan Publishing
House, 1982.
Heddendorf, Russell. *Hidden Threads: Social Thought for Chris-
tians.* Dallas: Probe Books, 1990.
Martin, David, John Orme Mills, and W.S.F. Pickering, eds. *Soci-
ology and Theology: Alliance and Conflict.* New York: St. Martin's
Press, 1980.
Storkey, Alan. *A Christian Social Perspective.* Leicester, U.K.: Inter-
Varsity Press, 1979.
Swatos, William H., Jr. *Faith of the Fathers: Science, Religion, and
Reform in the Development of Early American Sociology.* Bristol,
Ind.: Wyndham Hall Press, 1984.

Part Two
Mathematics and the Natural Sciences

5

Developing a Christian Perspective on the Nature of Mathematics

Harold Heie

THE NEED TO KNOW: WHAT A STUDENT TAUGHT ME ABOUT TEACHING

MOST OF MY EDUCATION has taken place after my formal schooling ended. As an engineering student, my postsecondary schooling was highly technical and specialized. The subjects that I never studied in college are legion, including history, philosophy, and all the social sciences. And following the pattern of my childhood days when I would rather play stickball on the streets of Brooklyn than read a book, I only read what I had to—the assigned reading in my courses. When I received my doctorate, I was about as illiberally educated as one could be. I had to do a lot of catching up. And that is what I was doing one day early in my teaching career at the King's College in Briarcliff Manor, New York, as I sat at my office desk reading the fifth edition of *Introduction to Psychology* by Hilgard, Atkinson, and Atkinson.[1] A student wandered by my office, a bright student who would flunk out of college in about six weeks. He was dumbfounded when he saw that I was reading the text for his Psychology 101 course, the cover of which he had not yet opened. He asked me why I was reading Hilgard, Atkinson, and Atkinson, and I told him. He then made an insightful comment that revolutionized my view of teaching: "The difference between you and me, Dr.

---

[1] Ernest R. Hilgard, Richard C. Atkinson, and Rita L. Atkinson, *Introduction to Psychology*, fifth ed. (New York: Harcourt Brace Jovanovich, 1971).

Heie, is that you have the *need to know*, I don't." His perception, unfortunately, was that the content of his psychology book had nothing to do with his life, and therefore, he did not need to know any of it. I was reading this book and numerous others every spare moment I could find and long into the night because I was struggling with a question that had everything to do with my life.

That question was "What is the relationship between law and liberty in a Christian ethic?" In brief, I was raised in a legalistic Christian tradition that emphasized rules for behavior, mostly proscriptive in nature. I could no longer accept that expression of the Christian faith. Neither could I accept the extremes of situation ethics in the 1960s that urged me to "just love," for some destructive behaviors were being justified in the name of love. So, as has often been characteristic of my intellectual pilgrimage, I sought that more nuanced middle ground between unacceptable extremes. I needed some understanding of psychology to deal adequately with this question. And I had to start from scratch.

At the same time that I was struggling with this question, I began to address questions about the nature of my teaching discipline of mathematics. In ways I did not anticipate, coherence ensued between the answers that emerged from my dealing with some of my math questions and the results of my struggle with the law and liberty question. But more about that coherence later. What I learned from my student was that developing a *need to know* is pivotal for effective learning and teaching.

WHAT DOES ONE NEED TO KNOW ABOUT MATHEMATICS?

At one level, what one needs to know about mathematics is obvious and beyond dispute. Students preparing for a variety of careers need to master pertinent techniques or formulas for doing mathematics, which points to the important instrumental function of mathematics. And at this level it is ludicrous to talk about Christian perspectives relative to mathematics. After all, the derivative of x^2 is $2x$ for all persons doing mathematics, independent of their particular faith commitments, religious or secular.

But there is a deeper level of discourse about mathematics that goes beyond the techniques or formulas for doing mathematics; a level that seeks to understand the fundamental nature of the discipline of mathematics. A philosopher friend of mine, David Wolfe, first introduced me to this deeper level of discourse many years ago when he asked me whether mathematical knowledge was created or discovered. My first reaction was "Who cares?" It seemed like an irrelevant question, at best. As an applied mathematician, I did mathematics. It all seemed to work out. What possible difference could any answer make?

I soon came to realize that this was only one of the foundational questions that could be asked about mathematics or any other academic discipline. It was the *epistemological* question— how one acquires knowledge in the discipline. There were related questions. What is the status of knowledge claims in a given discipline? Can they be asserted with certainty, or as highly probable, or what? And how does one deal with competing claims to knowledge? What criteria do practitioners in the discipline use to adjudicate between such claims?

My questions began to multiply. There were more foundational questions, including *ontological* questions about the nature of the entities mathematicians deal with, such as numbers. Of course, such ontological questions are not peculiar to mathematics; they can be asked about the entities of any discipline: written texts in literature; living organisms in biology; elementary particles in physics; individual persons in psychology; social groups in sociology. I was particularly drawn to *axiological* questions about the value commitments that may underlie mathematics or any other discipline. Are there value assumptions that inform the creation (or is it discovery?) of new forms of mathematics?

As I became increasingly interested in this foundational level of discourse about the nature of mathematics, I sensed that I did not have a lot of company. It seemed that so much philosophy of mathematics is of marginal interest to many teachers of mathematics, and I did not sense that many students in my math classes had a felt *need to know* about such matters. But I had a strong need to know, and I developed the conviction that my responsibility as a math teacher at a liberal arts college included nudging students toward a need to know something about this deeper level of discourse. I will now elaborate on my reasons for this conviction, based on my understanding of the phrase "integration of faith and learning." I will then make some concrete suggestions for initiating students into personal explorations of deeper foundational issues.

INTEGRATION OF FAITH AND LEARNING

The first few pages of the catalogs of many church-related colleges include a statement of commitment to the ideal of "integrating faith and learning" or words to that effect. However, if faculty members at such colleges are questioned about the meaning of the phrase "integration of faith and learning" and the implications of commitment to that ideal for their teaching, a variety of responses might be received. Some focus on an incarnational mode, where faith commitment informs a teacher's dealings with students, evidenced by deep care and concern for their well-being, both in and out of class, and by modeling the highest moral standards and aspirations for spiritual growth. This is indeed our important calling as teachers at church-related colleges, and such expressions of faith commitment need to be prominent in our interactions with students. But to limit the "integration of faith and learning" to this incarnational mode is to preclude the possibility that such integration can actually affect the academic subject matter being studied.

And yet what possible connection could there be between the subject matter of mathematics and one's beliefs as a Christian? One attempt at such a connection comes from an article on Christian day schools that used the following example "to explain how teaching in the [Christian] day school differs from teaching in public schools: 'two and two is always four . . . and God is always the same; you can depend on Him'" (deletion in original)[2]. Now, both the mathematical assertion and the theological assertion in this proposition may be true, assuming we

---

[2] David L. Wolfe, "The Line of Demarcation Between Integration and Pseudointegration," in Harold Heie and David L. Wolfe, eds., *The Reality of Christian Learning: Strategies for Faith-Discipline Integration* (Grand Rapids, Mich.: William B. Eerdmans Publishing Co., 1987), 4.

are counting in base ten and neglecting, for the sake of argument, the insights of process theologians and some evangelical theologians who have recently argued (persuasively, I think) for a more dynamic view of God.[3] But even assuming that both assertions are true, to place two truths side by side is not integration. Coexistence is not integration. The integration of theological and mathematical assertions does not occur until the integral relationship between the two assertions is explicated. Is there some integral connection between the certainty of number truths and the nature of God? I do not think so. But if someone else does, considerable argumentation and elaboration would be required to explicate the nature of the alleged connection.

What, then, is the nature of the scholarly aspect of "integration of faith and learning" that must complement the incarnational aspect? This is best explained in terms of one's *worldview*, defined here as one's comprehensive set of beliefs about the nature of reality and how one should live in the light of those beliefs. As formidable as that sounds, everyone has a worldview, although it is often neither examined nor articulated. The source of one's worldview beliefs are multiple, including knowledge gained from the academic disciplines, starting with one's own disciplinary specialization, and including relevant connections, hopefully, with other academic disciplines. One's worldview also includes beliefs emerging from one's faith commitment, be that religious or secular. In my case, that would include my biblical and theological understanding as a professing Christian.

I believe that I must seek coherence in my worldview beliefs. This requires that I seek to discover (or is it create?) connections or interrelationships between my biblical and theological understanding and academic disciplinary knowledge, for I believe that knowledge is all of one piece. The attempt to articulate the contours of that one piece, and to examine and refine this worldview, is what I mean by "the scholarly aspect of the integration of faith and learning."[4]

---

[3] See Clark Pinnock, et. al., *The Openness of God* (Downers Grove, Ill.: Inter-Varsity Press, 1994).

[4] I am indebted to Susan VanZanten Gallagher of Seattle Pacific University for the insight that the scholarly integrative task essentially involves the articulation and refinement of a worldview, although I bear full responsibility for the manner in which I have stated that insight in this essay.

A formidable obstacle to my focus on the importance of developing a coherent worldview is the perception that academic disciplinary knowledge is unrelated to the biblical and theological understanding of the Christian scholar. In many Christian traditions, we are socialized into being intellectual dualists. All too often neither our churches nor schools encourage us to formulate coherent relationships among these multiple sources of knowledge. And our graduate education often reinforces this compartmentalization. Against the backdrop of this persistent problem, I nevertheless propose that helping students to articulate and refine such coherent worldviews should be one of the fundamental qualities of Christian higher education. I propose this for two reasons. First, I think Christians are called upon to seek adequate understanding of the nature of all God's creation. Such understanding requires the articulation of a coherent worldview. Second, I believe we need such coherent understanding to inform appropriately our actions in a complex world as we seek to serve God and others as agents of redemption in all areas of life.

However, what does this worldview ideal have to do with my earlier claim that we need to expose math students to deep foundational issues about the nature of mathematics? My reasoning is simple: the most fruitful relationships among my multiple sources of knowledge are formed at the foundational level. In both the academic disciplines and the realm of biblical/theological understanding, foundational assumptions are made about the entities we seek to understand, ways of seeking understanding, and value commitments that inform this search for understanding. The fact that such foundational assumptions suffuse my various sources of knowledge holds promise for fruitful exploration of the relationships between these two sets of assumptions.

GETTING THE STUDENT'S ATTENTION: THE INTEGRATIVE QUESTION

The developmental worldview task I have outlined is daunting. I am suggesting that faculty at Christian colleges need to help students gain a reasonable level of competence in the sphere of academic disciplinary knowledge, whatever their major area of study, as well as reasonable competence in the sphere of biblical and theological understanding. As if that is not demanding enough, I then hope that students will seek to articulate and refine a worldview that exhibits coherence between these multiple sources of knowledge. And to compound the problem, I desire to instill these high expectations in students who typically do not come to college because of a keen interest in developing their worldview. Where, then, does a Christian teacher begin?

I suggest we begin by shedding the illusions that this integrative project is to be relegated to a course or two in the curriculum or that it is to be completed by graduation. It is actually a lifelong task. The best we can hope for is that our students be initiated into this lifelong quest. If we think initiation is too modest a goal, we probably have not tried it. R. S. Peters describes such initiation as follows.

> To be educated is not to have arrived at a destination; it is to travel with a different view. What is required is not feverish preparation for something that lies ahead, but to work with precision, passion and taste at worthwhile things that lie to hand. These worthwhile things cannot be forced on reluctant minds, neither are they flowers towards which the seeds of mentality develop in the sun of the teacher's smile. They are acquired by contact with those who have already acquired them and who have patience, zeal, and competence enough to initiate others into them.[5]

The tension in Peters's view is that the worldview project that I deem to be worthwhile may not be judged worthwhile by my students. And if I cannot convince my students that this task is worthwhile, they will never develop the need to know about such matters. It will not become a lifelong quest. So the goal of initiation requires that I help students see that the worldview project is worthwhile. That is much easier said than done. How does a teacher do that? A strategy that I have found to work, some of the time, is to pose an integrative question. By "integrative question" I mean a question that cannot be addressed ade-

---

[5] R. S. Peters, "Education as Initiation," in R. D. Archambault, ed., *Philosophical Analysis and Education* (London: Routledge & Kegan Paul, 1965), 110.

quately without formulating coherent relationships between academic disciplinary knowledge and biblical/theological knowledge.

For example, an integrative question in biology is "To what extent, if any, should genetic engineering be used to enhance human well-being?" A Christian biologist dealing with this question must seek coherent relationships between disciplinary knowledge in genetics and bioengineering and personal biblical/theological beliefs about the nature of "human well-being." The following are some illustrative integrative questions in other academic disciplines. *English:* What are the similarities and differences in interpreting the biblical text and interpreting other literary texts? *Sociology/Social Work:* To what extent are social problems caused by inadequacies in societal structures? To what extent by individual or group irresponsibility? *Business:* What social responsibility, if any, does a business enterprise have toward its employees and the geographical region in which the business is located? *Fine Arts:* What are the limits, if any, on the freedom of human creative expression? *History:* How do alternative views on the direction of history (linear, cyclical, teleological) fit or not fit with the Christian narrative? *Computer Science:* What are the ethical implications of the use of the internet? *Economics:* What is the relationship between the quest for profitability and the Christian call for compassion and justice? *Education:* What is the relationship between subject-centered and student-centered teaching pedagogies in light of a Christian perspective on personhood? *Physics:* What are the similarities and differences between the use of models in scientific inquiry and the use of models in theological inquiry?

Will students judge as worthwhile the exploration of integrative questions with the goal of developing a coherent worldview? Without seeking to generalize, I draw from my own teaching experience. I have found that after in-depth exposure to both disciplinary and biblical/theological understanding, many juniors and seniors have a keen interest in seeking to articulate a coherent worldview by exploring such integrative questions, possibly in a senior seminar course. But I have often found that many first-year students do not exhibit a strong need to explore possible responses to such integrative questions. Based on my judgment that students should be initiated into the worldview project early in their college careers, the challenge is to find pedagogical means that will inspire first-year students to begin exploring integrative questions. I have found that such early initiation was possible if I could establish connections between what these students believed they needed to know and what I as their teacher believed they needed to know in response to integrative questions. I now report on my attempts to establish such connections in introductory mathematics courses.

The Nature of Mathematics Course for Non-Majors

For many college students who are not majoring in mathematics, computer science, or one of the natural sciences, their exposure to mathematics is limited to one course, if that. Often that course focuses on techniques for using mathematics for problem solving and other applications in various disciplines (such as algebra, introductory probability and statistics, finite math, or calculus for business). Although students need these skills, is this the best use of one course in a Christian liberal arts curriculum? I think not. One course is better spent introducing the nonmath or science major to the nature of mathematics, with a focus on initiating students into exploring the possible relationships between mathematics and other areas of knowledge, including their biblical and theological understanding. Over many years, I taught various versions of such a first-year course, usually titled The Nature of Mathematics, and engaged students in a variety of relevant integrative questions, including the following examples.

Is the deductive method of the mathematician useful for Christian apologetics (defending the Christian faith)?

Because I sensed that many of my lower-division students did not have a felt need to explore the underlying nature of mathematics, I sought a connection I could make with something many of them seemed to be interested in—presenting arguments for the "truth" of the Christian faith. Therefore, I started the course with a major section on symbolic logic, in which students gained competence in testing deductive arguments for validity, and students did some elementary deductive proofs of theorems from axioms using the fundamental laws of logic. After this introduction to the deductive nature of mathematical reasoning, we then read an essay by C. R. Verno on "Mathematical Thinking and Christian Theology."[6] Verno proposes a presuppositional approach to Christian apologetics, in which Christian theology seems to emerge from certain fundamental assumptions in a manner analogous to the way a mathematician's theorems are deduced from axioms. A number of students liked this approach.

I then raised some possible objections to this presuppositional approach. If the truth of a theorem resulting from a valid deductive argument is guaranteed only if all the axioms are true, how does one establish the truth of the fundamental Christian assumptions? If they are the result of prior deductive arguments, then we have an infinite regress. Are these Christian assumptions self-evident? Inserting at this time my own version of a cosmological argument for the existence of God having the logical form $[(p{\rightarrow}q){\wedge}(q{\rightarrow}r){\wedge} \ldots {\wedge}(w{\rightarrow}x){\wedge}p]{\rightarrow}x$, where x is "God exists," I point out that axioms are often perceived as true, or self-evident, only by those who already accept the conclusion as true. I raise the possible objection that such a view of presuppositional apologetics insulates one's fundamental assumptions from the possibility of criticism and also does not take into account the role of experience in making judgments of the adequacy of any system of thought. Is not such an approach neglecting crucial empirical questions about whether Christian beliefs do indeed make sense of experience? Needless to say, we do not reach a definitive answer to my integrative question. But I have gained the students' attention. In the process of learning something about the method of the mathematician, they have been initiated into exploring possible connections with other areas of knowledge.

---

[6] C.R. Verno, "Mathematical Thinking and Christian Theology," *Journal of The American Scientific Affiliation* (June 1968): 37–41.

Is mathematical knowledge created or discovered?

Having introduced students to the deductive method of the mathematician, I then elaborated on the nature of an abstract mathematical system, which starts with undefined terms and axioms, and includes theorems proven from the axioms. (I sometimes started with nonsense syllables, such as "ogg" and "uff," as undefined terms, just to tempt my students into thinking this is all very silly). As a specific example of an abstract mathematical system, I chose the concept of "groups." After stating the undefined terms and axioms for groups, we proved a number of theorems. I then noted the numerous models for groups that result from interpreting the undefined terms, ranging from the addition of 2 x 2 matrixes to the symmetry of crystals to singing in the round. An important point was now made about the unifying value of an abstract mathematical system like groups: widely diverse calculations and phenomena can all be captured by one concise abstract system having a minimal number of undefined terms and axioms, and the theorems, proven once and for all in the abstract, are true for all of these models. Preparing students for a later integrative question, I even ventured the opinion that this economy of expression is elegant; it is "beautiful" (which was a new idea for many students).

But now we had a version of the chicken-and-egg problem. What comes first, the abstract mathematical system or models of the abstract system? I pointed out that historically mathematics has worked both ways. It has generally been the case that the existence of concrete models has preceded the axiomatization in an abstract mathematical system that unifies these models, as in the case of group theory. But, to the surprise of many students, I noted that in the development of non-Euclidean geometries, it was the abstract mathematical systems that came first, and at the time, people believed that no models of these strange geometries could possibly exist. After all, had not Euclid captured, once and for all, the nature of physical space? What were Lobachevsky and Bolyai and Riemann doing when they developed their hyperbolic and elliptic geometries? It looks like they were "playing games with marks on paper" in replacing Euclid's parallel pos-

tulate with axioms that seemed to have no connection to the nature of physical space. Why this flight of fancy? Stephen Barker
suggests that their dissatisfaction with the parallel postulate was
aesthetic: "the . . . [parallel] postulate looks out of place on account of its intricacy. It requires a much more complex sentence
for its formulation than does any of the other postulates."[7] But
there still was no apparent connection with reality, at least until
Einstein came along, many years later. Since his time, we have
not looked at physical space in the same way. In contrast to Euclid's capturing of the nature of local space, it now appears that
Riemann captured the nature of the space of the universe with
his elliptic geometry. So, the abstract system came long before
any model. A mathematician might be tempted to say that it
took many years for the physicists to catch up to a creative mathematician working from an aesthetic impulse.

What is the point of this story? And what does it have to do
with my integrative question of whether mathematics is created
or discovered? I have now prepared the students to envision the
two ends of the spectrum, as well as a possible middle way.
At the discovery pole, some mathematicians formulate abstract
mathematical systems that reflect the structures they discover
in a world external to themselves. At the creation pole, some
mathematicians create abstract mathematical systems independent of the issue of whether models exist in the "real world." I
suggest to my students that there is important mathematical
work to be done at both the discovery and creation poles. A
number of students are skeptical about the creation pole. Why
should a mathematician create an abstract mathematical system
that appears unrelated to the real world? I respond by asking
why an artist paints, or sculpts, or composes. Such human creations are artistic activities. As noted by Raymond Wilder, the
"aesthetic function" of mathematics, as an addition to the "instrumental function," is "to provide an aesthetically satisfying
structure allowing of advances by creatively minded mathematicians."[8] Then I dare to suggest that such artistic work can be a

---

[7] Stephen F. Barker, *Philosophy of Mathematics* (Englewood Cliffs, N.J.: Prentice-Hall, 1964), 32.

[8] Raymond L. Wilder, *Evolution of Mathematical Concepts* (New York: John Wiley & Sons, 1968), 118.

legitimate Christian calling, based on my belief that one of God's purposes is the creation of beauty and God's comprehensive purposes are accomplished by different Christians exercising their particular God-given gifts. At this point, at least some students have started thinking about a possible connection between their understanding of the discipline of mathematics and their biblical and theological understanding.

Finally, I point to the possibility of a more nuanced third way, based on my own interactionist epistemology, which suggests that much mathematical activity is neither pure discovery nor pure creativity. It is both discovery and creativity. Students who are looking for black-and-white distinctions find this suggestion unsettling, at best. Is it possible that Riemann, in creating/discovering an elliptic geometry that appeared unrelated to the external world, actually had an insight into the nature of that world long before his time? Is it possible that many claims to knowledge, not only in mathematics but in all disciplines, reflect an interaction between the known and the knower, thus calling into question the common bifurcation between objectivity and subjectivity? I think so. As my ultimate example of this claim, I suggest that the biblical record itself reflects such interactionism when I assert that "I believe the Bible to be the Word of God, mediated, by God's choice, through active human instruments, thereby reflecting the personality and culture of the writer, at the same time that it reveals God's truth." Students are thereby exposed to my own attempt to attain epistemological coherence relative to multiple sources of knowledge. This seems to get their attention.

Why should a Christian do mathematics?

This is a special case of the broader axiological question "What is of value?" For the Christian student, a more focused version of this question is whether doing mathematics is important in light of the values of the kingdom of God.[9] Although I have tried

---

[9] It appears to me that the most fundamental integrative question that Christian students working in any academic discipline should ask is "Is doing work in this discipline important in light of the values of the kingdom of God?

various ways to help students struggle with this most funda-mental integrative question, the best results have been achieved when I assigned *A Mathematician's Apology* by G. E. Hardy.[10] Hardy's story is a must read for anyone wondering about whether to do mathematics, vocationally or otherwise. Many students were deeply moved by this story. It raised some serious questions in their minds. Should a person do something only because he or she is very good at it? Should a person do some-thing only because it is a vehicle for creative expression? They were especially moved by the tragedy near the end of Hardy's life when he felt he had lost his youthful creative powers and decided he then had nothing more for which to live. Whatever their intended academic majors or vocational plans, students were initiated into serious reflection on the generalized version of my third integrative question: which activities, vocational or otherwise, are important enough in the light of the values of the kingdom of God to warrant my devotion?

My teaching of various versions of a course on the nature of mathematics for non-math majors focused on content related to the three integrative questions noted above. Some math teachers may argue that such a course focuses too much on foundational issues about the nature of mathematics, to the neglect of helping non-majors learn to do more mathematics. Others may not have the luxury of being able to design such a course, having been assigned the teaching of more traditional introductory math courses. For math teachers in either of these categories, I have a more modest proposal. Design one unit for one course around one integrative question of your choice. See how that works. If it works well, it could lead to an expanded use of integrative questions in your future teaching.

The Nature of Mathematics for Math Majors: A Spiral Strategy

One of the ironies that emerged in my life as a math teacher was that non-majors who were required to take my Math 101, The

---

[10] G. E. Hardy, *A Mathematician's Apology* (London: Cambridge University Press, 1969).

Nature of Mathematics, often left that course with a greater understanding of the nature and the structure of mathematics than first-year math majors who were more interested in getting down to the "real business" of doing more advanced mathematics (as in a calculus sequence) than in reflecting about the underlying nature of mathematics. For a year or two, I did teach a beefed-up version of Math 101 for math majors, with reasonable success. With or without such an introductory course, I eventually engaged math majors in substantial and sustained worldview inquiry in a capstone senior seminar course (more about that later). However, if I had the opportunity to do it all over again, I would propose a more radical approach that views the worldview project in terms of a coherent four-year curriculum for math majors rather than being reserved for one or two special courses. My proposal will be radical because it presupposes some coordination of subject matter across courses taught by different faculty in the math department, which is not a very common phenomenon.[11]

First, before any teaching begins, I would have the math faculty decide on a departmental list of integrative questions judged to be of such significance that by graduation, each student should have seriously reflected on them. This list of integrative questions should be revisited periodically since not all questions will be perennial; some will reflect current issues within the discipline. All first-year students intending to major in mathematics, or interested in exploring that possibility, should take a one-credit seminar in the fall semester. The primary focus of this course would be to introduce the students to the important integrative questions in mathematics. The class would include preliminary discussion of possible directions for student responses to these questions, commensurate with their intellectual maturity. The integrative question to be given the most extensive treatment would be "Why should a Christian do mathematics?" Each student would be required to submit an essay addressing this question at the end of the course, the thoughtfulness of which will determine the grade. Appropriate

---

[11] I believe that the strategy I propose for mathematics would be fruitful for any academic major.

readings will be assigned that introduce the students to chosen integrative questions.[12]

The math faculty should then review the course syllabi of all departmental courses for math majors to determine those places in the curriculum, prior to a capstone senior seminar course, where students will be expected to reflect on given integrative questions in a manner appropriate to the course content and the evolving mathematical maturity of the students. For example, in a course in abstract algebra, students could be expected to reflect on the integrative question of whether mathematical systems are created or discovered. Students could then be expected to come back to this question in a later course in advanced geometry that deals with non-Euclidean geometries. This strategy of returning to a question at various times at different levels appropriate to the student's emerging intellectual maturity is sometimes referred to as a "spiral approach" to teaching and learning. Note that this spiral strategy calls into question the naive assumption that what "integration of faith and learning" means is that something faith-related needs to be incorporated into each course being taught. My contrary position is that the faith-related integrative questions need to be included in a coherent four-year curriculum at appropriate and fruitful junctures, meaning that some courses (such as differential equations) may have no inclusion of integrative questions.

By now, you have surely surmised that my intended climax for this spiral integrative strategy is a capstone senior seminar course to be required of all math majors. I propose that this course be devoted to the deepening of individual student responses to a series of integrative questions, many of which (typically, the perennial questions) they will initially have been exposed to in their first-year math seminar with later exposure in appropriate courses taken prior to this capstone course. I have taught such a senior seminar for math majors on a number of

---

[12] At this introductory level for potential math majors, accessible books would include John D. Barrow, *Pi in the Sky: Counting, Thinking, and Being* (Oxford: Oxford University Press, 1992); Philip J. Davis, Reuben Hersh, et al., *The Mathematical Experience* (Cambridge, Mass.: Birkhauser Boston, 1995); William L. Schaaf, *Our Mathematical Heritage* (New York: Macmillan, 1963); Wilder, *Evolution of Mathematical Concepts*; Hardy, *A Mathematician's Apology*.

occasions, without the benefit of the prior spiral pedagogy pro-posed above. The syllabus typically included consideration of issues related to the three integrative questions that I proposed earlier for non-math majors, but at a more sophisticated level appropriate to senior math majors.[13] In addition, other integra-tive questions are appropriate for in-depth consideration at this more advanced level, including the three that follow.

What is the status of the classical laws of two-valued logic?

By the senior year, math majors have become adept at using the classical laws of two-valued logic (law of non-contradiction, law of the excluded middle) in doing mathematical proofs. It is now important to consider the metaquestion as to the status of these laws. We talk about the alternative views that these laws are a priori insights into reality, descriptions of operations of the mind, inductive generalizations, or conventions.[14] I propose for their consideration a transcendental justification that these laws are minimal preconditions for human discourse without confu-sion for those persons who wish to engage in the project of com-municating propositional knowledge. This raises the further interesting question as to whether there are other projects for which alternative multivalued logics are appropriate.[15]

---

[13] For one version of such a syllabus, including suggested readings, see Har-old Heie, "One Possible Outline For a First Undergraduate Course in Philoso-phy of Mathematics," 97–118, in Robert Brabenc, ed., *Proceedings of a Fourth Conference on Mathematics From a Christian Perspective* (Wheaton, Ill.: Wheaton College, 1983). The book I found most helpful at this more advanced senior seminar level was Barker, *Philosophy of Mathematics*. Other helpful books in-clude Reuben Hersh, *What is Mathematics, Really?* (Oxford: Oxford University Press, 1997); Robert J. Baum, ed., *Philosophy and Mathematics* (San Francisco: Freeman, Cooper & Co., 1973); Morris Kline, *Mathematics: The Loss of Certainty* (New York: Oxford University Press, 1980); Raymond L. Wilder, *Introduction to the Foundations of Mathematics* (New York: John Wiley & Sons, 1952); Harold Eves and Carroll V. Newsom, *An Introduction to the Foundations and Fundamental Concepts of Mathematics* (New York: Holt, Rinehart & Winston, 1965).

[14] 14 As summarized in Stephen F. Barker, "The Philosophy of Logic," in Stephen F. Barker, *The Elements of Logic* (New York: McGraw-Hill, 1965), 295–304.

[15] See Hilary Putnam, "Three-Valued Logic," in *Mathematics, Matter and Method, Philosophical Papers*, vol. 1 (London: Cambridge University Press, 1975),

*What is the meaning of "infinity" in mathematics, and is there any
relationship between the mathematician's use of "infinity" and the
meaning of the theologian who refers to God as "infinite?"*

As I have frankly told my students over the years, I have little
clarity about a possible cogent response to this question. Most
attempts at response appear to rely on analogies that I find un-
convincing. Furthermore, the idea of God being "infinite" is a
mystery that my limited understanding cannot grasp. I suspect
that the mathematician and the theologian are using the word
"infinity" in incommensurable ways, suggesting the probability
that there is no relationship between their respective uses.[16]
Some of my math majors have felt free to disagree.

*What is the status of the three major philosophies of mathematics
(Platonism, intuitionism, formalism), and do these philosophies
comport with a Christian perspective?*

This integrative question is the focus of the final paper required
of students in the senior seminar course. This paper is due at the
next-to-last class session. It is at this time that I give the students
my paper in response to this question, based on my conviction
that a professor does indeed "profess" a personal answer to integrative questions but not prematurely in a way that forecloses
the struggle of students to develop their own responses. In the
last session we discuss our agreements and disagreements. In
brief, I propose a philosophy of mathematics that encompasses
the total scope of activities carried out by mathematicians, including the activities of Platonists, intuitionists, and formalists,[17]

166–73. For an argument that the criteria for criticism of knowledge claims for
a given project are inherent in the nature of the project and are thus binding
on those who choose to engage in that project, see David L. Wolfe, *Epistemology: The Justification of Belief* (Downers Grove, Ill.: InterVarsity Press, 1982).

[16] For various views on how some prominent thinkers have reflected on the
meaning of "infinity," see the following selections from Baum, *Philosophy and
Mathematics*: Aristotle, 75–77, Descartes, 87–89, Newton, 136, 140–45, Leibnitz,
167–69, Berkeley, 189–92.

[17] For consideration of the major philosophies of mathematics, see Eves and
Newsom, *An Introduction to the Foundations and Fundamental Concepts of Mathematics*, 299–305; and Wilder, *Introduction to the Foundations of Mathematics*,
219–79.

and I profess a congruence between the aesthetic values under-lying these activities and the values to which I am committed as a Christian.

BEYOND PEDAGOGY

I have focused on the pedagogical strategy of posing integrative questions. But good teaching requires more than good pedagogy if it is to inspire a student's *need to know*. Such inspiration is most likely to occur if the teacher models his or her own *need to know*.

During my entire teaching career, I explored and continu-ously refined my own responses to the integrative questions I posed for my students. My own integrative questions deeply informed my teaching. My students knew that I was dealing with some of the same questions I expected them to address. They understood that I did not have all the answers, contrary to a popular myth about teachers. They found it liberating to know that the teacher was also on pilgrimage as a learner. At the end of each offering of Math 101, The Nature of Mathematics, I would typically give them a progress report on my attempts to respond to these shared questions, emphasizing the connections with my law and liberty question. In ways I did not anticipate, coherence ensued between the answers that emerged from my dealing with some of my math questions and the results of my struggle with the law and liberty question. I eventually came to view much of mathematics and all of Christian living as forms of art, not science, tied together by the integrative theme of "freedom within bounds."[18]

My students saw that my struggle with my integrative ques-tions was not an abstract intellectual exercise but was integrally related to my desire to live well as a Christian. I was trying to demolish the insidious bifurcation between learning and living so prevalent among students, not to mention faculty.

My ideal as a teacher, however imperfectly realized, was to model for my students my deep conviction that *learning, teach-*

---

[18] For an elaboration, see Harold Heie, "Mathematics: Freedom Within Bounds," pp. 206–30 in Heie and Wolfe, *The Reality of Christian Learning*.

ing, and living are all of one piece. My boldest venture exemplifying this conviction occurred when I was asked to teach an elective senior general education course titled Integration of Faith and Learning (not a math course). I decided to push the ideal of connecting learning with living as far as I could by asking each of the dozen or so students to submit one question that was most relevant to his or her present life. With the help of colleagues from many disciplines, I then developed an individualized, interdisciplinary program of study for each student that addressed that student's question. As I expected, their questions were integrative questions, as questions about life typically are, requiring that they draw on both their academic disciplinary understanding and their biblical and theological understanding. A year later, one student told me that the course was the first time she studied something because she "wanted to," not because she "had to." This marvelous teaching and learning experience convinced me that it is possible to create educational models that make an intimate connection between learning and living.

I hope that my students over the years have seen that my teaching proceeded from who I am as a person, consistent with Parker Palmer's assertion that "good teaching cannot be reduced to technique; good teaching comes from the identity and integrity of the teacher."[19] My ideal as a teacher includes caring deeply for the well-being of my students, but it also includes caring deeply for the subject matter—especially the scholarly integrative task of making fruitful connections between academic disciplinary knowledge and biblical and theological knowledge. It is my hope that because I modeled a need to know relative to this scholarly integrative task, some of my students developed their own need to know.[20]

SELECTED BIBLIOGRAPHY

Anglin, W. S. *Mathematics: A Concise History and Philosophy.* Berlin: Springer-Verlag, 1994.

---

[19] Parker J. Palmer, *The Courage to Teach* (San Francisco: Jossey-Bass, 1998), 10.

[20] I wish to thank my colleague and friend Dick Stout for his helpful comments on an earlier draft of this essay.

Aspray, W., and P. Kitcher, eds. *History and Philosophy of Modern Mathematics*. Minnesota Studies in the Philosophy of Science, vol. 11. Minneapolis: University of Minnesota Press, 1988.

Barker, S. F. *Philosophy of Mathematics*. Englewood Cliffs, N.J.: Prentice-Hall, 1964.

Barrow, J. D. *Pi in the Sky: Counting, Thinking, and Being*. Oxford, U.K.: Oxford University Press, 1992.

Baum, R. J., ed. *Philosophy and Mathematics*. San Francisco: Freeman, Cooper & Co., 1973.

Benacerraf, P., and H. Putnam, eds. *Philosophy of Mathematics*, 2d ed. London: Cambridge University Press, 1983.

Berlinski, D. *The Advent of the Algorithm: The Idea That Rules the World*. San Diego: Harcourt Trade Publishers, 2000.

Bradley, W. J., and K. C. Schaefer. *The Uses and Misuses of Data and Models: The Mathematization of the Human Sciences*. Thousand Oaks, Cal.: Sage Publications, 1998.

Brown, J. R. *Philosophy of Mathematics: An Introduction to the World of Proofs and Pictures*. London: Routledge, 1999.

Davis, P. J., R. Hersh, et al. *The Mathematical Experience*. Cambridge, Mass.: Birkhauser Boston, 1995.

―――. *Descartes' Dream: The World According to Mathematics*. New York: Harcourt Brace Jovanovich, 1986.

Ernest, P. *Social Constructivism As a Philosophy of Mathematics*. Albany: State University of New York Press, 1997.

Eves, H., and C. V. Newsom. *An Introduction to the Foundations and Fundamental Concepts of Mathematics*. New York: Holt, Rinehart & Winston, 1965.

Ewald, W. *From Kant to Hilbert: A Source Book in the Foundation of Mathematics*. New York: Oxford University Press, 1996.

Hardy, G. E. *A Mathematician's Apology*. London: Cambridge University Press, 1969.

Hersh, R. *What is Mathematics, Really?* Oxford: Oxford University Press, 1997.

Howell, R. and W. J. Bradley, eds. *Mathematics in a Postmodern Age: A Christian Perspective*. Grand Rapids, Mich.: William B. Eerdmans Publishing Co., 2001.

Kitcher, P. *The Nature of Mathematical Knowledge*. New York: Oxford University Press, 1983.

Kline, M. *Mathematics: The Loss of Certainty*. New York: Oxford University Press, 1980.

Putnam, H. *Mathematics, Matter and Method, Philosophical Papers*, vol. 1. London: Cambridge University Press, 1975.

Schaaf, W. L. *Our Mathematical Heritage*. New York: Macmillan, 1963.

Tymoczko, T., ed. *New Directions in the Philosophy of Mathematics*. Princeton, N.J.: Princeton University Press, 1998.

Wilder, R. L. *Evolution of Mathematical Concepts*. New York: John Wiley & Sons, 1968.

―――. *Introduction to the Foundations of Mathematics*. New York: John Wiley & Sons, 1952.

6

Christian Theism: Alive and Well in the Physics and Astronomy Classroom

Lois Kieffaber

My Pilgrimage and Underlying Principles

WHEN I BEGAN my teaching career at a state university, I received very little mentoring either in teaching or in my spiritual life. I lived a compartmentalized life, never mentioning my religious beliefs in professional settings and confining my spiritual life to Sundays and morning devotions. I accepted my present position at a church-related college without having given any serious thought to whether I *should* be attempting to integrate my faith with my academic discipline, much less *how* I should go about it. My learning curve went something like this: five years to consider whether integration was worth doing; five years of floundering about on my own, trying first one thing and then another in my classes; finally the most recent five years of intentional reading on integrative topics, attending conferences on science and religion, and discussing issues with like-minded colleagues.[1] This essay is an attempt to speed up the implementation process for others who have taken the first step of deciding that integrating faith and professional life is worth doing. My attempts to integrate issues of faith and values into my classroom teaching of physics and astronomy are guided by the three following principles.

---

[1] I am grateful to The Pew Charitable Trust for its support of the Calvin College Summer Seminars in Christian Scholarship, in particular the "Theology and the New Physics" seminar with Dr. John Polkinghorne, Summer 1998, which was devoted to connections between physics and theology.

Mutual respect

As a Christian scientist, I have attempted to respect both science and theology. Colleagues and students who share this position will rarely be distressed by anything I say about either science or religion in the classroom. But a teacher in a private school with a religious affiliation may well encounter more students who hold religious teachings in higher regard than science, whereas teachers in public institutions may have a preponderance of students who respect science more than religious teachings. My goal in either situation is to model respect for both arenas of knowledge and to challenge students to consider both science and religion as potentially legitimate sources of information helpful in forming a worldview. Mutual respect is critical to my integrative endeavors because Christ commands each of us to love God with all our heart, soul, mind, and strength (see Luke 10:27). To me this means that there are four channels—emotional, spiritual, intellectual, and physical—through which we may come to know more about God and thus love God better. To neglect any one of them is to limit unnecessarily our knowledge of God and God's creation.

Interdisciplinary connections

After decades of disciplinary territorialism, the educational tide is turning toward an intentionally interdisciplinary approach. This trend acknowledges that we have overestimated our students' abilities to make connections for themselves among their various subjects of study. Students seem not to connect the concept of a derivative from their calculus class with the definition of velocity or acceleration in their physics class. The spectra studied in chemistry are identical to those encountered in astronomy, and logarithmic scales abound in both physics and astronomy, but students are unable to interpret them across disciplines without a great deal of prodding. Realization that we must actively help students make these connections has given rise to interdisciplinary classes and team teaching.

It is not only higher education that can seem fragmented and compartmentalized to our students. The strategy of compartmentalism serves some of us well in our everyday lives also, with religion governing faith and practice while science governs our understanding of the physical world. But most of us would like to experience all areas of life as related and consistent. This synthesis is not fully achievable because there are always new experiences and information requiring reflection and integration, but I believe a consistent worldview is a worthwhile goal. The real world presents itself as seamless and undivided, and I desire my response to it to be similarly integrated.

Intellectual humility

It is easy for teachers to become accustomed to being the final arbiter on matters relating to disciplinary content. We need to be cautious about letting our sense of acknowledged disciplinary expertise carry over into matters of judgment and values. Just as newspapers distinguish opinion from news by placing opinion on the editorial page, teachers should label opinion and judgment as such. My belief in the centrality of intellectual humility comes from two considerations. The first arises out of my Quaker experience of community. Decision making is by consensus, not majority rule. Because the Holy Spirit is active in each of us, I can never assume that any single individual (including myself) has the full and complete truth. In matters of faith and practice, the understanding achieved by an individual must be validated by the faith community. Likewise in science, the findings of the individual must be validated by the scientific community.

A related consideration arises from a study of the history of science. In each particular age, those involved in the study of science were convinced that they had corrected the errors of the past and that their understanding of the nature of the physical world was true and would stand the test of time. Many of those cherished paradigms and theories, however, have been replaced with completely different models. There is no reason to expect our own understanding of the physical world to escape the same fate. With these three guiding principles as my integrative anchors, I turn now to the articulation of specific strategies that could be adapted to any physics classroom to facilitate integrative thinking, from general education courses for non-majors to upper-division specialty courses.

IN THE BEGINNING: GENERAL INTEGRATIVE STRATEGIES

If one believes that education should be integrative of the disciplines as well as of faith and learning, it is appropriate to introduce the notion of worldview early in the physics course. I sometimes tell my students that the purpose of their education is to construct an informed and integrated worldview that is consistent with what they have learned and experienced of life thus far. In science classes the emphasis is on the question, "What is the nature of the physical world?" We explore various aspects of the physical world using the criteria of rationality and congruence between what we see experimentally and what we believe the underlying physical reality to be like. Questions to ask students in this regard include:

- Is the universe orderly or chaotic?
- Is it friendly or hostile to human life?
- Are physical events determined or random?
- Did the universe have a beginning, or has it always existed?
- Is space finite or infinite?
- What authority figures in your life have helped shape your worldview (for example, parents, pastors, teachers, disciplinary experts, TV personalities)?
- What kind of information, data, or experiences would cause you to change one of your views?

Students may be asked to articulate answers to such questions in a written assignment to be shared in small groups, so they can get some ideas of the breadth of answers from among their colleagues. Or they may write in their own journals, in anticipation of an end-of-semester assignment asking them to compare their current views with their earlier views to see which, if any, have been confirmed, challenged, or changed.

Student beliefs about what it means to be human may also be included in a worldview discussion, because these beliefs will certainly color their responses to the issues with which we will concern ourselves in the course. One characteristic of being human that is pertinent to the study of physics is thinking. Einstein said, "I want to think God's thoughts." When we exercise our minds in the study of God's creation, we do in some small measure "think God's thoughts." We are endowed with mental capabilities that allow us to understand, at least in part, the world we live in. The so-called "Rationalist Credo" captures this notion well. It states that the world is orderly, knowable, and knowable best by human reason. Our minds, being part of the rationality or *logos* of the universe, are in tune with and thus able to understand that rationality to some extent. The Greek word *logos* is the same one used in John 1: 1 to describe the place of the eternal Christ in the universe. Rationality is a fundamental feature of the universe and of the intelligent creatures that inhabit it.

People of strong religious convictions do not all agree about the proper relationship between science and faith. A conceptual framework that helps students articulate these differences is provided by the following four models for the possible interaction between science and faith:[2] (1) conflict sees biblical literalism and scientific materialism as opposite ends of a spectrum, so that acknowledging the truth claims of one necessarily invalidates the other; (2) independence assumes two separate and autonomous domains that do not overlap and respect each other's turf, faith governing our relationship to God and others, while science tells us about the natural world; (3) complementarity holds that faith and science bring different perspectives to the same phenomena, neither invalidating the other because they are seeing through different lenses, and (4) qualified agreement claims that science and faith will agree in their account of phenomena, and in cases where they seem to disagree, better science or a revised interpretation of Scripture will eventually bring them into accord. When students can recognize and articu-

---

[2] Adapted from Ian G. Barbour, *Religion and Science: Historical and Contemporary Issues* (San Francisco: HarperCollins, 1997), 77–105. See also Steven J. Gould, "Nonoverlapping Magisteria," *Natural History* 106, no.2 (March 1997): 16–22, 60–62; William Provine, "Scientists, Face It! Science and Religion are Incompatible," *The Scientist* 2, no. 16 (Sept. 5, 1988): 10; Robert B. Fischer, *God Did It, But How?* (La Mirada, Cal.: CalMedia, c.1981; ASA Press, 1997) for examples of the models in action.

late the differences in assumptions that these models represent, they are less likely to feel threatened by people who do not agree with them.

I have also found it useful to ask students to differentiate between two questions: "How strongly do I believe something?" and "How sure am I that it is true?" It helps to picture the two questions as perpendicular axes on a graph. I may believe something scientific very strongly, such as that there are nine planets in the solar system, but simultaneously I may be very amenable to changing my mind if a tenth planet is discovered. The same is true in matters of religious belief. I may believe very strongly that the Noah story is a myth but am prepared to change my view if the remnants of an ark are discovered. That God is loving would rank highly on both scales within my belief system. On the other hand, the doctrine of the virgin birth falls somewhat lower on both scales.

Raising the above worldview considerations will delay the entry into the science content of the courses in our curriculum. But in our general education (non-major) science courses, it is particularly important to talk about the nature of science, its assumptions, and its limitations. The non-major science class may be the only exposure to science some students will have at the college level. Therefore, taking time to investigate the part played by values in assessing scientific theories can be a valuable integrative task. Ian Barbour notes four significant characteristics of a scientific theory.[3] Another such list of key features of a good scientific theory can be found in philosopher William Newton-Smith's book *The Rationality of Science*.[4]

Students could be asked to generate such a list. A fruitful class

---

[3] Ian G. Barbour, *Religion and Science*, 109. Barbour cites a*greement with data* (the most important criterion, but not sufficient to prove a theory true since other theories may also fit the data as well or better), *coherence* (consistency and interconnectedness with other accepted theories), *scope* (applicable to many different domains and supported by a range of evidence), and, *fertility* (the theory's ability to suggest new experiments, further elaboration, and new hypotheses).

[4] William H. Newton-Smith, *The Rationality of Science* (New York: Routledge & Kegan Paul, 1981) as quoted by Robin Dunbar, *The Trouble with Science* (Cambridge, Mass.: Harvard University Press, 1995), 80.

discussion will ensue if students begin to ask each other questions such as: Who decides what makes a good theory? What makes these characteristics the desirable ones? These questions are not scientific; rather they represent the values of the scientific community. Thus we immediately begin to question the assumption that science is a value-free enterprise. And we can ask students to be on the lookout in all their classes for those particular disciplinary assumptions (often unspoken) that are value based.

Students are very fond of quotations by scientists and about science. Start a personal collection today in some easily reached section of your computer's hard drive. An indispensable reference is *Physically Speaking: A Dictionary of Quotations on Physics and Astronomy*.[5] Quotations can be used as filler on exams and problem assignment sheets. They can be projected on an overhead or computer screen as a means of introducing a certain topic of discussion or when coming at a topic from a historical viewpoint. "Who cares about half a second after the big bang; what about the half second before?"[6] is a good quotation to call attention to the limits of science and to raise the question of whether physical or metaphysical questions are more important to most people in the long run. Some quotations are simply inspirational, for example Immanuel Kant's statement in *Critique of Practical Reason*: "Two things fill the mind with ever new and increasing admiration and awe, the oftener and the more steadily we reflect on them: the starry heavens above me and the moral law within me."[7]

Cartoons can be used in all the same ways. Sidney Harris's books of science cartoons are particularly useful,[8] another excel-

---

[5] *Physically Speaking: A Dictionary of Quotations on Physics and Astronomy*, selected and arranged by Carl C. Gaither and Alma E. Cavozos-Gaither (Philadelphia: Institute of Physics Publishing, 1997).

[6] Faye Weldon, as quoted by Paul Davies, *About Time: Einstein's Unfinished Revolution* (New York: Simon and Schuster, 1995; Touchstone Books, 1996), 129.

[7] Immanuel Kant, *Critique of Practical Reason*, trans. Lewis White Beck (New York: Liberal Arts Press, 1956), 166.

[8] Sidney Harris, *What's So Funny about Science?* (Los Altos, Cal.: William Kaufmann, 1970); *Chalk Up Another One* (Washington, D.C.: AAAS Press, 1992); *Einstein Simplified* (New Brunswick, N.J.: Rutgers University Press, 1988); *From Personal Ads to Cloning Labs* (New York: W. H. Freeman, 1993).

lent science cartoonist is Nick Downes.[9] Science journals are also good sources for cartoons, in particular *American Scientist*.

Sometimes a work of art can imaginatively express a scientific idea laden with metaphysical implications. Michelangelo's "Creation of Adam" on the ceiling of the Sistine Chapel is thought of as a work of art, but it also reveals the artist to be a scientist. Students can be asked to examine it for indications of scientific knowledge.[10] Many works of medieval art make it clear that science and religion were not always separate categories in peoples' minds.

Science fiction literature is also a way of raising issues of values and faith and may be less threatening to students because it is obviously not dealing with the real world. Science fiction fans will have their own favorites in this regard; a few of mine are *A Canticle for Leibowitz* by Walter Miller, "The Gentle Seduction" by Mark Stiegler in his book of the same title, C. S. Lewis's space trilogy, and the fiction of Madeleine L'Engle. The only anthology I have come across that is explicitly religious science fantasy is *Flame Tree Planet*, edited by Roger Elwood.

It has been said that it is easier for physicists and astronomers to be theists than for scientists in other disciplines. I think it is fairly easy to understand why this might be so. Physics became a separate discipline from natural theology in the early Renaissance when the dominant Western worldview included religious belief. Having students read biographies of scientists from this time period is one way to introduce the notion that science and religion are not incompatible and to suggest that the idea of any basic incompatibility is a relatively recent (eighteenth-century) phenomenon. Many students will be surprised to learn that Newton wrote more pages regarding scriptural prophecies than about scientific subjects. Or that Boyle gave vast sums of money to support missionary efforts in foreign countries. Michael Faraday was a member of a "a very small and despised sect of Chris-

---

[9] Nick Downes, *Big Science* (Washington, D. C.: AAAS Press, 1992); *Whatever Happened to "Eureka"?* (New Brunswick: Rutgers University Press, 1994).

[10] The background for the figure of God is the shape of the human brain, and the finger of God does not touch the man's finger but implies the passage of a divine "spark." And why does the first man have a navel?

tians, known, if known at all, as *Sandemanians*,"[11] who believed in spiritual equality for all. A good resource for interesting personal facts about scientists is *Asimov's Biographical Encyclopedia of Science and Technology*.[12] For further information, interested students can then be referred to other more definitive works.[13] A project may be assigned in which small groups research the religious/cultural background of a particular scientist. Such projects help students discover how the cultural context might have affected the interpretation of scientific findings. Results may be shared in the form of oral presentations or a poster session.

A second reason many physicists and astronomers are theists is their awareness that the physical world, including the large-scale features of the universe, seem to display order. The terminology "laws" of nature is common in these disciplines. In addition, physics, whether by happy coincidence or by design, emphasizes problems that have analytic solutions. It has an uncanny ability to ferret out those questions that can be answered while ignoring a host of others.[14] The lawlike behavior of certain aspects of the universe guided the work of St. Thomas Aquinas, the great thirteenth-century philosopher-theologian who undertook to synthesize the works of Aristotle with the Christian Scriptures. The similarity of laws of nature to moral laws, both with respect to their governing principles and their predictive abilities, has led many a theist to the conclusion that they have the same author; thus the concept of "natural theology." It is an easy step from laws to Lawgiver.

---

[11] From a letter to the Countess of Lovelace, as quoted by Geoffrey Cantor, *Michael Faraday: Sandemanian and Scientist: A Study of Science and Religion in the Nineteenth Century* (New York, St. Martin's Press, 1991), 5.

[12] Isaac Asimov, *Asimov's Biographical Encyclopedia of Science and Technology* (Garden City, N.Y.: Doubleday, 1964).

[13] For example, Stillman Drake, *Galileo* (New York: Oxford University Press, 2001); Richard S. Westfall, *The Life of Isaac Newton* (Cambridge: Cambridge University Press, 1993); Reijer Hooykaas, *Robert Boyle: A Study in Science and Christian Belief* (Lanham, Md.: University Press of America, 1997); Michael White, *Isaac Newton: The Last Sorcerer* (Reading, Mass.: Addison Wesley, 1997).

[14] Kepler attempted to understand how the period of a planet was related to its distance from the sun. Had he concentrated instead on finding a law for the spacing of the planetary orbits, or some way to predict a planet's average distance from the sun (a question still unanswered today), we might not be familiar with his name.

The Old Testament authors were also aware of orderliness in the universe, and to them, also, this order pointed to a reliable Creator/Sustainer. Psalm 19:1–6 can be used as an introduction to a class period during which the reliability of the physical universe will be addressed. Psalm 104:19–23 is also useful for this purpose. The notion of an orderly universe has never been seriously disputed by science; in fact science would be impossible without it. A lawful universe accounts for the repeatability of scientific experiments and for the assumption that similar causes will produce similar effects. This does not mean that we understand why it should be so. As Einstein remarked, "The most incomprehensible thing about the world is that it is comprehensible."[15] Mathematics is said to be the language of physics, and similar observations have been made about this very productive union. A distinguished group of French mathematicians writing under the pseudonym Nicolas Bourbaki said, "There is an intimate connection between experimental phenomena and mathematical structures; yet we are completely ignorant about the underlying reasons for this, and we shall perhaps always remain ignorant of them."[16] We do not understand why mathematics should be so effective in describing the physical world, but one explanation might be that the One who created mathematics also created the physical world and the human minds within that world, thus accounting for their consistency.

INTEGRATIVE OPPORTUNITIES AT THE FRONTIERS OF ASTRONOMY

Now that we have addressed some broad integrative strategies for physics or astronomy classes, I would like to turn to three topics in astronomy that can be examined for productive interactions with theology—big bang cosmology, the anthropic princi-

---

[15] Albert Einstein as quoted in Isaac Asimov and Jason A. Shulman, eds., *Isaac Asimov's Book of Science and Nature Quotations* (New York: Weidenfeld and Nicolson, 1988), 211.

[16] As quoted by Paul Morris in "Mathematics and Intuition," submitted for publication, 1999. Eugene Wigner explores this issue in his now-famous essay "The Unreasonable Effectiveness of Mathematics in the Natural Sciences," *Communications in Pure and Applied Mathematics* 13 (1960): 1–14.

ple, and the search for extraterrestrial life. Most students have some acquaintance with at least one of these because of recent media interest. They generate enthusiastic discussion, perhaps because they are seen as controversial and involve unanswered questions rather than unquestioned answers.

If one had set out specifically to create a scientific theory that was in harmony with Christian theology, one could hardly have done better than big bang cosmology. As first proposed, this theory of the origin of the universe sounded like nothing so much as the creation event described by theologians as "creation *ex nihilo*" (creation from nothing). The events that led to the paradigm shift from the reigning steady state theory, which holds that the universe is infinite, to the belief that the universe had a beginning and is finite in time and space make a wonderful story that demonstrates the interplay of theory and experiment.[17] In addition, the scientists who played key roles did not hesitate to express their preferences for the finite or the infinite universe; preferences that seem to be much more a matter of taste (governed by their values) than the result of examining the scientific evidence. One of my favorite quotations is by Dennis Sciama: "I must add that for me the loss of the steady-state theory has been a cause of great sadness. The steady-state theory has a sweep and beauty that for some unaccountable reason the architect of the universe appears to have overlooked. The universe is in fact a botched job, but I suppose we shall have to make the best of it."[18]

Another modern scientific theory that seems tailor-made to support Christianity is the anthropic principle. Examination of the physical constants governing the universe shows that if many of them were changed even slightly, the universe would be incapable of supporting carbon-based life. For example, if the nuclear strong force had been 2% stronger, stars would burn too fast for life to develop on planets; if it were 5% weaker, the deuteron would not be bound and fusion reactions in the cores of

---

[17] See Stephen G. Brush, "How Cosmology Became a Science," *Scientific American* (August 1992): 62–70, for an accessible review of this battle of cosmologies.

[18] As quoted by Martin Gardner in *The Relativity Explosion* (New York: Random House, Vintage Books, 1976), 185.

stars would be impossible.[19] The teacher can ask students to consider other physical constants (gravitational constant, fine structure constant, Planck's constant, or Boltzmann's constant, for example) and predict the physical consequences of increasing or decreasing each one. The format could be a class discussion, a homework assignment, or an essay question on an exam to evaluate their understanding of the role of constants in equations. Upper-division students can be asked more difficult questions. What if the photon were not massless? What would be the consequences of altering the mass ratio between electron and proton, or the ranges of the fundamental forces, or the masses of elementary particles? John Leslie's book *Universes* is a good reference for generating exercises of this sort.[20]

It seems that we inhabit a universe that has just the right parameters to allow us to come into existence. It is not just "any old world" but an extremely special one.[21] We may respond to this fact in a variety of ways. Some observers are indifferent: "We're here because we're here, what's the big deal?" This displays an extreme lack of intellectual curiosity, particularly in scientists whose instincts are to seek understanding of the physical world. Other observers acknowledge that if we inhabit the universe, its physical laws and constants must be consistent with our form of carbon-based life; this formulation is called the weak anthropic principle. It is hard to argue with that—or to feel satisfied by it. The strong anthropic principle, on the other hand, may seem to go too far. Barrow and Tipler state the strong anthropic principle in this way: "The Universe *must* have those properties that allow life to develop within it at some state in its development."[22] John Polkinghorne suggests a modified anthropic principle, which says that a fine-tuned universe is "an insight of

---

[19] John Leslie, "A Fine-Tuned Universe," pp. 297–311 in Robert J. Russell, William R. Stoeger, and George V. Coynes, eds., *Physics, Philosophy, and Theology: A Common Quest for Understanding* (Vatican City State: Vatican Observatory, 1997), 298.

[20] John Leslie, *Universes* (London: Routledge, 1989; paperback ed., 1996).

[21] John Polkinghorne, "A Potent Universe," pp. 105–15 in John Templeton, ed., *Evidence of Purpose: Scientists Discover the Creator* (New York: Continuum International Publishing Group, 1994), 112.

[22] John D. Barrow and Frank J. Tipler, *The Anthropic Cosmological Principle* (Oxford: Clarendon Press, 1986), 21.

significance that calls for some form of explanation."[23] Furthermore since it is the physical laws and constants themselves, presumably existing from the beginning of the universe, that are to be explained, we should expect the explanation to be metaphysical in character. Polkinghorne summarizes the need for an explanation by quoting an argument used by John Leslie:

> John Leslie, who is given to discussing philosophical questions in a parabolic mode, puts the issue clearly in his story of the firing squad.[24] I am due for execution by fifty crack marksmen. As the sound of firing dies away, I find that I am still alive. Here is a fact that calls for explanation. It is not enough just to say, 'Here I am, and that was certainly a close run thing.' There are really only two kinds of rational explanation of my good fortune: Either there were a great number of such executions and by lucky chance mine was the one in which they all happened to miss, or the marksmen are on my side.[25]

Responses to the particularity of our universe take the same two lines of thought. The many-executions explanation is similar to a group of theories called "many-universes" theories. The idea is that universes are very commonplace phenomena, boiling up and separating from a cosmic vacuum seething with energy, much the same way soap bubbles might rise and separate from a churning foam. If there are infinitely many of them coming into existence, each with its own random set of physical parameters, then there is a finite probability that *one* of them will have the conditions necessary for the existence of intelligent life. And that is our universe, very special to us, but purely random in the overall picture. The second explanation, that the fifty marksmen were on my side, is similar to the response that life exists because the universe was created by a benevolent Creator who designed it with us in mind. Because of God's intention and design, the universe is particularly suited to the development of human life.

In the early stages of scientific theories, when there is not yet any evidence to prefer one to another, it is natural that scientists

---

[23] Polkinghorne, "A Potent Universe," 114.
[24] Leslie, *Universes*, chap. 2.
[25] Polkinghorne, "A Potent Universe," 114.

should support the ones that are most compatible with their worldview. Thus Christian theists will find the inference of a loving Creator God a coherent and deeply satisfying explanation of the fine-tuning of our universe. Nontheists will prefer (and may be the creators of) many-universes theories, which avoid the implications of an intelligent designer. But scientists of integrity, no matter how strongly they believe one or the other to be true, will be willing to let future evidence, if any comes to light, be the final arbiter of which theory best describes the anthropic properties of our universe.

The third area that presents integrative opportunities is the notion of extraterrestrial life. Students can start with the number of stars in our galaxy (about half a trillion) and multiply by various probabilities to estimate the probability for the existence of other intelligent life. For example, what is the probability of the star being a solar-type star? (1 in 10) What is the probability of it having planets? What is the probability that one planet will be a suitable distance from the star and so forth, down to the probability that the life will be intelligent?[26] The estimates students make are likely to be very wide-ranging because of the uncertainty of most of the numbers and because, given a range, they will choose the one that helps drive the estimate in the direction they would like to see it come out. Other scientists do this also, and so there is no generally agreed-upon answer; it is another example of how values can affect what at first blush looks like a simple scientific calculation that would produce the same result for everyone.

A class period in which the possibility of extraterrestrial life is going to be discussed can be started by asking students (by anonymous ballot to avoid the influence of peer pressure) to place themselves on a numerical scale that runs from "I am sure there is intelligent life elsewhere in the universe" to "I am sure

---

[26] This is the so-called "Drake equation" found in most astronomy textbooks, but the purpose here is to think about how uncertain the various numbers that go into it are and how much a shift by one order of magnitude in several numbers can influence the outcome. The hope is that this discussion will prevent students from taking too seriously the statements of scientists who draw definite conclusions from this kind of data. (Because of the distances involved, there is probably no point in thinking about the probability of ever becoming aware of life in the other ten billion galaxies.)

there is no other intelligent life in the universe." If a quick tally of the responses is made, students can see the range of opinion among their classmates and, more importantly, discover that sincere Christians may end up on opposite ends of the scale. The teacher may allow or even encourage students to express how their worldviews support their position on the scale. Some students may be surprised to find that theistic arguments abound for both nonexistence and existence of extraterrestrial intelligent life. Similarly, nontheists will also bring philosophical arguments that support positions at both ends of the spectrum. We do our students a service if we help them understand that there is no one religious position on this (and many other) issues; instead there are religious positions. (The same is true for nonreligious positions, but students do not as easily make the assumption that the latter should speak with one voice.) With the understanding that others may disagree, and while the scientific jury is still out, it makes sense to adopt tentatively the perspective that best fits one's worldview, and I encourage my students to do so.

THEORETICAL INTEGRATIVE OPPORTUNITIES IN PHYSICS

Twentieth-century physics has given us a variety of theories that have turned the Newtonian mechanistic worldview of the Enlightenment upside down. A mechanistic, deterministic world fits well with a deist notion of God as the creator of a perfect machine that needs no further attention. But new physical theories emphasize unpredictability. In such a material universe, the actions of God may be hidden within processes that are not deterministic. These theories are much more compatible with a Christian interpretation of God's presence and immanence in creation than the eighteenth-century worldview. Let us now examine two strong contenders for the "causal joint," that is, the particular kind of event or situation in which God might act as agent in the world without setting aside any physical laws—chaos theory and quantum mechanics.

Chaotic behavior manifests itself in the time development of certain nonlinear systems and exhibits extreme sensitivity to initial conditions. Although the system develops deterministically, the tiniest variation in the initial conditions can result in wildly different behavior. Since we cannot accurately measure the initial conditions, we cannot predict what the behavior will be as a function of time. Polkinghorne and others are productively exploring the possibilities of divine interaction via this mechanism.[27] (Of course, not all physical processes are chaotic, and the fact that there is consistency and predictability in a large range of natural processes can be taken as an indication of God's faithfulness.)

A second source of indeterminacy and unpredictability comes from quantum mechanics, which exhibits itself primarily in the world of the very small. Here we confront our absolute inability to predict the outcome of certain measurements. This is not due to the imprecision of our measuring instruments; indeterminism is at the very heart of the matter. Quantum mechanics specifies a variety of possible outcomes for a particular measurement, each with a very accurately calculable probability of occurring. But it tells nothing at all about the result of any particular measurement. The mathematical formulation that carries the information about these probabilities is the wave function. When unobserved, the wave function representing a particle evolves continuously and gradually in a deterministic process described by Schroedinger's equation. But when a measurement is made, the interaction with the measuring device in some mysterious way eliminates all except one of the possible positions the particle could have, and the particle now has a location, in some sense produced by the measurement. This process is called "collapsing the wave function." Perhaps the mode of God's action in the world is to collapse wave functions at the atomic level, and the result is amplified into a macroscopic choice among several possibilities.

After coming to an understanding of the peculiarity of quantum mechanics, an upper-division class might be given an overnight assignment to imagine a world in which quantum mechanical phenomena became macroscopic. Students can fur-

---

[27] See, for example, John Polkinghorne, *Belief in God in an Age of Science* (New Haven, Conn.: Yale University Press, 1998), 61–75.

ther be asked to consider what aspects of quantum mechanics writ large might appear miraculous. For example, wave functions that extend into classically forbidden regions give rise to the phenomenon of tunneling; perhaps this is how Christ was able to pass through walls. Some students will bring analogies. For example, wave-particle duality may be analogous in some ways to the seemingly incompatible "fully human, fully divine" theological descriptions of Christ. After students present and discuss their ideas, the teacher should make the point that analogy is not evidence or even argument (unless the students have reached that conclusion on their own). This important point can be reinforced by asking students to analyze critically their own analogies and indicate the points beyond which they do not apply. Such analysis can keep students from taking simplistic analogies too seriously, for example, thinking that the three forms of water provide serious help in understanding the vastly more challenging concept of the Trinity.

I would like to touch briefly the subject of consciousness as it may relate to quantum mechanics, because consciousness remains unexplained in terms of basic physics and chemistry. Some have called it the last big question for our species. Consciousness is naturally interesting to us all, because we all have an experience of at least one mind—our own. The consensus model among neurophysiologists, biologists, and computer scientists working in the area of consciousness studies is entirely reductionistic, mechanistic, and deterministic. In other words, consciousness can be explained correctly and maximally in terms of the physical states and events of the brain under the operation of physical laws. That physics itself has moved away from reductionism seems to be a well-kept secret. A totally deterministic world cannot accommodate the theological notion of free will, but the fact remains that we all live as if we had free choice. Pragmatically, we still have to decide which job to take, what to wear each day, and what is the best way to present a certain idea to our students. If my actions and decisions, and those of others, do seem to be unpredictable at times and do seem to exhibit free choice, I would like my model of the physical world to include these possibilities. To have our students study quantum mechanics without thinking about what it might mean to their own worldview is to miss the fun of it.

A number of theories of consciousness that are based on quantum mechanics have been put forth.[28] Students in an upper-division quantum physics class can choose (or be assigned) a book expounding a particular quantum theory of consciousness as the subject of a term paper. The assignment can emphasize separating physics from metaphysics in the text. In lower-division courses, students may read descriptive books, affectionately known as "quantum-hype," which contain little or no math and are full of metaphysical interpretations. One example would be Fred Wolf's *Taking the Quantum Leap*.[29] Sometimes I have my upper-division students review such books for possible use in lower-division classes. Most students are excited to learn that certain physical processes are by their very nature underdetermined. This is quite different from the "God of the gaps" situation, in which our own ignorance is covered by proposing theistic interventions. There is an openness built into the universe at its most fundamental level. The known phenomena that incorporate indeterminism and unpredictability may in fact be avenues by which God interacts with creation.

TEACHING THE LIMITATIONS OF SCIENCE

Sometimes students are very forthright in stating their belief that the epistemology of science is the only reliable path to truth. One effective response to this rather facile affirmation is to draw attention to the restrictions inherent in the study of science. Science is an attempt to understand the working of the physical universe. Most scientists would acknowledge the inability of sci-

---

[28] See David Hodgson, *The Mind Matters: Consciousness and Choice in a Quantum World* (New York: Oxford University Press, 1991; paper ed. Oxford University Press, 1999); Michael Lockwood, *Mind, Brain, and the Quantum* (Oxford: Blackwell Publishers, 1989); Danah Zohar, *The Quantum Self* (New York: Quill/ William Morrow, 1990); Roger Penrose, *Shadows of the Mind* (New York: Oxford University Press, 1994); Henry P. Stapp, *Mind, Matter, and Quantum Mechanics* (Berlin: Springer-Verlag), 1993.

[29] Fred Alan Wolf, *Taking the Quantum Leap* (New York: Harper & Row, 1988). Zohar's book falls into this category also.

ence to produce ethics (what ought to be, particularly in human relationships) from observation of the natural world (what is). This line of demarcation between science and ethics is captured in the expression " 'Is' does not equal 'ought.' " Kant's categorical imperative[30] arises not from the world of nature but from the world of ideas. The world of ideas is populated by such virtues as love, beauty, equality, justice, duty, peace, morality, integrity, and other powerful notions that do not arise directly from the study of nature. These ideas have a long and venerable history, arising out of ancient societies, and they predate by far the serious study of the natural world, which for centuries was seen as merely a backdrop for the drama of human affairs.

One way students can be helped to understand that science does not attempt to explain all of reality is to identify questions that fall outside the limits of scientific inquiry. *Meta* (beyond) is a useful concept. The teacher may utilize responses such as, "That is a metaphysical question," or "That is not a question science can answer," or "Physics can give us a very accurate *description* of that phenomenon, one which has great predictive ability; but that is quite different from *explaining* what causes it." To name something is not to explain it, as Leibniz was quick to recognize when Newton failed to provide a mechanistic explanation for the action-at-a-distance that is characteristic of gravitation. Since Newton, scientific theories have been considered adequate if they explain what and how; they do not explain why (although some scientists may try).

Students also need to understand that the word *theory* has a special meaning in the sciences. When asked why Brian left the party early, someone may say, "Well, I have a theory about that," and listeners understand exactly what truth value to give to what follows. This everyday usage is easily carried over into the sciences, particularly regarding matters that are controversial outside scientific circles. Thus we hear our inexperienced students say (of biological evolution, for example, or of big bang cosmology), "Oh, that is just a theory." What they mean is that we are not required to respect it any more than we are required to agree about the reason for Brian's early departure.

---

[30] Roughly speaking, act only in ways that you would desire everyone in the world to act.

This tendency needs to be countered. The teacher can help by offering a gentle critique of students' use of the word, such as "This particular interpretation has not yet gained enough confirmation to be referred to as a *theory*." For example, in quantum mechanics, we would probably speak of the "hidden variables interpretation" rather than the "hidden variables theory." The teacher can remind students that the scientific method has an internal feedback loop that is repeated many times by many scientists before a hypothesis gains the confirmation necessary to be widely accepted as a theory. Bestowal of the title *theory* is the highest accolade that an explanatory principle can earn. It carries with it connotations of wide applicability to a number of different phenomena, the power of predictability, and a richness for suggesting further lines of inquiry. It is important for students to understand this, so that they cannot as easily reject as "just a theory" those powerful scientific principles that do not sit comfortably with their religious understandings. To dismiss scientific theories is in no way compatible with our attempts to integrate them with our faith.

Students should also be cautioned that while scientific experts can be considered authorities in their own field of study, that expertise does not necessarily extend to areas outside their training. When astrophysicist Carl Sagan described the formation of new stars from hydrogen clouds, I sat up and paid attention. But if he said that the human fetus does not have thought processes until the sixth month (and thus first trimester abortions are acceptable), I would be wise to be skeptical. I would be better advised to turn to experts in biology or medicine for my information about the development of the fetus.

Students can be asked to bring in stories from the media in which scientists make pronouncements in fields outside their own expertise. Then they can be asked whether they agree or disagree with the opinions expressed. Hopefully, they will find some comments persuasive and others less convincing. It should soon become evident that their worldview is of primary importance in whether they attribute authority status to the scientist in areas outside the scientist's disciplinary expertise.

Most of us understand that tradition plays a large part in religious belief. What may not be as well understood is that the same is true in the sciences. Researchers who base their work on theories that lie outside the current scientific paradigm can attest to the difficulty of obtaining research grants and publishing papers in peer-reviewed journals. Thomas Kuhn's book *The Structure of Scientific Revolutions* hypothesized that the reigning scientific paradigm is a cultural agreement that places strict boundaries on the kind of science that is done during most periods of history.[31] His theory was a serious critique of the Enlightenment principle that science was governed by nothing more or less than the search for truth. Students can consider that both scientific and religious claims rest on the twin pillars of authority (tradition) and experience. The major difference is that science requires that other researchers be able to repeat the experience (experiment), while religion respects the uniqueness of each believer's religious experience.

INTEGRATION BEYOND THE CLASSROOM

There is a growing body of literature written by Christian scientists who have taken seriously the challenge to integrate their faith with their disciplinary knowledge. They will probably have more credibility in the science classroom than will those theologians who have undertaken a similar challenge. When I was in graduate school training to be a nuclear engineer, the book *Physicist and Christian* by William Pollard, then head of Oak Ridge National Laboratory, was very meaningful for me because his scientific credentials were impeccable. Today the same can be said of scientists like John Polkinghorne, John Eccles, Ian Barbour, Robert John Russell, and Henry Stapp.

Teachers who are attempting to integrate their faith with their discipline should consider mentoring a younger faculty member who has the same goal or joining (creating, if none exists in the workplace) a group of like-minded colleagues. A support community is a great benefit in this task. Each person hears about the struggles and progress of others, and the questions asked by

---

[31] Thomas S. Kuhn, *The Structure of Scientific Revolutions* (Chicago: The University of Chicago Press, 1962).

others will encourage each person to articulate, clarify, and defend why integration is an important and worthwhile endeavor.

Opportunities to mentor will also arise during one-on-one contacts with our teaching assistants, lab assistants, research assistants, and advisees. These students will benefit greatly from witnessing our attempts to think through our experiences and unresolved issues and to respond to the continual flow of information. It is important for them to see that we are willing to struggle with troubling questions and to live with ambiguity while we wait for new information or interpretations to shed light on our present dilemmas. We do this because we strive for integrity and wholeness in our lives and consider it a worthy goal, regardless of whether or not we ever achieve it. We hope many of our students will choose to become our colleagues on this journey.

SELECTED BIBLIOGRAPHY

Barbour, Ian G. *Religion and Science*. New York: HarperCollins, 1997.

Carlson, Richard F., ed. *Science and Christianity: Four Views*. Downers Grove, Ill.: InterVarsity Press, 1990.

Dove, Jonathan, et al. "Contemporary Perspectives on Chance, Providence and Free Will." *Science and Christian Belief* 7 (1995): 117–39.

Eccles, John C. *How the Self Controls Its Brain*. Berlin: Springer-Verlag, 1994.

Gale, George, and John Urani. "Philosophical Midwifery and the Birthpangs of Modern Cosmology." *American Journal of Physics* 61 (1993): 66–73.

McKim, Mark G. "The Cosmos According to Carl Sagan: Review and Critique." *Perspectives on Science and Christian Faith* 45, no. 1 (1993): 18–25.

Polkinghorne, John. "*Creatio Coninua* and Divine Action." *Science and Christian Belief* 7 (1995): 101–8.

———. *The Faith of a Physicist*. Minneapolis, Minn.: Fortress Press, 1996.

————. *Quarks, Chaos and Christianity*. New York: Crossroad Publishing Co., 1994.

————. *Science and Theology*. Minneapolis, Minn.: Fortress Press, 1998.

Pond, Jean Bertelsen. "Catholic Frogs." *Faculty Dialogue*, no. 18 (1992): 83–90.

Russell, Robert John, and Carl M. York. *An Annotated Bibliography on the Relationship Between the Physical Sciences and Spirituality*. Available from The Center for Theology and the Natural Sciences, 2400 Ridge Road, Berkeley, CA 94709.

Russell, Robert John, William R. Stoeger, S.J., and George V. Coyne, S.J., eds. *Physics, Philosophy, and Theology: A Common Quest for Understanding*. Vatican City State: Vatican Observatory, 1997.

Sperry, Roger. "Search for Beliefs to Live by Consistent with Science." *Zygon* 26 (1991): 237–58.

7

A Careful Convergence: Integrating Biology and Faith in the Church-Related College

Lee Anne Chaney

Some Initial Parameters

I begin this essay with a healthy sense of inadequacy. The integration of personal faith with the content of one's discipline is not a skill included in the training of many academic professionals. It was not in mine. However, motivated by the mission of my college to promote the integration of faith and learning in all disciplines, I have attempted to engage my students in that endeavor.

While I do not attempt to introduce every core belief of my Christian faith into my biology courses, I do believe there are ample opportunities to assist students in recognizing the convergence of the discipline of biology with matters of Christian faith. My efforts to illustrate this convergence are animated by a desire (1) to identify values and beliefs that relate directly to the content or practice of biology or to the activities of teaching and learning, (2) to be intentional about including them as I plan class time and assignments, and (3) to make some of those values and beliefs explicit for my students in appropriate and legitimate ways. For twenty-two years, I have been fortunate to have colleagues who work at these goals and encourage me to do the same. Some approaches they use I will never pull off effectively; others I can use immediately or modify to fit my teaching style. This essay presents techniques I have found effective.

Before proceeding, I would like to clarify what this essay *is* and *is not* about. It *is not* about Christian apologetics or evangelism. The purpose of a biology class is to help students learn about organisms, not to defend Christian doctrines or to convert unbelievers. It *is not* primarily about the intellectual and spiritual work of exploring the overlap of my Christian faith and my field of specialization, which is plant genetics. Finally, it *is not* primarily about helping students deal with the issues of evolution and abortion. These are valid and important issues, and they are certainly the two most common areas of concern for students I have known. However, the interface of biology and Christian faith is much broader and more complex than these two issues. This essay *is* about how a teacher may encourage undergraduates in biology courses to give serious consideration to certain questions that arise when Christian faith and biological studies converge.

My Pedagogical Contexts: Denominational Perspectives

I grew up assuming that all thinking Christians paid attention to the natural world. Both of my parents modeled faith and a fascination with organisms. My father was a pastor who came from a farm family, so he was very attuned to patterns of weather and to cycles of life and death. He took time to examine and show us unusual plants and bugs. My mother was a nurse who read much in the spiritual classics and had a significant prayer life. As a result, I was in high school or perhaps even college before I really understood that there are Christians who do not consider the natural world wonderful and important.

My denominational background is in the Southern Baptist tradition. There are aspects of that heritage that made me very comfortable in studying and teaching biology. In the Baptist tradition, matters of faith are between the individual and God. There is an expectation that each person is able, free, and responsible for finding truth in Scripture, without having a special authority figure convey that truth to her. My tradition is not an authoritarian one in terms of belief. With regard to church governance, it is nonhierarchical and very democratic. This individualistic, democratic approach can cause disagreements, divisions, and sometimes fragmentation of congregations because not all believers will agree on the interpretation of Scripture, on church politics, or on money. In the best of the Baptist tradition, however, it is taken for granted that devoted, intelligent Christians may disagree about many matters—even matters of faith. These aspects of Baptist tradition mesh comfortably with the need for the individual scientist to consider the data and reflect upon them, to test hypotheses rigorously, and to explain or defend conclusions to colleagues whose data analysis may differ. The Baptists of my youth valued schooling generally, so the choice of an academic career was respectable. Baptists have been supportive of the applied sciences, especially agriculture and health care, as means of ministry. My sense of Baptist theology is that it is less theoretical than some other theological traditions, which seems to fit with encouraging young people to train in the practical sciences. Finally, mystery is not celebrated in Baptist worship as a general rule. The Baptist believer is to come to God with rational faculties, not mystical experience. This aspect of my faith background fits well with the empirical approach of the natural scientist. Until recently, post-World War II graduate training in science emphasized the need to deal rationally and objectively with the data. Subjective feelings about nature were seen as irrelevant. Thus in many ways, my home church heritage made me feel at home in the natural sciences.

While Baptists valued higher education, the tradition was or came to be somewhat anti-intellectual. Theoretical modeling of processes in the physical world seemed to be peripheral to Christian priorities of service. As a geneticist, my dealing with evolutionary theory made me suspect to many Baptists. Training to be a nurse, or even studying genes of crop plants to help feed the world, would have been a more natural fit with my Baptist heritage than studying genetic control of sexual reproduction in an obscure polyploid plant.

For the past eighteen years, I have been involved with Presbyterian and other more liturgical churches. I know less of their history and have absorbed less of their ethos, but there are differences I do perceive. These traditions include more focus on patterns and cycles in the church year. The more liturgical service has the potential to focus more on truth as it has been apprehended over the centuries and captured in creed or Scripture, and less on the insights of a particular preacher. These traditions acknowledge, even honor, mysteries about the world, about life, about God, and about our relationship with God. They have more liberal intellectual traditions, less fear of the notion of evolution, and perhaps more comfort with theoretical aspects of all sciences. These traditions seem to support exploring the natural world, not only for potential benefit to humans, but just because it is wonderful. They encourage me to be comfortable with the fact that we understand very little of the complex reality that exists.

MY PEDAGOGICAL CONTEXTS: VALUES AND ASSUMPTIONS

A few years ago I was asked to identify the values at the core of my discipline, the ethical issues related to this discipline, and the points at which my faith and my biology intersect. The choice of the verb *intersect* suggests a different mental landscape than would *converge,* or *overlap,* or even *permeate.* I am convinced that, at some times for some aspects of the faith-biology interaction, each of these verbs is appropriate. Indeed, many more verbs would be required to capture all of that interaction. But I use *converge* here, because it expresses hope for a growing integration. To be sure, undergraduates' experiences with science-faith integration may feel more like the meeting of a VW bug and a semi in the merge lane than the gradual, natural melding of two trails in a wood. But as we faculty members think about our own lives and development, as well as when we take the long-term view of helping our students mature, I think that *converge* can be a useful image.

Values and ethical issues related to biology are easy for me to identify. Biologists value truth, beauty, balance, diversity, curiosity, rigor, and integrity. Population pressures, land-use policies, water rights, unequal access to medical technology, control of human reproduction, conservation of organisms and habitats, and manipulation of genes and gene pools are just a few of the many ethical issues related to the life sciences. The obvious points at which faith and biology converge are fewer, especially if we are talking about what is unique to Christian faith. Students tend to see faith intersecting biology mainly when they study evolution or biomedical technology, neither of which seems to me to be central to the matter of what God does for us in Christ. Biology and the Jewish and Christian traditions certainly meet around the topic of creation. How biology interfaces with Christian redemption is less clear. When I reflect upon how the Spirit of God may interact with my being, I admit I wonder about how that happens. (For example, I ponder if there is any material change in the brain during prayer or after conversion). But these are not the areas on which my own work as a plant geneticist is focused.

My image of the teacher as host or guide is a critical component of the pedagogical context for helping students integrate faith and biology. The purpose of the class is to help all my students learn about organisms. Sometimes it is appropriate to indicate those aspects of my faith that relate to the course content or to model how I handle some questions that occur when my faith and my science interact. It is, however, inappropriate to use the lectern as a pulpit or to use class time to convert students to my faith. Because I have both Christian and non-Christian students in my courses, I do not use exercises that ask students to work in an exclusively or even consciously Christian worldview. Even if all my students came from religious backgrounds and agreed to some faith statement, I still would need to avoid pressuring students religiously in the name of faith-science integration. I may pose many difficult questions, as long as I make it clear that I am interested in their honest answers—not some church's party line.

Just as identifying presuppositions, values, and beliefs has helped me grow, students will benefit when presuppositions, values, or beliefs are made explicit in the context of a course. Not every one of these is appropriate for every class or every teacher. In any science class it would be suitable to remind students that we can learn real truths about the natural world by using our senses. A plant physiology class would, however, not be the most appropriate setting to talk with students about my belief that the human ability to study and to manipulate the natural world is part of our created nature, and therefore good, according to God's assessment in the Genesis account. But it could be a natural context to discuss the idea that organisms honor God when they operate as created, in all their complexity and diversity. A non-major ecology course might be an especially good class in which to remind students that organisms are beautiful and good and show us something about God. Faculty should probably take pains early in the college curriculum to state very clearly that even though many things are true, only things that can be known corporately can be known in a scientific way.

At points of interface between faith and science, our science and our faith affect each other. I see more need in evangelical circles for science to inform faith, than for faith to instruct science. Because I believe that God made the world and does not fear our study of it, what is true about the natural world can only enhance our appreciation of God. What is true about the natural world is surely part of that truth, which has been promised to make us free.

Science faculty in church-related colleges, more than others, need to help students grasp the differences among observations, interpretations, and beliefs. They must recognize the difference between observations and beliefs before they can exercise any critical analysis. For example, I observe that humans are organisms, finite, material, complex—more complex than our conscious minds can comprehend. As I look at organisms and the natural world, I see diversity and complexity, interconnections, patterns and order (but also chaos or randomness), terrifyingly destructive forces, and the mysterious power of new life in the development of organisms. When I look at nature, I do *not* observe evidence of righteousness, a personal God, forgiveness, mercy, or atonement; in other words, I do not see the attributes of a specifically Christian faith in the natural world. I believe that the human ability and inclination to know, to love, to perceive the world via our senses, to ponder, to worship, to make things and phenomena of beauty are there because of how God made us; they are built into us by God. I believe that God is pleased when we admire God's creative work, when we wonder about it, when we honor God by serious study of it.

CAREFULLY CONVERGING: PRACTICAL PEDAGOGICAL STRATEGIES

Integration of faith or values issues is more appropriate and do-able in some classes than in others. Generally there are more chances for faith-learning integration in non-major biology classes than in typical courses for majors. At Whitworth, most non-major biology classes have a topical focus such as human ecology, biology of women, and marine biology—some with in-herent values/ethics/faith connections.[1] In non-major courses with a traditional lab-science structure, the integration task is harder due to time constraints. But where the mastery of a cer-tain portion of an encyclopedic text as prerequisite information for the next course is unnecessary, some flexibility exists to con-sider deeper implications.

Within the major, some courses provide more opportunity for integration than others. Issues that connect to values, ethics, or faith are fairly common in courses like conservation biology (value of, human responsibility for, and human control of a spe-cies or habitat), genetics (genetic determinism and manipula-tion), animal behavior (human uniqueness) and evolutionary biology (mechanisms of change, humans as the pinnacle of cre-ation). Courses such as invertebrate biology, human anatomy, or plant physiology have fewer points at which matters of faith can be introduced naturally. I have found many potential points of convergence in some interdisciplinary courses, such as bioethics (cross-listed in philosophy and biology) and ecological imperial-ism (cross-listed in biology and history). An upper-division course in the Western scientific tradition, required of all stu-dents, has offered more opportunities for integration than any other course in my teaching experience, though not all are re-lated to biology.

---

[1] Significant values/ethics/ faith connections might raise questions like: Is the earth "for" human use? What questions should Christians consider as we ponder use of technologies to extend physical life? How does information about genetic and hormonal control of development mesh with the biblical notion that God forms the body in the womb? Is there any biblical basis for deciding which medical technologies are appropriate? Why should good bio-logical data about variations in sexual development and function not be in-cluded when Christians discuss sexuality?

One of the most direct ways to introduce integration concerns is to ask questions that have faith or values implications as an integral part of the class session. These questions might be part of a larger discussion. Plants in Culture, a course for non-majors, includes a unit on plants used in religious rituals. Some of the plants are valued in these rituals specifically because they have some chemical(s) that affect brain function. After covering fermented beverages, peyote, and marijuana, I ask students to compare and contrast the use of alcohol in the Christian West with the use of marijuana in Muslim Arab cultures and the use of peyote in the ritual of the Native American Church of North America, a specific denomination of Native American spirituality.[2] This line of inquiry prompts vigorous discussion—quite a bit of which is rather defensive of the tradition out of which many of our Christian students come. The contrast between two different ways of encountering the deity is clear and uncomfortable for them. Is the best, perhaps only, way to come to God with a clear, rational mind? Or is God so big and so mysterious that one must use more than the rational mind to be receptive to what God might do? Some of them discover in this discussion the tendency for some branches of Christian practice to assume that the word of God, as heard by the clear and alert mind, is God's preferred way of communicating with humans. They realize that the possibility of receiving grace or understanding or rebuke by means of vision is often discounted, especially if the person is under the influence of some mind-altering substance when the vision comes.

Questions can also serve as teasers to raise issues for students to think about later. Dr. David Hicks, a senior colleague of mine since retired, was a master of the perplexing teaser question. He would ask students in ecology classes whether we have more to learn from nature than nature does from us, or if it is the other way around. Many majors as well as non-majors would ponder quite a while, not realizing that for Dave, the answer was obvious. He always asked students to think about organisms in a

---

[2] Officially chartered as a church in 1918. See *The Columbia Electronic Encyclopedia*. 6th ed. (Columbia University Press. Licensed from Lernout & Hauspie Speech Products N.V., 2000). Accessed 10 August, 2001 http://www.encyclo pedia.com/articles/09028.html

new way, using a familiar line of reasoning. Non-majors in ecology classes are often concerned about the economic costs of protecting species. So he would ask them what a honeybee is worth,
and follow up by asking if we had to pay humans to pollinate
all our fruit and vegetable crops, would our GNP be enough
to pay their wages? Because he is convinced that complexity is
wonderfully provocative, he would ask if they could design
forty million kinds of living things. He would also ask whether
we might not have a better world if our political boundaries
matched our bioregions.

There are those professors among us who may desire to tell
students what they see as the important implications of the material they present as part of the lecture. I think that this works
best with a strong lecture style. For twenty-nine years, Dr. David
Hicks was a biblical prophetic voice in our department. Dave
spoke with intensity from his own experience with the Scripture,
with human behavior (individual and corporate), and with the
natural world. He did not ask students to agree with him, but
he did lay out his own perspective in pithy, pointed commentary. In a lecture for non-majors on interactions between humans
and nature, he would say that the bottom line really is not financial, as students have been taught all their lives, because economics is entirely derivative. Nothing that is bought and sold
has any value unless it is backed up by something in nature.
When he talked about culture and ecology, he described a city
as "a big animal that is sweating," as humans accelerate the consumption of energy and resources. He did not spare students'
cherished institutions but pointed out that political and religious
institutions in our culture are ecologically uninformed and environmentally unfriendly and that churches generally do not
spend time thinking about God as creator or about ways to live
more responsibly in the physical world. Many students were
comfortable with the claim that communists and socialists have
raped the earth but were taken aback when he included capital-
ists and Presbyterians or their own denominational group. Some
students, of course, were offended by his opinions, which included the suggestion that the most effective thing they could
do to make the world a nicer place for their grandkids would be
to quit living like U.S. citizens. Some were encouraged to act on

their own convictions about environmental issues. Some spent hours in his office in conversation about these matters. None left his class without having heard clear statements of biblical positions on the stewardship of and care for God's creation.

If it appears impossible to carve out class time for discussion, questions that incorporate worldview issues can still be posed as part of assigned work. My senior colleague Dr. Howard Stien was inclined to push students to grapple with provocative questions as part of the work for his classes. In a non-major life science class, the final evaluation might be a paper in which the student discussed, with specific examples, how the content of the class had influenced (changed, strengthened, challenged) his or her worldview. In a non-major human biology class, this final paper assignment might be to explain how being informed by biology could help one choose and act more responsibly in the face of human dilemmas, whether moral, political, economic, environmental or religious. I team-taught these courses with Howard when I was a new faculty member and he was a veteran. These assignments sounded intimidating to me, and I wondered whether we would get anything worth reading or even remotely gradable. We received a few papers that were trivial efforts and several that lacked sophistication. But students who had thought seriously about these matters turned in excellent work. Such paper assignments prompted more office visits and more wide-ranging conversations than research papers, extensive lab reports, or comprehensive final exams could have. Dr. Hicks sometimes had a non-major ecology class write an "essay on three current environmental issues you are interested in, but your name is Jesus Christ." Or he would ask them to identify examples of interactions between humans and nature that they considered to be sustainable and to calculate the balance sheet after about ten thousand years. After they had written about agriculture or timber, he would point out the features of these human activities that tend to make them non-sustainable.

One type of writing exercise that I especially like is the weekly reaction paper. I confess that I have not yet found a way to fit this particular writing project into a course for majors because of the grading time involved. But I suspect that majors may need this sort of reflection at least as much as non-majors do. These one- to two-page papers are graded mainly on whether the response shows evidence of real intellectual engagement. In some non-major courses, these papers might be the primary means of assessing student involvement. However they are used, the weighting of the assignment in the final grade should reflect a sense of their importance. It is much more interesting to read what students really think than to read what they assume I want them to say. To get honest responses, teachers must tell students that they will not be graded down because they disagree with or are troubled by the course material, conclusions, or the teacher's perspective. Initially many students may see this as a trivial assignment because it does not focus on mastery of scientific facts. Explain clearly the expectations for the papers and how they will be evaluated. The task for students is not to summarize the class notes, not to relate their immediate emotional response, but to present evidence that they have thought reflectively with regard to the course content or its implications. Eventually, many students, especially those from non-science disciplines, appreciate having this opportunity to demonstrate what they are thinking about the material. I write responses to their ideas in the margins of these papers. Some students never read my comments, but some do and will follow up in conversation or in their next paper.

Reaction papers can be a good technique if there is some uncertainty about how to introduce the integration of science and faith in biology classes. They let students construct their own connections to what they see and wonder about. Reaction papers therefore allow students to initiate the integration and will reveal where students are in their thinking about the convergence of biological topics and faith. If the goal is to encourage them toward integrative thinking, it is better to let students start with their own questions than with the instructor's favorite issues. Reaction papers provide at least the potential for a sort of ongoing paper dialogue between the faculty member and the student about questions important to the student. Sometimes students will not raise these questions in the class because they are shy, believe there is not enough class time, or fear the question will be, or at least will seem to be, peripheral. But they will address them in these papers. There would never be enough time to cover each question or implication that intrigues students during class, and it would be impossible to know ahead of time what special interests or experiences are present in those students. That is the beauty of the reaction paper project. One student may write about that dissonance she experiences as she thinks of how evolution is presented in class and in her church youth group. Another may be confused about the questions that are raised by the organisms we study; while a third might express uncertainty about his belief that God will continue to love him as he ponders these questions. Yet another student may write about the hard choices his farming family must make concerning irrigation practices that will eventually ruin the soil and the competing need to produce a large enough harvest to pay his college tuition. Some papers include gratitude that God allows humans to understand how to alter genes that cause disease, while others voice concern about the rightness of changing anything that God has made. Howard Stien considers reaction papers to be the most effective strategy he employed throughout nearly thirty years of teaching to help students integrate faith and science.

For certain courses it would be appropriate to identify in the syllabus some worldview or faith concerns that students may have with the course content and allow them an opportunity to respond. Dr. Craig Tsuchida teaches animal biology as part of our freshman majors' sequence. Craig's syllabus for this survey of the major metazoan phyla indicates that evolution will be the organizing framework for the course. After a few weeks, he conducts an anonymous survey in which the students have a chance to communicate their feelings about his framing the course around the concept of evolution rather than creation. It can be very helpful to students—especially beginning students—to acknowledge their concerns and to give them opportunity to articulate their feelings. Craig's survey serves as an invitation to conversation. This direct approach can lead to discussions outside of class that might not happen with the simple announcement that "the theory of evolution explains more of the data than any other scientific theory, so it is the basis for our study." The first time Craig used the survey, about half the students responded that they found it objectionable or at least uncomfortable, but only one said it was inappropriate at a Christian college. Most of his upper-division animal physiology students reported in a similar anonymous survey that they were comfortable with an evolutionary framework for that course, even if they did not "believe in it." I am not sure how much progress these particular majors have made in integration, if they have simply moved from being offended by the concept of evolution as freshmen to tolerating (but ignoring) it as juniors and seniors. At some point, they ought to wonder about the logic of studying hard in a class that is organized around a theory they claim they do not believe to be true. Perhaps they do wonder but are convinced that they must play along to be accepted in the department, or they reason that the descriptive information is good, even if the organizing theory is wrong. I think that many of our majors who arrive confident in their belief that evolution is wrong simply postpone dealing seriously with this question— some until the spring of their senior year, many until much later. Any approach that prompts students to engage in dialogue and look intently at data, theories, and beliefs, as opposed to dismissing either the science (as evil) or the faith (as stupid), should be worthwhile. One of our best students was surprised in her final semester when the consideration of evolutionary theory as a part of Western culture prompted her to review her work in the major. All the applications of the theory as presented in her biology courses had made sense, so she had to think about her belief that evolution did not occur. She wrote that she probably will be thinking about this question for some years to come.

A technique that is amusing and often surprises students is the use of cartoons to reveal cultural values and worldview issues.[3] I have used them most frequently in classes for non-majors and in the scientific tradition class. I use cartoons because they depend on common experiences, beliefs, biases, or worldviews for their hook. Sometimes I have non-major students locate items (cartoons, advertisements, articles) from the popular media that have some relationship to the course. They submit the item with

---

[3] I have found some of the best scientifically themed cartoons in daily newspapers. Sidney Harris's work in *American Scientist* is also very helpful in this regard.

written commentary about the connection they discovered. A variation on this project is to present a cartoon during class as the basis for a short writing assignment asking students to identify and comment on the value(s), ethical issue, or belief implicit in the image or sequence. In my Biology of Women class, I often reserve some of each three-hour class period for students to work in small groups on cartoons that I provide. I give each group three to five cartoons and ask them to discuss how the cartoon relates to the content of the class. Because the course includes reproductive function, sexuality, and cultural perceptions of women, it is very easy to find comics that are pertinent. However, cartoons can also be utilized in courses about photosynthesis, predation, food chains, genes, germs, evolution, development, behavior, or even senescence. Some cartoons may merely serve to remind students of certain course content, but others will bring into sharp focus cultural views and values and stimulate animated discussion about these pertinent concerns. Beyond that, students may begin looking more closely at what they see in the media for just such assumptions and value judgments, so that the integrative activity extends well beyond the classroom. The utility of this project, in whatever form, proceeds from the fact that it requires that students be more actively involved in thinking about the relationship between values/ethics/faith topics, popular media, and course content.

Another method helpful in generating student interest in exploring the convergence between biology and faith is the case study—if enough class time can be spared. In biology, the issues that relate directly to the course content are much more apt to be ethical or worldview issues rather than explicit faith issues. But students who are encouraged to think about the ethical implications of applied life sciences will be more apt to ponder questions about faith implications when they arise. In the Plants in Culture course, we discuss the relationship of plants in natural habitats to water availability and water quality. I ask students to consider a proposal that water from Montana, Idaho, Washington, and Oregon be diverted to California. They explain their response in writing, before we spend some class time discussing the proposal. Students talk about issues of value and ethics, such as equitable distribution, whether every item can or should be bought and sold, and whether we should have the freedom to use a natural resource as the majority might see fit. There is usually disagreement, even among the students from California.

In a genetics class, I have asked students to imagine that they sit on the board of an insurance company. The issue is whether to provide care for individuals with inherited diseases, such as cystic fibrosis, for which no cure exists at present and for which treatment costs many thousands of dollars. I ask them to consider the proposal that treatment for a child with cystic fibrosis be covered by the company on the specific condition that the couple will take measures to ensure that they not bring yet another cystic fibrosis sufferer into the world. When I want to prevent them from jumping on the abortion issue and ignoring everything else, I impose the condition that both parents be sterilized so that the gene simply cannot be transmitted again. After they have written about their decision and its basis, we discuss it as a group. Some students are very willing to air their opinions on this topic, but others who write articulately and with conviction will remain silent in a class of thirty peers. Generally, they will be far from unified in their responses. The concerns will always include the notion that no one should restrict human reproductive activity in any way—at least for a married couple, based on the claim that only God should interfere with human life. Other students focus on the responsibility parents have to care for offspring and do not see unlimited reproductive options as a part of God's plan or as an inalienable right.

The discussion may ultimately lead to ethical questions of broader economic responsibility (whether the population at large should pay higher insurance premiums to provide care for families who know they have heritable diseases) or to questions about what is the greater common good (having care for everyone with cystic fibrosis or being free of an insurance company's influence upon reproductive choices). Sometimes the discussion goes to the discernment of God's will, about which young people can be so confident even in the face of horrible dilemmas such as this. I want to ask them how they know the will of God regarding this policy that would affect thousands of people, not just themselves. Even though this is not a government or public policy class, it is appropriate to ask students to consider how the religious and ethical convictions of an individual board member might affect company policy.

Interdisciplinary student projects or reports can address issues of values and ethics as well as expand content coverage. In topical non-majors' courses, this can be particularly effective. In the Plants in Culture course, students may study specific plants used for religious purposes and reflect on the symbols or material aids to worship in their own religious tradition. In an infectious diseases course, student presentations can tie together ethics, history, and biology to consider ways of caring for persons with leprosy. Biology of Women students often use visual images as a basis for presentations on what a particular culture assumes and values about its female members. Global Environmental Issues students can examine the approaches of Christian and secular relief agencies to natural disasters like Hurricane Mitch or compare third-world and first-world agencies.

In interdisciplinary courses or courses targeted to specific audiences, it can be appropriate and helpful to require that all projects be pursued cooperatively and have some component addressing values, ethics, or faith. For example, in a microbiology course for nursing students, group projects on particular diseases might all include a component on ethical dimensions of disease prevention and treatment. In a course Dr. Arlin Migliazzo and I taught on ecological imperialism, students worked in groups that included both biology and history majors. Almost every project touched on some ethical or worldview issue related to the spread of Europeans and their associated organisms into many of the worlds' other bioregions. For many classes, such projects might be optional, either to replace another major assignment, generate additional credit, or provide part of an honors registration. In any case, it is important to remind students that the purpose is to integrate, not to use the project as a pulpit.

Readings and videos that incorporate issues of values, ethics, or faith can be used as the basis for short written reflections, longer papers, or class discussion. In genetics, I have used a twenty-minute section from a documentary on genetic screening that deals with a couple who discover that they both are carriers of the cystic fibrosis gene when their first pregnancy involves twins, both of whom have the disease.[4] Because the couple in this video speak for themselves about their experience and feelings, many questions and issues are immediately on the table: What if this happens to me? Is terminating a pregnancy when you do not see any way you can provide adequate care for the child a selfish or a responsible act? Are there kinds of information that God does not want us to have? If so, why does God give us the ability to learn about things? Typically I show the clip during class time and have the students write about it before the class discussion.

In the scientific tradition course, we have assigned biomedical case studies from the newspaper columns of biomedical ethicist Art Caplan.[5] These brief essays prompt vigorous conversations about ethics, economics, and what God wants. On what basis should our society prioritize the allocation of donated organs for transplantation? Who should have the right and responsibility to make decisions about technological maintenance of the very premature infant, the terminally ill, or the comatose individual? How ought we to partition our finite medical research efforts between increasingly sophisticated procedures for adults and preventive care for the poor in areas that lack medical treatment facilities? Does God want humans to try to cure every disease?

In this same course, we have used science fiction short stories that address issues about how cultures and governments plan for human use and misuse of technologies, or how technologies may change what we consider to be the essence of the human person or soul.[6] In Biology of Women, a short story about a Victorian woman going mad during a postpartum convalescence (enforced by her well-meaning physician husband) helps students consider the problem of the notion that women need to be protected against intellectual stimulation to insure their health.[7]

---

[4] *A Question of Genes: Inherited Risks.* Oregon Public Broadcasting, 1997.

[5] Art Caplan, *Moral Matters: Ethical Issues in Medicine and the Life Sciences* (New York: John Wiley & Sons, 1995).

[6] Tom Godwin, "The Cold Equations," pp. 543–69 in R. Silverberg, ed., *The Science Fiction Hall of Fame*, vol. I (New York: Avon Books, 1971) and Marc Stiegler, "The Gentle Seduction," pp. 221–47 in Marc Stiegler, ed., *The Gentle Seduction* (New York: Baen Publishing Enterprises, 1990).

[7] Charlotte Perkins Gilman, "The Yellow Wallpaper," pp. 46–61 in Barbara H. Solomon, ed., *The Experience of the American Woman* (New York: New American Library, MentorBooks, 1978).

In a microbiology class for nursing students, I have used a reading about a physician who first guessed that childbed fever might be caused by microbes but whose pleas for colleagues to wash their hands between autopsies and deliveries fell on deaf ears because of the prevailing medical opinion of the time that childbed fever was due to cosmic forces beyond medical control.[8] Both of these last two examples raise concerns about experts or professionals who are convinced that they know what is best for other people.

It is easier to find class time for videos or discussion of readings in non-major classes than in courses for the major. If there is not enough time to show videos or discuss readings during class sessions, students can be asked to turn in written responses to items in the media that relate to course material and that also address or raise questions about values, ethics, or faith. This approach has the advantage that students may be able to deal with issues that matter more to them than those raised in a particular case study assigned for the entire class. The assignment could be an ongoing one, spread over the entire term to even out the grading load. Students could turn in written summaries and responses or might be assigned to meet in small groups to discuss related issues—with or without the instructor present. But one way or another, students must have the opportunity to grapple with what they think and feel about the issues. Otherwise, they will conclude that issues crucial to them are either unimportant or are beyond the boundaries of appropriate inquiry. Faculty must not let this happen. We must legitimate student concerns and must model free inquiry on even the most challenging topics, because in doing so, our students will be drawn to find points of convergence between their personal lives and their study of the biological world.

Review questions can also assist students in thinking about ethics, values, or faith connections. The most straightforward type would cover the interaction between values, ethics, or faith in particular examples covered in class sessions or readings. After covering a particular controversy, it is absolutely appro-

---

[8] Neal D. Buffaloe and Dale V. Ferguson, *Microbiology*, 2d ed (Boston: Houghton Mifflin, 1981), 286–87.

priate for students to be examined on the specifics of that issue, for example: "Summarize the major arguments about the use of genetically engineered food crops, and indicate what values reinforce these positions." "What are the main points in the controversy over antibiotics and growth hormones used in animal feed?" "What valid concerns would each of these have regarding such use of antibiotics and growth hormones—a pharmaceutical company CEO, a rancher, a physician, a grocer, a parent?"

Review questions that incorporate faith, ethics or values can pull the material together and help integrate values or faith, even when these have not been the designated topic of class discussion. In the scientific tradition course, we sometimes ask students to ponder such issues as preparation for essay questions on the exam, even though they will not be graded on their personal position: "If you had been a university student during the time of Copernicus, which of his ideas would have been exciting for you and which would have been troubling? Explain why." "Which would cause more tension for your faith—strong scientific evidence that organisms have truly evolved or strong scientific evidence that there are intelligent creatures elsewhere in the universe? Explain." Students can also be given questions at the beginning of the course (or a unit) that will be the basis for some evaluation at the end. This can encourage students to work on integration throughout the course, not just while cramming for the exam: "How do these molecular regulations of developmental processes affect our understanding of what an organism is, or what its potential is? Does this apply to humans as well as to other organisms?"

Nothing works better than real organisms if the goal is to get students to see God's creations as marvelous works. Our personal example here is of the utmost importance. Give students as much contact with living things as possible, and let your awe for the organisms become palpable for them. Let students see that you are interested enough to squat down in the middle of the campus loop to examine a tiny plant or insect or bird's egg. When observing embryonic cleavage stages under the microscope, do not hesitate to express your excitement when something happens. Point out the amazing abilities of specific creatures, whether it is a starfish everting its stomach, a fern sporangium flinging its spores, or a seed absorbing water and breaking asphalt. Let your students witness your delight. Take them to habitats where lushness supports great diversity or where harshness requires unusual adaptations. Ask them questions until they begin to look and to know and finally to understand that successful living communities may involve not so much "nature red in tooth and claw" as cooperation, perhaps even symbioses—the more intimate the better. I am convinced that a faculty person whose manner reveals an ever-present sense of God will help students along the path of integrating faith and science as much as any of the more academic techniques I have described above. The exuberance of your own love for and fascination with plants or invertebrates or microbes will prompt students to let biology outgrow the purely academic boxes in their lives, some day to meet and join an expanding, growing faith.

Selected Bibliography

American Scientific Affiliation, Committee for Integrity in Science Education. *Teaching Science in a Climate of Controversy: A View from the American Scientific Affiliation.* Ipswich, Mass.: American Scientific Affiliation, 1986.

Bronowski, J. *The Common Sense of Science,* with a foreword by Sir Hermann Bondi. Cambridge, Mass.: Harvard University Press, 1978.

Diamond, Jared. *Guns, Germs, and Steel: The Fates of Human Societies.* New York: W.W. Norton & Co., 1999.

Eldredge, Niles. *Dominion: Can Nature and Culture Co-Exist?* Berkeley, Cal.: University of California Press, 1997.

Henry, Granville. *Christianity and the Images of Science.* Macon, Ga.: Smyth & Helwys, 1998.

Hyers, Conrad. *The Meaning of Creation: Genesis and Modern Science.* Atlanta: John Knox Press, 1984.

Larson, Edward J. and Darrel Amundsen. *A Different Death: Euthanasia and the Christian Tradition.* Downers Grove, Ill.: InterVarsity Press, 1998.

MacKay, Donald M. *Human Science and Human Dignity*, with a foreword by John R. W. Stott. Downers Grove, Ill.: InterVarsity Press, 1979.

Mangum, John M. *The New Faith-Science Debate: Probing Cosmology, Technology, and Theology*. Minneapolis: Fortress Press; Geneva: WCC Publications, 1989.

Miller, James B. and Kenneth E. McCall, eds. *The Church and Contemporary Cosmology: Proceedings of a Consultation of the Presbyterian Church (U.S.A.)*. Pittsburgh: Carnegie Mellon University Press, 1990.

Nobel Prize Conversations with Sir John Eccles, Roger Sperry, Ilya Prigogine, Brian Josephson. Dallas: Saybrook Publishers, 1985.

Pearcey, Nancy R. and Charles B. Thaxton. *The Soul of Science: Christian Faith and Natural Philosophy*. Wheaton, Ill.: Crossway Books, Good News Publishers, 1994.

Pond, Jean. "Catholic Frogs." *Faculty Dialogue*, no. 18 (fall, 1992): 83–90.

Wacome, Donald H. "Evolution, Foreknowledge and Creation." *Christian Scholar's Review* 26, no. 3 (Spring 1997): 306–21.

Wilcox, David L. "A Christian Integrative Framework for Biology." *Christian Scholar's Review* 12, no. 4 (1983): 339–48.

Wright, Richard T. *Biology Through the Eyes of Faith*. San Francisco: Harper & Row, 1989.

Part Three
The Fine Arts

8

"I Love to Tell the Story:" Teaching Theater at a Church-Related College

John Steven Paul

To Connect Theater and God

As part of my work at Valparaiso University, I direct a liturgical drama troupe called Soul Purpose. During the past ten years, Soul Purpose companies have traveled thousands of miles to churches across the country performing plays based on Bible stories in worship services. In addition to performing, the student-actors meet with members of congregations in their Bible classes or coffee hours where they talk about the process by which they create, rehearse, and present plays. They often speak about why they give so much of their time from which they earn neither money nor academic credit. On one of these occasions, Courtney, a very talented actor and the most advanced student in our theater department said matter-of-factly, "Before I came to Valparaiso University, I had never seen a way to connect theater and God. Soul Purpose has shown me how to make that connection."

As a theater person raised in the Lutheran Church, I have learned to look for connections between what Martin Luther declared to be God's two kingdoms. The heavenly kingdom, according to Luther, is the one in which God reveals and fulfills the divine plan for the redemption of the world. The second or earthly kingdom, sometimes called the "secular" world, is preserved and protected by God through such agencies as governments, families, and schools.[1] In Luther's view, education is an agency of God operating in the secular realm to foster people's capacity to learn and to enhance and enrich their lives. This view certainly encompasses the educational theater.[2]

Making connections is central to the art of the theater. In the theater event, an actor or actors connect with an audience,[3] and the nature of that connection has been the subject of scholarly analysis at least since the composition of Aristotle's *Poetics* in the fourth century B.C.E. Aristotle held that tragedy was the representation of a human action that effected the purgation of pity and fear in the spectator. Actors connect with the audience by enacting an "imitation," crafted by a poet, consisting of six parts—plot, character, thought, diction, melody, and spectacle.

Plot, said the philosopher, is the most important part of a tragedy, and the most successful connections between actors and audience are made when tragic poets arrange the incidents of the stories they have chosen to tell according to a particular formal pattern.[4] Then the poet gives it over to actors for performance. The poet's two-part creative contribution is to choose the story from the stock of myth, legend, or history and to shape the story into an effective form for presentation by actors. The poet is the story-maker, the actor the storyteller.

Theater, then, is storytelling, by one or more storytellers, to one or more people. And, as theater professors know, our students deeply love to stand before groups of people and tell stories. It is our job, first, to lead our students to stories that they may tell their own audiences. Second, we must teach students the techniques of telling a story to good effect. Finally, and this is of particular importance in the church-related institution, we

---

[1] See Richard W. Solberg's summary of Luther's doctrine of the two kingdoms in "What Can the Lutheran Tradition Contribute to Christian Higher Education?," pp. 71–81 in Richard T. Hughes and William B. Adrian, eds., *Models for Christian Higher Education: Strategies for Success in the Twenty-First Century* (Grand Rapids, Mich.: William B. Eerdmans Publishing Co., 1997), 76.

[2] See Thomas I. Bacon, *Martin Luther and the Drama* (Amsterdam: Editions Rodopi, 1976).

[3] Richard Southern, *The Seven Ages of the Theater* (New York: Hill and Wang, 1963), 21.

[4] S. H. Butcher, trans., *Aristotle's Theory of Poetry and Fine Art*, 4th ed. (New York: Dover, 1951), 39–43.

must think and talk with our students about this good effect for which we are all aiming.

THE HERITAGE OF WESTERN THEATER

Professors seeking to make connections between the theater and the divine need only teach the history of Western theater and drama. Nearly all anthropologists locate the origin of theater in religious ritual.[5] Western dramatic literature is replete with poets who explored the relationship between the mundane and the divine. The tragedies and comedies of ancient Athens were dedicated to the god Dionysus for whom both the principal theater and the primary civic festival in Athens were named. In the surviving plays by Aeschylus, Sophocles, and Euripides, a central question is the relationship between the gods and human beings. Most of the surviving dramatic texts from Medieval Europe, known as mystery, miracle, and morality plays, are religious in content and didactic in form. In the sixteenth century, the Society of Jesus (Jesuits) made extensive use of the theater in service of the Catholic religion and played an important role in the training of such major continental playwrights as Pierre Corneille, Molière, Calderón de la Barca, and Lope de Vega.[6] William Shakespeare often plumbed deep theological questions. No doubt, only the royal ban on plays with religious references kept Shakespeare from writing explicitly Christian plays of his own. In the later seventeenth century, French academicians promulgated a code of dramatic criticism grounded in Christian moral principles that governed European playwriting for two hundred years.

In the later nineteenth century, realist and naturalist playwrights such as Henrik Ibsen, August Strindberg, Henri Becque,

---

[5] See Oscar Brockett's review of the theories of ritual origin of the theater in *History of the Theater*, 7th ed. (Boston: Allyn and Bacon, 1995), 1–3. See also, Benjamin Hunningher, *The Origin of the Theater* (New York: Hill and Wang, Dramabook ed., 1961) and David Cole, "The Actor," in *The Theatrical Event* (Middletown, Conn.: Wesleyan University Press, 1975), 12–57.

[6] Margot Berthold, *A History of World Theater* (New York: Frederick Ungar, 1972), 427–32; William H. McCabe, S.J., *An Introduction to the Jesuit Theater* (St. Louis: The Institute of Jesuit Sources, 1983), vi.

and Anton Chekhov located their characters' motives for action entirely in the material realm. But for many twentieth-century tragic characters, it is precisely the absence of God that accounts for the aridity of the universe and their agonized search for something meaningful beyond the merely material, the physiological, and the psychological. The century's greatest playwrights continued to dramatize, if not the connections between human beings and God, then certainly humanity's spiritual quests. And if many recent plays seem relatively trivial, mundane, and vulgar, they represent a departure from the heritage of Western theater.[7]

LEARNING TO TELL THE STORY

Our theater students come to us with an intense desire for a life on the stage but without the slightest practical idea of what that life could be. Like Pirandello's six characters, they have come to our university in search of an "author" or at least a co-author to help them complete their stories. Now that they are here, what do we teach them?[8]

Educators who respect the tradition of Western theater will acquaint students with the historic role of the theater in providing its audience opportunities for theological exploration and spiritual experience. Lectures, discussions, and writing assignments on the drama will naturally lead students to struggle with issues of divine intervention, moral action, faith, hope, doubt, death, and redemption. Theater history and dramatic literature, however, might be taught effectively by history and literature faculties. Theater arts pedagogy addresses the questions of *how to tell the story*. At Valparaiso University, we have rooted our pedagogy in five fundamental principles to which our faculty subscribes.

---

[7] See, for example, Eugene O'Neill, "On Man and God," in Oscar Cargill, N. Bryllion Fagin, and William J. Fisher, eds., *O'Neill and His Plays* (New York: New York University Press, 1961), 115.

[8] On the importance of the college years as a time for the formation of commitments, see Sharon Daloz Parks, "Led to Places We Did Not Plan to Go," *The Cresset* 59, no. 6 (summer 1996): 7.

1. Theater pedagogy is most effectively delivered in the form of doing rather than talking.

Whenever possible we select teaching strategies that motivate students to learn by doing: sewing costumes, applying make-up, performing a scene for acting class, hanging a lighting plot, constructing a scenic flat, and directing a play are prominent examples. In dramatic literature classes, we spend considerable class time watching students enact pivotal scenes from the plays being studied. It is in doing that students make choices and establish priorities. Teaching through the participation *in* rather than the study *of* plays distinguishes theater pedagogy from other disciplines.

2. The actor-audience dynamic is the essence of theater art.

While we teach a comprehensive array of courses in all the theater disciplines, our pedagogical focus is the actor onstage. The majority of students who take our courses and participate in our activities is primarily interested in acting.

3. Theater is a community of artists and craftspersons formed around a project and committed to a goal. A play is projected into a community and will affect that community.[9]

It takes the work of many people to bring a play to fruition. Each new project, therefore, gives us as professors the opportunity to do more than divide the labor. We can also form an intentional community of student artists, craftspersons, and technicians. If we are successful in our formation, we will have transformed a group of unrelated individuals whose power is diffused into a new organism whose power is concentrated and enormous. This community must be educated to take responsibility for the power of the theater to edify, amuse, shock, offend, and even to harm an audience.[10] The intentional community, formed for the

---

[9] I am indebted to my colleague at Valparaiso University Walt Wangerin for his passionate articulation of this principle.

[10] Nicholas Wolterstorff, *Art in Action* (Grand Rapids, Mich.: William B. Eerdmans Publishing Co., 1980), 194.

purpose of presenting a play, is a subset of a larger community upon which it can have a wholesome or deleterious effect.

4. Art is the fruit of our labors and to God we owe the first fruits.

It is conventional wisdom that the theater performance is ephemeral, and thus it is hard to conceive of it as a product. While it is true that neither actor nor audience is in possession of something tangible that might sit on a shelf (apart perhaps from a video or audio recording), theater art is produced by the coordinated labor of many talented and trained people. The cultivation and ripening of the theater production requires as much care as does production in any field. The shelf life of the theater in the memory of its audience may be as long as any durable possession. Theater is what we do and what we make. And as children of God, we offer the best of our art to God.

5. Theater is a vocation; it is a calling that can be lived in any number of careers.

We understand the theater vocation, in the Lutheran sense, as a "valued channel of service."[11] Unfortunately, most students who are educated to be professional actors are unable to support themselves as professional actors. Though the employment possibilities are better in the allied crafts of scene and costume design, technology, directing, stage managing, and playwriting, the professional theater is still not a large enough industry to absorb every person who desires a job in it. But the theater calling can be lived out not only in the professional theater but also

---

[11] Richard W. Solberg summarizes Martin Luther's view of vocation in this way,

Just as each person possessed dignity as an individual, so every work or profession was a valued channel of service. Having been 'called' by God in baptism, the Christian was obliged to give expression to that call by faithful service in some useful secular 'calling' or 'vocation.' No hierarchy of services would distinguish one person's vocation from that of another. Faithfulness and integrity, not public honor or recognition, are the standards by which God judges a person's work. In the classic example cited by Luther, the faithful work of a scullery maid is as praiseworthy in God's economy as that of a learned scholar.

Quotation from "What Can the Lutheran Tradition Contribute to Christian Higher Education?" 78.

in such fields as education, the law, religion, civic and social work, and recreation. For our theater department, "vocational-ism" is an educational trend not to lament but to celebrate and to cultivate, for it is those students who identify the theater as their vocation who are most open to the myriad varieties of life in the theater.

True to the Lutheran tradition, there is much in these principles that would apply to theater pedagogy at any institution, for knowledge of the Gospel is not a prerequisite for excellence in theater. Yet Christian virtues can and do inform the theater profession and theater pedagogy in ways that are useful and, perhaps, salutary. In the following sections, I will explore the ways in which theater study and Christian practices intersect in our program. The five principles introduced above are woven into the fabric of our pedagogy and, when taken together, distinguish us as a teaching institution connected to the Church.

"Play Out the Play; I Have Much to Say"

Like Falstaff in Shakespeare's *Henry IV*, we in the theater department at Valparaiso University have much to say, and playing out the play is the way we say it. Play production is our department's most important and most distinctive pedagogical activity. It is our faculty's primary contribution to the enterprise of liberal arts teaching at Valparaiso University. Staging a classic play by Sophocles or Shakespeare is a uniquely effective way of leading our students—those on-stage and those in the audience—to the sources of our Western tradition.[12] A play onstage at our university theater reflects the mission of our department. In choosing a particular play to produce, the faculty decides to invest a significant amount of time, energy, and financial resources into this project as opposed to another. In the course of a play's preparation, departmental faculty shape and balance the skills students have learned in the studio and the shop, creating a community

---

[12] On this point, see Francis Fergusson's "Note on the Academic Theater," in *The Human Image in Dramatic Literature* (Garden City: N.Y.: Doubleday Anchor Books, 1957), 35. See also Mark Schwehn and John Steven Paul, "Theater as Liberal Arts Pedagogy," *Liberal Education*, 81:2 (spring, 1995): 32–7.

of artists and craftspersons to meet the challenge of a single, complex project. In short, it is through play production that we teach what we think is important for students to learn.

People often ask me, as the chair of the theater department, "What plays are you doing next year?" They are probably less interested in discerning the mission of our department than they are in whether they are going to enjoy the plays. Nevertheless, the answer would say a lot about what we want to teach and, thus, choosing which plays to produce is a very serious matter. Putting aside for the moment the vast number of plays that we could put onstage, we begin with the objectives that we wish to achieve with our productions. I believe that almost any well-produced play can be entertaining; theater must entertain, in the sense of holding an audience's attention. Still, some plays are more entertaining than others and will be more popular with audiences. We want our audiences to enjoy the theater and our audiences, like most U.S. audiences, love the musical theater. Though we *think* there is much to be taught by doing a U.S. musical, we *know* that presenting *Oklahoma!*, *Fiddler on the Roof*, or *A Little Night Music* will please the crowds, and that is one reason why we produce them.[13]

Another set of objectives is directed toward what we want our theater students to know. When, for example I chose to produce Bertolt Brecht's *The Good Person of Szechwan*, I did so because I wanted our students to appreciate Brecht's unique didactic approach to making theater and his brilliantly theatrical approach to teaching.

Brecht cared little for the audience's emotional involvement with his characters or story. Indeed, he believed that an audience needs to be emotionally distanced from the play to learn its lessons. Brecht was, however, a master entertainer, and his innovative uses of every possible theatrical resource were path breaking. Many of our students are, like Brecht, engaged in theatrical teaching through our theater outreach performances. Their participation in Brecht's overtly didactic twentieth-century

---

[13] The question of what will be popular with audiences overrides most other considerations for commercial theater producers. Academic theaters should not have to worry about this, but no one wants to bore the audience. On giving the public what it wants, see Wolterstorff, 194.

classic gave them an important historical perspective from which to view their theater work in schools and churches.

A third set of objectives has to do with what the play is about. Does the playwright have important things to say? In 1996, the first year in our newly constructed university theater, our department, in cooperation with the department of music, presented Michael Bennett's *A Chorus Line*. The show ran on Broadway from 1975–1990, and until recently it held the record as the longest running show in Broadway history. Here was a proven success with audiences—a contemporary classic with the cachet to snare the fancy of student performers at a time when the music and theater departments were attempting to boost a fledgling dance program. Here was a play about professional dancers that would certainly give our program visibility. More important, the subject of *A Chorus Line* also strongly recommended itself to those of us who chose it.

A Chorus Line is a play that leads student-performers to reflect upon their own life choices.[14] To make their characters live onstage, they have to consider how the reality of the present is

---

[14] The play is the story of a dance audition for a Broadway show. In the hard-driving opening number, a collection of twenty-four individual dancers is whittled down to sixteen. From this group, the director will choose eight to make up the chorus line for the show. Every one of the sixteen is technically good enough to be cast, but the director first employs another screening device, the question "Why do you dance?" In response to this simple question, the dancers recount, in monologue, song, and dance, the personal journeys that led them to this moment. Each story has a stunning air of authenticity, and several reveal a world of pain. As the dancers are being prepared for the final phase of the audition, one falls to the ground, victim of what threatens to be a career-ending injury. After the boy is carried from the stage, the dancers engage in an emotional exchange about the personal sacrifices they have made for an art form that values youth and physical agility above all else. These sacrifices, they sing, are "What I Did for Love," and it is their common experience of sacrifice that makes them less competitors than members of the same community. Inevitably, the director comes onstage to select the eight dancers for the show. The disappointed leave quickly, faced with new choices; those remaining take a deep breath of triumph and greet members of their new family, the chorus line.

A Chorus Line's authenticity can be traced to its origins in a series of taped interviews with dancers that Michael Bennett conducted at the New York Shakespeare Festival in 1974. Frank Rich, "Introduction" to *A Chorus Line: The Book of the Musical* (New York: Applause, 1995). Note also Gary Stevens and Alan George, *The Longest Line* (New York: Applause, 1995).

shaped by events and actions in the past. The production process offered them an opportunity to rehearse the feelings of the professional performing artist while still living in the relatively protected world of college. In post-show interviews, several cast members told me that the experience allowed them to survey their own resources of talent, skill, and even courage in a simulation of real life. In writing her spiritual autobiography as an assignment for her honors college senior colloquium, a student who had been in the show as a freshman revealed that the lyrics to one of the songs, which address issues of personal identity and meaning, came to have theological meaning for her in the discovery of vocation and was her clearest memory of her freshman year.

Acting Is Believing

In the finale of *A Chorus Line*, the entire company of dancers returns in flashy gold costumes, top hats, and canes to sing the song "One," the title song of the musical for which they have been auditioning. A closing tribute to *one* is an ironic ending for a play that has been about building a chorus. It points to a fundamental tension in the theater and in theater education. Though the actor is called upon to be part of an ensemble, her power ultimately depends on her ability to believe that she *is* the one, the "singular sensation."[15] That belief is an essential characteristic of an actor.[16]

The English theater historian and anthropologist Richard Southern has observed a basic duality in the actor's personality. In *The Seven Ages of the Theater*, Southern writes of public assemblies, alive with tension generated by the significance of the occasion. On these occasions, Southern writes, "two-fold"

---

[15] This fact is made abundantly clear in the first line of the song.

[16] "Acting is Believing" is the title of a respected acting primer by Charles McGaw, who was for many years the Dean of the Goodman School of Drama in Chicago. Charles McGaw and Larry D. Clark, *Acting is Believing*, 6th edition (Fort Worth, Tex.: Harcourt, Brace, Jovanovich, 1992). Belief is also a key concept for Constantin Stanislavski. See *An Actor Prepares*, trans. Elizabeth Reynolds Hapgood (New York: Theater Arts, Inc., 1936).

opportunities present themselves to those special persons in the assembly called "players" who seize

> the opportunity to *take* the power of the gathering to [themselves] and to dominate; this is a proud and selfish motive, and it is very characteristic of a player to show himself off. Or the opportunity to *give*, to seize the power of a gathering to convey to them . . . what? *A vestige of the godhead.* This, curiously, is a very humble motive; and even more curiously it is equally characteristic of the player—to give of himself without return.
>
> Thus we have the roots of the player's two main characteristics; his selfishness and his generosity.[17]

Experience teaches that many students do come to us with a mixture of these two characteristics. As faculty, we respect selfishness as an important source of the student actor's power, but we make systematic efforts to develop generosity. How?

We begin with love. Most of our students will say that they are studying theater because they love it. In response, we challenge the students with the words of another song from *A Chorus Line.* What will you do for love? What will you sacrifice for love? Your time? Your possessions? That is to say, will you invest the time necessary to learn to make good theater art, though it means you will have much less time for the other things you like to do? Will you be satisfied with less money and fewer things? Are you prepared for a life of unemployment? These are questions that few eighteen year olds are in a position to answer. Those who persistently answer "yes" may not actually know the meaning of love.

If it is difficult for students to grasp the implications of loving the theater, it is even more difficult for them to accept Richard Southern's notion that a player acts out of a humble motive. It seems to them, rather, that playing the heroic roles such as Oedipus, Medea, Hamlet, Phèdre, and Hedda Gabler would demand a display of what the Greeks called *aretē,* that success onstage would be the product of what Southern calls "the proud, selfish motive." Can we convince our young theater-lovers that humility, even Christian humility, is the beginning of theater art? What does it mean to love the theater?

---

[17] Southern, 27.

Constantin Stanislavski (1865–1938), the great Russian acting teacher and theorist, rendered his primer on acting in the form of a student diary. The student, whose reflections on acting are the text of *An Actor Prepares,* is not unlike the ones we see week in and week out—enthusiastic, serious, and full of hope, fear, and, most of all, a love of the theater. For his first assignment, the student prepares one of Othello's heroic monologues. Though the student believes his performance was a good one, his master teacher responds with severe criticism that devastates the student. What the student must understand is that a great performance results from a series of humble steps taken over "a long time."

> At the end of the discussion the Director announced that tomorrow, in addition to our work with him, we are to begin regular activities that have the purpose of developing our voices and bodies,—lessons in singing, gymnastics, dancing, and fencing. These classes will be held daily, because the development of the muscles of the human body requires systematic and thorough exercise, *and a long time.*[18]

Granting Southern's view that the selfish motive is the source of the actor's power, we at Valparaiso University work assiduously to develop the actor's other main characteristic—generosity. We have developed strategies to develop actors' generosity by choosing particular theater projects. The ethic of generosity can even be taught at a very basic level of the actor's training. For example, one of the first improvisational exercises that our actors are taught is called "The Mirror." In this exercise, two actors face one another at a distance of about eighteen inches and establish direct eye contact. One actor now begins to move her arms, head, and trunk, and the other actor attempts to move as close to simultaneously as possible to become a mirror for the first actor's movement. Many students who have not performed this exercise approach it as a competition; that is, they immediately move in such a way that their partners are unable to respond as a mirror. What I want the actors to do is not to trick the mirrors but to help their partners to mirror them. If there is a goal for this exercise,

---

[18] Stanislavski, 30. (Italics mine.)

it is for the pair to be moving with such sensitivity to one another that it is impossible for the onlooker to tell which of the actors is the leader and which is the mirror. Finally, I ask that the partners continue to move in a mirror relationship without either assuming the role of the leader.[19] This exercise is the first step in transforming the actor's focus from the self to the other, which will ultimately result in the building of an ensemble. It is also a metaphor for an entire approach to acting training and theater. We seek to educate the actor to believe that there is power in giving as well as taking. And, giving is the beginning of service.

"WHO *IS* MY AUDIENCE?"

In Luke, chapter 10, is the story of a lawyer who, having been told by Jesus that he must love his neighbor as himself, asks Jesus, "Who *is* my neighbor?" Jesus answers him with the parable of the Good Samaritan. In our theater department, we ask ourselves the question "Who is my audience?"[20] Our audiences, like those at most college theaters, are mainly comprised of students, faculty, other members of the campus community, and residents of the surrounding area. In the past, we have presumed very little about our audiences except that in coming to the Valparaiso University Theater they *have accepted our invitation to participate with us in the educational process.* Therefore, if they are entertained and edified, it will be a reflection upon this educational process.[21] But in the last five years we have tried to know

---

[19] For a series of mirror games see Viola Spolin, *Improvisation for the Theater* (Evanston: Northwestern University Press, 1963), 60–76.

[20] In *Theater Games for Rehearsal*, Viola Spolin, the inventor of the seminal approach to improvisation that gave birth to the Second City comedy troupes and the "Saturday Night Live" television program, has posed a useful series of questions for a director to ask before deciding to direct a particular play. The first question she poses is "Who will my audience be?"

[21] *A Chorus Line* received enthusiastic applause from its audiences and several standing ovations. But some audience members who spoke with me later found the play shallow and vulgar. The dancers do, in fact, speak with sometimes appalling frankness about their experiences both inside and outside the theater. For example, in one of the show's most famous songs, "Dance Ten, Looks Three," a small-town girl sings quite bluntly and cynically about the

our audiences in a different way; we have increasingly asked the lawyer's question, "Who *is* my neighbor?"

We usually think of audiences as those people who go to the theaters, including theaters on the campuses of universities like Valparaiso.[22] But recently, our department has identified the theater audience more broadly, as those people *from whom our students have most to learn* while engaged in the *service* of performing plays. To bring students into contact with a broader spectrum of audiences, we have designed two service-learning theater projects. With these projects, we have been able to demonstrate to our students the potential for a mutually educational relationship between actor and audience within a community[23] and the value of Christian outreach and service.[24] We have sought, in these projects, to relax our students' instinctive reflex to place themselves as actors against their audience by teaching them to think of *that* audience as *their* neighbors. To find our neighbors, we often must reach out beyond the walls of the Valparaiso University Center for the Arts.

In one of our service-learning projects, Theater Outreach Performances (TOP) companies of from four to six actors and a stage manager travel to elementary schools to perform *Little Bear,* an interactive play written by Don Yost at the Bridgework

---

kind of figure it takes to be cast in a show and what kind of cosmetic make over she underwent to become anatomically appealing. It is probably true that members of the audience who were offended by the play's language were not edified nor did they see the play as the worthy pedagogical vehicle that the faculty did. The spectators' presence in the theater testifies to a bond of trust between them and the producers—the audience trusting the producers' care for the educational process and the producers the audience's willingness to be educated. The producers must be aware of the real power of live theater to break that trust by giving offense. The residual effects of an offensive production tend to be lasting and may rest on future projects. While we at Valparaiso University do not modify a play's language or content once we have chosen it, we do ask another of Viola Spolin's questions, "Is the play in good taste?"

[22] This has not been exclusively true, for there have always been theater companies willing to perform anywhere there was flat ground available, including streets and marketplaces.

[23] For an insightful discussion of the audience's role in theater performance, see Herbert Blau, "Odd, Anonymous Needs,"in Herbert Blau, *The Audience* (Baltimore and London: The Johns Hopkins University Press, 1990), 1–49.

[24] On Martin Luther's view of vocation and service, see H. Richard Niebuhr, *Christ and Culture* (New York: Harper and Row, 1951, Harper Torchbooks Edition), 174–75.

Theater of Goshen, Indiana. In the play, Little Bear is the victim of unwanted sexual advances from Big Bear. With the help of friends Little Moose and Big Moose, Little Bear learns a strategy for coping with such abuse. We began this program in 1991 when three social workers from nearby school districts came to my office to ask for help. The sexual abuse of children, often in the children's own homes, was a growing problem in their community and children needed to know how to protect themselves. Videotaped productions of *Little Bear* were not communicating effectively to first and second graders, yet the schools could not afford to hire a professional company to perform the play. Could we help? At that time, one of our theater majors was also majoring in psychology. She was eager to direct the play and take it to the schools. Another theater and psychology student designed and built the set. In the first year, the company performed for sixteen schools. Eight years later, we now have three companies doing *Little Bear* for thirty schools a year, and we find ourselves unable to serve all the schools that would like us to perform.

A year after we began touring with *Little Bear,* our university sponsored a series of events designed to raise the consciousness of students about the serious matters of acquaintance rape in conjunction with alcohol abuse. The university's student affairs office commissioned a play from the Theater Department and the *Little Bear* team set to work on developing a new piece, which they called *The Chartreuse Dress.*[25] This play follows the experiences of six university students, one of whom, a freshman, becomes the victim of a sexual assault by an older male student who she thought was a friend she could trust. Like *Little Bear, The Chartreuse Dress* is an interactive play; that is, at certain points the spectators are invited to address the actors who remain "in character." The *Chartreuse Dress* sounds an alarm for young people of high school and college age that "against her will is against the law" and that crimes will be prosecuted. Like *Little Bear, The Chartreuse Dress* also offers the sexual assault vic-

---

[25] *The Chartreuse Dress* was developed in a workshop directed by Kari-Anne Blocher Innes. Ms. Innes later revised the play and is now credited as the author.

tim a specific program of response. The latter play goes a step further than the former by offering the emotional support of the community to the victim. By sponsoring annual performances of the play at freshman orientation, Valparaiso University says to victims that their legal rights and physical health are important, but that it also wants to restore them to wholeness and health and in a community which attempts to emulate Jesus in its love for the hurting and the downtrodden. By performing *Little Bear* and *The Chartreuse Dress* we provide our students the opportunity to embrace their vocation as actors uniquely qualified to serve their community.

SOUL PURPOSE

In addition to TOP, our theater students at Valparaiso may also participate in Soul Purpose, a liturgical drama troupe begun in 1987. The intention of Soul Purpose is to provide students with the opportunity to follow the command of Exodus 23:19: "The choicest of the first fruits of your ground you shall bring into the house of the LORD your God." The first play Soul Purpose performed was adapted from a sermon by the Rev. David H. Kehret, associate campus pastor at Valparaiso University. Its title, *The Man Who Was Not Far from the Kingdom of God* came from the Rev. Kehret's text, Mark 12: 28–34. Three subsequent plays which the troupe continues to perform are also adaptations of his homilies.[26] In its twelve-year existence, Soul Purpose has introduced nine new plays to the liturgical drama repertoire. The liturgical drama genre is defined by its service to the liturgy and most of the troupe's performances are given at that point in a liturgical service where a homily would be offered.[27] The plays, like homilies, elaborate upon a Scripture reading appointed in

---

[26] *The Man Who Was Not Far from the Kingdom of God*, from Mark 12:28–34, a play for the chancel by John Steven Paul adapted from a sermon by the Rev. David H. Kehret.

[27] Wolterstorff, 185. Wolterstorff offers a succinct and useful definition of liturgical art: "Liturgical art, much of it participatory in character, is the art of a community, at the service of its liturgical actions and not at the service of artistic contemplation." See Wolterstorff, 188.

the common lectionary to be read for given day in the Church Year.[28]

One of the program objectives of Soul Purpose is to guide students through a workshop method of new play development. All the plays in the troupe's repertoire have resulted from this process. As the director, I present a selection of possible workshop projects from which the troupe chooses one. The choice is based on the interests and concerns of members of the troupe. I advise them on the potential of each project for service to the Church. The most recent play we have completed through the workshop process is entitled *Zacchaeus: For the Lord He Wanted to See*. This play is based on Luke, 19: 1–10, the Gospel reading for the twenty-fourth Sunday after Pentecost in the third year (C) of the three-year lectionary cycle, though we have performed it at various times during the church year.

All our workshop sessions begin with a prayer for guidance. We understand that when the play is finished, we will be invited to perform it as a way of preaching the Gospel to congregations. It is a solemn responsibility. We read the story carefully, aloud, and discuss its scriptural and historical context, often bringing learned commentary to our discussions. These discussions invariably bring new insights, some of which will have substantial impact on our dramatization of the story. In the *Zacchaeus* workshop, for example, we were surprised to learn how near to the end of his ministry Jesus met the tax collector. According to Luke, Jesus goes directly from Jericho to his triumphal entry into Jerusalem where within a week he would be crucified.

Following a discussion of the Zacchaeus story, workshop participants identified salient images—a short man, his possessions, and, of course, the sycamore tree. Next we considered the characters in the story—Jesus, Zacchaeus, the people of Jericho and Jesus' disciples as well as the relationships among the characters. From these conversations we discovered that the sharpest conflict in the story was not between Jesus and Zacchaeus, but between the people of Jericho, who resented Zacchaeus's "taxation

---

[28] For an explanation of and guide to the lectionary, see Martin Connell, *Guide to the Revised Common Lectionary* (Chicago: Archdiocese of Chicago, Liturgy Training Publications, 1988).

policy," and Jesus who went to dine with him. "All who saw it began to grumble and said, " 'He has gone to be the guest of one who is a sinner' " (v. 7). At the time we were developing this play, a young male theater student had just been expelled from Valparaiso University for repeated, serious harassment of younger female theater students. There was no one whom the students resented more and whom they found harder to forgive. "What would you think," I asked, "if Jesus came to Valparaiso and invited himself to share a meal with 'Jim' at his apartment?" Suffice to say, the issue moved immediately from the abstract to the concrete! The neighbors would have much to say in this Zacchaeus play. And, further, I said, "could you imagine being married to Zacchaeus?" Now, in our play, there would be a new character who does not appear in Luke's story and in whom the town's revulsion would be crystallized. Her name would be "Sarah," wife to this son of Abraham (v.9).

Reading forward from Luke 19:1–10 suggested to us that Jesus's visit to Jericho was part of a longer story that could be dramatized. We were struck by the significance of the two trees, the sycamore in Zacchaeus's story and the tree on which Jesus would be crucified. Zacchaeus had climbed a tree to see Jesus; was it stretching the imagination too far to present a reversal of the situation to show Jesus climbing the tree of the cross so that *he* could see everyone who believed in *him*? We thought not. As it is written, the play follows Zacchaeus from his stunning meeting with Jesus in Jericho to the foot of the cross where he kneels with other characters from Luke's gospel: the centurion from Capernaum, the widow and her son from Nain, the Samaritan leper, and the blind man whose sight Jesus restored just before his meeting with Zacchaeus. In the workshops, *Zacchaeus* went through seven drafts, each read aloud by the company, re-drafted and read again. After the fourth reading, I staged the play. We rehearsed a working draft of the script and tried it out for the folk service at our university chapel. In the following year we began performing *Zacchaeus* for churches around the country.

Another program objective of Soul Purpose is to provide students with opportunities for spiritual development and the benefits and support of a Christian community. The community forms during the two weeks of rehearsal in September. At least once during that period, we break bread together and at the close of the period we celebrate Holy Communion. Trips to churches, though they require sacrifices of time and sleep, are times of fellowship, fun, and personal, as well as spiritual growth. But the challenge of sustaining a community of eighteen busy college students over the course of a seven-month season is not an easy one. Some of the bonding work happens on Saturday mornings, but generally only the six or eight actors who are performing that Sunday will come to the Saturday morning rehearsal. In short, Soul Purpose actors spend much more time apart than together. This is where student leadership becomes critical. It is the students who hold the Soul Purpose community together. One of the songs we sing is "Here I Am, Lord," which contains the promise to follow where the Lord leads, always remembering the Lord's people.

I refer to Soul Purpose as a "drama ministry," and the order of the words is important. This ministry is distinct from the University's chapel or counseling ministries. The student members of Soul Purpose understand that their vocation as actors distinguishes them from seminarians and social workers. What makes their Christian ministry peculiarly effective is their faithfulness to their Lord *and* to the disciplines of the theater. In its early years, actors and director tended to think of Soul Purpose as something we did in addition to our other theater work. After all, Saturday and Sunday came at the end of a week of work. Through its evolution, we have begun to turn that way of thinking around. On Sunday, the first day of a new week, we offer our performances as the first fruits of our labor. As the words of the Soul Purpose prayer remind us:

Merciful God,
We offer with joy and thanksgiving what you have first given us—
our selves, our time, and our possessions, signs of your gracious love.
Receive them for the sake of him who offered himself for us,
Jesus Christ our Lord. Amen

Shaping Communities

The shaping of a community to meet its goal is a critical phase of the enterprise of bringing a play to the stage and an important educational goal for our department. We want our students to appreciate the power of community, to accept responsibility within a community, and to be able to shape communities of their own.[29] As a theater director, my job is to make the artistic choices and to direct the actors' movement, gesture, and speech in ways that will communicate the intentions of the playwright to the audience. At the same time, I work to shape the community that will produce the play by employing a deliberate pedagogical strategy. Early in the rehearsal period, I invest a great deal of personal time in the shaping process. I convey to the cast what I think is the value of the play, my artistic goals, and a schedule for our progress. I also install a structure of student leadership for the production—a dramaturg, an assistant director, a stage manager, a warm-up captain—and publicly invest these students with my confidence. The shaping process continues well into the rehearsal process, but once accomplished, I concern myself exclusively with my artistic responsibilities. And then I withdraw from the leadership of the community in what I hope are imperceptible increments. It is my goal to be able to arrive at the theater on the opening night of the production at about the same time as the audience with the confidence that the community has achieved its goal.

In the spring of 1997, the Valparaiso University Theater produced *The Book of the Dun Cow*, a musical by Mark St. Germain and Randy Courts based on the award-winning novel by Walter Wangerin, Jr.[30] Shaping a community for the *Dun Cow* was especially difficult for several reasons. First, the work had never been produced other than in a staged reading. It was, in fact, in draft

---

[29] See Larry Rasmussen, "Shaping Communities," in Dorothy Bass, ed., *Practicing Our Faith: A Way of Life for a Searching People* (San Francisco: Jossey-Bass, 1997), 119–32.

[30] Walter Wangerin, Jr., *The Book of the Dun Cow* (New York: Harper and Row, 1978). In the fantastic story, a group of barnyard animals, led by a noble rooster named Chauntecleer and his mate Pertalote, fight against an ancient subterranean evil that threatens to devour their world.

Walt Wangerin is currently a member of the Valparaiso University faculty. St. Germain and Courts wrote the musical as an anniversary gift to the New Harmony Project, an annual two-week workshop in New Harmony, Indiana. At the workshop the works of playwrights are prepared for public staged readings under the guidance of a Board of Directors committed to the promotion of Christian values on the stage, in films, and electronic media.

form only. As with any play adapted from a novel, only a fraction of the original work finds its way to the stage. The exact nature of that fraction had not yet been determined. The music existed in the form of a piano-vocal score only and needed to be orchestrated. The playwright and the composer, who wanted further input into the book and music, lived and worked in New York. The actor who would play Chauntecleer lived in Los Angeles and would come in for the last two weeks of rehearsal only. Walt Wangerin, the on-stage narrator, was himself available for only two of the five rehearsal weeks. The stage designer lived in Memphis, Tennessee.

One of the major artistic goals of this production was to assist the playwright and composer with the development of their new work by giving them the opportunity to see the play fully produced at a high level of competence. That we achieved this goal, in spite of the challenges facing us, was due, in no small part, to the skills brought to the production by actors from the Soul Purpose company who comprised the core ensemble for *The Book of the Dun Cow*. In addition to their extensive experience in developing new plays from non-dramatic sources, these actors understood how to bond a community against the multitude of centrifugal forces that whirl around the typical college student. Their willingness to be open to one another, to correct one another, to pray for one another, in short, to be responsible for one another provided the basis for this complicated project.

We have learned a great deal about the value of community from TOP and Soul Purpose, both about the way it allows us to impart critical knowledge and necessary skill to our students and the way it nurtures the spirits of members of those outreach companies. The lessons of TOP and Soul Purpose inform our pedagogy in two ways. First, the faculty has developed two new courses for our curriculum, "Service-Learning in the Theater Arts: Society" and "Service Learning in the Theater Arts: Church."[31] These courses will cover the tradition, philosophy,

---

[31] These course titles are explicitly linked to Valparaiso University's mission statement, which describes the university as "a private institution of higher learning distinguished by its Lutheran heritage of scholarship, freedom, and faith, provides strong programs of liberal and professional studies well-grounded in the arts and sciences by a faculty dedicated to challenging teach-

discipline, and methods peculiar to each outreach company with a special emphasis on the creation of new plays for the audiences that the companies serve. The goal of these courses will be 1) to prepare students systematically to join these companies, and 2) to clarify the core values of the companies and their general applicability to work in the theater.

While the service-learning courses are in their pilot stages, a weekly Colloquium required of majors has been in place for nearly two years. The syllabus for the Colloquium reflects the faculty's commitment to the five fundamental principles that have been articulated above. The mission of the departmental Colloquium is the shaping of a community of artists, crafts-people, and technicians who relate to their brothers and sisters in the field not as competitors for jobs but as friends and members of the same community from whom they can draw strength and support. At its best, the Colloquium is a weekly reminder that theater is the product of collaborators and a reaffirmation of the bond that exists among us as theater teachers and students.

Nothing tests this bond more strenuously than the regular "post-mortem" discussions of theater productions presented by students and faculty in the department. Artists, especially student artists, are extremely sensitive to criticism of their work. Criticism of one's art, especially criticism not charitably and skillfully offered, can sting. But critical reflection upon artistic expression, followed by correction and improvement, is at the heart of theater arts pedagogy. When conducted in community, such criticism fosters students' growth and strengthens the community itself.

RENEW A RIGHT SPIRIT WITHIN ME

Professors and students will search the scriptures in vain for teachings on theater technique. And, though there have been many acting teachers and theater gurus who have addressed the

---

ing and care for the individual in a residential setting where its students can develop as whole persons, *motivated and prepared to serve both church and society*."

spiritual dimension of theater art, we will not find there what H. Richard Niebuhr calls "the right spirit of service, of confidence and hopefulness, of humility and readiness to accept correction."[32] What we do, as professors at Valparaiso University, is to assist our students to see the connection between theater and God by applying to their vocation such Christian values as humility, generosity, responsibility, and community. As professionals responsible to our own discipline, we teach our students the special methods and discipline necessary for the creation of theater art. Finally, we pray *for* ourselves and our students—and, we hope, *with* our students—the words of the offertory:

> Create in me a clean heart, O God,
> and renew a right spirit within me.
> Cast me not away from your presence,
> and take not your Holy Spirit from me.
> Restore unto me the joy of your salvation,
> and uphold me with your free Spirit.

The right spirit comes as a gift to us by grace through faith. We repeatedly seek renewal of that spirit in the sharing of word and sacrament, and the blessing of the Spirit in our efforts to shape community, do service, and tell the story.

Selected Bibliography

Allen, Robert A. *Don't Give Up the Script: Writing Original Sketches for the Church*. Colorado Springs, Col.: Meriwether Publishing, Inc., 1984.

Benedetti, Robert L. *The Actor at Work*, 3d ed. Englewood Cliffs, N.J.: Prentice-Hall, 1981.

———. *Seeming, Being, and Becoming: Acting in Our Century*. New York: Drama Book Specialists, 1976.

Bennett, Michael. *A Chorus Line*. New York: Applause, 1995.

Bondi, Roberta C. *To Love as God Loves: Conversations with the Early Church*. Philadelphia: Fortress Press, 1987.

Brook, Peter. *The Empty Space*. London: MacGibbon & Kee, 1968.

---

[32] Niebuhr, 176.

Dolan, Jill. *Geographies of Learning: Theory and Practice, Activism and Performance.* Middletown, Conn.: Wesleyan University Press, 2001.

Driver, Tom F. *The Magic of Ritual: Our Need for Liberating Rites That Transform Our Lives and Communities.* New York: Harper-Collins, 1991.

Fergusson, Francis. *The Human Image in Dramatic Literature.* Garden City, N.Y.: Doubleday; Anchor Books, 1957.

———. *The Idea of a Theater.* Garden City, N.Y.: Doubleday, 1949.

Hardison, O. B., Jr. *Christian Rite and Christian Drama in the Middle Ages.* Baltimore: The Johns Hopkins University Press, 1965.

Kehret, David H. *Can These Bones Live? Contemporary Dramas for Lent and Easter.* Minneapolis: Augsburg Fortress, 1999.

———. *Worshiping Through Drama.* Kansas City, Mo.: Lillenas Publishing Co., 1999.

McCabe, William H., S.J. *An Introduction to Jesuit Theater.* Ed. By Louis J. Oldani, S.J. St. Louis: The Institute of Jesuit Sources, 1983.

Miller, Arthur. "On Social Plays," pp. 51–68 in Robert A. Martin and Steven Centola, eds. *The Theater Essays of Arthur Miller.* New York: Da Capo, 1996.

Niebuhr, H. Richard. *Christ and Culture.* New York: Harper & Row, 1951.

Pederson, Steve. *Drama Ministry.* Grand Rapids, Mich.: Zondervan Publishing House, 1999.

Perry, Michael. *The Dramatized New Testament: New International Version.* Grand Rapids, Mich.: Baker Book House, 1993.

———. *The Dramatized Old Testament: New International Version.* Vol. I, *Genesis to Esther.* Grand Rapids, Mich.: Baker Book House, 1994.

———. *The Dramatized Old Testament: New International Version.* Vol. II, *Job to Malachi.* Grand Rapids, Mich.: Baker Books, 1996.

Price, Reynolds. *Three Gospels.* New York: Simon and Shuster, 1997.

Solberg, Richard W. "What Can the Lutheran Tradition Contribute to Christian Higher Education?" pp. 71–81 in Richard T. Hughes and William B. Adrian, eds. *Models for Christian Higher Education: Strategies for Success in the Twenty-First Century.*

Grand Rapids, Mich.: William B. Eerdmans Publishing Co., 1997.

Spolin, Viola. *Improvisation for the Theater*. Evanston, Ill.: Northwestern University Press, 1963.

———. *Theater Games for Rehearsal: A Director's Handbook*. Evanston, Ill.: Northwestern University Press, 1985.

Stanislavski, Constantin. *An Actor Prepares*. Trans. by Elizabeth Reynolds Hapgood. New York: Theater Arts, 1936.

Steiner, George. *Real Presences*. Chicago: University of Chicago Press, 1989.

Von Balthasar, Hans Urs. *Theo-Drama: Theological Dramatic Theory*. Trans. by Graham Harrison. Vol. I. *Prolegomena*. San Francisco: St. Ignatius Press, 1988.

Wolterstorff, Nicholas. *Art in Action*. Grand Rapids, Mich.: William B. Eerdmans Publishing Co., 1980.

9

Toward a Christian Pedagogy of Art

Edward Knippers

After receiving a B.A. and an M.F.A., and after eight years of teaching art to undergraduates and periodically studying abroad, I became a full-time artist. From the time of my first painting at the age of eleven and throughout the succeeding forty-plus years, I have been forced as a committed Christian to both question and explain my place in the modern world of art and in the ancient world of faith. It is my hope that the following will help young professors of art to bridge the gaps and avoid the pitfalls that make up the contemporary no man's land between the studio and the Church as they attempt to pass on our remarkable artistic heritage to a new generation.

In Defense of the Teaching of Art in Church-Related Higher Education

Chaim Potok, the Jewish author, was asked why there had been relatively few Jews in the visual arts until the last two hundred years. His answer was that until the rise of secular democracy "art was a Christian endeavor." Jaroslav Pelikan, in his *Imago Dei: The Byzantine Apologia for Icons*,[1] explores this question: How did the sect of a culture that rejected images because of a strong prohibition against idolatry, while accepting that prohibition,

---

[1] Jaroslav Pelikan, *Imago Dei: The Byzantine Apologia for Icons*, Bollingen Series (Princeton, N.J.: Princeton University Press, 1990.) The A. W. Mellon Lectures in the Fine Arts, delivered at the National Gallery of Art in Washington, D.C., in 1987.

form a civilization that has given the world its greatest outpouring of images? The answer, Pelikan explains, was worked
out by the Church over a six-hundred-year period and in numerous ecumenical councils. In short, the answer was the fact of a
true Incarnation—God with us in human flesh in the person of
Christ Jesus. If God came in the flesh, then he could be pictured.[2]
Pelikan's argument explains how Potok's statement can be true.

For centuries, the very reason for the making of art in the West
proceeded from the most fundamental of Christian doctrines—
the Incarnation. Then came the paradoxical sixteenth century.
Ironically, on the one hand, the Protestant Reformation pro-
voked the great outpouring of art during the Catholic Reformation. On the other hand, much of the Protestant Reformation
soundly rejected in practice the teachings of the ancient Church
councils on the use of visual images. In Protestantism, the Word
and the invisible interior of the heart comprised the template of
earthly faith. Images merely fed the lust of the eyes and, at
worst, led to idolatry. A seventeenth-century primer written by
American Puritans clearly illustrates this schism. The primer
contains a dialogue between Christ, a youth, and the Devil. The
Devil describes the downward fall of youth through various sinful activities, culminating in this couplet:

> If you will but be ruled by me
> An Artist you will quickly be.[3]

We are seeing the results of this abandonment of art to the
Devil's care, and it is devastating. The Church is no longer a
central patron of the arts. Art has, at best, become a secular endeavor to the point that not infrequently contemporary gate-
keepers of the arts establishment are hostile to a Christian
worldview. (Yet even in such a deplorable circumstance, Christian artists may discover an unintended blessing. We are placed

---

[2] In fact, the Eastern Orthodox tradition would say that if images are not
used in worship, the Incarnation has been denied.

[3] A Christian college president shared this with me many years ago as a
challenge to my presentation at his school on Christianity and the visual arts.
He later sent me a copy of the text, which I misplaced after committing it to
memory. The context in which I received this couplet is further evidence that
the Protestant prejudice against images is still alive in some Christian college
circles.

in a somewhat parallel position with the early Christians as they found their way in a bustling pagan world. As a friend observed on a recent trip to Asia Minor, Antioch might well have been the ancient world's Malibu.) One can hardly blame church-related college and university administrators for their wariness regarding the influence of the arts on campus. If contemporary art and its supporting institutions have become so thoroughly secularized, the question now seems to be not if art may be practiced by non-Christians but *if art can any longer be Christian at all*.[4]

Certain subjects are required in what has become the Christian liberal arts curriculum. Science, history, literature, language arts, the Bible, and even music—all have defensible positions in the educational offerings of even the smallest church-related college. Visual art, though, has been a stepchild. Art history—let alone studio art—is often a luxury, perhaps added to the curriculum as the institution becomes established and financially sound. In a Protestant worldview based on the primacy of the written word, the nonverbal is suspect.

This state of affairs suggests that the visual arts are of less significance to a sound Christian education than other fields of study. To some in Christian higher education, such a perspective is simply self-evident. Painting, sculpture, and printmaking seem more engaged in the craft of making physical objects than in the mind, focused on skill development rather than intellectual development. This perception, however, has been challenged by recent studies of the brain. The visual arts (and the fine arts, as distinct from the crafts in particular) simply demand intellectual engagement of a different sort from that of the verbal world.

The criticism that art lacks the intellectual rigor of other fields has faded in recent years as the church-related liberal arts college and the academic world in general have become market oriented, attracting new student consumers seeking as many

---

[4] Historically, the arts have been held in much higher esteem in Roman Catholic institutions than in Protestant ones. Consequently, the remarks that follow, while addressed to all church-related colleges and universities, will most likely have special meaning for Protestant institutions. Eastern Orthodoxy's embrace of icons and wariness of Western artistic development is a special case beyond the scope of this essay.

practical applications of their college years as possible. In an atmosphere in which the career marketplace exerts more influence over undergraduates than intellectual nurture, it is hard to be a purist in curriculum formation. It is difficult to build a traditional liberal arts case for eliminating the hands-on activities of the ceramics studio at a school in which business administration majors have become the financial cornerstone. Yet in a bottom-line, cost-per-student environment, the visual arts still have a difficult time because of the physical and financial requirements of space, tools, and equipment for teaching them.

Of all the subdisciplines, art history has the strongest claim to legitimacy in the Christian liberal arts curriculum. It is unassailably true that an individual does not need art to be a worthwhile person—leading even an abundant life rightly related to God, family, friends, and community. But civilizations *do* need art, and it is here that art history can stand firmly in the educational enterprise. It is the art produced by a people that often provides our major understanding of who they were, what they believed and desired, how they saw themselves and others, and what they felt was worthy of preservation. Art history is about all of this and more. But the making of art is qualitatively different from studying what has been made within a historical context.

Art may also be touched upon in Christian colleges in courses under the general title of Art Appreciation, a misnomer that further trivializes the arts. (The implication is that art does not have content to be learned. Can you imagine courses in Physics Appreciation or New Testament Appreciation?) In such settings, art is used to give "culture" to the students. In the past it was even seen as morally uplifting. Although we no longer see a relationship between art and moral elevation (cultural refinement as next to godliness), I must hasten to add that art can greatly enrich the life of the individual who wants to learn from it. In fact, in the light of studies of the human brain, the case can be made for the sacred arts (those used in worship) as helping to fulfill the biblical injunction to worship God with our *whole* mind. It is also through the arts that Christians can understand and even participate in cultural formation as we try to signal Christ's presence in our world. For these reasons, as well as others that will be explored later, I firmly maintain that the visual arts need not take an inferior position in relation to any other field of human inquiry.

In this essay, I will lay a foundation for teaching art from the perspective that Western art in fact grows from a Christian worldview. This understanding applies to studio art as well as to art history. Indeed, my major concern will be for building a theoretical as well as a practical foundation for the teaching of studio art at church-related liberal arts colleges and universities. In *The Greek Experience,* C. M. Bowra writes:

> The primary impulse in the arts is to give permanence to the fleeting moment, to bid it stay because we cannot bear to lose it, to defy mortality by creating something which time cannot harm. The Greeks expressed this by comparing poetry to such inanimate objects as pillars or temples or gold or ivory or coral. But they saw too the paradox that though it must have the permanence of such lifeless things, it is also in some sense alive, that it not only *is* but *does,* that it both exists in itself and affects us, that for all its finality of form it still moves and acts. That is why they also compared it to such living things as flowers, birds, bees, chariots in motion, and athletes at their games. But beyond this they saw something else, which they could express only in the imagery of fire or light.[5]

This same impulse to preserve and pass on is at the heart of Christian faith. The visual arts have been, and can still be, a major component in accomplishing these ends. For example, we still gain inspiration from the art of the catacombs and are instructed by it regarding the earliest beliefs of the Christian community as it moved past the apostolic period.[6] Although I would reject the extremes to which Bowra's somewhat overly romantic views might lead, the venerable view of art that he expresses sheds valuable light on a Christian art pedagogy. As Christians, we have much that has been entrusted to us to preserve and pass on in a form that is intellectually and emotionally viable for the present generation and the generations to come. But how does one teach the concept that preservation is a good thing to a gen-

---

[5] C. M. Bowra, *The Greek Experience* (Cleveland and New York: The World Publishing Co., 1957), 126.

[6] This raises the questions, What record are we leaving for future generations as to the presence of our believing community? What are we preserving and why?

eration reared on the throwaway virtuality and instant gratification of television and video games? The answer, I believe, is to be found in returning to primary things.

THE HUMAN FIGURE AS THE CORE OF THE CURRICULUM

Artists begin with the real world. The current generation is an image generation. But for its members, images are for information or entertainment, not meaning. They are interchangeable—virtual illusions divorced from objective reality. Therefore, as an antidote, the artistic educational process should begin with still life. A cup on a table can tell us much about the physical presence of the real world and from that, about the mind of God, for God was free to create the world to divine liking. God chose to give us four dimensions, including time. Much about composition, color, shape relationship, and design can be learned from still life. It is truly an artist's art. Yet this is only the beginning. An art of meaningful images will eventually lead to the human body.

The one irreducible component of the human experience is our physical being. Without the body, there would be no*body*. The fact that it is through the body that we have continuity suggests an underlying human truth that ironically counters an existential worldview that says we live our lives in fragments. In the body we are always a part of a greater whole. Furthermore, the body's universal existence stands against nominalism and the denial of universals by its contemporary cousins. This affirms the traditional understanding of human universals that has laid the foundation for our greatest art. The body is the one artistic subject of consequence that can focus the attention as nothing else can. For in dealing with the human form artistically, we are basically dealing with ourselves—with our humanity.

From the body we establish our position in the world: we become self-aware. From it we derive our sense of scale and proportion. The classical style in both sculpture and architecture is derived from the ideal of a composite of human proportions. This might explain why we deem the style "classical" and why it endures.

The body is necessary to the Christian understanding of the person. It is the shape of that wonderful creature with whom God wants to commune. It reflects the image of God. It is the form that God took eternally in Christ, without which there can be no true Incarnation. Using the body as subject matter in art inevitably leads to the larger questions of human existence. Our Christian view of time as salvation history places us in a line of physical persons with whom God has personally dealt. The sacrifice of Christ for our sins marks each person with incalculable worth. Christ was resurrected bodily, and so it will be with us. This reality must be presented to students from the beginning of their studies, first in lectures, then in practical reminders as they draw and paint from the figure. I once heard a university professor refer to the model as "it." This is unacceptable for Christians. Never letting the students lose sight of the humanity of the model is central to teaching why drawing the figure is important.

Students should also be made aware that our sense of morality grows from God's expressed caring about what we do with our bodies. The human body reflects a transcendent reality that speaks even in the face of unbelief. Take for example the nudes of Lucian Freud. His figures are unmistakably earthbound. Yet they allude to something more—a something more of which one suspects Freud does not approve. "Prove to me that there is a transcendent reality," he might say. I would answer, "Look at your portraits." He cannot completely control and possess the figures he paints in the way that he does, say, the plants, which somehow magically become his under his paintbrush.

The visual arts start with the concrete, with the perceivable, and the figure is inescapably concrete. Form is always implied in the creative arts, no matter how abstract the work might be. The perception of form sets the work of art apart from that in the world which is not art. Form does not make something art, but intentional form is the beginning of the artistic endeavor. Even Barnett Newman's huge red canvas has its edges and an installation—in other words, it has its limits. How would one attempt to paint the human soul without a body? How would a landscape be painted without at least the essence of its form? From the study of the human body the developing artist can uniquely learn the implications of creating artistic form, for the human body is the epitome, in complexity, form, and beauty, of the created order—that concrete perceivable world in which we live.

The body is not to be worshipped, but neither can it be ignored. It is who we are in the most practical earthly sense, and certainly who we are visually. The fact that we are creatures who are fearfully and wonderfully made tells us much about the mind of our Creator. It is with the study of the human body, therefore, that we must begin in formulating a Christian art curriculum.

There are those in the Christian arts community who might question the centrality of the human figure in art pedagogy.[7] Designers, ceramists, and others may imagine a false limitation because their artistic expression historically uses the figure less than painting or sculpture. In suggesting that the figure should be the core of the visual arts curriculum, I am arguing that it is time to return to the basics—to reestablish a time-honored foundation for the teaching of art. In dealing with a subject as important as the human form, developing a basic knowledge of design, putting objects in space, eye-hand coordination, skills of observation, interrelationships of light, texture, form, and other elements of artistic creativity are all heightened in significance.[8]

---

[7] The secular art community also has its naysayers. The New York Academy of Art, an educational institution devoted to the artistic study of the human figure, was turned down by the National Endowment for the Arts for a modest educational grant. "The NEA Director for Visual Arts informed . . . the staff of the Academy: 'Teaching students to draw the human figure . . . is a revisionist approach that would stifle creativity in young artists.'" (Letter from the NEA, Susan Lubowsky, Director of Visual Arts program, 20 December 1989, as quoted by James F. Cooper in "*Pietà* at the Cathedral," *American Arts Quarterly* 14, no. 4 (fall 1997): 7.

[8] In Michelangelo we find a supreme example that the study of the nude from life liberates one in all that one might do in the visual arts. Michelangelo was a master of sculpture, painting, and architecture. "His style in all three arts is wonderfully consistent. The key to that consistency may be found in his own words: 'The members of an architectural structure follow the laws exemplified in the human body. He who . . . is not a good master of the nude . . . cannot understand the principles of architecture.' His whole inspiration came from the beauty and majesty of the human body: the visible aspect of the human soul." Horst de la Croix and Richard G. Tansey, *Gardner's Art Through the Ages*, 8th ed. (New York: Harcourt Brace Jovanovich, 1986), 622.

There are other objections that will be raised in Christian settings. Figurative art (more specifically, the use of the nude)[9] on a Christian campus remains a major problem for administrators as well as for many in college constituencies and in the larger body of Christ. Christians are often quite uncomfortable with the body. Can anyone—but especially 18-year-olds at the height of their sexual energy—look with purity on a naked body? Should we not teach art without getting into this questionable area with its pagan ancestry? These questions are posed most often by those who have not studied drawing in a figure studio—those who have no idea what is required to place a complicated form such as the human body on a two dimensional surface. They do not understand that the concentration required leaves little room for the mind to wander. Nonetheless, such questions persist.[10]

Another objection to the centrality of the human figure is its supposed non-Christian origin. It is simply not accurate to dismiss the study of the nude for having pagan roots. Timothy Verdon, in a lecture given at the National Gallery, traced the rise of the figure in Western Christendom *not* back to the ancients, but to St. Francis. In his enlightening address, Verdon argued persuasively that it was this saint who emphasized the emotions of the believer in his reenactment of the crèche. Of course, the container of these emotions was the body. It should also be

---

[9] In this essay, I use figurative art and nude studies virtually interchangeably. To the degree figures are clothed, the subject is cloth, not the figure. One recalls Michelangelo's query, "What is more noble, a man's shoe or his foot?"

[10] One such question is how to find models for study. Using nudes for study in the studio at most Protestant and some Roman Catholic institutions may well not happen any time soon. If they are, professional models, not students, should be hired. Some parents may not mind if their daughter or son draws from a nude, but they are less likely to approve if their child *is* the nude. Lists of available models can be obtained from local universities or art leagues that have life classes. In many communities there will be a network of artists that can provide leads.

If the nude cannot be used, drawing from students in bathing suits will be a distant second best, adequate only to a point for the classroom. Again, students might well find friends willing to pose nude in the dorm or might be able to set up same-sex drawing situations that will not offend the administration. This is a very sensitive area. Take on only what you think is doable and in the best interest of the department. Even on very conservative campuses, though, faculty and administrators can be made allies in the use of studio nudes if a strong theoretical foundation can be established.

noted that it was during the era of St. Francis that excavations of ancient art were being done on the Italian peninsula at places such as Pisa. As Verdon pointed out, such excavations of the pagan past became the instructor—taught artists *how* to use the form—while St. Francis and others gave the theological impetus—the *why*—for the resurgence of the realistic human form in art. It is not a surprise to realize that Giotto, the father of Western painting, was closely associated with the early Franciscan community and its theology of the goodness of God's creation.

Building upon the Verdon Lecture, art historian John Walford of Wheaton College has further noted that it was during St. Francis' time that there arose a more literal reading of Scripture than had been the case with the earlier Scholastics. This theological trend demanded a closer look at and a more realistic depiction of nature in art. These scholars build a strong case for the Christian foundation of the centrality of the human figure in the art of the West.

Paul Klee provides a useful analogy of the artist as the trunk of a tree. The leaves and the limbs are his work; the roots are grounded in all of his experience. The leaves and limbs do not reflect the ground, but they draw their nourishment from the ground. Klee reminds us in this analogy that the artist has much latitude. In my advocacy for the primary importance of the human figure in art pedagogy—its ground if you will, I am not proscribing the limits of Christian involvement in the visual arts. A Christian artist by definition is not necessarily a figurative artist. A Christian artist is simply a Christian whom God has called to work in the arts. A Christian artist, therefore, seeks to do only what God requires of the talent given in the first place. There are many media and modes for making art. There are none, though, that will not benefit from the unique honing of the perceptual ability that figure study alone provides. I am simply saying that the figure is the tiller of the soil around the artist-tree.

CHALLENGING THE ARTISTIC PERSONA

There are no shortcuts to the teaching of art anymore than there are shortcuts to making good art. Many students will come to you wanting to *be* artists but not wanting to *become* artists. It is therefore of great importance that the emphasis in the studio be on verbs rather than nouns, on words that emphasize work—such as making, creating, painting, sculpting, drawing—instead of on the artist or art. Always emphasize doing over being. The twentieth century viewed the artist as a seer and prophet, an autonomous creature who lives by self-made rules, a superior being who rightly snubs the rest of us. No wonder some students want to be seen as artists. Living a life of no rules, yet being praised for whatever you deign to produce as long as you call it "art," has its appeal. Such a view is based on the very non-Christian assumption of the autonomous, self-defining individual. We may be made in the image of God, and Christ has offered to every person the possibility of also being a child of God. But we are not God. We are always dependent creatures living in an orderly universe—a world of rules and laws. Your students may try to reject such a world as overly restrictive. A world without rules and laws, though, would be bondage indeed, for we could count on nothing. Our freedom would be the freedom of floating in outer space with nothing to guide us or to push against. The laws and rules of the universe give us the freedom to act. Thankfully, art making also has rules. I sometimes refer to them as "tools" instead of "rules." But the fact is, to be an artist with the freedom to exercise the breadth of the artistic imagination, one must have as many concrete skills at hand as possible. Therefore, one should try to keep the game of role playing the "artist" to a minimum. Make the students truly earn the name of "artist" as a term applied to them after people see what they make, not how exotically they dress, nor how erratically they act. Communicate this through lectures and discussion and through exhibiting a low tolerance for capricious or irresponsible behavior.

Minimize the preciousness of what the students make, particularly at first. Construct problems that will force them to work on each other's drawings or paintings. Change easels during a life session or have them work collaboratively on projects. One life drawing instructor at a major art school has the students destroy their work after each session. This may seem somewhat extreme, but the point is that the students are there to learn, not to parade their abilities. For those of us in the visual arts, the pre-Renaissance view of the artist as artisan, worker, or skilled craftsman, rather than prophet or seer, is a much healthier and a much truer model. This is especially true during the student years. The making of art is hard work. The designation of students as workers and artisans will help them understand that one becomes an artist through what one makes. An "artistic personality" counts for little.

SELF-EXPRESSION

Related to the contemporary elevated view of the artist is the perception of art as self-expression. It is assumed that if an artist is special in the human race, then the mere expression of that special self is all that is required. I have been asked, after someone views a dark or violent painting that I have done, if I am all right, if I am sleeping well at night. The fact that I am painting the Passion of our Lord, a dark and violent subject, does not seem to be considered. Freud has made demi-psychologists of us all. In such a society, it should be no surprise that the college art student comes with the expectation of self expression as the beginning and end of the artistic life. This expectation can impede learning in the studio, for it places the art making squarely at the dead end of the constantly fluctuating emotional life of the student instead of at the richly open-ended physical world—that training laboratory for eyes. The student will probably not believe you at first, but artistically the self is not very interesting in the long run. The best students will find, though, that being expressed in what we make is quite different from limiting all that we make to the self.

The emphasis on the objective world in teaching art is helpful here. It is not that emotions are to be avoided in the studio, but for the student the objectification of the emotions—depending on observable reality to clarify and to formalize the formless intuitions of the emotional life—will be a significant education for a lifetime. Assign drawings from life that are fifty to eighty percent light or seventy-five to ninety percent dark. These projects will have emotional content, but they will not be directly dependent on the student's feelings.

If self-expression is the end of the art-making endeavor, on what grounds can criticism be made of an object sincerely created? How can one teach? The emotional life of the student can cause major problems in developing an objective inner critic that will stand the student in good stead for the years to come. It is the creating and development of an interior disinterested objectivity—an inner critic—that is the goal of art education. We are trying to instill in the students a realistic artistic judgment of their own work that will make their instructor less important as time goes on. Without this independence how will the student continue to develop artistically after graduation?

To this end, make students constantly point out their best and worst work and articulate why they have made that judgment. They should also do this with each other's work as well as the work of "known" artists. Make them be as objective as possible, realizing the subjectivity of the task. The key is to insist they first use artistic criteria and then other criteria that are consistent with judgments of beauty, truth, reality, and goodness. In doing this, the students must learn to set aside as much as possible their incidental feelings about their own work and that of others so that they can see clearly.

When still an undergraduate, I had a professor at the Pennsylvania Academy of the Fine Arts who came up to my easel in the figure drawing studio and said dismissively, "Oh, you are trying to feel. Students don't feel." This was a somewhat shocking way of getting at this rudimentary truth—the students' primary concern should be not their own personal feelings but how the solid world of real things can be a vehicle for human universals.

ON LOOKING

The visual arts deal with the eyes and the language of the eyes. Developing artistic expression not only requires seeing the natural world for what it is, but also learning the refinements of the visual language developed over the centuries by the masters of our craft. Therefore, if a museum is nearby, students should visit often and with direction. They should have the benefit of the professor's eyes and experience in touring the collection. Discuss questions such as: What are your favorites *and why*? What is the historic importance of a given work? How does a work relate to your studio assignments, to your own work, to the faith? What is the context, content, and meaning of the work? Students should write about the collection over a number of visits. One way to accomplish this objective is to ask for a paper on their favorite work from certain galleries in the museum or have them choose a religious work and explore how faith and theology are expressed. Even in the many Christian schools that are in isolated locations with no nearby museums, tours can be planned during breaks or long weekends. Build touring abroad into the curriculum. In one way or another, make sure your students can experience directly the original works that have formed our artistic consciousness.

The less feasible it is to go to museums and other centers of art, the more important it is to bring original art to the students. A gallery is essential. If mounting special exhibitions is not possible because of time and financial restraints, there are many touring shows available from organizations such as Christians in Visual Arts (CIVA).[11] Start a permanent collection of original works for your college or university. This might be quite modest at first, but with persistence it can grow. Original graphics can be important and are affordable. Also, buying from the shows in the college gallery is often possible. And do not forget donations that might be available if only the artists and collectors know that the college is serious about creating a permanent collection. A permanent collection need not be confined to a gallery. Ideally, offices and general spaces such as dining rooms and rooms in the student commons should all have original art.

Augment the viewing of original works with the holdings of the college library. Build an art library that is broad and deep.

---

[11] Christians in Visual Arts, P.O. Box 18117, Minneapolis, MN 55418. CIVA has a mailing list of over 6,000 individuals and institutions. It is a valuable resource for those in art education.

Get to know the library staff and help them to catch your vision for the visual arts collection.[12] Be sure that your students use the collection, not only by doing research in the library but also by bringing books to class to share with each other. For example, each week ask students to bring reproductions from an artist about whom they knew little or did not know at all.

ON DRAWING

Michelangelo was called divine, not for his sculpture, painting, or architecture, but for his drawing. All art students should have a sketchbook at hand during all of their waking hours. Carrying and using a small sketchbook could well be a standing assignment throughout the first two years of study. This practice should become a habit for the most serious students. It should become second nature to think with a drawing instrument recording what is before the eyes. Since I suggest the figure as the core of the visual arts curriculum, at *least* one night a week should be set aside for drawing from the figure in a studio setting, more if there are generous funds for models.[13] Consider making a certain number of these sessions mandatory each term for all art students, no matter what other classes they have.[14]

---

[12] Order books, and with appropriate sensitivity, do not worry overmuch about staying within your personal library budget. You will be helping library staff members use the budgetary surplus left by those departments that do not order much, since they would rather buy what they know a faculty member has requested than order something that might seem important but will not be used.

[13] A classroom note on looking and the model: in France the length of poses started with forty-five minutes, then thirty-minutes down to five and then to one. This is the opposite from what is done in most studios in the U.S. In starting with short poses, we want to "warm up" the hand. In starting with long poses, the French want to "warm up" the eye. For them, looking is the important thing.

[14] One caution: students can draw themselves in a mirror, or they can draw each other, roommates, and friends, but they should *never* draw from photographs. Working from photographs short circuits necessary lessons, particularly learning how to place a figure in space. Also the subtleties of surface differences are often lost in the photo. A student can copy a photo perfectly and receive much praise from peers but will learn little about drawing in the process. The point is that an artist should build a life-long habit of drawing from life.

On New Materials and Technologies

Superficially, we seem to live at a time of ever increasing artistic possibilities. New materials and technologies in image making are being developed at a rapid pace. With each new innovation new techniques need to be taught. Since much in art must be learned though the making of visual objects instead of through lectures, there is always a great temptation for the studio professor to retreat into a technique-centered mode of teaching. Techniques need to be taught in order to give the students as wide a range of tools as possible. But it is easy, particularly in exploring a new material or medium, to divorce the technique from the perception of the real world of artistic concerns—that intersection of the eye and the idea. By all means, explore new materials, but always explore the nature of a new material in the light of a perceptual need in order to discover what it can uniquely do. Be wary of substitutions that are shortcuts to an old end—"it's fast and it looks just like. . . . " But will it *be* just like?

Also be alert to the dangers of the overly long way around. Although the melding of art and idea—the synthesis of heart and mind and eye into something never before seen—most often happens in the making, process should not be an end in itself. As a rule of thumb, we as artists should follow a principle of subsidiarity of materials—make all art using the simplest and most appropriate material, medium, or technology for the richest embodiment of the subject. The art object should emerge from a symbiotic relationship between the subject (idea) and the material that forms it. Without a principle of subsidiarity of materials, the material may well seem inappropriate to the subject, thereby producing inferior art.

Toward a Christian Art

Many Christian students who rightly take their faith seriously want to make "Christian art" immediately upon arriving from high school. Many students will have come from secular schools and will be relieved to experience a general acceptance of their faith. Often, for these students, Christian art means explicitly

Biblical subject matter. Unfortunately, few young students have the artistic tools with which to give form to profound faith. Therefore their work trivializes and demeans that which they hold precious. As a rule of thumb, especially for beginning students, I would suggest that: 1) There should be no use of religious subject matter until the tools of artistic perception and expression are well in hand. Sincerity alone does not make good art; 2) There should be no "spiritual expression" apart from solid observation. Even God, after all, came in the flesh in order to teach us about the spiritual; 3) There should be no attempt to convey propositional content apart from the life and language of the eyes. The visual arts are limited. Most theology is difficult for the visual to hold except in the way the Gospels do—through stories. Therefore assignments in the visual presentation of narrative will be helpful as the student develops personal skills, but keep the subject as neutral as possible—emphasize the how more than the what.

From the beginning of the educational process, though, give assignments that will make the students confront the great Christian art of the centuries. Writing papers that deal with comparisons of different artistic treatments of the same Biblical subject, for example, will introduce the students not only to our artistic heritage but also to the artistic language on which they must build if they are to deal with the Bible. Flannery O'Connor said that her faith was the light by which she saw, not the subject she wrote about as a Christian writer.[15] This is a very helpful guide for a more profound Christian art than that of which most earnest young students conceive. Eventually, some may very well be called to hold Biblical subjects vitally before our society. My own work as a painter is almost exclusively of Biblical accounts. But a broader definition of Christian art is needed if the true vitality of the Christian faith is to find the depth of expression it demands in our time.

The affirmation of the goodness of the creation that our Lord came to redeem can speak of His presence as much as explicit depictions of sin and salvation. I would hasten to point out,

---

[15] Flannery O'Connor's book of essays, *Mystery and Manners* is a must read for students concerned with faith and the arts.

though, that the more generally his revelation is depicted, the less clearly "Christian" the work will be read in our secular society and the more open to pantheistic interpretation it will be. A portrayal of a fallen tree might well evoke the Fall in Eden to the seventeenth century Dutch society, but it will most likely read as an environmental event to modern Americans.

The Classroom and the Professor's Studio

Art is a subject that may be more appropriately caught than taught. The professor can teach the elements and principles of design, explain various techniques and methodologies, develop assignments that hone skills and provoke discoveries, and expose students to great art. But as with other subjects, art may be beyond the student's ability. Lack of coordination or spatial perception may be an insurmountable handicap. Even more, the student may never be able to grasp the essential nature of art. Drawing an adequate picture does not make one an artist any more than throwing a good curve ball makes one an athlete.

Nurturing a student's innate ability to become an artist, when such ability is there, is often impossible within the confines of conventional classroom hours, formal syllabi, and a detached professor/student relationship. As much as possible, consider appropriating the apprenticeship model, at least in attitude. You are a master artist, your studio is the real classroom, and the students are apprenticed to study and work with you. This model shifts many assumptions. The assessment of art is never quantifiably objective; this makes clear that your informed judgment, albeit subjective, will determine the students' grades. Because they are in your studio and not a generic classroom, you should feel free to paint or draw or sculpt on anyone's work as necessary to make your point. This pedagogical strategy provides a healthy antidote to the excessive "preciousness" that students hold about their art. If students know that they are coming each day to study in your studio, they very likely will come with a different kind of seriousness—perhaps even pride. Later, in recounting their time with you, they can rightly say that they studied in "the studio of _____." But for this identification to have any worthwhile meaning, we as artists are under a burden to become masters worthy of the name—we must have active studios from which we can extend the classroom.

THE PROFESSOR'S LIFE

An active studio is also one of the best ways not to go stale—to stay focused. One of the most difficult parts of teaching (and life) is the day-to-day repetition. How do you continue to sound, let alone be, interested in your subject after telling dozens of classes the same introductory material that will prove to be foundational to their lives as artists, yet is self-evident to you?

Much of teaching is just good acting. In the same way that a professional actor stands before an audience night after night saying the same lines as if they have never been spoken before, so the professor must remember that the students in the class are new to the material no matter how many of their fellows have come before.

This being said, even actors have a life offstage and it is from there that they gain professional strength. You must find your own rhythm of renewal. For the called and committed artist, the studio is central to staying alive while teaching. But also your creativity should be used to vary class assignments—invent new ways to get at old and basic ideas. This is a way of using your student's ingenuity to stimulate in you new avenues of thought. Traveling, seeing the great masterpieces, and getting with artistic colleagues as often as possible will also help you not to fall into the trap of thinking your college is the universe. The academic life is a breeding ground for the ingrown. Do not try to fight this problem alone. Get out. Our Lord has given us the great banquet of life; therefore, we should not try to live on bread and water. Eat and be grateful.

All of this, though, must be wrapped in a strong and active life of prayer for it is from God that true renewal and refreshment comes.

We teach in all that we do. For Christians, *example* is our watchword. One does not take seriously the words, "Thou shalt not steal," from a minister with his hands in the collection plate.

Likewise, should a student take seriously the pronouncement that "Art is an important use of your time" from a studio professor who rarely if ever makes art? The demands of time in the contemporary Christian college are formidable. With the computer, the forms and paper trails have only multiplied. Committees and extracurricular activities demand much time and energy. And this does not even consider family, friends, church, and other obligations. Yet to fail to set an example for students through a productive studio is to cheat not only them but also ourselves as their mentors. They want to know not only what we say but also what we do. This means making art and exhibiting it. The better our own work, the more authority we will have in what we teach. The balance is delicate and hard to maintain. Family, for example, is more important than art and is a prior commitment. This, too, is an example to be set before students. But art should not come last on our list. If it is our calling, we should embrace it, and our love for art should show in how we conduct our affairs. Is the artistic life that we hold before our students important to us—important enough that sacrifices are in order? If not, why should our students forego other college activities in order to complete a difficult and time-consuming studio assignment, let alone make a life of art making?

An active studio will not let the artist live too comfortably in the academic ivory tower of theory divorced from action. It will demand that we always move from theory to practice. I have always tried to model life as a working artist for my students. Many of the concepts about teaching art that I have presented here are caught by students observing this model. Tell your students about problems you are solving in your studio. Show them how you pray over and wrestle with your image making. If possible, invite students into your studio to keep an eye on your work as it develops.

I have emphasized that the artist should love art. For the Christian this sometimes creates an apparent conflict of interest. There is a fear that your art will become too important and will damage your Christian life and your commitment to God. One answer may be that it is not a problem of loving your art too much but loving God too little. The underlying issue is your identity and where it is found. If you see yourself as an artist who happens to be a dedicated Christian—if your worth and identity comes first from your being a painter, or a sculptor, or a printmaker, or a craftsperson—then you do not have your priorities straight. In being an artist who happens to be a Christian, instead of a Christian who happens to be an artist, everything becomes a point of compromise. Adding a "Christian" modifier to the term "art" compromises to some degree your artistic commitment in the world's eyes. And what of your Christian commitment? What does it mean to be a Christian in the arts? Do you do a work once in a while for a Christian cause? If so, does that mean that your other artistic work (that done without a Christian cause in mind) is not Christian, at least not wholeheartedly so? All becomes right when we allow our artistic commitment to be consumed by our Christian faith. If our art making is a call from God, then we are artists by vocation not career. This is the point. We must give up art. And only then will we *perhaps* receive it back as a calling from God for our lives. The most important part of teaching art from a Christian perspective is to convey to your students the paradox that for one to have true freedom as an artist, one must have an all-consuming commitment not to art but to Christ and his calling, whatever that might be. This may never be easy to do, but we must remember that art makes a lousy god.

Selected Bibliography

Barzun, Jacques. *The Use and Abuse of Art* (A. W. Mellon Lectures in Fine Arts; Bollingen Series, vol. 35, no. 22). Princeton, N.J.: Princeton University Press, 1989.

Bustard, Ned, ed. *It Was Good, Making Art to the Glory of God.* Baltimore, Md.: Square Halo Books, 2000.

Dvorak, Max. *Idealism and Naturalism in Gothic Art.* Trans. with notes and bibliography by Randolph J. Klawiter. Notre Dame, Ind.: University of Notre Dame Press, 1967.

Dyrness, William A. *Rouault, A Vision of Suffering and Salvation.* Grand Rapids, Mich.: William Eerdmans Publishing Co., 1971.

Maritain, Jacques. *Creative Intuition in Art and Poetry* (Bollingen Series, vol. 35, no. 1). New York: Pantheon Books, 1953.

O'Connor, Flannery. *Mystery and Manners: Occasional Prose.* Ed. by Robert and Sally Fitzgerald. New York: Farrar, Straus, and Giroux, 1969.

Pelikan, Jaroslav. *Imago Dei: The Byzantine Apologia for Icons* (Bollingen Series, vol. 35, no. 36). Princeton, N.J.: Princeton University Press, 1990.

Rubin, William S. *Modern Sacred Art and the Church of Assy.* New York and London: Columbia University Press, 1961.

Wolfe, Gregory, ed. *IMAGE, A Journal of the Arts & Religion*, Seattle, Wash.: Center for Religious Humanism, published quarterly.

10

Music Pedagogy and the Christian Faith: A Twenty-Year Journey of Discovery

Charlotte Y. Kroeker

A JOURNEY

MY JOURNEY OF EXPLORING the relationship of faith to the teaching of music began as I was finishing doctoral work and starting to teach piano and music theory in a small Mennonite college in central Kansas. I taught my students what I had learned from my formal education—respect for the score, a sense of historical context, good habits of practice and interpretation, and knowledge of the repertoire. One day a student casually mentioned to me that she was going to play in church that Sunday. When I asked if she would like to play the piece for me, she said it did not matter, as it was "just for church." For this student, because it was "just for church," and "people don't really care what I play," the quality of the music as well as the quality of the performance apparently did not require further attention. I could not have been more shocked. Indeed, this was a defining experience in my professional life. What was I doing, or failing to do, that allowed a student to discredit her church music but take the study of Bach and Chopin very seriously? How could her commitment to serious music fail to be reflected in her practices of worship? Why had my teaching failed to convey to her the importance of music in Christian worship?

Twenty years later I continue to pursue the answers to these questions. During this period I have had the opportunity to see the intersection of the Christian faith and the field of music from many different perspectives. These perspectives include fourteen years of music teaching, seven years of music administration, four years as artist-in-residence at a Presbyterian college, hundreds of performances in a myriad of concert settings, twelve years of service in Episcopalian and Presbyterian churches as minister of music, choir director, and organist, together with academic presentations and publications on musical topics. More recently, a research project on the use of piano in worship and the organization of a national church music conference for pastors, church musicians, and academic musicians have crystallized my awareness of the needs in this field and have led to a longer-term, multidenominational project in church music.

During all these years, the questions have not changed very much. If we have a faith commitment, should that not inform every area of our work and life, including our educational pursuits? In this essay I will indicate some of the insights I have gained during my journey. Of course, neither the journey nor the insights are complete. My suggestions represent a stop along the way. I offer them in the hope they may be of benefit to my fellow travelers.

PERSONAL DILEMMAS OF THE STUDENT MUSICIAN

It may seem a bit odd to begin an essay on faith and learning by addressing concerns about relationships and personal development. But I think this is where we must begin, at least in the field of music. Our discipline is structured to train students by giving them heavy doses of modeling and mentoring. Their successful acquisition of the skills involved in the craft of music making is a prerequisite to the creative process or at least a companion to it. These musical skills are best taught in ways that are analogous to the relationship between apprentice and master. So then, what kind of masters will we be? How can we spend our time most profitably with our students during their four to five years of undergraduate music study? Will they learn Christian ways of being musicians from us? How will they define their faith as musicians? These questions are sobering to a committed,

Christian teacher. Faculty members who are mentors can surely
be highly influential in shaping students' values and orienta-
tions. The way we nurture our students has the potential to affect not only their development as musicians but also their
development as persons and Christians.

Perhaps it is necessary to understand why this is so. Student
development studies indicate that long after the content of a
class is forgotten the more profound influences of the teacher
remain. Indeed, most professional musicians could probably cite
numerous examples (both positive and negative) that illustrate
the lasting impact our own teachers have had on us and on our
colleagues, far beyond the content of their teaching. Our pastoral concerns, our values, our enthusiasms (and eccentricities) do
not go unnoticed. Thus the suggestions that follow will not be
confined solely to practical strategies for implementing a faith-
related pedagogy in the music curriculum. They also will presume a continuing effort on the part of faculty members to understand and live out a faith that is interwoven with their lives
as musicians. They assume a commitment of faculty members to
each other for mutual support and continuing dialogue in this
endeavor. They presuppose a deep commitment to nurturing the
development of their students as whole persons. They recognize
that a faculty member's attention to the coherence of faith and
the music profession may be the very best gift we can give our
students.

An important area to consider for students, and one that is
rather unique to the field of music, is the development of their
gifts of music in the context of their development as persons, as
professionals, and as Christians. The expression of the individual's musical ability and self-perception are closely related. Artists seem particularly vulnerable to stunted, warped, or
debilitating career paths for reasons to be explored shortly. Fortunately, they also have the opportunity to live meaningful,
thoughtful, and unusually multifaceted lives. The direction of
this development, I am convinced, can be strongly influenced
by the relationships music students have with their professors
during their undergraduate years. It is generally understood
that for artists to practice their craft successfully, they must be
sensitive. Sensitive people react to many types of stimuli that

others might not even notice. How they learn to process these stimuli will influence their emotional stability and their ability to function as creative, productive artists. How many of us have known talented artists with skewed personalities that prevented them from attaining a level of achievement that their talent suggested was possible, or worse, prohibited them from being functional at all? Why might this be so?

From my experience, musicians have to deal with situations that other professions avoid or at least seem to encounter less frequently. Learning to deal with these situations is a necessary but tricky part of musicians' training. First, the criteria for evaluation of quality work in the arts are not always clear. Point of view and circumstance can have a great deal of influence in any determination of value and can be far from objective. It may be hard for a student to understand what these judgments mean. Their interpretation by a kind professor can help enormously.

Also, the distinctiveness of individual musical ability can make any evaluation of work seem like an evaluation of personhood. For example, the properties of a person's voice are unique to that person, even though training can affect the way the voice is used. Similarly, the physical characteristics of an instrumentalist will affect the nature of the performance on a particular instrument. While the interpretation of music requires an understanding of style, an appropriate contribution from the individual is still required for it to be successful in its final form. Thus the assessment of a student's talent, performance, or composition can easily be misconstrued as an assessment of personal worth, which can be devastating when the evaluation is negative.

The one-chance character of live performance can be tremendously stressful. Months of intensive practice culminating in one short performance puts enormous emphasis on that performance. For students who have not had years to accumulate performance experiences, the importance of this singular opportunity can be skewed, especially if it does not go well. At the same time, the one-chance character of music is also its glory and can give live performance deep aesthetic and spiritual meaning. It can be one of the most exhilarating experiences of a musician's life. Capturing balance and perspective with regard to performance is a necessary part of the development of a musician.

The capacity of technology to produce recordings that are close to perfection provides a rigorous standard for a student striving for good performance quality. Those students who cannot attend a variety of live performances must rely on recordings as an aural guide to performance. A recording creates unrealistic expectations of perfection not possible in live performance. I have often recounted to my students the story of a conductor and pianist who were listening to the final recorded product after several days of recording one concerto. The various takes and retakes were at last spliced into one consecutive performance. As they listened to the final product, the conductor said to the pianist, "Don't you wish you were really that good?"

Music competitions can be traumatic for talented, sensitive performers in our culture that is so laden with the win-lose metaphors of sports competition. It is difficult to understand that music competitions are often idiosyncratic, and rarely assess accurately either the overall quality of the musicians competing or their ability to contribute to their art over long periods of time.

If a student is a church musician, the relationship between performance ego and service in the church can be difficult to negotiate. How can the natural confidence needed for polished performance be combined with the need for the music to be a vehicle for worship but not the object of it? Even if appropriate self-motivation is achieved, how does one deal with applause or accolades following performance? How can appreciation for the talents of the musician be recognized, while at the same time acknowledging the source, the Creator?

The common difficulty of making a living as a musician calls into question the reasons for giftedness if, at times, there appears to be no means for using it. That is, why is one given talent—and the desire to use it—when there may not be any apparent way to make a living by using that talent?

Finally, the perception that music is play (as in we "play" an instrument) or that it is not a worthy occupation for a Christian can be devastating to a serious student. Equally hazardous is the idea that music is a gift that needs neither study nor discipline. ("You either have talent or you don't.") Our culture tends to view music as entertainment and musicians as entertainers. We would benefit from the inclusion of arts education in the general curriculum both prior to and during college. We should encourage our very best musicians on the faculty to teach music appreciation courses and advocate for a strong arts component in interdisciplinary core courses. The larger malaise of the arts in our society is not an issue the music faculty can ignore. By finding ways to address larger issues when opportunities arise, we provide valuable modeling for students who can do the same in their careers.

At times colleges, seminaries, and churches abandon their responsibilities to identify giftedness and to recognize the need for its expression in many areas. They especially tend to do so in music. While the importance of seminary training for ministers is generally recognized, the parallel importance of training for church musicians, or musical training for ministers, is less often recognized. Although music is a large part of any worship service, an informal approach to music is much more often tolerated than would be acceptable in the pulpit. Colleges, seminaries, and churches generally do not approach church music with the same intentionality that they do pastoral ministry.

In a similar fashion, music programs in the public schools are not afforded the same attention as the rest of the curriculum. Students need to understand that these problems are systemic rather than a negative reflection on their own abilities as musicians. They need creative means to use their gifts in the best possible way. They need our help in discovering ways to express the importance of the arts to those who do not understand them. At the same time, students need to understand that music study can be an invaluable basis for a career in other fields. The traits and skills that build a musician transfer well into a variety of occupations. And music study is equally valid for those not intending a career in music, if only for the discipline and character that it can build.

The personal skills required to be a successful musician demand the hiring of music faculty who are capable of helping students acquire these skills. Clearly, faculty must be personally mature and sufficiently motivated to navigate the complex personal and professional issues faced by musicians. The field of music is somewhat unique in the low student-to-faculty teaching ratio that is necessary for the development of individual skills, giving faculty quality time with students. The demanding music curriculum requires that students spend much of their time in the music facility and with other musicians, both students and faculty. These circumstances present the opportunity for faculty to know their students well, which in turn creates opportunities to help them discover their gifts, to explore the ways their giftedness can be useful to them and to others, and to help them determine their Christian calling. Faculty members who enjoy working together can provide a model of professional collegiality for students. Church-related college music departments seem especially well positioned in this regard. It is my happy observation that good departmental relationships and emotionally balanced faculty are common in church-related colleges. We must treasure our sense of community for the sake of ourselves, our students, our music, and our faith.

FOUNDATIONAL PREMISES FOR FAITH AND MUSIC

Few of us would disagree with Josef Pieper that "music prompts the philosopher's continued interest because it is by its nature *so close to the fundamentals of human existence.*"[1] But the nature of giftedness, its meaning, and its source, need to be clearly understood both by faculty and the students they teach. Elizabeth O'Connor, in her book that addresses giftedness and creativity, is helpful here:

> We ask to know the will of God without guessing that his will is written into our very beings. We perceive that will when we discern our gifts. Our obedience and surrender to God are in large part our obedience and surrender to our gifts. . . . Our gifts are on loan. We are responsible for spending them in the world, and we will be held accountable.[2]

---

[1] Josef Pieper, *Only the Lover Sings: Art and Contemplation* (San Francisco: Ignatius Press, 1990), 39.

[2] Elizabeth O'Connor, *Eighth Day of Creation: Gifts and Creativity* (Waco, Tex.: Word Books, 1971), 15.

She continues,

> Since the first day of our beginning, the Spirit has brooded over
> the formless, dark void of our lives, calling us into existence
> through our gifts until they are developed. And that same Spirit
> gives us the responsibility of investing them with him in the con-
> tinuing creation of the world. Our gifts are the signs of our com-
> missioning, the conveyors of our human-divine love, the
> receptacles of our own transforming, creative power. A primary
> purpose of the Church is to help us discover our gifts and, in the
> face of our fears, to hold us accountable for them so that we can
> enter into the joy of creating.[3]

Could not we argue that, in the case of the talented undergraduate musician, the music department, its faculty, staff, and students, is indeed the Church, insofar as it is charged with the
discovery of gifts? Nicholas Wolterstorff in *Art in Action* speaks
of the responsibility we have for our gifts:

> Whether they be those of the artist who composes or those of the
> public which uses, they are to be actions in which the earth is
> responsibly mastered, actions in which the fulfillment of our-
> selves and others is responsibly served, actions in which God is
> responsibly acknowledged. The artist is not to pick up his respon-
> sibilities when he lays aside his art—he is to exercise his responsi-
> bilities in the very production of his art.[4]

The theological underpinnings for our work as musicians are
usually absent in professional music training but are mandatory
if we intend to see our vocation as musicians in a holistic framework. Richard Viladesau, a priest and professor at Fordham
University, in *Theology and the Arts: Encountering God through
Music, Art and Rhetoric,* makes a convincing case of the manner
in which music gives us access to God in his first chapter entitled, "God and the Beautiful: Art as a Way to God."[5] Calvin Johansson, trained both as a musician and theologian, provides
explanations of the doctrines of creation, the *Imago Dei,* the incarnation, and the concept of mystery and awe in his book *Music*

---

[3] O'Connor, *Eighth Day of Creation,* 17.

[4] Nicholas Wolterstorff, *Art in Action: Towards a Christian Aesthetic* (Grand
Rapids, Mich.: William B. Eerdmans Publishing Co., 1980), 78.

[5] Richard Viladesau, *Theology and the Arts: Encountering God through Music,
Art and Rhetoric* (New York: Paulist Press, 2000), 11–58.

and Ministry: A Biblical Counterpoint.[6] Another direct linkage between theology and the arts is explored in Jeremy Begbie's *Voicing Creation's Praise: Towards a Theology of the Arts.*[7] Dorothy L.
Sayers in *The Mind of the Maker* suggests a Trinitarian view of the
role of the writer that transfers easily to that of the musician:

> Every work of creation is threefold, an earthly trinity to match the
> heavenly. First, there is the Creative Idea, passionless, timeless,
> beholding the whole work complete at once, the end in the begin-
> ning: and this is the image of the Father. Second, there is the Cre-
> ative Energy begotten of that idea, working in time from the
> beginning to the end, with sweat and passion, being incarnate in
> the bonds of matter: and this is the image of the Word. Third,
> there is the Creative Power, the meaning of the work and its re-
> sponse in the lively soul: and this is the image of the indwelling
> Spirit. And these three are one, each equally in itself the whole
> work, whereof none can exist without the other: and this is the
> image of the Trinity.[8]

PROVIDING STUDENTS WITH FOUNDATIONS
AND GROWING OUR OWN

How can these ideas be transmitted to students? First, it is important that music faculty be reading, thinking, and talking with
each other about such weighty matters. This is not an easy or
necessarily a natural task. We are not trained to think philosoph-
ically or theologically when we study in graduate school to be
music historians, conductors, performers, or theorists. We do not
always encounter the riches of intellectual thought prevalent in
other arts and humanities. We are busy honing specific musical
skills! It is easy, therefore, to drift through graduate school and
then through a career as a music professor without really thinking about the reasons or context for our work. But we constantly
need underlying meaning for that work, as do our students. If

---

[6] Calvin M. Johanssen, *Music and Ministry: A Biblical Counterpoint*, 2d ed.
(Peabody, Mass.: Hendrickson Publishers, 1998).

[7] Jeremy Begbie, *Voicing Creation's Praise: Towards a Theology of the Arts* (Edinburgh: T&T Clark, 1991).

[8] Dorothy L. Sayers, *The Mind of the Maker* (San Francisco: Harper & Row,
1987), 37–8.

we expect our students to construct meaningful lives through reflection on their musical studies and performances, we must be in continual reflection and re-creation of our own. Our modeling of thoughtful reflection on vocation, or lack thereof, will translate to our students.

One of my most formative experiences as a young faculty member was the weekly breakfast meeting of the music department at Tabor College. Each Wednesday morning we met to discuss ideas or music that intrigued us, to pray and to plan for our work together at the college. We learned to know each other, to trust each other, and to infuse individual and corporate meaning into our frantically busy lives of teaching, writing, performing, and, of course, recruiting. We supported each other personally and professionally. We provided healthy modeling for the students who learned the importance of community. Because they knew the faculty supported each other, they were encouraged to support each other as well.

Another means of communicating such ideas can be the regular departmental performance class. Early in the semester, when students are not yet ready to perform, or when a visitor to campus is available, opportunities arise to explore topics other than those in the established curriculum. Seminars in the performance field also can address subjects related to specialized fields. Seminars specifically targeted toward freshmen or seniors are another rich opportunity for such reflection. But more important than formal classes is the ability of faculty members to draw on their own conceptual resources when talking with individual students as they sort through what it means to be a musician. Well-thought-out ideas will surface in informal ways when students are struggling with class work, their futures, competition with other musicians, or performance difficulties. They will be empowered to build their lives as musicians in this Christian context, and to establish foundations upon which they will continue to build for the rest of their lives.

TEACHABLE MOMENTS IN THE CURRICULUM:
PEDAGOGICAL CONSIDERATIONS

Most of the following ideas address ways in which religious music and music making can be incorporated into the day-today activity of music study. I would never want to suggest, however, that a musician's life can or should be divided into Christian and non-Christian segments. Professional music and Christian service are frequently seen as two different realms with different standards applied to each, with Christian service considered the only truly Christian realm. On the contrary, church music deserves the highest quality of music—complexity is a separate issue—and high quality of preparation. Are we willing to say that God is deserving of less? But we must also understand, as Dr. Karen DeMol states in reflecting on church music practice, that

> the rest of professional musical life is also Christian service, as part of our use of God's gifts of talent and opportunity to serve others, to serve our culture. All of music-making—the concert and study life as well as service to worship music—is done before the face of the Lord, and is part of our life of worship and service.[9]

Private Lessons

One setting with great possibility for integrating the Christian faith with music is the studio lesson. It is here that teacher and student spend hours honing their craft; it is here that the masterworks are taken apart, put back together, discussed, interpreted, technically mastered. And it is here that teacher and student work week after week and year after year. If a healthy relationship develops, it can be a most wonderful part of nurturing a student toward personal and musical maturity. As part of this ongoing one-to-one relationship, natural opportunities will arise to help the student to know his or her own strengths and weaknesses and to face those honestly and openly in a supportive environment.

It is possible for the student to build a repertoire that can be used in service to others, and particularly in service to the Church. A studio teacher can make sure that students study at least one significant piece of music each semester that could be used in church. Discussion can occur about how that piece could be used. Is it most appropriate for a prelude, an offertory, a post-

---

[9] Personal letter, Karen DeMol to Charlotte Kroeker, October 17, 1998.

lude, communion, a wedding, an Easter celebration, a funeral or memorial service? What are the characteristics that make it appropriate for various parts of a service? Organists and vocalists benefit from a long historical association with the Church and have a standard repertoire that is naturally compatible with music appropriate for church. The rest of us must work a little harder.

For example, the organ-plus literature for organ and instruments (organ and trumpet, organ and brass ensemble, organ and flute, and so on) provides a wealth of repertoire often unexplored by instrumentalists who are studying only their own repertoire. Organ repertoire literature arranges nicely for brass quintet. Slow movements of sonatas, or selected portions of them, can be fine choices for communion or an offertory. Last movements of sonatas can be energetic, rousing postludes. Within the repertoire for each instrument, or repertoire translated from other venues, there will be that basic, serious repertoire that has application for a church service. It serves both for the mastery of the repertoire of the instrument that is a part of the musician's formation and for creating a deposit of music from which the student will draw again and again to use in church. Assisting students in gathering settings of hymn tunes that are finely crafted for the particular instrument they are studying is another valuable opportunity for music faculty to be of service. This repertoire brings questions of validity: music publishing houses can produce these collections voluminously and sometimes with seemingly little regard for quality. But even publications of lesser quality provide an opportunity for students to hone their skills of aesthetic judgment and recognition of quality music. This valuable skill is particularly important at present given our commercially driven religious music industry, as compared to the denominational publishing houses of former years.

It also will be important for students to have opportunities to share the music they study with others. This is true for any developing musician but particularly for Christian students who desire to serve God with their talent. Developing appropriate channels through which students can offer their gifts is a must. The departmental recital hour is the normal venue for performance, but finding others can enhance the performance art, can be a vehicle for service, and often can move a student out into the real world of music making. Church music jobs are sometimes available for students on a part-time basis. Retirement centers are often open to student performances either individually or in groups. Dinner music requests often come the way of the music department office and can be offered to students who can benefit from that experience. (I admit a reluctance to validate dinner music as a legitimate form of music making, but I acknowledge its value for students in need of low-pressure performance opportunities—or cash!) Service clubs need musicians and music for special events. Such windows for service can help students use their gifts and refine their skills.

Students from any one studio or performance area can combine their talents in performance. This can take the form of special performances or it can be informal. For example, one Christmas, my students and I borrowed from the title of Eugenie Rocherolle's lovely collection of intermediate level Christmas carol arrangements, "Christmas Around the Piano."[10] We called it "Twelve Hours of Christmas Around the Piano." We moved the best piano we could find in the student center (this can be challenging!) into the lobby and each of us, professor included, took turns playing non-stop Christmas music from 7:30 A.M. to 7:30 P.M. on one day in December. The event was announced several weeks in advance and members of the campus community planned their lunch hour and other breaks so they could listen to the music. The event itself served a number of purposes. It was a way to help the students develop sight-reading skills while preparing the literature. It also gave them a repertoire of Christmas music for church or other settings. Finally, it became our Christmas musical gift to the campus community. And our endeavor affirmed the performing skills of each participant. Such holidays, communal gatherings, or special events on campus are times when musicians can add to the sense of community and help to set the emotional tone for the event.

---

[10] Eugenie Rocherolle, *Christmas Around the Piano.* (San Diego, Cal.: Neil A. Kjos, 1982).

Performance Groups

Commonly desired goals for performance groups are to develop students' awareness of literature and their ensemble performance skills. A less common goal is to help them develop awareness of how such literature and ensembles could serve the Church, or be used as an expression of the Christian faith. While not all churches have members capable of being soloists, they often have members who can play in an instrumental ensemble, sing in a choir, or perform in small chamber groups. If college performance group conductors select literature that lay church musicians can play or sing, and use rehearsal techniques that illustrate how the piece could be introduced in a church setting with a volunteer group, they will do their students a great service. Students then leave their undergraduate study with repertoire and rehearsal skills they can use with amateur musicians. As part of their tours, student groups often perform in churches. Choral or instrumental settings of hymns are welcome repertoire to a congregation, and academic musicians have access to the finest arrangements. This literature can be programmed for such performances, modeling for students a setting that is most appropriate for its use.

Conductors of performance groups have an enormous effect on the students in the way they present reasons for choosing repertoire, assign solo work or make chair assignments, positively motivate players or singers to excel, and create community within the organization. Conductors are frequently viewed as power brokers by the students. Careful use of that power can model Christian virtues such as fairness, consistency, and charity—characteristics not always found in conductors elsewhere.

Music Theory, History, and Composition

The natural connection between the general history of Western music and the history of music in the Church allows for in-depth exploration of issues of Christianity in the normal course of music study. Prior to the mid-eighteenth century, a preponderance of traditional Western art music was associated with the

Church, first in the Catholic tradition and later in Protestant churches. Additionally, world music can have special significance for Christian colleges. Perhaps there will be personnel from international church organizations who bring music to campus that is used elsewhere in the world. Music of the faith from other cultures gives an alternate window from which to view our own and supplies rich new repertoire for the worship experience. Music history and the history of music in the Church are wonderfully compatible, though texts do not often reflect this compatibility. Standard music history texts can be accompanied by parallel study in the music of the denomination or tradition with which the college or university is affiliated. Since church music texts and practices are often specific to denominations or other identifiable traditions, it is natural to expand the study of music history, literature, or hymnody to include the religious background of the institution where the students are studying music. Many theological traditions have contributed substantially to art music in the religious setting, and to explore and celebrate these contributions enrich and deepen the understanding of the role of the Church in music. For example, a particular denomination's historical development, contemporaneous issues, and theological understandings that affected the music of worship at any one historical moment can be brought into the study of secular music history at relevant points in the course. Why and how, for instance, are there different musical traditions in the Catholic, Lutheran, Calvinist, Methodist, Anabaptist, Pentecostal and Anglican/Episcopalian Churches? Knowing that these differences exist, how can we think more wisely about music in our particular church or denomination?

Hymns are a natural source of repertoire for early study of harmony and composition, providing a rich source of repertoire for analysis. The texts of hymns provide rhythm and form for early composition exercises. While standard music theory texts include hymns and chorales, the hymnal of the denomination of the institution can be used as a supplemental text. It will acquaint the students with the relationship among biblical references, text, meter, and hymn tunes, and will help them understand that music is useful in real life. It also allows the contributions of the college's denomination to be explored in greater depth. Students can thus learn to use a hymnal creatively and appropriately. Examples of good hymns and poor ones can be contrasted. Using good examples first will set a standard; analysis of less satisfactory ones can be introduced gently later. For example, when studying harmonic rhythm, choose a hymn in which the text demands a slower tempo but the harmonic rhythm then grinds to a deadly pace. Re-harmonize this hymn as an individual or class project.

INTERDISCIPLINARY STUDY OF MAJOR WORKS

Exploration of a major religious work from different disciplinary perspectives can be a particularly effective and coherent educational experience for students. Handel's *Messiah* is such a work and may be a wise choice because it is so commonly known and highly regarded. Students will likely encounter this work many times, from choral society performances to annual sing-alongs. Knowing it intimately will be to their advantage. The work has much to recommend it for an undergraduate Christian liberal arts music curriculum. A prime consideration is that the work is textually accessible because it was originally written in English. It is valuable from a Christian point of view because the text is directly from Scripture. The *Messiah* can be done with either a small orchestra or organ (or even piano) and sections can be excerpted. Since it is rarely performed in its entirety, the ability of the singers and instrumentalists can be accommodated by the choice of movements. It is especially appropriate for Christmas or Easter season celebrations. And movements can be used in a variety of settings other than in a performance of the work itself. The work is accessible for analysis as early as first-year music theory and literature classes. It has value for conducting classes because of the inclusion of chorus, recitative, aria, and orchestral accompaniment, for repertoire development of performance groups, and for the study of continuo realization for keyboardists. Movements of the *Messiah* may be appropriate for students who are studying voice privately. Because the text deals with three of the major Christian observances, Christmas, Passion

Week, and Easter, it embodies the heart of Christian belief in a musical setting that has worn well over the ages.

Another example of a major work that can be studied in an interdisciplinary setting is J. S. Bach's *B Minor Mass*. My original study of the work with a Bach scholar was part of a FIPSE[11] project with the goal of creating common texts that crossed disciplines. As a result, the *B Minor Mass* was studied by students in religion classes as a religious text, in literature classes for its literary content, in music appreciation classes for listening acquaintance, and in music theory and literature classes for its musical characteristics, including harmonic, formal, and tone-painting analysis. Because the work is thoroughly religious, it gives an in-depth view of a devout Christian, J. S. Bach, as he gave his life to God through composition, music study, and performance. *Soli Deo Gloria*, as Bach signed his works, has new meaning when a critical study of his *B Minor Mass* is completed. (A friend once said he learned more about how to be a Christian musician by studying Bach than through any other avenue.) Though this work is more complex in many ways than Handel's *Messiah*, it offers a rich example of one of Western culture's most important masses. I used it with great success as a regular part of the curriculum for sophomore-year theory and literature class and scheduled its study during Passion Week for its devotional value.

These are only two examples of how major works with significant religious content could be included in a music curriculum. The particular works cited are not as important as the concept of integrative work that crosses parts of the music curriculum. They have even more value if they can be used in non-music curricula as well. The music will enhance religious experience, and the religious nature of the works will give richness to the study of the music. The broader context for placement of the work in historical or literary perspective will vitally link the study of music to the other liberal arts. Musicians who feel less than qualified to cross into another discipline such as literature or history will be gratified by the response of colleagues in En-

---

[11] Fund for the Improvement of Postsecondary Education, a division of the U.S Department of Education.

glish or history departments. Lecture exchanges with colleagues from another department, or even combining classes to team-teach several sessions when material is similar, provide rich learning environments for students and faculty alike.

OUR CONTEMPORARY CHALLENGE: CHURCH MUSIC

Few trained musicians would disagree that church music has changed over the last quarter-century, though we may not agree about whether the change has been positive. It is hard to know how to approach issues in church music when everyone has an opinion, regardless of whether it is informed. Seminaries rarely train ministers in church music beyond basic hymnody. Fewer and fewer churches offer music programs that consider an historical perspective. A smaller percentage of the general public has an appreciation of art music. Denominations with definable traditions are losing membership to non-denominational movements. Mainline denominations, with their longer history and deeper traditions, are not as influential as they once were. The demise of denominational publishers has created an environment that commercial music publishing houses are eager to replace—the popular Christian music market. Given these conditions, it seems incumbent upon the church-related colleges to give music students, and the general college student population, an understanding of the basic concepts and literature of church music and worship. Until the past few decades the church provided a setting for music composition and performance inspired by spiritual beliefs and informed by the best of music practice and history. Contrary to current trends, the flow between the concert hall and sanctuary, and even the living room and the sanctuary, was a constant for much of Western music history. The elder members of our churches are testimony to this. They have a genuine regard and appreciation for music, and many have participated in music as highly skilled, non-professional performers, in church choirs, as concertgoers, and as collectors of recordings. They have upheld and defended strong music traditions in churches. But with the passing of time, the number of the aesthetically literate has decreased. Simultaneously, pastors increasingly measure their success in terms of the numbers of seekers who populate their pews. As a result, tradition and reflection on the purpose of church music has narrowed to a popular culture ethos: give the people what they like and they will stay. Young, idealistic students are particularly susceptible to this ethos, particularly if they have a serious faith commitment and are interested in evangelism.

Thus, at this juncture in history, I believe that departments of music at church-related colleges and universities can play a critical role in addressing these perplexing issues. Perhaps they are the final hopeful venue—ministers and churches cannot solve the problem alone. Church-related colleges and universities carry on a musical tradition steeped in history and can be thoughtful about faith in intellectual dialogue. Colleagues can help us think through the issues and devise means of resolving these problems. Students can be helped to see the deeper issues at stake. They, in turn, can then influence the larger Church. One practical way to meet the current challenges to our collective Christian musical heritage is to bring together students and faculty leadership teams to design chapel worship services that are thoughtful in their use of music. Unfortunately, on some campuses the gulf between the chapel personnel and the music department is wide, mirroring the gap between historically based church music and what happens each Sunday in some contemporary church services. We must, however, try to bridge the gulf on our campuses. If we cannot, who will? If we are successful, we will involve students in meaningful worship practice and model for them the use of musical gifts for the glory of God. Such a collaboration will also provide opportunities for musically gifted students to offer their gifts to the people of God. As a background for beginning this process, I suggest Calvin Johansson's *Discipling Music Ministry*.[12] Prophetic in nature and honest in confronting issues, Dr. Johansson gives much insight into current dilemmas while suggesting positive alternatives.

Finally, I would issue a call to music faculty members to work together even harder to share best practices, both within the col-

---

[12] Calvin M. Johansson, *Discipling Music Ministry: Twenty-first Century Directions* (Peabody, Mass.: Hendrickson Publishers, 1992).

lege and between colleges, and to encourage each other in the vocation of teaching music at a Christian college. Collegial relationships can be a support in finding strength for the journey. We have much to gain in sharing our insights and pedagogical experience. All of us, as Christian music educators, want to give our students an education that prepares them for a life of meaningful music making. As we listen to each other and to our students and reflect on our task, we may find the voice of God speaking. And then we will find our way.

Selected Bibliography

Alperson, Philip, ed. *What is Music?: An Introduction to the Philosophy of Music.* University Park, Pa.: Pennsylvania State University Press, 1994.

Barnby, Bertram L. *In Concert Sing: Concerning Hymns and Their Usage.* Norwich, U.K.: Canterbury Press, 1996.

Begbie, Jeremy. *Voicing Creation's Praise: Towards a Theology of the Arts.* Edinburgh: T&T Clark, 1991.

Best, Harold M. *Music Through the Eyes of Faith.* San Francisco: HarperCollins, 1993.

Brown, Frank Burch. *Good Taste, Bad Taste, and Christian Taste: Aesthetics in Religious Life.* New York: Oxford University Press, 2000.

Copland, Aaron. *What to Listen for in Music.* New York: McGraw-Hill, 1939.

Faulkner, Quentin. *Wiser than Despair: The Revolution of Ideas in the Relationship of Music and the Christian Church.* Westport, Conn.: Greenwood Press, 1996.

Johansson, Calvin M. *Discipling Music Ministry: Twenty-first Century Directions.* Peabody, Mass.: Hendrickson Publishers, 1992.

———. *Music and Ministry: A Biblical Counterpoint,* 2d ed. Peabody, Mass.: Hendrickson Publishers, 1998.

Jones, Ivor H. *Music: A Joy For Ever.* London: Epworth, 1989.

Klee, Paul. *On Modern Art.* London: Faber and Faber, Ltd., 1962.

L'Engle, Madeleine. *Walking on Water: Reflections on Faith and Art.* Wheaton, Ill.: Harold Shaw Publishers, 1980.

O'Connor, Elizabeth. *Eighth Day of Creation: Gifts and Creativity.* Waco, Tex.: Word Books, 1971.

O'Connor, Flannery. *Mystery and Manners.* New York: Farrar, Straus and Giroux, 1969.

Pieper, Josef. *Only the Lover Sings: Art and Contemplation.* San Francisco: Ignatius Press, 1990.

Routley, Erik. *Church Music and the Christian Faith.* Carol Stream, Ill.: Agape, 1978.

Sayers, Dorothy L. *The Mind of the Maker.* San Francisco: Harper & Row, 1987.

Viladesau, Richard. *Theological Aesthetics: God in Imagination, Beauty and Art.* New York: Oxford University Press, 1999.

———. *Theology and the Arts: Encountering God through Music, Art and Rhetoric.* New York: Paulist Press, 2000.

Westermeyer, Paul. *The Church Musician.* New York: Harper & Row, 1988.

———. *Te Deum: The Church and Music.* Minneapolis: Fortress Press, 1998.

Wolterstorff, Nicholas. *Art in Action: Towards a Christian Aesthetic.* Grand Rapids, Mich.: William B. Eerdmans Publishing Co., 1980.

Part Four
The Humanities

11

An Ignatian Approach to Teaching Philosophy

Elizabeth Murray Morelli

THE PURPOSE of this volume of essays is to gather practical pedagogical strategies that may be of use to professors in religiously affiliated universities and colleges. I have been asked to reflect upon how issues of faith and issues raised by faith are woven into the teaching of my courses. I have been teaching philosophy at Loyola Marymount University for over a decade. During that time I have developed a number of approaches and assignments that seem effective. Because I am a professor of philosophy at a Jesuit university, my approach to teaching has been strongly influenced by the Ignatian ideal of pedagogy. The influence of this ideal on my teaching has been subtle and gradual and, until recently, implicit. I was a product, beneficiary, and instrument of the Ignatian spirit that pervades Jesuit education before I became aware of the explicit ideal of Jesuit education. Because the context of my undergraduate education and my teaching is Jesuit higher education, it might be helpful to review the general outlines of this influence on my pedagogy.

THE IGNATIAN HERITAGE

"St. Ignatius was aware of the wide cultural impact of universities and chose to send Jesuits there, as places where a more universal good might be achieved."[1] This basic Ignatian commit-

---

[1] "Decree Seventeen: Jesuits and University Life," *Documents of the Thirty-Fourth General Congregation of the Society of Jesus* (St. Louis, Mo.: The Institute of Jesuit Sources, 1995), 189.

ment to higher education has been affirmed throughout Jesuit history. In the words of University of Central America President Ignacio Ellacuria, S.J., "A university is inescapably a social force; it must transform and enlighten the society in which it lives."[2] In an amazingly short time, Ignatius and his companions founded a number of schools in Europe—thirty-five by the time of Ignatius's death in 1556. By 1640, the centenary of the founding of the order, there were three hundred Jesuit institutions of higher education. Currently, there is a network of two hundred Jesuit schools worldwide, including the twenty-eight Jesuit colleges and universities in the United States. "Someone once quipped of Jesuits that if two arrived in a new town in the morning, one had a high school started by noon, the other a college by dark, and both taught in the night school after dinner."[3]

The ideal and basic principles of Jesuit education were first formulated by Ignatius of Loyola and his companions in the Society of Jesus in the sixteenth century. They have been reformulated and affirmed in official documents of the Jesuit order in the twentieth century. The best source for the explicit and direct thought of Ignatius on the apostolate of education can be found in the *Constitutions* (specifically, the revised version of the fourth part) of the Society of Jesus, which Ignatius composed in the last years prior to his death in 1556. In this document, Ignatius developed the ideal of *magis* (the more). It is not sufficient to do well, one must strive to do better. This striving always to do better is not for self-aggrandizement but *ad majorem Dei gloriam* (for the greater glory of God). The ideal is to educate the whole person, to form men and women of competence, conscience, and compassion for the service of others.[4] The spirit of Ignatius, captured in his *Spiritual Exercises*, was reflected in his idea of the teacher. He modeled the relationship between teacher and student on the relationship between the director of the *Exercises*

[2] Jon Sobrino, S.J., *Companions of Jesus: The Jesuit Martyrs of El Salvador* (Maryknoll, N.Y.: Orbis Books, 1990), 149.

[3] David G. Schultenover, S.J., *The Ethos of Jesuit Education: Ignatius to Hopkins to Ellacuria* (Omaha, Neb.: Creighton University Press, 1997), 11.

[4] Peter-Hans Kolvenbach, S.J., "Ignatian Pedagogy Today" (April 29, 1993) in Carl E. Meirose, S.J., ed., *Foundations*, 260–69 (Washington: Jesuit Secondary Education Association, 1994), 265.

and the person making them. The teacher must get to know the student personally so as to aid the student's moral and religious as well as intellectual development. Ignatius also viewed the teacher as a role model, to use today's parlance. In the fourth part of the *Constitutions*, Ignatius places the *"teacher's personal example* ahead of learning and rhetoric as an apostolic means to help students grow in values."[5]

The Jesuit ideal of critical engagement with the secular culture reflected the basic premise of the Renaissance humanist tradition that religious and moral inspiration could be found in secular subjects, even in the works of pagan authors. The earliest Jesuit schools were inspired by the lived experience of the *Spiritual Exercises* and modeled on the course of studies and methods of the University of Paris. In 1599 an international committee of Jesuits completed the definitive version of the *Ratio Studiorum*, a handbook to assist teachers and administrators of Jesuit schools. In the preface to the *Ratio*, Francesco Sacchini, S.J., remarks, "Among us the education of youth is not limited to imparting the rudiments of grammar, but extends simultaneously to Christian formation."[6]

The directives of the *Ratio* not only outline general objectives, but also detail specific approaches. One directive that may be of interest to anyone who has labored on a curriculum committee regards the structure of the overall curriculum: "The curriculum should be so integrated that each individual course contributes toward the overall goal of the school."[7] Other directives focus on procedures in the classroom. The following directive, for example, sounds like a sixteenth-century lesson plan for a critical thinking course: "The pedagogy is to include analysis, repetition, active reflection, and synthesis; it should combine theoretical ideas with their applications."[8] One that I particularly like, because the end of the semester seems to sneak up on me sooner and sooner every year states that "It is not the quantity of course

---

[5] Ibid.

[6] Ibid., 263.

[7] The International Commission on the Apostolate of Jesuit Education, "Go Forth and Teach: The Characteristics of Jesuit Education" (1987), 129–68 in Meirose, *Foundations*, 152.

[8] Ibid.

material covered that is important but rather a solid, profound, and basic formation."⁹

In 1986 the International Commission on the Apostolate of Jesuit Education produced a document titled "Go Forth and Teach," outlining twenty-eight distinctive, but not necessarily unique, characteristics of Jesuit education. While the direct focus of this document is secondary education, its principles are applicable with some modification to college and university education. Some of the principles address administrative policies; others regard specifically the religious formation of students. The following principles are those I consider most applicable to Jesuit institutions of higher education in the United States today and that may be helpful to colleagues in other church-related colleges and universities.

The first set of principles state the foundational premises: Jesuit education is "world-affirming; assists in the total formation of each individual within the human community; includes a religious dimension that permeates the entire education; is an apostolic instrument; and promotes dialogue between faith and culture."¹⁰ In relation to knowledge of self and world, Jesuit education is "value-oriented, encourages a realistic knowledge, love and acceptance of self; and provides a realistic knowledge of the world in which we live."¹¹ In relation to students, it "insists on individual care and concern for each person; emphasizes activity on the part of the student; and encourages lifelong openness to growth."¹² Regarding service orientation, Jesuit education "prepares students for active participation in the church and the local community for the service of others; is a preparation for active life commitment; serves the faith that does justice; seeks to form 'men and women for others;' and manifests a particular concern for the poor."¹³ In terms of a community of learning, it "relies on a spirit of community, and takes place within a structure that promotes community."¹⁴ In sum, the ideal of Jesuit ed-

---

⁹ Ibid., 153.
¹⁰ Ibid., 134.
¹¹ Ibid., 139.
¹² Ibid., 137.
¹³ Ibid., 141, 144.
¹⁴ Ibid., 147.

ucation is "the well-rounded person who is intellectually competent, open to growth, religious, loving, and committed to doing justice in generous service to the people of God."[15] This entire endeavor is to be carried out in the above-mentioned spirit of the *magis*: it "pursues excellence in its work of education and formation, and creates an ambiance, which will promote excellence"[16]

More recently, the Thirty-fourth General Congregation of the Society of Jesus in 1995 formulated decrees for the guidance of members of the order including directives and suggestions regarding higher education. The *Documents of the Thirty-Fourth General Congregation of the Society of Jesus*[17] deal directly with the changing role of Jesuits in the universities they founded and in higher education in general. The *Documents* encourage Jesuits to continue to engage in their traditional work in higher education and to respond creatively to current challenges. Specifically, they are encouraged to respond to the challenge of the changing structure of universities: "Jesuits must continue to work hard, with imagination and faith and often under very difficult circumstances, to maintain and even to strengthen the specific character of each of our institutions both as *Jesuit* and as a *university*."[18] Regarding the institution *qua* university, Decree 17 affirms "a commitment to the fundamental autonomy, integrity, and honesty of a university precisely as a university: a place of serene and open search for and discussion of the truth."[19] Regarding the institution *qua* Jesuit, the decree further strongly affirms a commitment to fostering the Jesuit identity and mission of any Jesuit university: "A Jesuit university can and must discover in its own proper institutional forms and authentic purposes a specific and appropriate arena for the encounter with the faith which does justice."[20] A Jesuit university has as its central ideal the unfettered pursuit of truth in all fields integrated with a faith that does justice. The reaffirmation in the twentieth

---

[15] Ibid., 143.
[16] Ibid., 145.
[17] See note 1.
[18] "Jesuits and University Life," 191.
[19] Ibid.
[20] Ibid., 192.

century of the need for critical engagement with the culture simply continues the spirit of the very first Jesuit colleges in which students studied subjects ranging from philosophy and theology to astronomy and classical ballet.

How does this Ignatian ideal actually work itself out in the daily life of the present-day Jesuit university in the United States? In the past two decades numerous national meetings, conventions, institutes, commissions, and publications have been devoted to just this question. I will not attempt to summarize the results of these ongoing conversations here. Even a description of how the Ignatian ideal operates concretely at Loyola Marymount is beyond the scope of the practical purposes of this volume. I will therefore, limit my remarks to how the Ignatian ideal of pedagogy has influenced my own teaching. First, however, I would like to recount how the Ignatian spirit subtly infiltrated my outlook to operate as an implicit ideal of my pedagogy.

THE IGNATIAN IDEAL: A PERSONAL HISTORY

I came under the influence of the Ignatian ideal of pedagogy in at least three ways before it became explicit for me. First, as an undergraduate at Santa Clara University, I breathed the atmosphere of the Jesuit tradition. I encountered models of compassion and genuine concern; I was encouraged to pursue the disinterested love of learning for its own sake; and I enjoyed the true freedom to develop in a converted community. As I read now the directives for teachers set forth in the *Ratio* of 1591, I discover that I had the good fortune to be taught by a master of Ignatian pedagogy, Timothy Fallon, S.J. I thought his concern and love for me as his student was unique, but I understand now that his profound influence on my intellectual, moral, and religious development was exactly in line with the Ignatian ideal of the teacher. In his attention to students, Father Fallon exemplified one of the overriding principles of Jesuit pedagogy, namely, *"alumnorum cura personalis* (a genuine love and personal care for each of our students).''[21] What was unique, perhaps, was

---

[21] Kolvenbach, "Ignatian Pedagogy Today," 265.

his excellence and total dedication as a teacher. He undermined my half-baked preconceptions and repeatedly challenged me to self-transcendence and personal commitment. In short, he transformed a student floundering for meaning into graduate-school material. A community of students formed around him and his philosophy classes. As an indication of his influence, six of us from that one group of friends went on to pursue graduate studies. The pedagogical finesse of Father Fallon provided an unforgettable model of teaching excellence.

My second indirect introduction to the Ignatian ideal of pedagogy was through my encounter with the thought of the twentieth-century philosopher and theologian Bernard Lonergan, S.J. I was first introduced to Lonergan's philosophy at Santa Clara University. Lonergan's thought was the focus of my graduate studies in philosophy. I had the opportunity to attend a number of Father Lonergan's formal talks and workshops, to meet with him occasionally, to take one of his graduate courses, and to edit and publish a set of his lectures under his direction.[22] My philosophic pursuits have introduced me to many other thinkers, but none have had the profound and continuing impact of Lonergan on the methodology and direction of my own work. I was not attracted to Lonergan's work because he was a Jesuit, or even a Catholic, but because he directly addressed my own philosophic questions.

As I learn more about the Jesuit tradition, I am discovering just how consonant Lonergan's work is with the overall Ignatian spirit.[23] His central notion of the self-appropriation of one's own rational self-consciousness is continuous with the Ignatian aim of growth in self-reflection and discernment in the *Spiritual Exercises*. Lonergan's focus on method can be seen as the full blossoming of the pedagogical directives of the early Jesuits. His articulation of the three kinds of conversion—intellectual, moral, and religious—and the centrality of values to his thought, echo

---

[22] Lonergan, Bernard, S.J., *Understanding and Being: The Halifax Lectures on Insight*, edited by Elizabeth A. Morelli and Mark D. Morelli (1980), revised by Frederick E. Crowe (Toronto: University of Toronto Press, 1990).

[23] For an introduction to the works of Bernard Lonergan, S.J., see Mark D. Morelli and Elizabeth A. Morelli, eds., *The Lonergan Reader*, (Toronto: University of Toronto Press, 1997).

the concerns of both pre- and post-Vatican II Jesuits. Lonergan's integration of developments in post-Einsteinian science into his worldview and his treatments of developmental and depth psychology, historical theory, and hermeneutics exemplify critical engagement with the culture. His lifelong concern with fundamental problems in economics reveals his commitment to justice and his concern for the systemic plight of the poor. These examples may suffice to demonstrate how a prolonged study of Lonergan's thought might tend to imbue one with Ignatian concerns.

Finally, when I began teaching at Loyola Marymount, I found a spirit of faculty cooperation and encouragement quite different from the atmosphere of my graduate school. It took me a few years to begin to unlearn the habit of guarded suspicion and the expectation of self-interested competition. Similarly, after years in a secular environment, I was pleasantly surprised in classroom discussions and student essays by unabashed remarks by students concerning their faith, love of God, grace, or prayer. I began to realize that I did not have to exclude serious reference to the transcendent in my philosophy courses. I found myself in an academic community, ethnically and religiously diverse but unified by a subtle Ignatian spirit. It was some time before the change in atmosphere was reflected in my teaching.

THE IGNATIAN IDEAL AND PEDAGOGICAL APPLICATIONS

Over the past several years, I have been drawn into discussions on the mission and identity of Loyola Marymount. This has led me to pursue the question of the nature of Jesuit higher education, and further to pursue the question of the nature of church-related higher education in general. In the process, I have become aware of certain catch phrases that recur in conversations, addresses, and readings—"educating the whole person," "forming men and women for others," and "finding God in all things." These are not the only key notions, nor do they necessarily represent the most important Ignatian aims, but they are the ones that most readily capture the intent in my courses.

Prior to the recent establishment of our philosophy graduate program, I have been teaching lower- and upper-division under-graduate courses in philosophy. Two of the courses I teach regularly are required for all Loyola Marymount students— Philosophy of Human Nature, a lower-division introductory course; and Ethics, an upper-division course. I also teach upper division courses in Ancient Greek Philosophy, Lonergan, Phenomenology, and Existentialism. In all of these courses, my underlying aim is to aid in the self-appropriation of the students—to "educate the whole person." This self-appropriation includes growth in understanding their own moral characters and responsibility, and so it aids in their development as "men and women for others." Materials for study in my courses include the works of major philosophers in the Christian tradition as well as the thought of non-Christians and atheists. My students are invited to reflect upon high intellectual achievements in the history of thought and on dimensions of popular culture. In this way, I set up the opportunity for them to follow the Ignatian ideal of "finding God in all things."

As a philosophy teacher, I am primarily concerned with students familiarizing themselves with their own intellectual life. I do not consider this focus to be alienated from moral, social, political, or religious concerns. Awakening students to the history of the discovery of mind and to their own desire to know— their own wonder and critical doubt—aids in the development of virtuous habits of the mind and the heart. In Philosophy of Human Nature, I focus on the role of wonder in the advancement of thought from the pre-Socratics to St. Thomas and in the role of doubt from Descartes to contemporary thinkers.

In one such course recently, a young woman from south central Los Angeles came to see me during office hours. She did not have a problem with the quizzes or with her essays; she was doing well in class. She told me that she was the first in her extended family and in her neighborhood to attend college. She was a single mother on welfare as were her mother, her two aunts, and her grandmother. She told me how she had always asked questions, how she yearned to understand more, to read and to learn more. Her aspirations were denigrated by her friends and family. They called her "uppity" and worse and more or less ostracized her. But she did not come to my office to complain. She came as one struck with an amazing self-discovery—that this wonder, this infinite desire to know, this *eros* described by Plato, Aristotle, and St. Thomas was her own desire and motivation.

The moral relativism that Allan Bloom decried in *The Closing of the American Mind* seems to be more pervasive with each group of incoming freshmen. On the first day of class in my Ethics courses, I ask students to fill out a sheet with their name, major, previous familiarity with philosophy, and the answer to two questions: "Can we really know what is right?" and "Are we free, or are we determined?" Ninety percent of the students respond that no one can say what is right or good. It is all relative. Yet, just as many typically respond that each of us is free to decide what to do. The consensus seems to be that we do not know what to do, but we are definitely free to do it anyway. I save these initial responses, which are normally quite definitive in tone, and return them to the students after we have dealt thoroughly with the problems of relativism and determinism.

In dealing with moral relativism, I tell them a story that always generates much discussion. In the seventies, a graduate student in anthropology reportedly traveled to the Amazon and lived with a previously undiscovered aboriginal group. He adopted their lifestyle as much as possible, while secretly recording their practices. After living with them for nearly a year and developing their trust, he was invited to partake in an initiation ritual to become a member of their tribe. He felt honored and agreed to join in the elaborate preparations. He engaged in ritual intoxication and dancing, in the hunting and killing of a neighboring tribesman, and in the festive, cannibalistic meal that followed. Afterwards he stole away from his newly adopted community, returned to New York, and wrote a stunning dissertation. When one of the examiners at his oral defense questioned how he could have engaged in murder and cannibalism, he responded, "Don't worry. I wouldn't do that in Manhattan." I ask my students to interpret his response and to determine whether they think his actions were defensible. The discussion that follows is invariably lively. Cultural relativists adamantly defend the actions of the tribesmen in their own culture, and extreme relativists argue that the graduate student's actions were equally justified: "When in Rome. . . ." A few brave souls venture to suggest that his actions were wrong for various reasons, not the least being that he betrayed the trust of his newly adopted tribe. At this point, the class is engaged. The issue of moral relativism has become more than simply academic. One purpose of this exercise is to help the students become aware of the moral positions they already assume.

Helping students to get in touch with their own questioning and more importantly with the notion that there is actually something to be known, that all knowledge and value judgments are not subjective or relative, that there is truth, and that it is possible to reach objectivity even in moral matters, counteracts a pervasive sense of futility. Once awakened, a basic intellectual hope can lead to increased academic interest and effort. I also challenge students to admit that they do in fact know certain things to be true, that they can make objective judgments. This requires the risk of commitment and so a degree of courage. I tell my students, for example, that the phrase "Who is to say?" is not an acceptable response or conclusion in my class; that it is simply a verbal shrug of the shoulders; and that, as future leaders in the community, they are the "ones to say."

A number of virtues can be encouraged in the classroom. And, as Aristotle warns, such encouragement is critical: "It is no small matter whether one habit or another is inculcated in us early on; on the contrary, it makes a considerable difference, or, rather, all the difference."[24] In addition to hope and courage, I will mention one more—humility. In line with the phrase, "finding God in all things," I encourage students to seek the truth in the works of whichever thinker we study. I invariably need to remind students that just because they were born in the late twentieth century, they cannot assume that they have surpassed thinkers of the past. When I introduce the pre-Socratics, I try to help students recapture the sense of wonder they felt as little children asking about the world. In one such lecture, I invite the students to put themselves back into a naive frame of mind, and ask the basic question "What is everything made of?" I usually receive

---

[24] Aristotle, *Nicomachean Ethics* II.1 (1103b20–25), translated by Martin Ostwald (Indianapolis: Bobbs-Merrill, 1962), 34–35.

the semi-educated response, "Molecules or atoms." Not long ago, a student, newly arrived in the United States from his home in an Indonesian fishing village, responded, "Water." When I proceeded to introduce the thought of Thales, students did not react with the typical derision directed towards the thought of the ancients.

The education of the whole person involves, then, the appropriation of the students' own intelligence and rationality, an introduction to or a heightening of historical consciousness, and the fostering of appropriate attitudes regarding their own present achievement and capabilities. College-age students are perhaps most ready to appropriate the moral dimension of themselves. The Ethics course and especially the Existentialism course I teach are geared to the student's appropriation of his or her own moral consciousness. In my classes, this involves learning about conscience, moral reasoning, feelings and values, choice, anxiety, commitment, responsibility, self-constitution, and moral conversion. In addition to introducing the ethical theories and principles of thinkers such as Aristotle, Kant, Mill, Scheler, Kierkegaard, and Lonergan, I integrate a reflective component into assignments and examinations.

In Ethics, after dealing with issues of relativism and determinism, we study Aristotle's notion of virtue and vice. I have developed two assignments that require reflection on one's own moral character. The first is a one-night homework assignment. I ask the students to make a complete chart of the virtues and their corresponding vices described by Aristotle in his *Nicomachean Ethics*. Then, I challenge them to add to this list any virtues not mentioned by Aristotle that they consider to be significant. This simple assignment opens the door to a major discussion of the difference between our Judeo-Christian culture and that of the ancient Greeks. Aristotle does not describe compassion or patience, for example, not to mention the modern virtues of punctuality or efficiency. As the course proceeds, the students become more aware of the difference between ancient Greek morality and Christian morality. I take this opportunity to challenge them further by introducing Nietzsche's defense of the spirit of ancient morality. Nietzsche charges that Christianity is simply a slave revolt in morality, the flower of *ressentiment*. The effort to differentiate their virtues and values from those of the ancient Greeks, and then to defend Christian virtues and values as truly good and not corrupt, effects a deeper appreciation of their own Christian heritage.

I also ask the students to write an essay on how one becomes virtuous (or vicious), and to describe a person who exemplifies for them the virtuous (or vicious) person. Students have written fascinating accounts of everyone from César Chávez, Mohandas Gandhi, Martin Luther King, Jr., Mother Teresa, and Oprah Winfrey as heroes to Idi Amin, Andrew Cunanin, Mike Tyson, and 'George' on *Seinfeld* as villains. Occasionally, the same individual will be the epitome of virtue for one student and the epitome of vice for another. This assignment tests their comprehension of Aristotle's account of virtue and uncovers their own heroes and the values they represent. Even students who are struggling with the theoretical rigor of a philosophy class readily apply themselves to rich descriptions of their heroes. By acknowledging the admiration they feel for these exemplars, students are appropriating the structure of their own hearts, discovering what is important to them.

In my Existentialism course, I assign a philosophic journal, which is to consist of the student's reflections on the lectures and the readings. Invariably, some one issue central to the student's intellectual, moral, and religious development crystallizes in the course of these reflections. The underlying question is often one of faith. This is perhaps a function of the challenge of reading Kierkegaard in conjunction with Nietzsche and Sartre. Students who come into the class with an unquestioning acceptance of their religious background are sometimes shocked and challenged by the views of Nietzsche and Sartre. On the other hand, those who come to the course with the rebelliousness of the atheistic neophyte are challenged by Kierkegaard's insistence on the self's essential relation to God. The discussions in class and, especially, the more private reflections in their journals manifest their ongoing struggle with their relation to God. For a final examination essay, I ask them to provide a critique of Kierkegaard's views from the standpoint of Nietzsche or Sartre and a critique of Nietzsche's or Sartre's views from the standpoint of Kierkegaard. This strategy requires that they not only understand each philosopher's basic categories and distinctions but that they write from a perspective with which they themselves disagree.

Another issue that is of particular importance to students of college age is commitment in personal relationships. In the Ethics course, we read Aristotle's treatment of the three basic forms of friendship and what is meant by true self-love. Students are too familiar with so-called friends who are only friends of pleasure or utility. They are particularly disturbed by Aristotle's notion of the friendship between unequals, because most insist that everyone is equal. This opens the door to a discussion of envy and competitiveness in our society and in their own relationships. We also discuss Aristotle's claim that human beings cannot be in a friendship with the gods. This raises the issue of the basic difference between the ancient Greek notion of love as *eros* and the Christian ideal of love as *agapē*.

In the Existentialism course, I address the issue of relationships and forms of love through Kierkegaard's "Diary of the Seducer" and his account of romantic versus conjugal love in *Either/Or*. Class discussion can be quite revealing and surprising to students. One student, for example, declared that he could never commit to any one woman, because she could always lose her looks in a few years. The film *Enemies: A Love Story* illustrates the difference between romantic and conjugal love, and it focuses on the fundamental issue of free will and the need to make a commitment. Existential thinkers provide the terms with which students can express their anxiety in facing the decisions they must make about relationships and careers. Students sometimes use the course itself as an occasion for making decisions. Students will shear off, grow out, or radically dye their hair, grow or shave off facial hair, or appear with new tattoos or body piercings. More seriously, a student once came to me with the idea that he should break off his engagement and put an end to the wedding plans underway, even though he claimed still to be in love and the invitations had already been sent. He earnestly desired to become a genuine Knight of Faith by renouncing what was dearest to him, as Kierkegaard had done with Regina!

Such situations remind us of the responsibility we have as teachers in the formation of our students. Fortunately, the responsibility we bear is limited. While I have a role in helping my students practice certain activities to develop certain intellectual and moral virtues, I am aware that it is a small role. I am only one of their many teachers, and university professors are not the greatest influence on their lives. I realize that I can help only so much, and I have had occasion to refer students to campus ministry or to counseling services. To paraphrase a saying with popular currency, it takes a whole university to educate a whole person. I might add, it also takes a whole person to educate a whole person.

One great advantage of teaching topics in metaphysics, ethics, and epistemology is that such fundamental subject matter is flexible in application. A deeper meaning almost always can be found in the familiar and mundane. A philosopher has objectification of the everyday in common with a stand-up comedian. In the spirit of "finding God in all things," I use whatever authors, texts, films, news stories, and personal anecdotes may assist in the student's self-appropriation. Diagramming the relations of terms on the board is useful for student notes, but it is stories and anecdotes that best facilitate their insights into the material. I draw upon my own experience for anecdotes to illustrate points. In addition to films, I occasionally use short stories to illustrate the subject matter for discussion and reflection. Finally, I integrate current events into class discussion and assignments. Often on final examinations it is the details of these stories that students, even those who are struggling in the course, recall most exactly.

I often draw upon examples from concrete experience in my lectures. As an Ethics professor, I have the advantage of having a sister who is a cardiac care nurse in a major hospital. Her sometimes harrowing stories have provided a number of dilemmas and situations to analyze. To apply Kant's and Scheler's principles, I present the following case. A forty-year-old woman, mother of three school-age children, was putting her groceries in the car one afternoon, when she suddenly dropped to the ground in cardiac arrest. Paramedics rushed her to the hospital, and she ended up in my sister's unit. The hospital's most respected cardiac surgeon had recently been successful in procuring a state-of-the-art heart monitor for that unit at great expense to the hospital. The woman had the fortune to be hooked up to this most advanced monitor. My sister was walking past the woman's bed when she noticed all the signs of cardiac arrest. My sister immediately called a code and hospital personnel rushed in, including the surgeon who had persuaded the hospital to buy the monitor. After they administered the emergency drugs and shocked the woman's heart back to a normal rhythm, my sister mentioned to the doctor that the monitor had malfunctioned. He did not believe her and insisted that the machine must have functioned properly. To prove the point, he applied pressure to the woman's neck with his gloved fingers and induced another arrest. Those attending immediately repeated the lifesaving procedures and were able to revive the woman. The machine again malfunctioned as my sister had described. The doctor became more irate. He proceeded to induce yet another cardiac arrest in the woman to retest the monitor. The woman did ultimately survive.

It is not difficult for students to apply Kant's practical imperative to this case—the patient was clearly being treated as a means, not an end. But I also point out to the students how they reacted as I told the story. Students typically gasp and shake their heads before we have even begun to analyze the case. This gives them a concrete experience of Scheler's point that the heart responds to values and disvalues before the mind articulates reasons. With this exercise, I attempt to aid the students in the appropriation of their spontaneous affectivity. Despite avowed moral relativism, students do react spontaneously to injustice.

In discussions and assignments, I sometimes employ short stories and films to provide images for student's understanding and application of principles. For example, when we study Plato's account of the death of Socrates in the *Phaedo*, I have the students read Sartre's "The Wall" for comparison and contrast. Both Socrates and Sartre's character Pablo have been tried and sentenced to death unfairly, both face execution in a few hours, and both men have companions with whom to interact. But, the differences in their attitudes, responses, and actions in this situation are both subtle and profound. Socrates is a devoutly religious man who knows on the basis of faith and reason that he will survive death. Pablo is a materialist and atheist, whose ultimate horizon is death. I ask students to reflect upon the difference that one's understanding of the soul or self has on one's approach to death and on one's interactions with others.

When I use film for the sake of class discussion or essays, I have the students view the film outside of class. Screening films takes up too much valuable class time. I have had students apply the principles of Kant, Mill, and Scheler to the question of capital punishment using the case portrayed in *Dead Man Walking* and to the question of euthanasia using the film *The English Patient*.

As the occasion warrants, I will also employ current events and topical issues as pedagogical opportunities. While we were experiencing the series of Northridge earthquakes, I asked students in my Phenomenology class to write a phenomenology of an earthquake. This exercise required self-reflection on their immediate experience, which is an aid to self-appropriation. When the verdict in the O. J. Simpson criminal case made the news, the atmosphere on campus was charged. Students gathered in the commons to watch the outcome on television. There were groups of students cheering on campus. In my classes students were self-conscious and polarized. We were studying Plato's *Republic* at the time, so I passed out clippings of remarks regarding justice made by key attorneys in the case. Our detached analysis of the various notions of justice helped to defuse tensions in the class. Similarly, I used news of the mass suicide of the Applewhite cult to have the students reflect on what it means to doubt and to be critical. We were working on Descartes's *Meditations* at the time. I had them write a fictional response to Mr. Applewhite, as if he had invited them personally to join his group. The letter was to provide a critique of his views and students' reasons for declining his invitation. At the time of the news story, there also happened to be a problem with a cult vigorously pursuing students on campus, and I knew that at least two of my students had attended these cult meetings.

There is a tradition in Jesuit education of critical, even countercultural engagement with one's sociopolitical world. Perhaps the most dramatic instance of such critical engagement was the November 1989 executions of six Jesuits and their two housekeepers at the University of Central America in San Salvador by members of the Salvadoran military. There are many social, political, economic, and environmental issues that warrant such countercultural engagement in the universities and colleges in this country. For one local example, the Los Angeles riots were a dramatic occasion for reflection on problems of the inner city and the tensions of changing demographics. The diversity in Los Angeles is reflected in the student body of Loyola Marymount University. There is also economic diversity, from very wealthy students to those holding down two jobs to support themselves and stay in school. I have students who are the children of famous Hollywood figures or who are themselves young film stars sitting next to exiles from the impoverished, war-torn mountains of Central America and children of migrant farm workers sitting next to children of the CEOs of multinational corporations. There is also a small but growing number of openly gay students in classes.

I generally do not address racial or sexual orientation issues directly in my classes, because I have found that such discussions tend to make members of the minority in question uncomfortably self-conscious. I do integrate into my lectures some reflection on the attitude toward women in the history of thought. I can use myself as an example in these cases. The central focus of all of my courses is what is universal in all persons regardless of religious, economic, gender, sexual, or racial differences. I work toward elaborating the foundations of our common ground. I believe that the respect I show to each student regardless of differences and the students' own collaboration in class discussions and group projects contribute indirectly to a growing respect students have for each other. Not every subject matter and course allows for the flexibility I enjoy in my philosophy courses. Yet I think the demands of distinct disciplines can be met and the distinct subject matter enriched through reflection upon the social and political situation, popular culture, the arts, current events, and the professor's own personal experience.

Finally, the Ignatian principle of "finding God in all things" has a deeper significance than finding metaphysical, epistemological, and ethical meaning in the world around us. It expresses the distinctively Catholic awareness of the sacramentality of the world. It is the sense that ultimately all things are manifestations of Mystery, that in the words of the Jesuit poet Gerard Manley Hopkins, "There lives the dearest freshness deep down things." My aim is to encourage students beyond a one-dimensional self-understanding. Ultimately, I hope to contribute to their developing awareness of the divine undercurrent of the everyday and to provide them with the critical tools necessary to discriminate between the nonsensical and the intelligible, the ridiculous and the rational, the purely selfish and the self-transcending.

SELECTED BIBLIOGRAPHY

Buckley, Michael J., S.J., ed. *Faith, Discovery, Service: Perspectives on Jesuit Education.* Milwaukee: Marquette University Press, 1992.

Byrne, Patrick H. "Paradigms of Justice and Love." *Conversations on Jesuit Higher Education*, no. 7 (spring 1995): 5–17.

Cunningham, Lawrence S. "Gladly Wolde He Lerne and Gladly Teche: The Catholic Scholar in the New Millennium." *The Cresset*, vol. 55, no. 7B (June 1992): 4–10.

Curran, Charles E. "The Elusive Idea of a Catholic University." *National Catholic Reporter* (October 1986): 12–15.

Documents of the Thirty-Fourth General Congregation of the Society of Jesus. St. Louis, Mo.: The Institute of Jesuit Sources, 1995.

Donohue, John. *Jesuit Education: An Essay on the Foundations of Its Idea.* New York: Fordham University Press, 1963.

Hesburgh, Theodore M., C.S.C., ed. *The Challenge and Promise of a Catholic University.* Notre Dame, Ind.: University of Notre Dame Press, 1994.

Himes, Michael. "Living Conversation: Higher Education in a Catholic Context." *Conversations on Jesuit Higher Education*, no. 8 (fall 1995): 21–7.

Hollenbach, David, S.J. "Is Tolerance Enough? The Catholic University and the Common Good." *Conversations on Jesuit Higher Education*, no. 13 (spring 1998): 5–15.

Kolvenbach, Peter-Hans, S.J. "Ignatian Pedagogy Today." Address to the International Workshop on Ignatian Pedagogy: A Practical Approach (April 29, 1993). Reprinted in Meirose, *Foundations* (see ref. below).

————. "The Service of Faith and the Promotion of Justice in American Jesuit Higher Education," *Studies in the Spirituality of Jesuits* 33, no. 1 (January 2001): 13–29.

Lonergan, Bernard, S.J. *Topics in Education: The Cincinnati Lectures of 1959 on the Philosophy of Education*. Robert M. Doran and Frederick E. Crowe, editors. Toronto: University of Toronto Press, 1993.

Meirose, Carl E., S.J. ed. *Foundations*. Washington: Jesuit Secondary Education Association, 1994.

Newman, John Henry Cardinal. *The Idea of a University*. New York: Doubleday, Image Books, 1959.

O'Brien, David J. *From the Heart of the American Church: Catholic Higher Education and American Culture*. Maryknoll, N.Y.: Orbis Books, 1994.

Schultenover, David G., S.J. *The Ethos of Jesuit Education: Ignatius to Hopkins to Ellacuria*. Omaha, Neb.: Creighton University Press, 1997.

Sobrino, Jon, S.J. *Companions of Jesus: The Jesuit Martyrs of El Salvador*. Maryknoll, N.Y.: Orbis Books, 1990.

12

Teaching Literature as Mediation: A Christian Practice

Arlin G. Meyer

THE ACADEMIC VOCATION AS PERSONAL JOURNEY

WHEN MY FATHER DIED several years ago at the age of ninety, I shared some recollections of him at the funeral service, reflecting on his four most admirable qualities—his patience, equanimity, sense of righteousness, and his lived faith.

As a farmer, my father knew the importance of time, and he knew something of the regularity of time. He was never in a hurry, never frantic, and seldom harried. He was endlessly patient with his seven children. As much as we tested his patience, he always remained unperturbed, almost stoic in his demeanor. His equanimity demonstrated itself in his calm and even temperament. He seldom exhibited extreme highs or lows and always kept his emotions under control, thus providing stability in the family. If I imagine my father as a boat, he was even-keeled, seldom rocking and never tipping. Dad possessed a supreme sense of righteousness. In all aspects of life, he had a vision of fairness, justice, and rightness. Whether it involved the planting and cultivation of corn, the education of his children, or the proclamation of the gospel in church, Dad knew there was a right way of doing things. To live righteously and to practice justice was for him a credo, a way of living. And for him God was the measure of righteousness, the yardstick against which all of our human activities are measured. Despite all of the trials and adversities in his life, Dad never questioned God or God's plan for his life. He seemed to know, in a way few of us do, that if he put his trust in God, his own life would be both fulfilled and fulfilling.

I concluded my tribute to my father by saying that for me, and for other family members, he was, if not a preacher, then a teacher and a mentor, a guide for our life journeys, and a living witness to the presence of God in our lives. Perhaps it is true that as we grow older we become more like our parents. I realize in retrospect that I identified those qualities in my father that I not only most admired but also have tried to emulate in my own life and in my vocation as a teacher.

My father was a Calvinist, and I was born and raised in the Christian Reformed denomination. I attended Dordt College for two years and then completed my undergraduate education at Calvin College, both colleges sponsored by the Christian Reformed Church. After teaching high school English for four years at Holland Christian High School, I completed my graduate education at the University of Michigan and Ohio University, institutions that were becoming increasingly secularized in the 1960s although at least half of my professors were practicing Christians. Consequently, I did not experience the open hostility toward the integration of faith and learning in graduate school that most of the postdoctoral fellows with whom I have worked for the past eleven years in the Lilly Fellows Program have reported. In 1967 I began my college teaching career at Valparaiso University, a Lutheran institution.

Unlike many of my younger colleagues, my understanding of my vocation as a Christian teacher and scholar was forged and fostered in environments that were either openly supportive of or hospitable to the relationship between my personal faith and my work as an academic. However, like most college and university professors, I received very little advice or mentoring about a philosophy of teaching that integrated Christianity and the academic profession. My own sense of vocation was fashioned after important role models—undergraduate teachers at Calvin, selected professors at Michigan and Ohio, colleagues at Valparaiso University, and, I think, my father as a farmer. For the past thirty years I have taught at a Lutheran university, an institution that honors the doctrine of the two kingdoms. As Richard W.

Solberg explains this doctrine, Martin Luther declared that God is the

> ruler of two "kingdoms" or "realms." The heavenly kingdom is a spiritual one, in which faith rules over reason and in which God reveals His plan for the redemption of the human family. . . . The earthly or secular kingdom is the created world, pronounced by God at the creation as "good," but since marred by sin and awaiting its ultimate redemption at the "end time" through the recreating act of God.[1]

For Lutherans education is squarely in the domain of the secular kingdom. My own approach to teaching has always been more Calvinist, based on the belief that all academic disciplines are part of Christian education. Thus, my teaching philosophy is more perspectival in the sense that my own Christian faith provides the lens through which I see the whole creation and perceive my vocation as a teacher.

In "The Fiction Writer and His Country," Flannery O'Connor states: "I am no disbeliever in spiritual purpose and no vague believer. I see from the standpoint of Christian orthodoxy. This means that for me the meaning of life is centered in our Redemption by Christ and what I see in the world I see in its relation to that. I don't think that this is a position that can be taken halfway or one that is particularly easy in these times to make transparent in fiction."[2] I have always viewed my vocation as a teacher in a similar way: what I see in the world of academia, in the world of literature, and in the world of writing, I see in relation to my life as "centered in our Redemption by Christ."

In an essay entitled "Faith and Fiction," Frederick Buechner notes that both the practice of faith and the writing of fiction are creative, ongoing practices, perhaps even journeys of discovery. "The living out of faith. The writing out of fiction. In both you shape, you fashion, you feign. Maybe what they have most richly

---

[1] Richard W. Solberg, "What Can the Lutheran Tradition Contribute to Christian Higher Education?" 71–81 in Richard T. Hughes and William B. Adrian, eds., *Models for Christian Higher Education: Strategies for Success in the Twenty-First Century*, (Grand Rapids, Mich.: William B. Eerdmans Publishing Co., 1997), 76.

[2] Flannery O'Connor, *Mystery and Manners*, Sally and Robert Fitzgerald, eds. (New York: Farrar, Straus & Giroux, 1970), 32.

in common is a way of paying attention."[3] Faith, then, is not a possession but an integral part of who one is and who one is becoming. I have always been uneasy with the phrase "the integration of faith and learning" because it seems to imply that both faith and learning are possessions rather than essential aspects of our being and becoming. This is true, I believe, for both students and teachers. In *The Night Is Dark and I Am Far From Home*, Jonathan Kozol argues that "What the teacher 'teaches' is by no means chiefly in the words he speaks. It is at least in part in what he *is*, in what he *does*, in what he seems to *wish to be*. The secret curriculum is the teacher's own lived values and convictions, in the lineaments of his expression and in the biography of passion or self-exile which is written in his eyes."[4] Both of these quotations, particularly Buechner's phrase, "a way of paying attention," and Kozol's phrase, "written in his eyes," reinforce my own understanding of the perspectival aspect of my faith and teaching.

As I have been troubled over discussions concerning the integration of faith and learning, I am also reluctant to describe techniques or strategies of teaching, particularly as these descriptions attempt to link faith concerns with pedagogical practice. Yet that is the challenge given those of us commissioned to write essays for this book, so I will describe some of my own practices as a teacher, knowing that these practices have not always worked successfully for me and realizing that each teacher must discover her own distinctive style of teaching and her own pedagogical practices. As Robert Inchausti concludes in *Spitwad Sutras: Classroom Teaching As Sublime Vocation*:

> Classroom teaching is a great existential art, if we would only own up to what a serious and difficult craft it really is. The best teachers know this; that's what makes them the best teachers. But beginning teachers have to be reminded that their vocation is sublime—bigger than they know, bigger than anyone knows. And though there will be times when the pettiness of one's circum-

---

[3] Frederick Buechner, *The Clown in the Belfry: Writings on Faith and Fiction* (San Francisco: HarperCollins, 1992), 26.

[4] Jonathan Kozol, *The Night is Dark and I Am Far From Home* (Boston: Houghton Mifflin, 1975), 101.

stances seems overwhelming, those circumstances are the very stuff of self-creation.[5]

When Parker Palmer published *To Know As We Are Known* in 1983, I wrote out his definition of teaching ("to teach is to create a space in which obedience to truth is practiced") and taped it to the lamp on my desk where it became a mantra with which I began each academic day.[6] In that book and in his more recent volume, *The Courage To Teach*, Palmer describes his own practice of teaching in the triangular relationships between teacher, students, and subject matter, concentrating on the space the teacher needs to create. Palmer's expositions on teaching confirmed my own unarticulated goals and practices and emboldened me to become more reflective about the art of "teaching from within."

Although teachers have numerous roles or functions, four are essential to my own style of teaching. These roles are: (1) to create an inviting and dynamic classroom environment; (2) to identify and understand the individual needs of students in a particular class; (3) to select appropriate texts so that students can engage meaningfully with the subject matter of a course; and (4) to serve as a mediator or conduit between the truth embodied in the subject matter and the students' search for identity and meaning in their own lives. This articulation of my role as a teacher may not, on the surface, reveal my understanding of myself as a Christian teacher, but my expectation is that I can accomplish each of these roles in a manner that is consistent with my beliefs and practices. If one's faith is embedded deeply in the fabric of one's being, then that faith will inform the way in which that person conducts all activities in life, including the teaching of one's classes.

I and Thou: Personalizing the Classroom

The first two roles I mentioned are integrally related. An appropriate classroom environment must be established to meet the

---

[5] Robert Inchausti, *Spitwad Sutras: Classroom Teaching As Sublime Vocation* (Westport, Conn.: Bergin & Garvey, 1993), 148–9.

[6] Parker J. Palmer, *To Know As We Are Known: A Spirituality of Education* (San Francisco: Harper & Row, 1983), 69.

individual needs of students in each class. The particular personalities of students in a given class will determine, to some
extent, the environment of that class. My overall goal at the beginning of each course is to establish a communal and collaborative atmosphere. I try to create this atmosphere from the very
outset, using a number of different strategies to draw students
out of themselves and into the communal space of the classroom. Frequently, I have the classroom arranged before students
arrive for the first class so that everyone can see each other—
either around seminar tables or in a circle. I have name cards,
printed on folded 4x8 note cards, at each desk so students can
immediately attach names to faces. This personalizes the classroom and quickly allows students to address each other by
name. I use these name cards, rearranging them in different
desks or chairs each day, until all students know each other by
name. If the classroom is to become a community, where individuals can exchange ideas, feelings, and convictions honestly,
then an atmosphere of openness and trust must exist. A prerequisite for such a classroom is personal recognition.

To establish a community of trust and a hospitable atmosphere, I typically begin by sharing aspects of my own life with
my students, usually before I ask them to disclose anything
about their lives. Most often I do this in the form of stories drawn
from my growing up on the farm, my relationships with my
siblings, my struggles with doctrines of Christianity as a high
school student, my own undergraduate days at Calvin College,
and my experiences as a high school teacher. All of them know
that I am an aging professor; what I want them to sense is that
the stories of my life are not dissimilar from their own narratives. These stories also reveal to them my own process of becoming—becoming an adult, becoming a Christian, becoming a
teacher. This kind of self-disclosure is a form of intellectual and
spiritual witness uniquely possible and appropriate in the kind
of classroom I attempt to create at a church-related university.
In essence, it is an extension or expansion of my name card that
hopefully allows students to believe in me as part of the learning
community they have entered. This strategy is particularly apro-
pos in literature courses where we will be reading fictional stories together. I then encourage students to recall and share their

own stories so that we can connect the narratives we read to our own evolving lives.

To assist everyone in getting to know each other, I also use other techniques during the first week of class. For instance, in a freshman seminar entitled Personal Lives: Autobiography, Biography, and Autobiographical Fiction, I ask students to complete autobiographical data forms that request personal information. Some of this information is factual—name, campus address, hometown—but much of it is more subjective and disclosing— favorite author, most powerful film you have seen recently, best book you have read, person you most admire. I tell students beforehand that some of their responses on these sheets will be made public. On some occasions, I have reproduced student responses in an abbreviated form and distributed them to all members of the class. At other times, I pair students off and ask them to talk with each other about their responses. Then I ask the students to introduce each other to the entire class on the basis of the information on the autobiographical data forms and their conversations with each other. This little exercise accomplishes several purposes: (1) it requires every student to speak (and others to attend and listen) during the first or second class period; (2) it allows everyone in the classroom to begin to know each other on a personal basis; and (3) it establishes a practice of interaction and self-disclosure. I am always amazed at how much students are willing to reveal about themselves in these opening dialogues.

The purpose of this seminar is to examine the personal lives of several twentieth-century authors to see how their lives are revealed in autobiographies, biographies, and novels. For instance, the last time I taught this seminar we studied James Baldwin, Sylvia Plath, and John Updike, using *Go Tell It on the Mountain*, *The Bell Jar*, and *Of the Farm* as examples of highly autobiographical novels.[7] In each case, the authors have written autobiographical accounts of experiences fictionalized in these novels. We also read biographical accounts of these experiences.

---

[7] Good teaching editions of these novels are: James Baldwin, *Go Tell It on the Mountain* (New York: Dell Publishing Co., Inc., 1985); Sylvia Plath, *The Bell Jar* (New York: Bantam Classics, 1983); John Updike, *Of the Farm* (New York: Fawcett Crest Books, 1987).

Together we learn a great deal about these three authors—something about how people's lives are revealed differently and similarly through autobiography, biography, and fiction—and ways in which we can disclose and understand our own lives through various forms of writing.

Because this seminar focuses on personal lives, it seems particularly appropriate to establish a classroom climate in which we examine our own lives as well. Like the authors and protagonists in the novels we read, students in the seminar also have emotional and spiritual lives, and I provide them with opportunities to write—biographically, autobiographically, and fictionally—about emotional traumas like those Esther Greenwood experiences in *The Bell Jar*, spiritual crises like those John Grimes undergoes in *Go Tell It on the Mountain*, or family breakdowns like those of the Robinson family in *Of the Farm*. If issues of faith, belief, and spirituality are introduced through texts in which authors address these matters openly and honestly, whether in autobiographical or fictional form, students are much more likely to explore similar crises through their own writing. However, this kind of self-examination and self-disclosure is not likely to occur unless an atmosphere of trust and mutual respect has been established in the seminar from the beginning.

Although a personal and communal atmosphere seems particularly appropriate to a seminar entitled Personal Lives, I find this kind of environment is equally important in all the classes I teach. Consequently, in every class, I attempt to know and understand the individual needs of my students and establish a classroom atmosphere that is appropriately responsive. In her wonderful book, *The Peaceable Classroom*, Mary Rose O'Reilley spends considerable time describing her practices in attempting to forge classroom communities for disparate groups of students. In an early section of the book entitled "A Preliminary Sketch of Principles," she identifies her own primary goals as a teacher:

> The first goal of education—if we think it has anything at all to do with values— is to bring students to a knowledge of the world within: its geography and anthropology, depths and heights, myths and primary texts. To foster this process, you don't even have to put your chairs in a circle.

Our second goal should be to help the student bring his subjective vision into community, checking his insights against those of allies and adversaries, against the vision of the texts he studies, and in general against the history of ideas. The classroom, then, must be a meeting place for both silent meditation and verbal witness, of interplay between interiority and community.[8]

This sense of community—of fellowship and sharing—can exist in individual classrooms but certainly extends beyond the walls of the classroom as well. The classroom is not always the most appropriate setting for students (or faculty) to discuss their personal problems, their most deeply held convictions, or their personal faith. Reflection or conversation about such issues may often be precipitated in the classroom but may then spill over into other communal settings—residence halls, faculty offices, the student union, or the chapel, to name other communal settings on my campus.

As teachers we often forget that students have rich and complex interior lives that they bring with them to the classroom. Although there is much about each student's personal life that I do not want to know, I also believe that I can teach students more effectively if I know them as individuals, and this often includes sharing some of their personal pains and struggles. These kinds of experiences are most often shared outside the classroom, but a teacher's awareness of these situations often affects the tone and nature of a discussion in the classroom as well. Just as our lives as teachers are related to all other aspects of our lives, so a person's life as a student in the classroom is connected with the rest of his life. Some of my most fulfilling accomplishments as a teacher have occurred with students whose lives I knew interiorly and intimately and with whom I worked closely beyond the boundaries of the classroom.

A Question of Texts

The third role of a teacher is to select texts that will enable students to engage the subject matter meaningfully. As professors,

---

[8] Mary Rose O'Reilley, *The Peaceable Classroom* (Portsmouth, N.H.: Heinemann, 1993), 32.

we often discover which texts are appropriate through trial and error, perhaps because we do not adequately gauge our students' needs, interests, and readiness. One of the postdoctoral fellows teaching in the Lilly Fellows Program at Valparaiso University recently shared with me the student evaluations from an introductory theology course. In every area, the students evaluated the course very highly with one exception—the textbook used for the course. I was struck by this set of evaluations because the teacher and the course were unanimously praised while the textbook was uniformly criticized. It was clear from student comments that the textbook in this course was not effective for the students in this class.

Because my primary teaching area is literature and I teach many courses in fiction, there are literally hundreds of novels to select from in courses like The Novel or Twentieth-Century Fiction. One of my selection criteria is that the novel be good literature. And what is good literature? When I was learning to read and appreciate fiction as an undergraduate at Calvin College, Henry Zylstra, a professor of English, provided the following guidelines for assessing novels, which I have used profitably in my own reading and teaching ever since:

(1) A novel is literature if a comprehensive view of life, sensitively perceived, is given aesthetic embodiment in it.
(2) A novel is literature if it is an appropriately embodied narrative that touches powerfully on life at many points.
(3) A novel is literature if an imaginatively gifted person of unusual magnitude of mind presents an interpretation of reality in it.[9]

All literature allows the reader escape into or access to another world—in the case of fiction, the imagined world of the novel or short story. Great novels, however, are distinguished by a comprehensiveness of vision, the significance of their examination of life, and the degree to which they contain an interpretation of reality. Such works of literature allow readers to see their own

---

[9] Henry Zylstra, *Testament of Vision: Reflections on Literature and Life, Education and Religion* (Grand Rapids, Mich.: William B. Eerdmans Publishing Co., 1958), 52. Some of Zylstra's essays, speeches, and notes were published in this collection shortly after his untimely death in 1956.

world in relationship to the world embodied in the novel. C. S. Lewis comments on the power good literature has to make us live another's experience without fragmenting our own. He says:

This, so far as I can see, is the specific value or good of literature considered as Logos; it admits us to experiences other than our own. They are not, any more than our personal experiences, all equally worth having. Some, as we say, "interest" us more than others. . . . Literature gives the *entrée* to them all. Those of us who have been true readers all our lives seldom fully realise the enormous extension of our being which we owe to authors. We realise it best when we talk with an unliterary friend. He may be full of goodness and good sense but he inhabits a tiny world. In it, we should be suffocated. The man who is contented to be only himself, and therefore less a self, is in prison. My own eyes are not enough for me, I will see through those of others.[10]

Novels too provide new perspectives on our own lives. A great novel embodies a microcosm of the world, but the world created by a writer of great magnitude of mind is also macrocosmic. It enlarges our vision, expands our horizons, increases our range of experience, and deepens our self-understanding. It deals with all aspects of human experience. As a Christian teacher, I attempt to introduce my students to these fictional worlds. For instance, in a seminar I teach on William Wordsworth and Thomas Hardy, we read half a dozen Hardy novels and a selection of his poetry.[11] Geographically, the world of Hardy is small, limited to a part of England called Wessex. But within that microcosmic world, all the basic questions of human nature are explored—one's relationship to nature, the value of labor, the varieties of love, familial relationships, the existence of evil, one's relationship to the past, the meaning of suffering and death, the fickle nature of fate, the existence of God, and the

---

[10] C. S. Lewis, *An Experiment in Criticism* (Cambridge, U.K.: Cambridge University Press, 1961), 139–40.

[11] When I taught this seminar recently, I used the following texts by Thomas Hardy: *The Mayor of Casterbridge* (New York: Houghton Mifflin, Riverside Edition, 1962); *The Return of the Native* (New York: Houghton Mifflin, Riverside Edition, 1967); *Tess of the D'Urbervilles* (New York: Houghton Mifflin, Riverside Edition, 1960); *Selected Short Stories and Poems* (New York: Everyman's Library, 1993); and *Under the Greenwood Tree* (New York: Penguin Books, 1986).

destiny of humankind. To read Hardy's novels and poetry is to have entered a universe comprehensive in scope and intensive in quality. It is, in the words of Zylstra, "to have confronted the moral issues of human existence, not in the skeleton of theory or the bones of principle, but in the flesh and blood of concrete experience."[12] It is a vision of life profoundly seen, artistically embodied, and deeply felt.

Thomas Hardy is not a Christian writer: his world is grimly pessimistic, a world governed by fatalism and pessimism. However, I believe it is vital for Christians to inhabit worlds not lit in precisely the same way as their own. Great fiction enables readers by vicarious experience to bring to bear on their own lives myriads of lives not their own. By immersing oneself in the experience of others, there is more of oneself that can be Christian than there was before. Because Hardy was a writer of considerable mind and imagination who created a fictional world that contains a comprehensive view of life, sensitively perceived and richly embodied, a reader's life should be expanded after reading Hardy. As a result, there is more of that person's life with which to be Christian than there was before and, perhaps, even more conviction in the reader's own view of the world.

I enjoy teaching courses in which we examine a number of works by one or two authors precisely because this allows the class to extrapolate the worldview embodied in the author's works. To explore the world of Hardy, a late Victorian writer, against the backdrop of the world of Wordsworth, an early Romantic, also forces students to compare and contrast the worldviews embodied in the writing of these authors. Students are prompted to reexamine their own views of the major questions of life in relationship to those embodied in the literature of Wordsworth and Hardy. As part of the final examination, I ask students to compare and contrast the worldviews of Wordsworth and Hardy and to critique them from their own perspectives. The most important outcome of this exercise is that students begin to expand the boundaries of their own construction or formulation of a philosophy of life.

I also teach a seminar entitled John Updike, Toni Morrison,

---

[12] Zylstra, *Testament of Vision*, 66–67.

and Contemporary America, in which we read many of the major works of two of the most important and widely acclaimed contemporary U.S. writers.[13] Although one of the primary goals of this course is to discover how U.S. culture and society are portrayed by two very different writers, both Updike and Morrison are also deeply religious writers who create characters engaged in a quest for meaning in a world that often appears to be devoid of meaning. Because Morrison and Updike are contemporary novelists, the worldviews embodied in their novels and short stories come closer to approximating the world in which my students live. And because both writers powerfully raise questions about the existence of God, the presence of evil in human nature and society, the ability of love to transform human relationships, and the quest for meaning in an irrational world, students must come to terms with their own answers and responses to these questions.

My own inclination, then, in selecting texts in the fiction courses I teach is to choose the best short stories and novels I know that will both engage and challenge my students. In my Twentieth-Century Fiction course I usually begin with a group of writers—James Joyce, D. H. Lawrence, Virginia Woolf, E. M. Forster—who rejected Christianity, but I also include more contemporary writers—Flannery O'Connor, Graham Greene, John Updike, Larry Woiwode, John Irving—who either write from a Christian perspective or deal explicitly with issues of faith.[14] Almost all great works of literature deal with fundamental moral issues and to that extent are religious works. I am less interested in the author's beliefs or the explicitly Christian content of a

---

[13] To provide a representative sampling of these two authors I have used the following texts by Toni Morrison: *The Bluest Eye* (1970), *Song of Solomon* (1977), *Beloved* (1987), and *Jazz* (1992), all published as Plume paperbacks by Penguin Books; and the following texts by John Updike: *Rabbit, Run* (1960), *Pigeon Feathers and Other Stories* (1962), *Couples* (1968), *Marry Me* (1978), *S.* (1988), and *Rabbit at Rest* (1990), all published as Crest paperbacks by Fawcett Crest Books.

[14] Representative works by these authors would include James Joyce, *Dubliners* or *A Portrait of the Artist as a Young Man*; D. H. Lawrence, *Sons and Lovers* or *The Rainbow*; Virginia Woolf, *Mrs. Dalloway* or *To the Lighthouse*; E. M. Forster, *Howards End* or *A Passage to India*; Flannery O'Connor, *A Good Man Is Hard To Find* or *The Violent Bear It Away*; Graham Greene, *The Heart of the Matter* or *The Power and the Glory*; John Updike, *Rabbit, Run* or *In the Beauty of the Lilies*; Larry Woiwode, *Beyond the Bedroom Wall*; and John Irving, *A Prayer for Owen Meany*.

novel than in my students' engagement in the novel and their interaction with the world of the novel.

Some critics argue for the necessity of divorcing one's personal views of life and beliefs from one's response to a literary work, and to an extent this is necessary. To appreciate a novel, a reader must give himself up to it. But total separation is finally impossible. One cannot ultimately separate life attitudes from aesthetic judgments precisely because one's view of life is all encompassing. Just as every work of art has what Giles B. Gunn calls its own informing or presiding assumption, its embodied vision, its metaphysic,[15] so every mature reader has her own worldview, her vision of reality, her set of beliefs. And if I do my task properly as a teacher, then it is precisely the interaction or direct confrontation of these differing visions of the world that makes the reading of fiction such a powerful, transformative, and profound experience for my students. Reading fiction will likely not make students more (or less) religious, nor will it make them better (or worse) Christians. But fiction can make them more fully aware of who they are, of the rich potentialities of life, of what it means to be more fully human. When brought into direct contact, both literature and Christianity have a way of informing and transforming each other.

THE TEACHER AS MEDIATOR

Having created an appropriate classroom environment for the individual needs of students in a particular class and having selected texts that engage students meaningfully with the subject matter of a course, the rest of teaching should be easy. But it never is! The more one teaches, the more one learns that success is never predictable. What works in one class may fail in the next, and a strategy that opens the minds and hearts of one group of students can close those of another class. Even a brilliant lecture that stimulates a class of students one semester may fall on deaf ears the following semester. But should we not ex-

---

[15] Giles B. Gunn, "Introduction: Literature and Its Relation to Religion," in Giles B. Gunn, ed., *Literature and Religion* (London: SCM Press, Ltd., 1971), 29.

pect that to be the case? Each group of students is different, and each class develops its own group dynamic, so teachers should anticipate that no single pedagogy or methodology will meet the needs of all classes. The key, perhaps, is fluidity or flexibility—the capacity to be responsive to expectations, needs, and situations as they develop in the classroom.

Adopting Parker Palmer's identification of student, teacher, and subject as the three essential components of a teaching situation, I tend to locate myself between the students and the subject matter, perceiving my role alternately as a conduit or a mediator. In some ways, this image seems wrong because I do want students to be in direct contact with the subject matter. By placing myself as teacher between the two, I can, of course, stymie or distort that relationship; however, my goal is to facilitate, enliven, and enhance the relationship between students and subject matter. In a lecture on "The Grace of Teaching" at the national conference of the Lilly Fellows Program several years ago, Mary C. Boys said that "Teaching is fundamentally about relationships, about not imposing oneself upon the subject or upon the learners, but in fashioning an appropriate response to both."[16] For me, this statement captures the ideal intermediary role of the teacher. I would add that the teacher is also a mediator among students. A colleague of mine compares this aspect of teaching to being a host, bringing people together in a social setting, introducing them to each other and the subject matter and getting them to speak. Then the host steps back or gets out of the way to allow for more direct interaction. The key for a Christian teacher—as for any teacher in a broader sense—is to determine in any given classroom situation what an appropriate response to both the subject and the learner might be.

As an intermediary, one of my roles is to provide maximum occasions and settings for students to engage in meaningful relationships with the subject matter of a course. One strategy that I have used with some success is to involve students collaboratively in structuring the response to and dialogue about the subject matter. In a course on Twentieth-Century Fiction, I assign seven novels to be read by the entire class. Let us assume the

---

[16] Mary C. Boys, "The Grace of Teaching," *The Cresset* 59, no. 6 (1996): 12.

novels for a particular semester are James Joyce's *Portrait of the Artist as a Young Man*, D. H. Lawrence's *Sons and Lovers*, E. M. Forster's *Howards End*, Virginia Woolf's *To the Lighthouse*, Flannery O'Connor's *The Violent Bear It Away*, John Irving's *A Prayer for Owen Meany*, and Louise Erdrich's *Love Medicine*. I design a syllabus in which we devote four or five class periods to each of the seven texts. I then work out panels for each novel with three or four students on a panel. For each panel, I meet with students at least once, at which time we decide how to approach a particular novel in a panel presentation. The students may decide to focus on four different aspects of the novel (plot, characterization, point of view, imagery and symbolism); or they may provide four different critical approaches to the novel (feminist, deconstructionist, psychoanalytic, moralist); or they may identify four central themes or ideas in a novel. If we devote four class periods to a novel, I reserve the first and last class period for myself and the middle two class periods for the students. In the first class period, I provide a background lecture, introducing the author, providing the setting for the novel, and contextualizing the work under consideration. Since I have met with the panel, I can anticipate in this introductory lecture their presentation, which occurs in the second class period. In a fifty-minute class period I limit their presentation to approximately thirty-five minutes to allow for immediate response from the rest of the class. The third class period is devoted to an open discussion, sometimes moderated by the panel members (occasionally even in four small groups) but at other times moderated by me. In the fourth class period I provide a concluding lecture, attempting to draw together in some kind of meaningful way the questions that have been raised and the issues that have been opened up in the panel presentation and subsequent discussions.

I have had considerable success with this format primarily, I think, because it allows and encourages the students to raise the important issues they wish to discuss. I may have some input into the way they design the panel presentation, and I do participate in the discussions, but the issues discussed are primarily those that resonate with their reading and research of the novel and grow out of their relationship with the subject matter of the course. Students tend to respond more actively and more naturally to questions raised by their classmates than those I might ask as a teacher. Because I have read most of the novels I teach numerous times, I may be too far out ahead of the students in terms of my own responses. So it seems to work better to begin with their questions and responses and relate them to my own responses in the concluding lecture.

This combination of lecture and discussion is effective in a course in which novels are the primary texts, but I think this format could be adapted to other kinds of courses as well. As O'Reilley says in *The Peaceable Classroom*, "We have a lot to tell our students, but I believe our primary job should be to bring them to asking, by whatever means we can devise, the questions that will elicit what they need to know. Students do not really listen well to the answers to questions they have not learned to ask."[17] Interestingly, when a class is structured so that students generate the questions and issues for discussion, the topics are more personalized and genuine than if I had raised them. Invariably, students introduce the religious dimensions of novels like *Sons and Lovers* and *Howards End*, examine the spiritual journeys of Stephen Dedalus in *Portrait* and Owen in *A Prayer for Owen Meany*, and argue vehemently about the deleterious effects of Christianity in *The Violent Bear It Away* and *Love Medicine*. This provides me with the opportunity to engage in discussion of these matters with the students and spares me the criticism that the professor is always trying to impose a religious or Christian interpretation on the texts. Some of the deepest and most animated discussions about matters of Christian faith and doctrine have emanated from student presentations. These discussions also provide me with an opportunity to address these questions and issues in the concluding lecture on each author. What I have learned from this practice is that if a teacher provides opportunities for students to engage great works of literature directly and meaningfully, the fundamental questions about the meaning of life will surface. Once these issues are raised, the teacher can truly assume the role of mediator between the student and the subject.

Even without such an elaborate format, there are other strate-

---

[17] O'Reilley, *The Peaceable Classroom*, 34.

gies to elicit the questions about texts that students are most interested in raising. If one class period is devoted to a short story or a poem, for instance, I will sometimes ask students beforehand to come to class with one or two questions about the text they would like to address in class. Often these questions will be ill conceived or simpleminded. However, the questions usually fall into half a dozen patterns or clusters; and if I take a little time at the beginning of class to put students with similar questions into small groups, asking them to reformulate or sharpen their questions, not only do they come up with better and more profound questions, they also begin to provide answers to those questions. These questions can then be used as a way to approach the poem or short story in a class discussion. Because literary works tend to evoke personal responses, the questions students raise will usually be more self-disclosing about their personal beliefs and convictions than their responses to questions raised by the teacher.

Discussions of pedagogy tend to focus on the classroom as a forum where the teacher lectures and moderates discussions. We seldom talk about how important the art of listening is to effective teaching. Because any class consists of disparate students with different personalities and learning styles, a teacher must be sensitive to the various ways in which students respond to what is going on in class. Some students are bold and assertive, others are shy and passive. Some students talk too much, others say nothing. Some students appear to be actively engaged, others appear withdrawn and inattentive. Without discounting the possibility that some students really are disengaged and disinterested, a teacher must listen for and to all of the voices in a classroom, even those that are seldom heard. At times students who are seemingly uninvolved are internally more engaged with the questions and issues under discussion than those who participate more actively. Every teacher has had the experience of observing a student in class who has sat quietly in the back row for the first five or six weeks of a course and then writes a paper or an examination that belies her apparent lack of interest or attentiveness.

Because students are not equally comfortable engaging in class discussions or voluntarily raising questions that are on their minds, teachers need to be attentive to these quiet voices and find ways of hearing them as well. This is especially true when discussions turn to matters of moral conviction, personal interpretation, or private belief. I attempt to create numerous opportunities to engage students on a personal basis. Whenever possible, I arrive in class early and stay until the last student has left. Not only does this encourage students to arrive on time, it allows me to talk with students as they enter the classroom and linger afterwards. These casual conversations seem trivial, but they often lead to more extended dialogues and empower shy students to voice their opinions in class. Inviting students to my office early on in the semester will also prompt the timid student to make an appointment on his own when he is struggling with a problem or issue. Often these discussions can lead to the construction of paper topics that are more responsive to the student's own interests and convictions.

Additionally, I create occasions for students to respond personally to the subject matter of the course. If we are beginning a discussion of a short story or poem, I may ask the students to complete a sentence like the following, selecting one noun and one adjective from the words in parentheses: "On the basis of reading Flaubert's 'A Simple Heart,' the (choose one: situation, idea, issue, question) I find most (choose one: powerful, troubling, intriguing, tragic, interesting) is. . . ." I will then ask each student to read his sentence and ask students to respond to each other's assertions. Since students have committed themselves in writing to a particular proposition or point of view, they are more likely to defend their own positions and challenge those of others. This leads immediately to multiple viewpoints on a text but also assists students in clarifying their own interpretations and convictions.

On the surface, these little techniques and strategies have nothing to do with the integration of faith and learning or with teaching as a Christian vocation. My experience, however, suggests that students will only consider the relationship of their own beliefs and faith to the learning process if we as teachers know each student individually and create appropriate opportunities for them to respond personally. In addition to an intellectual self, every student also has an emotional and spiritual self.

Christian teachers can be most effective if they are responsive to the whole student. The effect a teacher has on a student is often not discernible during the semester in which the teacher has a particular student in class. As teachers we desire immediate gratification, but this response is not always present in the student evaluations at the end of a semester. However, the effect of an experience in a class may become apparent in a student's life later. I will provide three quick examples.

A discussion I had with a student in a Twentieth-Century Fiction class about Peter De Vries's *The Blood of the Lamb* led to an independent study project entitled "Searching for God: Responses to the 'Death of God' in Novels by Flannery O'Connor, John Updike, Peter De Vries, and John Irving." Recently I received a letter from a former student who remembered a lecture on Christianity and literature I gave in a course on Politics and Literature, which led him to continue to read novels by Graham Greene, Franz Kafka, and Nadine Gordimer as he practices his own vocation as a politician.[18] Because I attempt to discover the specific interests and needs of my students, I make a practice of giving them individual books to read when they leave my class or graduate from college. A student who graduated several years ago recently attended chapel when she was visiting campus. When she graduated, I gave her, at her request, a list of twenty good novels.[19] In fact, I gave her copies of many of these

---

[18] The gist of this lecture, as I recall, was to enumerate various ways of construing the relationship between Christianity and literature—a biographical approach that limits the relationship to those writers who are professing Christians; a thematic approach that identifies works dealing with Christian or religious themes; a definitional approach that shifts the terms from Christianity and literature to theology and literature; and a reader-response approach, which places emphasis on the relationship of the reader to the literary works. As should be clear from the earlier sections of this essay, I am most sympathetic to the last approach.

[19] The books on this personalized list were Frederick Buechner, *The Book of Bebb* (New York: Atheneum, 1984); Hugh Cook, *The Homecoming Man* (New York: Mosaic Press, 1989); Peter DeVries, *The Blood of the Lamb* (New York: Penguin Books, 1982); Annie Dillard, *The Living: A Novel* (New York: HarperCollins, 1993); Clyde Edgerton, *Killer Diller* (New York: Ballantine, 1992); Louise Erdrich, *Love Medicine* (New York: HarperCollins, 1993); John Gardner, *The Sunlight Dialogues* (New York: Random House, 1987); Graham Greene, *The Heart of the Matter* (New York: Viking Penguin, 1991); John Irving, *A Prayer for Owen Meany* (New York: Ballantine Books, 1989); Toni Morrison, *Beloved* (New

books. She has read almost all of them and was eager to receive a new list. One reward of being an older professor is that the satisfaction of having touched the minds, hearts, and souls of former students such as these three becomes a more common experience.

Concluding Reflections

I began this essay by reflecting on the qualities exhibited by my father in living out his vocation, noting the influence he had on my own life. Along with other teachers I admired as I grew up, my father was a role model as I developed my own understanding of teaching as a Christian vocation. As teachers, we are often reluctant to think of ourselves as role models, but many of our students will ultimately perceive us in that way. To the extent that teachers are role models, their public lives and personal relationships with students are, in the end, more influential than their pedagogical practices. Jonathan Kozol reflects on the opportunity he had, for one year at Harvard, to work with the distinguished Christian educator, Paulo Freire. Commenting on the profound effect Freire had on him, Kozol concludes:

> I think the reverence that we feel for men and women who have been true teachers, and the way *that* love can change our lives, our vision, our perception of all things we know, and open up new areas of freedom and imagination we have never felt, after certain periods of loneliness that we have never undergone—that this is, in the long run, what education *is* and nothing else *but* this.[20]

In an article entitled "The Spirit of Teaching," Mark Schwehn argues that "though teaching is closer to an art than it is to a

---

York: Plume/Penguin, 1988); Flannery O'Connor, *The Violent Bear It Away* (New York: Farrar, Straus, & Giroux, 1960); Walker Percy, *The Second Coming* (New York: Ivy Books, 1990): Chaim Potok, *The Chosen* (New York: Fawcett, 1987); J. F. Powers, *Morte D'Urban* (New York: Popular Library, 1963); James C. Schaap, *In the Silence There Are Ghosts* (Grand Rapids, Mich.: Baker Book House, 1995); Isaac B. Singer, *The Slave* (New York: Farrar, Straus, & Giroux, 1988); Muriel Spark, *The Takeover* (London: Macmillan London, Ltd., 1976); John Updike, *Rabbit, Run* (New York: Ballantine, 1991); Walter Wangerin, Jr., *Miz Lil and the Chronicles of Grace* (New York: Harper & Row, 1988); Larry Woiwode, *Beyond the Bedroom Wall* (New York: Farrar, Straus, & Giroux, 1975).

[20] Kozol, *The Night Is Dark and I Am Far From Home*, 195.

techne̅, and though it certainly involves mysterious transactions, it is nevertheless a public activity that is improvable through practice and criticism."[21] In his earlier book, *Exiles from Eden: Religion and the Academic Vocation*, Schwehn describes the degree to which, even in the modern university, the conduct of academic life, including teaching, "still depends upon such spiritual virtues as humility, faith, self-sacrifice, and charity."[22] When these virtues are grounded in a lived faith and a sense of righteousness, like the patience and equanimity exhibited by my father, they become the essence of both the art and the practice of teaching. Our teaching will be more genuinely Christian if these virtues become the habits of our hearts that guide our relationships with students, our practices in the classroom, and all of our collegial responsibilities.

Selected Bibliography

Boys, Mary C. *Educating in Faith: Maps and Visions*. New York: Harper & Row Publishers, Inc., 1989.

———. "The Grace of Teaching." *The Cresset* 59, no. 6 (summer 1996): 11–16.

Buechner, Frederick. *The Clown in the Belfry: Writings on Faith and Fiction*. San Francisco: HarperCollins, 1992.

Cunningham, Lawrence S. "Gladly Wolde He Lerne and Gladly Teche: The Catholic Scholar in the New Millenium." *The Cresset* 55, no. 7B (June 1992): 4–16.

De Boer, Peter, Harro W. Van Brummelen, Douglas Blomberg, Robert Koole, and Gloria G. Stronks. *Educating Christian Teachers for Responsible Discipleship*. New York: University Press of America, 1993.

Dupré, Louis. "The Joys and Responsibilities of Being a Catholic Teacher," 61–70 in James L. Heft, ed., *Faith and the Intellectual Life* Notre Dame, Ind.: University of Notre Dame Press, 1996.

---

[21] Mark Schwehn, "The Spirit of Teaching," *Conversations on Jesuit Higher Education*, no. 10 (fall 1996): 6.

[22] Schwehn, *Exiles from Eden: Religion and the Academic Vocation* (New York: Oxford University Press, 1993), 44–65.

————. "On Being a Christian Teacher of Humanities." *The Christian Century* 109 (April 29, 1992): 452–55.

Dykstra, Craig. *Vision and Character: A Christian Educator's Alternative to Kohlberg.* New York: Paulist Press, 1982.

Gallagher, Susan V., and Roger Lundin. *Literature Through the Eyes of Faith.* San Francisco: HarperCollins, 1989.

Gunn, Giles B. "Introduction: Literature and Its Relation to Religion," 1–33 in Giles B. Gunn, ed., *Literature and Religion.* London: SCM Press, Ltd, 1971.

Holmes, Arthur F. "Teaching as Formation." *The Cresset* 58, no. 7B (June/July 1995): 12–17.

hooks, bell. *Teaching to Transgress: Education as the Practice of Freedom.* New York: Routledge, 1994.

Inchausti, Robert. *Spitwad Sutras: Classroom Teaching as Sublime Vocation.* Westport, Conn.: Bergin & Garvey, 1993.

Jackson, Philip W. *The Practice of Teaching.* New York: Teachers College Press, 1986.

Kozol, Jonathan. *The Night Is Dark and I Am Far From Home.* Boston: Houghton Mifflin, 1975.

Lewis, C. S. *An Experiment in Criticism.* Cambridge, U.K.: Cambridge University Press, 1961.

O'Connor, Flannery. *Mystery and Manners,* Sally and Robert Fitzgerald, eds. New York: Farrar, Straus & Giroux, 1970.

O'Reilley, Mary Rose. *The Peaceable Classroom.* Portsmouth, N.H.: Heinemann, 1993.

Palmer, Parker J. *To Know As We Are Known: A Spirituality of Education.* San Francisco: Harper & Row, Publishers, 1983.

————. *The Courage to Teach: Exploring the Inner Landscape of a Teacher's Life.* San Francisco: Jossey-Bass, 1998.

Parks, Sharon Daloz. "Led to Places We Did Not Plan To Go . . . ." *The Cresset* 59, no. 6 (summer 1996): 5–9.

Schwehn, Mark R. *Exiles from Eden: Religion and the Academic Vocation in America.* New York: Oxford University Press, 1993.

————. "The Spirit of Teaching." *Conversations on Jesuit Higher Education,* no. 10 (fall 1996): 5–15.

Simon, Caroline J. *The Disciplined Heart: Love, Destiny, and Imagination.* Grand Rapids, Mich.: William B. Eerdmans Publishing Co., 1997.

Solberg, Richard W. *Lutheran Higher Education in America*. Minneapolis: Augsburg Publishing House, 1985.

———. "What Can the Lutheran Tradition Contribute to Christian Higher Education?" 71–81 in Richard T. Hughes and William B. Adrian, eds. *Models for Christian Higher Education: Strategies for Success in the Twenty-First Century*. Grand Rapids, Mich.: William B. Eerdmans Publishing Co., 1997.

Timmerman, John H. and Donald R. Hettinga. *In the World: Reading and Writing as a Christian*. Grand Rapids, Mich.: Baker Book House, 1987.

Zylstra, Henry. *Testament of Vision*, Grand Rapids, Mich.: William B. Eerdmans Publishing Co., 1958.

13

Faith, Learning, and the Teaching of History

Shirley A. Mullen

I COME to this essay on faith, learning, and the teaching of history as a seeker. What I will share is a brief narrative of how I came to this place, several affirmations that characterize my current thinking on the relationship between Christian faith and the academic discipline of history, and several specific ways that I have sought to facilitate the integration of faith and learning in my own classes.

I grew up in the Holiness tradition—a tradition that is known more for emphasizing clean living and personal piety than theology, doctrine, or the life of the mind. It is a tradition that might well, and often does, lead to a fairly dichotomized vision of faith and learning—a view that sees one's Christianity and one's discipline operating in quite different spheres each with its own presuppositions and ways of proceeding. My background, however, was not the stereotypical Holiness background. For I grew up in a family that cared a great deal for intellectual rigor and even more so for intellectual honesty. When I encountered my first crisis of faith in high school, my father encouraged me to ask the tough questions, to read, and to study church history. My father was a keen John Wesley enthusiast and taught me early that there was much more to Wesley than a warm heart. Wesley was an avid reader in a wide range of disciplines and an eager student of the latest scientific discoveries of his day. Just before I moved from Houghton College to attend graduate school at the University of Toronto, my grandfather, himself a Holiness preacher, said to me, "Shirley, as you continue in school, if you run into anything that really seems to you to be true that conflicts with your current understanding of Christianity, you have to go with truth and you will come out right in the end." This is not an uncomplicated affirmation, and especially so when set in the context of postmodern sensitivities. Nevertheless, it confirmed in me a sense that faith cannot be kept in a compartment and separated from learning.

Another set of voices, besides family ones, made my Holiness upbringing somewhat unusual. When I was in the seventh grade, we moved to the college town of Houghton, New York. I heard about Art Holmes's *The Idea of a Christian College,* and the affirmation that "all truth is God's truth" long before I took any classes at the college. In Houghton, I came under the influence of Dr. Charles Finney and his wife Anne. Dr. Finney chaired the music department at Houghton College for many years and also played the organ for my church. Anne Finney for many years taught the junior high Sunday school class in our church. From the Finneys I heard again and again—not always fully understanding what was being said—the message that our art, our music, and our work must be excellent before it can be pleasing to God. Sincerity is not enough. Our art, our music, and our work must be good on their own terms before they can be appropriately offered to God. This, too, is not an uncomplicated affirmation, but it insured that by the time I entered Houghton College as a student in the fall of 1972, I already had a strong inner desire to explore how the life of the mind and the life of the heart—and how excellence and sincerity—went together in the life of the Christian disciple.

At Houghton, I honestly do not remember a lot of conscious discussion about "integration of faith and learning," but that integration was incarnated in my teachers. I think especially of Professor Katherine Lindley in history and Professor Warren Woolsey in religion. In the content of their classes, in the style of their teaching, and in their attitude to their work, they showed me an integrated vision in which the life of faith informs our learning and where learning informs and enlarges faith—and in which both learning and faith inform our daily lives. It was also at Houghton that I discovered Blaise Pascal—in my freshman Western Civilization text of all places—and also Augustine, Aquinas, C. S. Lewis, John Milton, D. L. Sayers, Lesslie Newbigin, and many other members of the community of saints from other times and places who have sought to live lives of wholeness that brought together the mind and the heart, intellectual integrity and devotion.

All this is to say that I was enticed into the enterprise of faith and learning over a long period of time. And I am still a true believer in this enterprise. I react quite viscerally to comments that seem to suggest that faith and learning or faith and work can somehow be separated, that faith is "out there" or something that we have "in addition to" our learning and knowledge. I respond similarly when it is implied that what makes a Christian college "Christian" is that chapel is required or that professors pray before class or that the concerns of "faith and learning" are for those faculty who are not doing the "real" work of disciplinary research.

But this legacy of family and college has shaped my thinking in another way as well. For this integrative vision of faith and learning came to me, not in a systematic or highly cognitive package—nor even in a particularly self-conscious way. This vision of integration came to me through watching the lives of particular people—wanting to be like them and to have what they had. The enterprise of faith and learning was not presented as an add-on—as something that Christian thinkers might elect to be involved with if they chose. It was simply a matter of seeking to be whole. It was a matter of bringing one's whole self to one's work. So at this point in my life, I also react with equal passion to any discussion of integration of faith and learning that seems mechanical, formulaic, or highly defensive and apologetic in nature. I would caution against being overly eager to see a Christian perspective on this or that, as if it is some peculiar perspective—separate from simply seeing *clearly* and *deeply* and *sensitively* (though this too is complicated, for we do not want to say that only Christians can see clearly, deeply, and sensitively.)

In short, after more than fifteen years of teaching history at Westmont College, I find myself convinced that integration of faith and learning is very important, but at the same time, I am very suspicious of any contrived way of engaging in this enterprise. I have many questions, and I am more comfortable with the idea that the integration of faith and learning should manifest itself in lively dialogue and in the ongoing presence of a certain set of questions in our life together rather than in pat answers, or solutions, or "*the* Christian perspective" on any given set of issues.

SOME SIGNIFICANT CONSIDERATIONS

First, integration of faith and learning must be more than integration of piety and learning—though it must be at least that. That is, a professor may want to pray in a class or present a devotional thought. Often that is what students expect, and it is a way of building trust so that they can be invited into a richer understanding of integration of faith and learning. I have found a reluctance in some colleagues my age—especially those who went to Christian colleges—to have prayer at the beginning of classes on the grounds that they got very tired of it during their own education and felt that it became merely routine. It is also perhaps their way of indicating that integration of faith and learning is more than juxtaposition of piety and learning. Both of these reasons are understandable, but it is important to remember that many of our students are not reacting to the same things as their professors. Furthermore, it is up to us as professors to be careful that our prayers and our devotional readings are not trite but fresh and compelling. So, though integration of faith and learning is not merely nor even primarily the adding of expressions of piety to learning, it must be clear to our students that we do care about living a life of faith. And that life of faith can often be exhibited in a choice to pray when it is appropriate and to present devotional thoughts. (I will make some specific suggestions about this issue in the next section.)

Second, it is clear to me at this point that integration of faith and learning or a life of wholeness of mind and heart ultimately happens inside a person. Though reconciling potentially conflicting propositional content or conflicting presuppositions between the Christian faith and one's discipline can be an important task, it is not the only task of the integration of faith and learning. I would even suggest that it is not, finally, the most important task. Certainly, becoming aware of how content and presuppositions of the Christian faith might be reconciled with one's discipline can be a preliminary step to an internalized personal integration of faith and learning. Professors can provide information and address intellectual challenges to faith that are part of having a large and integrated vision of faith and learning. But at some point, all we can do as professors is to invite, to facilitate, to witness, to create curiosity, and to present the questions that invite integration to take place. Jesus' model of teaching in parables seems to hint at a style of pedagogy that invites rather than cajoles, that challenges the listener while still allowing the person space and freedom to come closer to truth at her own pace.

Third, I also believe that before one can offer an integrated vision of history and faith, one must be certain that one is doing good history. This assertion takes me back to Dr. and Mrs. Finney's affirmation—that something must be excellent before it can be truly good or pure in heart. Before history can be Christian history, it must be good history. But someone might ask, "How do we know objectively what constitutes 'just being a good historian' apart from all the other identities that one carries around—one's class, one's religion, one's family, and so on?" My point here is simply that integrating one's faith and history must result in history that honors the regulative principles of the discipline. In many areas of history, it is not entirely clear how integrated Christian teaching differs from just plain good history teaching that is characterized by efforts to be fair minded, efforts to bring to my work a wide range of moral and spiritual sensitivities, efforts to be appropriately self-critical about my own biases, and efforts to see with merciful and gracious eyes. I believe that the Fall operates on our thinking and our ability to see clearly as well as on our ability to act rightly. And I believe that the truths of revelation and the work of the Holy Spirit can provide us with insight that is not available to the unbeliever, but the notions of *common grace* and *natural revelation* suggest that there is significant common truth available to the believer and unbeliever alike. It seems to me that we ought to work as Christian historians—and to teach students—in such a way that we are not shown to be obviously or carelessly deficient in the skills, sensitivities, and methodology that characterize the common ground between believer and unbeliever. In short, we must do history in a way that it is seen to be good history.

Fourth, I believe that the present language of "integration of faith and learning" may not be the most helpful language at this point in time. It can suggest that faith and learning are things out there—apart from ourselves—like separate entities waiting to be fitted together like so many pieces in a puzzle. There is, as we have already said, a cognitive aspect to this task of integration. But to the extent that Christian truth is incarnational, the integration of faith and learning must take place, finally, in a life. The traditional language of integration also seems to partake of a certain defensiveness on the side of faith. This is perhaps understandable, given the assumptions of the modern epistemological vision that knowledge (to count as knowledge) must be arrived at from a neutral, objective perspective. This language seems to assume that one has the option either to integrate or not to integrate. We are more aware now that our worldview is in our learning whether we choose to have it there or not. So the language of integration is not fully satisfactory. And we may need a new set of words to help us think more creatively and less tritely in these areas.

But the language still serves to call attention to the fact that as Christians in the world, we are shaped by more than one worldview. We are shaped both by the worldview of our place and time and by the worldview of the Kingdom. Integration language calls our attention to the fact that the mind of the World is not the mind of the Kingdom, that we need to have our thinking transformed by the renewing of our minds (see Romans 12:2), and that we, as responsible agents in the world, have a role in this transformation. Calvinists and Arminians would no doubt understand our role in this process quite differently, but all Christians would agree, I believe, that we need to be transformed in our thinking to have the mind of Christ.

So in the end, there *is* a task for the Christian student of history (or any other discipline) that is different from the task of the non-Christian. The Christian student is to be conformed to the image of Christ, to think in the patterns of the Kingdom, and not in the patterns of the World. Until we have better language, the language of "integration of faith and learning" reminds us of this task.

FROM THEORY INTO PRACTICE

I believe that integration of faith and learning operates in three aspects of the classroom experience: first, in the content we teach; second, in the style and policies of our classroom; and third, in the attitude with which we approach our discipline and encourage students to approach it. In the section that follows, I will illustrate how I work out my thinking on the integration of faith and learning. I will organize this section in accord with the three aspects of the integration task that I have just identified— the area of content; the area of pedagogical style; and the area of attitude toward the work. In each case, I will provide some examples from my own teaching.

Content

One obvious way to integrate faith and the study of history is to make use of the framework of history to enlarge students' vision of the community of saints and students' sense of the rich heritage of hymnody and literature that is available as resources for their spiritual growth. In this case, it is the study of history that is speaking to their faith, more than it is faith speaking to the study of history. In my English history class, I often begin class with either a hymn or a prayer or a passage from a sermon from the period of time that we are studying. In the context of the class, I make use of the text for devotional purposes, rather than for strictly historical ones. But the effect is to enlarge the students' sense of identification with the historical period in question. This practice also serves to acquaint them with particular believers in other times and places, so that they see the Church as an institution that transcends time as well as place. (*The Ox-*

ford Book of Prayer is a wonderful resource for finding prayers.[1] Any good hymnal is a ready source for appropriate hymns. I use both Presbyterian and Methodist hymnals in my teaching.)

For example, when studying medieval England, I have used several prayers by Alcuin of York. Usually we talk about the prayer first, discuss the imagery that is used, and look for ways in which the prayer might be instructive about the time period. Then we pray the prayer as a class. For the seventeenth century I have used poems by John Milton, ("On His Blindness"), and poems ("Holy Sonnets") and sermons by John Donne. For the eighteenth century, I have employed various hymns of John Wesley ("And Can It Be," "Oh For a Thousand Tongues to Sing") and Joseph Addison ("When All Thy Mercies, O My God"). For the nineteenth century when we study the Oxford Movement, I have had the students work with John Henry Newman's hymn, "Lead Kindly Light."

In the case of both the hymns and prayers, I utilize them partly for devotional purposes in the class. But I also take time with the students to look for ways in which the Christian faith is embodied in the texts differently from the language of today and, perhaps, for ways that the texts can be lenses through which we might understand more completely the times that we are studying. In a world civilization class, I have made similar use of prayers from *An African Prayer Book*.[2] With this resource, students have opportunity to understand not only how Christians of a different time have framed prayers but also how believers of a different culture think about God.

A second strategy for integrating faith and the study of history in the area of content is to be intentional about including topics of study that are of obvious interest to Christians and that might otherwise receive less attention in academic contexts in which there is less sensitivity to the concerns of the Christian faith. For example, in Russian history we do a unit on the Orthodox tradition within Russia and its significance for Russian history. I have found Timothy Ware's book on Orthodoxy to be very helpful

---

[1] George Appleton, ed., *The Oxford Book of Prayer* (New York: Oxford University Press, 1985).

[2] Desmond Tutu, ed., *An African Prayer Book* (New York: Doubleday, 1995).

in introducing students both to Orthodoxy as a branch of the Christian Church and to the role of Orthodoxy in Russian history.[3] In working with the text, I ask them to focus first on points of similarity and difference between Orthodoxy and Protestantism, which is the predominant branch of Christianity among our students. This discussion naturally leads to their gaining a greater understanding of Roman Catholicism as well. In this course, I also direct their attention to the different historical relationship between state and Church in Russia and the West. This comparative approach provides a framework for discussing ways in which the Church as an institution and the faith of its individual believers can be affected by the relationship between religion and political power. We talk about advantages and disadvantages of being tied to the state for Christian faith and witness. In addition, we discuss particular ways in which Russia's Orthodoxy, especially during the czarist years, shaped its foreign policy. I have also invited the class to visit a local Russian Orthodox church. I did not require this, primarily because I am reluctant to require attendance at a worship service but also because I do not want to turn a worship service into an object for study. I suggested that if students would like to worship in that tradition that would be great. After the service, the local priest (whom I had called prior to our arrival) met with our class and offered additional instruction in Orthodoxy.

In the world civilization course, an area of obvious interest to Christian students is the work of Christian missions—especially to the non-European world. One book that is particularly powerful in raising questions about the nature of missions and how mission work can get inextricably intertwined with westernization is Shusako Endo's novel *Silence*.[4] This simple and beautifully written book lends itself to inquiry on a number of themes. I have the students read the story individually. Then I assign written projects that must address questions such as: What is the essence of the Christian faith that transcends culture? Discuss Rodrigues's (a Portuguese priest and the protagonist) interaction with the Japanese. To what extent would we want to emulate his

---

[3] Timothy Ware, *The Orthodox Church* (Baltimore: Penguin Books, 1964).
[4] Shusako Endo, *Silence* (New York: Taplinger Publishing Co., 1969).

style in presenting the gospel to another culture? What does it mean to be true to the gospel? Did Rodrigues do the right thing? This last question, which is the simplest, invites students to wrestle with all the other ones as well. After the students have written their essay, we spend up to two full class sessions on the book. Sometimes I have then asked students to do a supplementary essay that reconsiders their own initial essay in the light of our class discussion.

In English history, a number of themes raise concerns for students that are part of their lives today. The vast literature on Puritanism raises for us questions about the relationship of law and morality and about the balance of purity and unity in the Church. One book that has worked quite well with students is David Underdown's *Fire From Heaven—Life in an English Town in the Seventeenth Century*.[5] I invite students to write a traditional historical book review on it, and then we discussed the book in class. In the context of that discussion, we move into an investigation of how religion actually functioned in the daily lives of people, especially in the areas of motivating action and providing explanations. Though the book is particularly focused on the era of the English Civil War and how religion functioned in that conflict, these concerns are relevant today in considering how faith actually pertains to daily life.

In the Victorian period, a study of William Gladstone provides a framework to look at the work of a devout person in politics and to consider how his faith and his leadership style intertwined.[6] We talk not only about what Gladstone did but also about the way he was viewed by his contemporaries. We also consider the extent to which we would want to model our lives after Gladstone in balancing concern for principle and concern for people. In the Victorian period, I also enjoy spending time on the Oxford Movement. This topic allows us to consider again how the Church is called to function in the world relative to politics. In addition, it also invites us to explore questions

---

[5] David Underdown, *Fire From Heaven—Life in an English Town in the Seventeenth Century* (New Haven, Conn.: Yale University Press, 1992).

[6] To provide a basis for this discussion, David Bebbington's *William Ewart Gladstone: Faith and Politics in Victorian Britain* (Grand Rapids, Mich.: William B. Eerdmans Publishing Co., 1993) might be used.

about the conflict between loyalties and conscience and to look at patterns of generational conflict in faith development. In working with this issue, I would highly recommend David Newsome's *The Parting of Friends: The Wilberforces and Henry Manning.*[7]

A final example of where the content of English history can raise issues of concern for Christians today is in the area of social reform. I think especially of the work of William Wilberforce, Hannah More, the Salvation Army and the Christian Socialists. I have recently made use of two different books on this general topic: Boyd Hilton, *The Age of Atonement: The Influence of Evangelicalism on Social Reform and Economic Thought 1785–1865*[8] and Gertrude Himmelfarb, *Poverty and Compassion: The Moral Imagination of the Late Victorians.*[9] The first invites students to explore how Christian faith was used in public policy debates and in the development of economic theory to deal with industrialization. The book is especially interesting because it makes clear that Christians used arguments from theology and Scripture to support quite different positions, which raises very provocative questions: How, in fact, does Scripture actually function to give guidance for our lives? Does it just serve as a way of reinforcing positions that have already been arrived at for other reasons? Himmelfarb presents a wide-ranging discussion of the moral and religious motivations for dealing with poverty in late Victorian England. With each of these monographs, I have the students read first on their own. Then I let these issues emerge in freewheeling class discussions.

In modern European history, there are a number of issues that are naturally of concern to Christians. I will mention only a few examples. First, there is the controversy over secularization—whether or not the modern age is an increasingly secular age. I have found Owen Chadwick's book on secularism to be helpful here.[10] He presents a very clear discussion of the controversy and

---

[7] David Newsome, *The Parting of Friends: The Wilberforces and Henry Manning* (Grand Rapids, Mich.: William B. Eerdmans Publishing Co., 1966).

[8] Boyd Hilton, *The Age of Atonement: The Influence of Evangelicalism on Social Reform and Economic Thought 1785–1865* (Oxford: Clarendon Press, 1988).

[9] Gertrude Himmelfarb, *Poverty and Compassion: The Moral Imagination of the Late Victorians* (New York: Alfred A. Knopf, 1991).

[10] Owen Chadwick, *The Secularization of the European Mind in the Nineteenth Century* (New York: Cambridge University Press, 1990).

then argues for his position. Second, there is the experience of state churches. I have already mentioned the case of Orthodoxy in Russia, but the experience of the Catholic Church in France and the role of religion in the French Revolution is another obvious example. Dale Van Kley's *The Religious Origins of the French Revolution* can be helpful in this discussion.[11] I draw special attention to events related to the Church such as the Civil Constitution of the Clergy and invite students to reflect on what we might learn from the French experience about the relationship of Church to the power structures of an age. A third example from European history that I believe ought to have special relevance to Christians is the art of peacemaking. I have always tended to spend more time discussing the causes of World War I than the strategies of peacemaking at the Treaty of Versailles. Recently I asked my students to write a paper focused on identifying and analyzing strategies of peacemaking in light of the circumstances that had given rise to the war in the first place.

In addition to viewing history as an invitation to students to expand their faith perspectives and an opportunity to draw attention to areas of content that are of particular concern to Christians, I try also to be intentional about raising questions from history that encourage moral and theological reflection. Questions of this sort call us to reflect on what we can learn about the human condition from the experience of various historical figures and events. As with many of the large human questions, these questions rarely lead to definitive answers. Nevertheless, in the process of reflecting with others on the questions, students come to a clearer sense of their own thinking and to a clearer sense of the complexity and ambiguity of the fallen world in which we live.

The types of questions that I am thinking about are implied in the previous section. But I will list a few examples here as well. First, what can we learn about being a Christian in politics from the life of Gladstone? Or Cromwell? Second, what can we learn about Christian activism from the life of William Wilberforce? Third, how do we think about the relationship of the Church to

---

[11] Dale Van Kley, *The Religious Origins of the French Revolution* (New Haven: Yale University Press, 1996.)

the power structures of an age? Is there a way that the state can be appropriated for moral and spiritual purposes? If not, why not? Are there limits to our obligation to civil authority? Fourth, how does God work in history? Can the historian, as historian, see God at work? What sort of knowledge claim is it to say that God has acted in history? Fifth, what can be learned from a study of historical attempts at peacemaking (Vienna, Versailles) about how to be peacemakers in the world?

I also believe that concern for integration of faith and the teaching of history draws us to be as inclusive as possible in allowing students to learn about the past from as many different perspectives as possible. If we take all of creation—including different cultures, and different individuals—as manifesting God's presence in their experience in ways that are distinct to their particular needs and circumstances, then we should expect that there would be much to learn about history and human experience by hearing from different voices. If we take seriously the doctrine of human fallenness, we should not expect that we see the past with perfect clarity from any one perspective. Thus, there is a theological mandate for Christians to seek to study the past from a range of perspectives. Sometimes this diversity of perspective comes through readings that speak from a range of cultural, gender, and class perspectives. Sometimes it comes from guest speakers. This past year, in the world civilization class, we heard from two Japanese-American Christians who had been interned in the Japanese internment camps in California during World War II. This learning experience called students very powerfully to empathize with fellow brothers and sisters in Christ who had been treated as outsiders here within the United States.

Pedagogical Style

Integrating faith and the study of history is not only a matter of working with content. It is also a matter of pedagogy—of cultivating in students not only the information that they ought to know as Christians but also the virtues that ought to characterize their lives as Christians. For one thing, we want to encourage in our students an attitude of humility and clear vision about the nature of their own perspective on the world. We want them to be aware of their own location in place and time—their own biases and their own perspectives—as a way of inviting them to a larger, more multifaceted perspective on the world. To nurture this self-awareness that I believe produces humility, I have tried a range of assignments. For example, I have invited students to do two brief essays—one at the beginning of a world civilization course and one at the end—on their views of the world and their own place within the world. Sometimes I have assigned students the task of writing an essay that connects their own family history to the larger historical picture. This often involves students conducting oral history interviews with family members.

There are not only virtues but also certain sensitivities that ought to characterize the Christian historian. One such sensitivity is an awareness of complexity, ambiguity, and mystery in the historical process. This seems to be the point of Jesus' parable of the wheat and the tares. Things in this world are not always black and white. Good and evil are inextricably intertwined. There are tensions, paradoxes, and different visions that may never be satisfactorily resolved in this world. Part of being Christian is always to be engaged in the task of sorting—discerning where good is, where truth is. Sometimes the good and the true are to be found in surprising places. One way I begin developing in students strategies for dealing with complexity and ambiguity is to have them read two books dealing with the same set of events and then to invite them to do a comparative book review. In an English history class, I assign the accounts of Christopher Hill and Conrad Russell on the causes of the English Civil War. I ask students to compare the differing interpretations offered in these two books and then to explain what might account for the differences.

A second sensitivity that Christian students of history ought to bring to their work is an awareness of human responsibility in the historical process. One topic that lends itself very well to the promotion of reflective thinking on human responsibility is the appeasement policy of the Allies after World War I. We work particularly with A. J. P. Taylor's controversial assessment that shifts the blame for World War II from the fascists to the Allies.[12] The question of how much we bear responsibility for preventing evil or holding one another accountable is a fascinating one. (There is a helpful discussion along these lines in Michael Walzer's *Just and Unjust Wars*[13] dealing with the question of how we should think about the participants in the perpetration of the Holocaust who were "only obeying orders.")

Attitude Toward the Subject Matter

In thinking about the integration of faith concerns and the study of history, we are also invited to consider how we as historians are to think about the biblical message of history as the arena of God's special activity. One pervasive message in the Scriptures is that God acts in human history. In the same way that we speak of God's handiwork in nature, so we want to think of God's activity in history. And yet once we move outside the biblical framework, it has always been unclear how Christians are to know where God is acting in history. Are we, as Christian historians, to take into account God as a factor in historical causality? If so, what would that mean? If not, then what is the value of affirming God's activity—indeed, God's sovereignty—in history? Herbert Butterfield's essay, "God in History," is a helpful discussion starter on this topic.[14] In upper-division classes, I have had students write a reflection paper on their own philosophy of history. In case they are intimidated by that language, I assign questions like the following: What are your thoughts on the meaning of history? How do we account for change in history—through forces, structures, individuals? What biblical teachings or theological doctrines have implications for your thinking about history?

It would seem that part of cultivating a Christian attitude to

---

[12] A. J. P. Taylor, *The Origins of the Second World War* (New York: Atheneum, 1968).

[13] Michael Walzer, *Just and Unjust Wars: A Moral Argument with Historical Illustrations* (New York: Basic Books, 1977).

[14] C. T. McIntire, ed., *Herbert Butterfield: Writings on Christianity and History* (New York: Oxford University Press, 1979).

our subject is cultivating a sense of the individual people in history as particular objects of God's love and mercy. This is something that can be done very powerfully through working with autobiographies. I do not think it is so important which autobiography is used, but it should be one that helps the student feel what it is like to be that person in space and time. The point here is not that the subject of the book be Christian but that the student come to see that person through the eyes of grace and mercy—to look at the person with compassion, in the same way as God looks at that person. Personally, I have found Vera Brittain's *Testament of Youth* on the experience of her generation in World War I to be very helpful in allowing students to see the participants in the Great War as individuals—particular objects of God's grace caught in a particularly painful period of history.[15] The book helps them to empathize with those individuals and to see World War I not as an impersonal event but as a context in which individuals were shaped in ways that have eternal consequences. This awareness of the relationship of the temporal and the eternal in the lives of individuals seems to be one of the fundamental aspects of Christian thinking about history.

CONCLUSION

After nearly two decades of teaching history, I feel I am only beginning to understand what it means to cultivate the integration of faith and learning. Part of that understanding is to realize that, as professors, we can only sow the seeds of integration. A much larger process is going on in the lives of our students than the education that we are trying to give them in the classroom—a process that we have very little control over and that operates sometimes through us, and—as humbling as it is to realize—sometimes in spite of us. I speak of the work of the Holy Spirit—the Comforter, who is sent to guide us into all truth and who is at work in us and in our students to bring about the integration and wholeness that we so imperfectly seek.

---

[15] Vera Brittain, *Testament of Youth* (New York: Penguin Books, 1933).

Selected Bibliography

Bebbington, David. *Patterns in History: A Christian View.* Downers Grove, Ill.: InterVarsity Press, 1979.

Butterfield, Herbert. *Christianity and History.* New York: Charles Scribner's Sons, 1949.

Marsden, George, and Frank Roberts, eds. *A Christian View of History?* Grand Rapids, Mich.: William B. Eerdmans Publishing Co., 1975.

McIntire, C. T., ed. *Herbert Butterfield: Writings on Christianity and History.* New York: Oxford University Press, 1979.

Newman, John Henry Cardinal. *The Idea of a University.* Notre Dame, Ind.: University of Notre Dame Press, 1982.

Wells, Ronald A. *History Through the Eyes of Faith.* San Francisco: Harper & Row, 1989.

———, ed. *History and the Christian Historian.* Grand Rapids, Mich.: William B. Eerdmans Publishing Co., 1998.

14

Christian Faith and the Teaching of Speech Communication

Michael T. Ingram

Some Professional and Personal Considerations

I teach at Whitworth College in Spokane, Washington, which is affiliated with the Presbyterian Church (U.S.A.). Many of the fifteen hundred undergraduate students have some Christian background. Some students are very committed to Christ and a local church, some are committed to Christ with no strong allegiance to a particular group, some are nominal Christians, and some profess no religious faith. Thus there is a wide range of faith perspectives on my campus.

My religious heritage is Southern Baptist. This faith tradition regards the Bible as the inspired authority for all areas of human activity. Many Southern Baptists value 2 Timothy 3:16, which affirms that "All scripture is inspired by God and is useful for teaching, for reproof, for correction, and for training in righteousness, so that everyone who belongs to God may be proficient, equipped for every good work." Scripture provides instruction on spiritual matters such as prayer and worship. It also provides instruction on topics like marriage, money management, and relationships. Southern Baptists emphasize discipleship and following Christ in all matters of life. Thus it is natural for Southern Baptists to examine the Bible for guidance on human communication.

As will be demonstrated in this essay, there are numerous biblical texts that consider the manner in which Christians should communicate. These passages provide clear instruction to humans on how to communicate with each other. Many of them address the power of the spoken word, the necessity of integrity and honesty in human transactions, and the promotion of respect for others. Thus communication themes are directly addressed in the Scriptures and in standard communication course textbooks. If Baptists and other Christians are to follow God by obeying God's commands, then the lessons of faith should permeate our life, thoughts, and understanding of our academic disciplines.

Students learn several skills in the discipline of speech communication. They learn how to speak persuasively, how to advance arguments, and how to present themselves interpersonally. The skills themselves are neutral. They can be harnessed for the good and for the Church. Students might use communication skills to encourage and edify other Christians, to present the gospel clearly, and to listen respectfully to the concerns of others. But the same skills may just as easily be appropriated to propagate the evils of manipulation, lying, or deception. To insure that students understand the full range of possible uses to which the skills they learn may be put, it is important that they receive instruction on the spiritual dimensions of their communication abilities. This essay will focus on the integration of faith in teaching three different course areas in speech communication—interpersonal communication, small group communication, and communication ethics.

Assumptions

In the current legal and social climate, many state schools do not actively seek or even permit discussions on the relationship of faith and assumptions in the disciplines—including communication. This is based on both a respect for all students regardless of their religion (or lack thereof) and a fear of bridging the wall of separation between church and state, which would appear to preclude any such discussion. Hence students are denied the full exploration of ideas.

Private schools have the luxury of expanding the discussion of topics to include a religious dimension without fear of legal sanction. The manner in which professors explore faith dimensions should be both bold and respectful. My approach has been to present an idea and its faith implication and invite students to address it. I look for vocal students, both religious and nonreligious, to speak up. I do not call on students directly in these discussions, thus preserving the autonomy of the nonreligious or nominally religious to choose whether to participate in such a discussion. This is a deliberate attempt both to present ideas for intellectual consideration and to be sensitive to those who do not subscribe to religious views.

I do state that all students, especially in the senior-level communication ethics course, must give an account of what they do with Christ and his ideas, just as they must with Immanuel Kant or John Stuart Mill or the textbook author. Rather than indoctrination, the presentation of Christian interpretation of class concepts and their relationships to spiritual topics is an expansive act consistent with the liberal arts tradition. Students regardless of religious background should be exposed to major religious thinkers and their influence on thinking in the discipline. Universities often consider the religious or metaphysical ideas of Aristotle and Plato across courses in several disciplines. Why not those of Christ as well? Why not in speech communication?

INTERPERSONAL COMMUNICATION

Interpersonal Communication is a freshman-level course at Whitworth College. Many students take it to meet the college oral communications requirement. I make at least five connections between faith and course content as the term progresses. The first connection considers the power of language. Many textbooks in the discipline present the Sapir-Whorf hypothesis that language shapes thought.[1] This leads to a discussion on the

---

[1] The Sapir-Whorf hypothesis is also referred to as "linguistic determinism" or "the linguistic relativity hypothesis." It is found in textbooks like Joseph A. DeVito, *The Interpersonal Communication Book* (New York: Longman Press, 1998); Steven A. Beebe, Susan J. Beebe, and Mark Redmond, *Interpersonal Communication: Relating to Others* (Boston: Allyn & Bacon, 1996); John Stewart and Carole Logan, *Together Communicating Interpersonally* (New York: McGraw-Hill, 1993); and John Caputo, Harry Hazel, and Colleen McMahon, *Interpersonal Communication: Competency Through Critical Thinking* (Boston: Allyn & Bacon, 1994).

causal effect of language, its power in shaping thought and belief, and thus its effect upon communication styles and choices. The class examines studies that support the claim that hearing particular words or images often enough strongly influences people's perceptions.

A standard lecture explains how the use of racist and sexist language by speakers can cause listeners to develop racist or sexist attitudes and exhibit related behaviors. I discuss how the term *mailman* has become *letter carrier*. This language change allows us to think that women and men could deliver the mail. I discuss the term *gook* and how its use during the Korean and Vietnam wars led some Americans to regard the enemy as less than human. I also discuss how universities no longer recruit *foreign* students (who are very different than we are) but recruit *international* students instead.

I demonstrate Sapir-Whorf in discussing the language of God, how humans name God, and how religious language can create barriers in interpersonal and intercultural relationships. The class considers the growing presence of diverse religious groups and views in the United States and how language creates meaning in our pluralistic society. Students may have had their own religious views shaped by language without conscious recognition of this fact.

A frequent class discussion compares the more traditional term *God the Father* with the more contemporary *God the Parent* or even some denominations' use of *God as our Mother*. Students consider the following terms:

TABLE 1. TERMS FOR GOD

Traditional	Contemporary	Functional
God the Father	God the Parent	Creator
God the Son	God the Offspring	Redeemer
God the Holy Spirit	God the Spirit	Sustainer

The first column describes God with traditional names and roles, which most students recognize. The second column describes God with contemporary and gender-neutral names and roles, which students from more liberal backgrounds recognize. The third column describes God by function rather than assigning anthropomorphic names. A rich discussion follows about what the various names do for our understanding of God. It can lead to an ontological discussion of God's being and qualities. This discussion can suggest that perhaps language, or our use of it, causes us to believe that God has a gender.

The key principle of the Sapir-Whorf hypothesis is that language is causal. Our class discussion of it reveals how language shapes our theological understandings and how we choose different faith communities. Why are some attracted to traditional hymns and language use, while others are attracted to newer expressions? How does being raised in one faith-language community shape a person's theology and understanding of God? Students enjoy comparing hymns in which the traditional term *men*, such as in "Good Christian Men Rejoice" and "Brethren We Have Met to Worship," becomes the gender-neutral language of "Good Christian Friends Rejoice" and "Christians We Have Met to Worship."

A discussion of cursing and the acceptance of profanity in modern U.S. culture also connects to Sapir-Whorf. Students list current favorite movies and television programs and compare that list to their favorite programs when they were younger. The discussion invariably leads students to acknowledge the increasing frequency of profane and impure speech and the heightened force with which such language is expressed in the entertainment industry. Our collective reflection concludes that profanity has been accepted in most forms of entertainment and helps to shape social attitudes. A discussion of rap music is always exciting here. Students must decide how using repeated words, images, and phrases will or will not shape the attitudes of listeners. An examination of teachings in Matthew chapter five, or in James chapter three, is often helpful here in analyzing cursing and how Christians view speech. Students then wrestle with their own language use and must evaluate the merits of what they consider entertainment. If Sapir-Whorf is true, then students must consider how the language of their entertainment choices shapes their own beliefs.

The second connection considers the propriety of assertiveness. Many textbooks, like Joseph DeVito's *The Interpersonal Communication Book*, address the communication styles of assertiveness, nonassertiveness, and aggressiveness.[2] In class discussion, students typically list the verbal and nonverbal behaviors that accompany each style. They then decide which style they would employ in various settings ("people behind you at the movies are talking loudly" or "your restaurant food arrives cold instead of hot" or "you are attracted to someone in the class and want to ask him out on a date"). The conventional assumption is that assertiveness is the preferred North American response style. It is clear, direct, and reflects a cultural value of affirming individual rights.

It is interesting to question students about the styles Jesus might employ and under what conditions. Some make the argument that Jesus would teach nonassertiveness. Students consider passages in Matthew chapter five to turn the other cheek and go the second mile, which suggest a theme of dying to self and placing the concerns of others above personal ones. It is easy to read these examples from the gospel and believe Christians are called to be nonassertive. A few students argue that Jesus showed aggression, certainly in Matthew 21 when he overturned the tables in the Temple in anger. Passages in which he says that his followers should love him more than their parents (for example, Matthew 10:37) and that he comes to bring division (Luke12:51) also suggest that Jesus causes conflict. This appears quite aggressive to some students. Frequently students agree that one of the two great commandments is based on an assertive principle. The command to "love others as you love yourself" appears based on the premise that you love yourself. The voyage of Jesus across the Sea of Galilee in John chapter six, demonstrates self-love by protecting the time that he needed for himself. He was not available to the crowds all the time. Students discuss how Jesus protected his needs in this and similar situations. The point of the discussion is to get students to connect their view of a speech communication topic, in this case assertiveness, to their own faith and not merely to accept uncritically the dominant view of assertiveness as normative.

---

[2] Joseph A. DeVito does this explicitly in his textbook, *The Interpersonal Communication Book* (New York: Longman Press, 1998).

A third connection examines the spiritual dimensions of relationship. All interpersonal communication textbooks emphasize the centrality of relationships, understanding relationships, and discovering ways to strengthen them. Some textbooks like John Stewart's *Bridges Not Walls* include the ideas of the Jewish philosopher Martin Buber.[3] Buber addresses the desire to have "interhuman" relations where two people meet each other and connect in deep ways, as opposed to a mere "social relationship" that does not require any depth of person-to-person contact. Buber argues for being present, genuine, and authentic with other people, thereby fostering the interhuman.

Scripture teaches us that God calls us together to be God's people and to live together as God's Church. Scripture has many passages about people connecting with each other and reconciling with God to live together in peace.[4] Buber's ideas are consistent with biblical ideas that God made us for relationship with God and with each other. Students hear the idea that God made each one of us in God's image. Therefore we should treat each person with dignity and respect because we come from God. In relationships we must show respect to each person. Students read the excerpt (and helpful outline) of Buber's essay in *Bridges Not Walls* and respond to questions like these:

1. Explain how Buber distinguishes "being" from "seeming." (This helps students grasp the foundation of Buber's central idea.)

---

[3] John Stewart, ed., *Bridges Not Walls* (New York: McGraw-Hill, 1995). Buber's ideas are also developed in other course areas, such as communication ethics. Richard Johannesen covers the I-Thou relationship in his classic *Ethics in Human Communication* (Prospect Heights, Ill.: Waveland Press, 1996) as do James Jaksa and Michael Pritchard in *Communication Ethics: Methods of Analysis* (Belmont, Calif.: Wadsworth, 1994).

[4] Matthew 5:21–24 calls Christians to leave offerings at the altar and be reconciled to our brothers (and sisters) before worshipping God. Matthew 5:43–48 calls Christians to love our enemies and those who persecute us. This sounds like an imperative for pursuing conflict management with our enemies and others for whom we harbor ill will. Luke 17:4 calls Christians to forgive an unlimited number of times, which suggests the ongoing pursuit of unencumbered relationships. Romans 12:17 warns Christians not to pay back evil for evil or take revenge. This sounds like an imperative for doing good and extending kindness in all relationships. 1 Peter 3:8–13 specifically calls Christians to be kindhearted.

2. Explain what Jesus taught about "being" and "seeming." (Connections can be made here to Jesus' indictments of the Pharisees for their false talk and false ways of presenting self, especially in matters of prayer, and his praise for genuine persons who were honest and present.)
3. With whom do you interact in the "seeming" way that Buber and Christ indict? With whom do you interact in the "being" way?
4. Explain how racism conflicts with the idea that we are all made in God's image.

Christ calls us to know one another intimately in committed relationships. He models this by pouring his life into the disciples and commanding them to make more disciples. These discussion topics help students to see the spiritual dimensions of communication relationships.

John Stewart and Carole Logan, who wrote *Together: Communicating Interpersonally*, summarize Buber's list of five qualities that distinguish the personal from the impersonal across cultures.[5] The impersonal approach regards people as objects and mere parts of a whole while the interpersonal sees people as individuals and pays attention to their distinctions. Standard assumptions in interpersonal communication classes suggest students should treat humans like persons and not objects. A colleague of mine organized Stewart and Logan's ideas into a continuum that looks like this:

TABLE 2. IMPERSONAL VERSUS INTERPERSONAL VIEWS OF PEOPLE

Impersonal—see people as objects	Interpersonal—see people as individuals
Interchangeable—like car parts	Uniqueness—people are distinct
Measurability—physical description tells all	Unmeasurable—must include spirit or psyche or cognitive patterns
React Only—respond to stimulus	Able to choose—can select own responses regardless of stimulus

---

[5] John Stewart and Carole Logan, *Together: Communicating Interpersonally* (New York: McGraw-Hill, 1993).

| Unreflective—unaware of surroundings | Reflective—aware of surroundings |
| Not Addressable—people can be talked about | Addressable—people can be talked with |

Students come to understand how they make a range of communication choices about how they interact with various people. Students then assess their relationships using this continuum and consider how to move their behavior from the impersonal approach to the interpersonal approach. I ask them to describe how they interact on this continuum with various people, such as parents, best friends, professors, bookstore clerks, classmates, and romantic partners. Students discuss how treating people in these ways ("I treated the clerk as interchangeable, as it really did not matter who I paid for the books" or "I gave my best friend the opportunity to choose how to respond to me") promotes an interhuman or social relationships response.

The self-reflection of students regarding where they placed their relationships along the continuum is helpful in gauging both communication styles and spiritual considerations. Students consider John chapter eight, in which Jesus teaches us a new way to consider the woman caught in adultery. The Pharisees were not interested in her as a person. They used her as a tool or object against Christ (or impersonally). Jesus responds and shows us that the woman is not to be used in this way. She is to be regarded as a person—a person in need of grace. Students then consider their own communication behaviors and how they treat others.

A fourth connection is the clear tie between Scripture and conflict management and reconciliation. Several lessons connect biblical mandates on peacemaking to practical implementation. The charge to engage in peacemaking comes from the Sermon on the Mount, in which Jesus teaches that peacemakers are blessed and Christians are to initiate reconciliation. In Romans 12 the Apostle Paul teaches Christians not to take revenge. I teach that conflict management should be done not only because it helps groups accomplish their goals but also because Christians are commanded to be peacemakers. That is who we are to be. The pragmatic justifications for peacemaking exist in addition to the scriptural call to be God's people. In discussing particular conflict management techniques I make connections to Christian values. Specific scriptural ideas include:

1. Christians should deal with conflict in a timely fashion without delay. Ephesians 4:26 teaches "Do not let the sun go down on your anger." I present this as an imperative to deal with anger and conflict and to solve problems immediately. This passage suggests deliberate action. It also implies that Christians should initiate reconciliation. This is the opposite of avoiding conflict.

2. Christians should communicate with people in a direct fashion. Matthew 18:15–17 teaches that, when in conflict with an individual, Christians should talk to the person first and try to solve the problem directly. If there is no resolution, we should first take one witness, then take the issue to a group, and then to the public. Following a private model then increasingly more public models of conflict management is both scriptural and conventional in its wisdom.

3. Christians should be careful of judging others. Matthew 7:1–5 calls us to "notice the log in your own eye" before preparing to "take the speck out of your neighbor's eye." Students must consider their own failings and the ways they may have contributed to the problem before rushing to judge others. Some honest self-evaluation is in order before one makes accusations about another person's responsibility in the affair. In *Together: Communicating Interpersonally*, Stewart and Logan suggest abandoning the concepts of fault and blame. This perspective suggests everyone has a part in a conflict, and parties should avoid scapegoating each other. Each person should look inward before going outward.

4. Christians should engage in "carefronting" instead of confronting. In confronting, students raise a topic of concern in a relationship with an eye to solving the problem from their own perspective. In carefronting, the attitude is such that while students are raising a topic of concern in the relationship, they are also displaying concern for the other person and for the relationship. The approach is not simply a list of reading one's own rights and asserting one's own way but also a concern for the other person and what will minister to her needs. This also connects the conventional ideas of rhetorical sensitivity toward others with the biblical command to love others.

I find a fifth connection in addressing family communication. Textbook chapters on this topic tend to start with several definitions of family. Historical definitions (nuclear, extended, step) are often compared with emerging contemporary definitions (unmarried persons living together, domestic partnerships, homosexual unions). Students are usually asked to define "family" and talk about what kinds of family structures they desire to have in the future. This topic provides students an opportunity to examine Christian understandings of familial relationships and how their definitions compare with Scripture. Such opportunities are important in light of contemporary challenges to marriage and its role in society. With cities and states recognizing unmarried couples in a very similar way to married couples, the advent of "domestic partners," and a movement legally to validate homosexual unions, the traditional biblical definition of "marriage and family" is being questioned. In completing an assignment to define a "family," students are encouraged to consider their answers in light of their faith. They then must provide reasons for their perspectives regardless of the position they take.

Small Group Communication

Small Group Communications is a sophomore-level course. Several students take it to meet the college oral communications requirement, though most of the students are majors in the department. I also teach a junior-level version of the course to adult students enrolled in a six-week cohort program. I raise faith issues in four distinct contexts and connect them appropriately to course content.

A first connection occurs in the discussion of negotiation with an emphasis on the ideas of Roger Fisher, William Ury, and Bruce Patton in their book *Getting To Yes*.[6] They build their notion of "principled negotiation" on four main ideas: a separation of the people from the problem, a focus on interests and not posi-

---

[6] Roger Fisher, William Ury, and Bruce Patton, *Getting to Yes: Negotiating Agreement Without Giving In* (Boston: Houghton Mifflin, 1991).

tions, the invention of options for mutual gain, and insistence on using objective criteria. They argue negotiators should move away from both "soft" bargaining (emphasizing the relationship at all costs) and "hard" bargaining (emphasizing the result at all costs). Negotiators should focus instead on the principles that value both the process and the relationship.

Some students argue that principled negotiation is consistent with a Christian understanding of fairness, including the command to treat everyone fairly. Some argue that separating the people from the problem is consistent with a Christian "love-the-sinner-hate-the-sin" approach. Christians should focus on people and their needs and should work to get people to collaborate as problem solvers rather than as adversaries or enemies. Principled negotiation complements Christianity in its deliberate engagement in peacemaking and in its regard for the needs of all parties. It requires us to see whole persons and all of their needs. A frequent exam question asks students to argue for or against the statement "principled negotiation is consistent with Christian beliefs" or "principled negotiation is inherently ethical."

A second connection occurs in the discussion on communication rules. In *Theories of Human Communication*, Stephen Littlejohn discusses the place of communication rules and the concept of regulative rules.[7] Regulative rules provide guidelines for acting out already established behavior and suggest what is appropriate in a particular context. When one encounters behavior A, behavior B is the normative response. Everyone expects behavior B. Littlejohn uses the example of a host opening the door for a guest who is leaving. In the classroom, a regulative rule is to raise one's hand or have the eye contact of the professor before speaking. Another rule is not to interrupt a person who is speaking.

I ask students to describe Sunday morning worship services at Catholic, Presbyterian, African-American Baptist, and Pentecostal churches paying particular heed to styles of singing, type of liturgy, role of audible or silent prayers, and role of the audi-

---

[7] Stephen Littlejohn, *Theories of Human Communication* (Belmont, Calif.: Wadsworth Publishing Co., 1989), 119.

ence in responding to the sermon. (Students respond to this question from their own experiences and memories.) I pose questions to the class about the regulative rules they have observed. How does each church socialize members to its communication rules for worship services? How does each church handle people who violate group communication rules? Are there connections between the communication rules for the worship service of each church and the various small groups of each church? This discussion supplies another example to illustrate how communication rules work (along with secular examples I supply in class) and connects a communication theory to practice in the life of the church.

A third connection appears in comparing groupthink and Christian decision making. The classical definition of groupthink from Irving Janis is "a deterioration of mental efficiency, reality testing, and moral judgment that results from in-group pressures."[8] The conventional premise is that critical thinking and the presence of disagreement is extremely important to groups. Standard textbooks teach students how to identify and prevent groupthink. Solutions often include creative thinking and asking for honest feedback. In light of these proposed solutions, I ask students how they believe Christian groups, especially close-knit groups, should make decisions. For many churches and faith traditions—even non-Christian ones—a lack of disagreement is interpreted as a sign of God's spirit and blessing. The presence of disagreement can be interpreted as divisive and as evidence of someone's standing in the way of God's will.[9] Students are asked how they make sense of Bible studies in which everyone agrees all the time and if that agreement reflects more of God's spirit or of groupthink. Questions arise about how to promote critical thinking in the church. I ask students to comment on their experiences and to imagine ways to promote Christian unity while avoiding groupthink.

A fourth connection appears in the broad and overt applica-

---

[8] Irvin L. Janis, *Groupthink: Psychological Studies of Policy Decisions and Fiascoes* (Boston: Houghton Mifflin, 1983).

[9] Bill Strom makes this overt connection between communication conflict and spiritual observations in his textbook *More Than Talk: Communication Studies and the Christian Faith* (Dubuque, Iowa: Kendall Hunt, 1996), 115.

tion of many course ideas to Christian small groups, like Bible study groups, prayer groups, mission teams, and church committees. Class activities here include direct application of course concepts to specific religious settings. For example, discussions on how to lead meetings, how to recognize personality types, and how to plan an agenda are reviewed in the particular context of ministry groups.

Students are encouraged to see how all the course ideas can be used in Christian contexts. Topics include various processes of decision making, how to run meetings, types and styles of leadership, how to observe and analyze groups, models of problem solving, how to assess meetings, how to observe roles group members play, how to recognize communication rules, how to manage conflict, and how to conduct negotiations. I discuss how to lead youth meetings, how to manage personality types in summer missions teams, and how to plan an agenda for a dorm Bible study meeting. Frequently the summary lecture connects most class topics to practical steps of implementation for Christian small groups.[10] For non-Christian students, the summary merely provides another illustration of ways the class ideas can be applied in different contexts.

COMMUNICATION ETHICS

Communication Ethics is a senior-level capstone course, required for communication studies majors. Here my objective is for students to reflect on all the skills they have learned in four years and decide how they will use these skills. The metaphor of the knife is used as an illustration. A knife can be used to rob or kill someone, to carve wooden furniture, or to heal injuries as a surgeon's scalpel. The knife itself is morally neutral. How one uses the knife is the moral question. Faith issues intersect course content at two significant junctures.

---

[10] In recent years this lecture has been shortened, as my colleague developed a new Communication in Ministry course. My sophomore-level Small Group Communication course provides a basic introduction to groups. My colleague develops more faith connection ideas in the junior-level Communication in Ministry course for students with a special interest in such direct applications.

A first direct connection is made in our discussion of integrity. The tongue can tell the truth or lie. There are several passages in James that speak to the role of the tongue, and several Old Testament Proverbs address liars per se. Students read *Lying* by Sissela Bok and grapple with difficult topics including white lies, lying to liars, lying to enemies, and lying to protect clients and preserve confidentiality.[11] Bok discusses famous historical lies like President Dwight Eisenhower's about U-2 flights over the Soviet Union. I ask students how they regard the lies of President Eisenhower and those of subsequent presidents.

Bok also presents typologies of lies offered by St. Augustine and by St. Thomas Aquinas. Students read the following quotation from St. Augustine that appears in Bok:

> It cannot be denied that they have attained a very high standard of goodness who never lie except to save a man from injury; but in the case of men who have reached this standard, it is not the deceit but the good intention that is justly praised and sometimes even rewarded. It is quite enough that the deception should be pardoned, without its being made an object of laudation.[12]

Here I make the discussion of intentions personal. I ask, "Suppose Jenna and Adam are throwing Deanna a surprise birthday party in the dorm on Friday. Deanna sees Adam on Tuesday and asks him how he is doing and if Jenna is planning a party for her birthday. What would you say if you were Adam?" Frequently the discussion leads the class to accept this white lie. I connect class answers back to the discussion on presidential lying and relevant Scripture verses. My goal is to encourage students to be consistent in their thinking. Students must reconcile lies and justifications of lies with their own faith understandings and interpretation of Christian Scripture.

The justification of lies is a key theme in class discussions all semester. I give students several scenarios and case studies and ask them how they would judge these lies. One example concerns the hiding of Jews from the Nazis in occupied Holland during World War II. Students role-play Dutch citizens hiding

---

[11] Sissela Bok, *Lying: Moral Choice in Public and Private Life* (New York: Vintage Books, 1989).
[12] Bok, *Lying*, 33.

Jews in the basements of their homes. The Gestapo knocks on the door and asks if they are hiding any Jews or know the location of any Jews in Holland. Most students elect to lie to the Gestapo. The justifications are usually based on the moral evil of the Nazis or the pragmatic position of saving Jewish lives. In another context, I relate the plight of illegal immigrants in the U.S. Southwest. After considering accounts of the 1980s "Sanctuary Movement," I ask students if they would lie to U.S. immigration officials about illegal immigrants they might be hiding in a house or in a church building.

I ask students to consider their lying in light of several Scriptures that command Christians not to lie. I ask them if they would side with Immanuel Kant in an absolute rejection of lies. Then students hear how Rahab lied to the King of Jericho and hid the Hebrew spies Joshua and Caleb in the Book of Joshua, chapter two. The Hebrews honored Rahab, and she is an ancestor of Jesus Christ. Students must then decide if lying to save God's people is justified. The point of the exercise is to help students understand how they use reason to justify their own lying and how they might reconcile their actions with the tenets of their faith.

The class also considers political rhetoric and examines the public lies of political, social, and religious leaders. Students assess lying both for its results, which could either be effective or ineffective, and for its ethical ramifications. They frequently begin the course concerned that political leaders lie, though some have simply accepted it as a way the world works. We then discuss whether lying reflects or does not reflect our respect for the spoken word and our respect for each other. Good questions for discussion include: How do lies respect persons made in the image of God? How do lies honor God? How do lies help or harm community?

I also address the problematic nature of embellishment. I offer the example of a man claiming to be a Vietnam War veteran who had collected artifacts and money from veterans and opened a war museum in San Antonio, Texas, in 1989.[13] Newspaper re-

---

[13] Roberto Suro, "Collections" reprinted in the *The Spokesman-Review*, December 3, 1989.

porters proved that the man lied and never served in Vietnam. He embellished some facts and freely added other "facts" to the "truth." I encourage students to make an ethical judgment with regard to this man and his actions. Then the question is turned to, "Suppose another man embellished the truth about a past event to raise money for Christian missions. Would he be justified?" The intent of the second discussion is to help students examine their justification of the first lie and to consider how a lie in the name of God or the Church would stand up under close scrutiny and again to consider how they reconcile their actions with the tenets of their faith.

The second crucial connection occurs when students see the Christian faith as authoritative for making ethical decisions. It is important for students to see how Christianity should or could influence their ethical views. Given the secular nature of contemporary life, they may not have considered the relationship that Sunday morning faith should have on Thursday evening ethical decision making. I introduce students to classical theories of ethical decision making (the deontological ideas of Kant, the utility of Jeremy Bentham and John Stuart Mill, the pragmatism of John Dewey). We discuss the role of ethical standards as well as the absence of standards (as in cultural relativism and egoism). Students are also exposed to theories that rely on natural and on supernatural (that is, religious) authority for making ethical decisions. I operate on the working assumption that Scripture is a reliable authority for ethical decision making. The Southern Baptist tradition calls Christians to examine the Bible and discover verses and passages that speak to moral prohibitions and to moral duty.

Near the end of the course, students must write an eight-page paper on their personal system of ethical principles in speech communication. This paper outlines their preferred foundation of ethics (utility, pragmatism, hedonism, or otherwise) and explains how they would make decisions in certain situations. For example, students could write how they view utility and explain three reasons why they find that perspective appealing. Then they explain how utility would guide them when faced with the option of lying to an enemy or to a dying relative.

This assignment provides both clarity and closure. For an entire semester, students have considered many perspectives on ethics. In this project they must choose the single view they find most compelling. They must demonstrate understanding of the perspective and how it would be lived out. In reviewing first drafts of the paper, I encourage students of faith to explain how the perspective they chose fits or does not fit with their faith principles. Some students attempt to mix several ethical theories together to create their own ideas about how things should be. Many work to create a Christian-utility perspective or a Christian-deontological perspective. Most of the students create exceptions to the rules they have developed, such as "Lying to enemies is wrong except when terrorists have nuclear weapons." The conference time is a good opportunity to encourage students individually to make the connections between their faith and learning.

Usually I teach this class with a journalism colleague, and we do our best not to reveal our own beliefs and struggles. We attempt to play the devil's advocate and ask questions on all sides of whatever issues arise. Then on the last day of class, we answer any question the students put to us. Many recall particular readings and scenarios we have posed and ask us to respond to them at this time. The reason for this approach is not to tip our hand too much and lead some students to believe that they must concur with our ethical positions during the semester. This discussion on the final day allows students to hear our struggles. They have opportunity to hear how we make judgments and decisions about the class topics and how we try to connect our faith and our learning.

Conclusion

This essay has discussed eleven different intersections of Christian faith and the course content in Interpersonal Communication, Small Group Communication, and Communication Ethics. There are many ways to connect biblical imperatives with the content and skills development included in human communication courses. At Whitworth College, where the motto is "An education of the heart and mind," students in Communication

Studies also receive some biblical instruction on how to use the tongue.

SELECTED BIBLIOGRAPHY

Bok, Sissela. *Lying: Moral Choice in Public and Private Life.* New York: Vintage Books, 1989.

DeVito, Joseph A.. *The Interpersonal Communication Book.* New York: Longman Press, 1998.

Fisher, Roger, William Ury, and Bruce Patton. *Getting to Yes: Negotiating Agreement Without Giving In.* Boston: Houghton Mifflin Co, 1991.

Jaksa, James, and Michael Pritchard. *Communication Ethics: Methods of Analysis.* Belmont, Calif.: Wadsworth Publishing Co., 1994.

Janis, Irvin L. *Groupthink: Psychological Studies of Policy Decisions and Fiascoes.* Boston: Houghton Mifflin, 1983.

Johannesen, Richard. *Ethics in Human Communication.* Prospect Heights, Ill.: Waveland Press, 1996.

Littlejohn, Stephen. *Theories of Human Communication.* Belmont, Calif.: Wadsworth Publishing Co., 1989.

Shultze, Quentin J. *Communicating for Life: Christian Stewardship in Community and Media.* Grand Rapids, Mich.: Baker Book House, 2000.

Stewart, John, ed. *Bridges Not Walls.* New York: McGraw-Hill, 1995.

——— and Carole Logan. *Together: Communicating Interpersonally.* New York: McGraw-Hill, 1993.

Strom, Bill. *More Than Talk: Communication Studies and the Christian Faith.* Dubuque, Iowa.: Kendall Hunt, 1996.

Suro, Roberto. "Collections." Reprinted in the *The Spokesman-Review* 3 Dec. 1989.

Conclusion: A Prudent Synergy: Pedagogy for Mind and Spirit

Arlin C. Migliazzo

FOR MOST OF WESTERN HISTORY, the central purpose of this book would have been questioned as misguided or ignored as redundant. Until the recent past, Christian educators from the fifth century forward would not have perceived a need for a volume of disciplinary essays linking academic content to faith perspectives. General cultural norms derived from the dominant Christian ethos made unnecessary any explicit exposition of distinctly religious themes and values in academic subjects. Educators of a more naturalistic bent, whether in Plato's Academy, the Parisian salons, or the latter twentieth-century ivies, would be less than enthusiastic about the ability of anyone committed to a religious community to participate (much less encourage students to participate) in the unfettered pursuit of knowledge. For them, membership in either community—the academic or the religious—precluded vital membership in the other. In contradistinction to critics of either stripe, the contributors to this anthology have demonstrated both the necessity of thoughtful intentionality on the part of Christian educators and the fallacy of epistemologically dichotomous thinking and teaching. They each point us toward a holistic pedagogy of mind and spirit—a pedagogical practice that values both critical rationalism and theistic authority by embracing such pairings as the empirically verifiable objective and the personally verifiable subjective, disciplinary content and keystone ethical values, intellectual knowledge and emotional/spiritual wisdom, logical reason and supernatural faith—in other words, truth as both *veritas* and *alētheia*.[1]

The distinctions between *veritas* and *alētheia* truth as well as the complementary relationship between them proceed from exquisite theoretical and hermeneutical exegesis. But without direct, explicit, and coherent praxis before students in our church-related colleges and universities, exegesis is still only exegesis, and our church-related institutions will be pressured to mime dominant educational patterns instead of being sources of the types of transformative teaching advocated by Parker Palmer and others. I am reminded of Professor Mullen's candid rejoinder to her grandfather's confident declaration of her ability to discern truth from error when critical rational learning seemed to challenge directly her understanding of Christianity. She said simply that his sentiment was "not an uncomplicated affirmation." I find her refreshing candor invigorating because it admits to the daunting task always before us.

In this passionately holistic vision of the enterprise of higher education, there is much that binds together the contributors to this volume, though they come from an array of Christian faith

---

[1] The Latin word *veritas* corresponds to what Albert C. Outler calls "discursive truth," that is, the types of inquiry described herein as the results of critical rationalism. For nearly two millennia, *veritas* truth was a complement to truth of a spiritual nature—that which has been called theistic authority in this study. The Greek term *alētheia*, used nearly one hundred times in the New Testament, denotes truth of this nature. The term itself translates roughly "without a veil" and, as Ben C. Fisher writes, signifies "truth as unveiled mystery." Truth of this type proceeds from God's initiative and is known through Scripture, Christ's incarnation, and the work of the Holy Spirit. It is "the source of human comfort, ground for hope, and assurance of eternal life." *Alētheia* truth is never to be confused with *veritas* truth. Neither is it to be "in conflict with new facts or insights gained by reason, but its frame of reference must include the transcendent." These two dimensions represent the integration of human aspirations to know different kinds of truth. There is no double truth here, "no hierarchical subordination of one to the other," and no rivalry. But there is validation of the search for each type of truth, as well as acceptance of the methods whereby the truth is accessed. Given the realities of U.S. higher educational culture, it is probably only in the context of Christian institutions that such holistic learning might be possible. See Albert C. Outler, "Discursive Truth and Evangelical Truth," pp. 102–6 in Lloyd J. Averill and William W. Jellema, eds., *Colleges and Commitments* (Philadelphia: The Westminster Press, 1971), 103–4. Quotations from Ben C. Fisher, *The Idea of A Christian University in Today's World* (Macon, Ga.: Mercer University Press, 1989), 36–37.

traditions. Each essayist speaks with that thoughtful intentionality noted above regarding both disciplinary perspectives and faith commitments. Whatever the strategies shared, whether Professor Paul's shadow exercise, Professor Mullen's use of hymnody, Professor Wilber's group projects, or Professor Heie's culminating seminar paper, the goal is to move beyond simply a content model of teaching to awaken an understanding of something deeper than mere mastery of text or procedure. The values and virtues cultivated by these innovative strategies proceed from the Christian faith assumptions of each practitioner. One cannot read the essays by Professors Morelli, Van Leeuwen, or Kirkemo and not come away impressed with the depth to which they have built their entire pedagogical practice around the richness of their commitment to Christianity as expressed in the Roman Catholic, Reformed, and Wesleyan traditions respectively. These traditions serve as guideposts for college and university teachers, no matter what the discipline taught, providing important doctrinal vantage points from which to view not only the content of each discipline, but also the assumptions embedded within it. The clearly articulated Anabaptist convictions that animate Professor Chaney's explorations of the natural world with her students are just as evident in Professor Ingram's use of biblical texts in speech communications. And so it is with each author. The bedrock convictions of each expression of Christian faith represented here find their way into the overarching goals and pedagogical strategies of each contributor. It is this intentional connection of faith and disciplinary study that should be the hallmark of the pedagogy generated by faculty members at church-related institutions. Christian colleges and universities would be hard pressed to justify their existence (and cost!) without this explicit and holistic education of the mind and spirit.

Each essayist also shares the conviction that an epistemological compartmentalization of knowledge in higher education is inappropriate, if not impossible, though the patterning of their integration of critical rationalism and theistic authority would certainly differ in context, degree, and intensity. For example, Professor Meyer might be more attuned to pursuing affective knowledge as it proceeds from rigorous study of literary texts within the bounds of the classroom and would turn to more overtly Christian topics in other contexts. Professor Clark, on the other hand, with important qualifications, would appear to feel at home melding distinctly Christian topics directly into classroom discussions of pertinent topics. Professor Knippers provides perhaps the most intriguing example of the blending of empirical technique with Christian assumptions in his pedagogy and his productive output while Professor Kieffaber's willingness to address specific Christian doctrines at opportune moments allows her the freedom to speak compellingly for both empirical and supernatural ways of knowing. In each case, the teaching strategies of the essayists allow students to recognize that knowledge has both cognitive and spiritual origins. This integration of mind and spirit upholds both epistemologies as valid pathways to understanding and wisdom.

LEVELS OF INTEGRATIVE PEDAGOGY

At one level or another there are attempts at this sort of educational wholeness going on all across the Christian college and university network. What I would encourage those of us in church-related higher education to do is to go further, to build on the solid base we already have, to be even more intentional, more sophisticated, and more creative in linking beliefs and values to our respective academic disciplines.[2] Once we clearly understand the levels at which integration occurs, we can build into our courses appropriate discussions, projects, lectures, or readings that truly stimulate our students to take their religious beliefs with them into all of life's challenges.[3]

Integrative educational wholeness, as I have come to under-

---

[2] Faith-discipline integration as a topic of ongoing discussion in church-related higher education has an extensive history. For a helpful survey of the discussion from a Protestant vantage point, see William Hasker, "Faith-Learning Integration: An Overview," *Christian Scholar's Review* 21, no. 3 (March 1992): 234–48.

[3] The following discussion of the levels of integration is adapted from my earlier essays on the subject. See Arlin C. Migliazzo, "Teaching History as an Act of Faith," *Fides et Historia* 23 (winter/spring 1991): 10–18 and "The Challenge of Educational Wholeness: Linking Beliefs, Values, and Academics," *Faculty Dialogue* no. 19 (1993): 43–63.

Faith and Learning Integration Levels

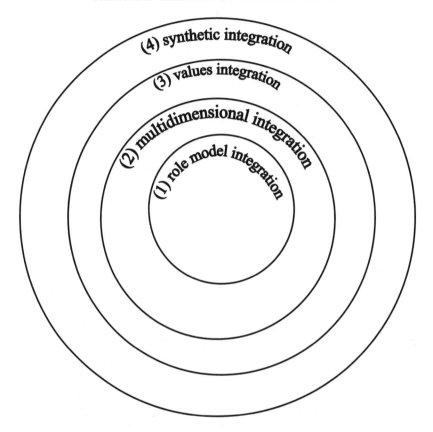

(4) synthetic integration

(3) values integration

(2) multidimensional integration

(1) role model integration

stand it, can happen at four different levels.[4] Each level builds on successful utilization of the preceding levels—and in fact presupposes the professor's appropriate application of disciplinary content and pedagogical methods at those levels. The levels of integration are mutually coherent, not mutually exclusive, as demonstrated by the diagram. Many professors probably shift back and forth between different levels, perhaps without con-

---

[4] For a different perspective on faith-discipline integration see Ronald R. Nelson, "Faith-Discipline Integration: Compatibilist, Reconstructionalist, and Transformationalist Strategies," 317–39, in Harold Heie and David L. Wolfe, eds., *The Reality of Christian Learning: Strategies for Faith-Learning Integration* (Grand Rapids, Mich.: Christian University Press and William B. Eerdmans Publishing Co., 1987).

sciously realizing it. The contributors to this present volume operationalize for us just how that switching back and forth might look in terms of pedagogy itself, for all the essayists demonstrate their considerable skills at multiple levels of integration. At each level, there is a greater intensity of faith-discipline integration generally correlated with Bloom's Taxonomy of Higher Levels of Learning, which implies increasing degrees of confrontation with interpretive and value questions because teaching strategies are made progressively more explicit to these issues. It is also important to note that integration at the first three levels is applicable either to the secular or Christian learning environment. The fourth level is only applicable at the church-related institution because of its explicit concern with Christian faith.

The beginning point of integrative thinking occurs at the level of role model integration. Some scholars would dismiss this level of integration as no integration at all because nothing is said in class that could be construed as having any explicit Christian content and no explicit linkages are made between disciplinary learning and faith concerns. Yet, I would argue that integrative activity begins here, because professors at this stage are acutely aware of the imperatives of both faith and disciplinary expertise. Many of them desire to model both with deep integrity, but they are unwilling or unable, for a variety of reasons we will explore later, to make explicit connections between the academic subjects they teach and the faith they treasure. Those who integrate at this level do not seek to point to or to raise questions about ultimate issues of human life and purpose beyond perhaps a rhetorical question or two but seek to transmit solid knowledge within the discipline to the next generation of citizens and to pursue respectable scholarship in the field. By modeling good teaching and rigorous scholarship, professors in this category reflect their commitment to Christ. By assuming their responsibilities as respected members of the academy, they seek to honor Christ. The only time issues related to faith are broached is when students approach the professor. Even then there may be some reluctance to share too specifically with the searching student. Since this is where all integrative thinking begins, the three succeeding levels are predicated upon the conscious awareness of the professor of her position as a role model for students. The danger at this level is the potential to perceive role-model integration as an end in itself and not a means to the next level of integrative activity. Should this occur, students have no way of knowing what motivates the professor to model teaching excellence, academic fairness, and personal integrity, unless they are willing to ask—and very few do. While it is clear from his essay that Professor Meyer moves well beyond the role-model level of integration in his teaching of literature, he is also most articulate in explaining how this particular level of integrative activity is reflected in his pedagogy.

The second level of increasing integrative sophistication I have chosen to call multidimensional integration, which comports well with the current postmodern academic milieu. This second level of integration occurs when the professor validates the possibility of multiple views of reality. The Christian scholar understands that humans operate under the influence of many different and often competing priorities at the same time. We are not solely noble or rational creatures. But neither are we the opposite, because the creation, though fallen, retains the imprint of the Creator. Professors integrating at this level might challenge materialistic or deterministic answers to aesthetic, scientific, and humanistic questions of knowing and being by questioning through lectures, discussions, or directed readings the underlying assumptions of monocausistic interpretive perspectives. They also might validate religious motivation on its own terms and not solely as a manifestation of psychosis, misogyny, or economic power. Christianity provides the scholar at this level with a theoretical framework for interpreting knowledge and life just as minimalists, Marxists, behaviorists, or deconstructionists find their theoretical interpretive ground in their own set of presuppositions. These professors may utilize various Christian doctrines on such topics as human nature to interpret knowledge and life but will not announce explicitly to their students their theoretical assumptions. Professors may also use Christian readings as counterpoint to readings from other theoretical perspectives. This second level of integration begins to address issues from underlying Christian assumptions, but as with the role-model level of integration, students will not necessarily know why the professor gives credence to religious issues unless they press the issue. If the issue is pressed at public institutions, the Christian scholar may be hesitant to disclose his rationale during class time, perhaps out of concern for church-state separation issues. Unfortunately, at many church-related colleges and universities, however, the same hesitancy occurs, which may reveal an inability to move beyond the multidimensional level to the next stage of integrative sophistication. All the contributors to this anthology have moved well past this second integrative level, and Professors Kroeker, Chaney, and Knippers provide excellent examples of multidimensional integration in significant sections of their respective essays.

Values integration comprises the third level of educational wholeness. Here we find the professor exploring deep value assumptions of an ethical, moral, philosophical, or spiritual nature in the classroom. Lively discussions oriented toward values questions can make integration at this level much more stimulating for students than the essentially straightforward presentation of material in lecture form as is often the case at the second level of integration. Values-based teaching can also demonstrate the relativity of values if they are only based on social consensus. As such it can provide a forum for spirited debates regarding the basis or anchor for values, which could lead directly to religiously oriented exchanges. Professors might guide these discussions such that issues of faith could ultimately arise but might hesitate to share in class just why the values discussed were chosen for discussion or what grounds the particular values as prescriptive for fear of approaching indoctrination or overstepping appropriate boundaries. These types of issues lend themselves handily to even larger questions related to the personal worldviews of students and their implications for an assortment of beliefs and behaviors.

It is at this level of integration that students become actively involved. Lecture material can and should emphasize values but such information should be introduced in such a way as to elicit student responses so that they might make that connection with their own thinking on these issues. The focus on values may most simply be achieved by the use of supplementary readings. Class discussions based on these readings often allow students to confront the bases for their own attitudes toward such topics as world religions, environmentalism, minimalism in the arts, the impact of technology on cultural norms, deconstructionism, the pursuit of leisure, and sexism. Small group worksheets centered on value-based, open-ended questions give rise to lively dialogue in class. Sometimes splitting the class into opposing camps to debate critical issues works well as a way to review key readings and to enter the domain of value-centered teaching—as long as the professor can serve as an effective moderator. All the essayists model the power of this third level of integrative pedagogy. Among them, perhaps Professors Chaney, Paul, and Morelli demonstrate most ingeniously the tremendous potential for a deeply value-oriented teaching philosophy.

At this values level of integration, some discussion of the mechanics of a worldview would also be appropriate. The sophistication of the discussion must fit the analytical capacities of the students and be respectful of all responses, but even lower-division students can be challenged with basic questions—the answers to which will be the domain of worldview thinking.[5] All these opportunities allow students to comprehend more coherently their own assumptions about the value decisions they make and the beliefs that motivate them as well as to discern more readily the worldviews of others. This third level of integration addresses holistic education by allowing students opportunities to explore their own values and beliefs but stops short of introducing distinctly Christian categories. As a result, even this third level of integration is appropriate for the professor at public institutions without fear of transgressing church-state boundaries. At church-related colleges and universities, this third level provides an entrée to the deepest level of integration, which should serve as the unique contribution of Christian institutions to the enterprise of higher education.

This fourth and most satisfying level of integration links val-

---

[5] I have attempted to keep the number of questions to a minimum so that students are not overwhelmed by the complexity of understanding their own worldview and yet, in discovering their answers to the questions they will have successfully ventured into epistemology, metaphysics, and axiology—the core areas of worldview thinking. The two questions I now use are: (1) What do I believe to be true and real and how do I know it? and (2) How do I act and expect others to act based upon what I know to be true and real?

ues directly and explicitly to the examination of a Christian worldview. This is the level at which church-related institutions should excel. At this synthetic integration level, value assumptions are directly addressed in relation to historic Christian doctrinal and worldview concerns. Since this final integrative step relies heavily on a strong values orientation, many techniques noted previously will be of great help to those seeking to demonstrate that historic Christianity provides a consistent foundation for the values to which humans should aspire. Professors may use this level to challenge students to compare contemporary theoretical views in the natural sciences, arts, humanities, or social sciences with biblical views of these same fields by encouraging students to grapple with the implications of a Christian worldview that addresses aesthetics, critical literary theory, the most recent thinking in theoretical physics, or the concepts of work and play. To do this, professors might wish to provide what they conceive to be fundamental components of a Christian worldview so that students can contemplate their answers to worldview questions in this context.[6]

Course content will be influenced by the desire of the professor to link faith concerns directly to the discipline. Questions proceeding from the operating assumptions of the discipline are fertile fields of inquiry. Supplementary readings for class and small group discussion can be more direct in addressing issues from a Christian worldview. These readings can range from dis-

---

[6] I have adopted an eight-point Christian worldview statement for my students. Others might add a few more points depending on their particular faith tradition. 1) God created all things and created them good, 2) God's creation has a purpose (that is, there is a reason for creation to exist), 3) Humans are God's creation and are a distinct part of the created order, 4) God is holy and loving and cares deeply for the creation, 5) God's holiness and love means that God is both just and compassionate toward the creation, 6) Human sinfulness has corrupted God's creation, but it still has intrinsic worth, 7) God intervened in human history through God's Son, Jesus Christ, whose death and resurrection healed the breech between sinful humans and holy God, satisfying God's demand for justice and giving evidence to God's love, 8) The Old and New Testaments are God's spoken words to humans and contain what we need to know to be restored to a right relationship to God, other humans, and to the rest of God's creation. I am especially indebted to Arthur F. Holmes, *Contours of a World View* (Grand Rapids, Mich.: William B. Eerdmans Publishing Co., 1983) for my formulation of these issues and others I address when speaking of a Christian worldview.

tinctly Christian analyses of pertinent disciplinary concerns to works that explore the enduring questions of science, human creativity, and life. Course assignments also could reflect a greater emphasis on analyzing issues from a Christian perspective. Personal response projects will be especially instructive here, but the professor must be very careful not to judge a student's personal beliefs. If a certain level of professional detachment cannot be achieved, then this type of assignment should be avoided. Another project that would be appropriate for senior students in a capstone course would be to have them compose their philosophy of the discipline. In the guidelines to introduce such an assignment, the professor must again be careful not to prejudge the outcomes but merely to make sure the student understands that such an assignment cannot be done in a vacuum. The student's philosophy of the discipline must proceed from personal answers to worldview questions, even if the connections are not immediately obvious to the student.[7]

It is at the synthetic integration level that the concrete articulation of a Christian worldview, presented sensitively and compassionately, will demonstrate to students the real basis of their value assumptions, whether they are Christians or not. Such an articulation also can help Christian students recognize where their worldview is at odds with their profession of faith. True synthetic integration, in theory and in practice, will also help heal the breach in the minds of the Christian professoriate between faith and professional learning and will ultimately lead to the reinterpretation of Christian intellectual life.

At both the values integration and synthetic integration levels, pedagogical inquiry can take four different but complementary

---

[7] The most sophisticated project I assign at the synthetic integration level is a paper that each of my senior history students must complete. This philosophy of history/history of education paper comes after we have investigated thoroughly the impact a worldview has on beliefs and activities. In the guidelines provided, I emphasize the intensely personal nature of the project and the importance of maintaining a conscious linkage between the philosophy of life (worldview) and the philosophy of the discipline/profession. My assessment proceeds not from the ideas presented but from the congruency of the worldview principles articulated to the disciplinary/professional philosophy articulated. Students are peer advisors for each other during the entire process to help with these issues. They also are given strict guidelines as to their role as advisors.

forms. Incidental inquiry occurs serendipitously as the class session unfolds. No teacher can plan for these opportunities, because they occur without warning, embedded in the unsolicited questions and comments of students. Incidental inquiry occurs most often in the context of class discussion or cooperative projects. Unlike incidental inquiry, analytical inquiry requires substantive planning on the part of the teacher, for it is based upon an examination of topics through the lens of a particular value, aspect of church teaching, or worldview perspective. Students might be encouraged to analyze certain policies, cultural norms, or ethical dilemmas through this lens in discussion or assignments. Professors Clark, Wilber, Kieffaber, Mullen, and Ingram provide a wide variety of examples illustrating the diversity of possibilities for analytic inquiry. Presuppositional inquiry at both the values and synthetic levels of integration cut to the very foundations of the disciplines we study and the world in which we live. This mode of inquiry encourages students to ponder the very bases of human knowledge, faith, and community and drives them to evaluate their particular assumptions about the deepest issues of human concern. Professors Heie and Van Leeuwen have crafted among the most deeply creative strategies in this volume to engage students presuppositionally. While presuppositional inquiry might be called an immersion of the spirit and the intellect, experiential inquiry could be termed an immersion of the spirit and the body. In this mode of inquiry, students find themselves out in the "classroom beyond the college," where their values and faith perspectives are tested and refined in the living of life beyond their comfortable boundaries. Essays by Professors Paul and Kroeker in the fine arts and Professors Clark and Kirkemo in the social sciences most clearly illustrate integrative learning of this nature.

THAT HOLY TENSION

As is apparent from the preceding discussion of the levels of integrative activity, holistic educational opportunities can take a wide variety of forms and exhibit numerous characteristics. Yet, the notion of integration is also a problematic one for Christian educators. Among the contributors to this volume, at least five (Professors Van Leeuwen, Heie, Chaney, Meyer, and Mullen) struggle with the concept itself. There are other writers who might even challenge the contention that each essayist is here pursuing integrative linkages.[8] I believe that beyond the issue of semantics there are legitimate reasons for the concerns generated by the idea of the integration of faith and learning. One proceeds from the splendid diversity underneath the umbrella of contemporary Christendom. In the past, each of the five major divisions within the Christian tradition highlighted in this volume have diverged from each other in substantial and all too often violently iconoclastic ways. To make matters more complex, each of the five has become the fountainhead of multiple theological and denominational strains of thought, so that while each claims Jerusalem as home, the ways to (or from) Athens are legion. It is presumptuous of one tradition to tell another where the true path lies. Yet, there is opportunity for encouragement along the way from others on a parallel but somewhat more adventurous route. Ecumenical dialogues on individual campuses as well as at regional and national conferences facilitate such encouragement. The common denominator, however, must always be explicit intentionality and epistemic duality. Without the tensions present engendered by these all-important priorities, the delicate balance necessary for synergy to occur between critical rationalism and theistic authority cannot be maintained, and Christian higher education loses its raison d'être.

A second concern emanates from Tertullian's grand dilemma regarding the proper steerage between Athens and Jerusalem, the Church and the Academy. The debate has lasted nearly two millennia because, as Nicholas Wolterstorff has recently reminded us, neither Tertullian's answer nor any alternative has been the object of universal acceptance.[9] History, however, has been replete with numerous attempts at resolution. In retrospect, most appear hopelessly optimistic or inordinately defensive. But why is this the case?

---

[8] See for example David L. Wolfe, "The Line Between Integration and Pseudointegration," 3–11, in Heie and Wolfe, *The Reality of Christian Learning.*

[9] Nicholas Wolterstorff, "Tertullian's Enduring Question," *The Cresset* 62, no. 7 (June/July 1999): 6.

Others more learned than myself have written lengthy volumes on the theoretical and institutional processes involved in the continued erosion of theistic authority in the academic community of Christian colleges and universities. I would like to add a more mundane factor to the mix. F. Scott Fitzgerald once noted that the test of a first-rate intelligence is the ability to contemplate seriously two opposing ideas and still retain the ability to function. We are, after all, creatures of extremes. As my respected high school English teacher Mrs. Alice Rydeen once said, "We shun the middle way." It is so much easier to make our abode either Athens or Jerusalem. It is a much more difficult matter to commute adroitly between them. Whether the scholar chooses the epistemic hegemony of Augustine's theism, the modernist's objective empiricism, or the postmodernist's individualistic relativism, the end result remains constant. There is little need to contemplate the possibility of even limited complementarity among apparently opposing worldviews. Given the opportunity to engage in ongoing, vexing, and pointed dialogue with competing epistemological assumptions, most of us suffer from the same malady. We would much rather assume Peter's supine position during Christ's agony in the Garden of Gethsemane than Jacob's active role in his encounter with the angel. But until more of us in Christian higher education can grant simultaneous legitimacy to both the Church's commitment to theistic authority and to the secular academy's commitment to critical rational method—each in their appropriate contexts—the kind of synergistic pedagogy illustrated by the essays in this anthology will continue to suffer setbacks even as the culture around us looks to our colleges and universities for some coherent values beyond content and technique.[10]

I am not so naive as to believe that mere recognition of epistemic duality will alleviate our uneasiness or solve all our problems. Indeed, I would expect our dilemmas to increase and our concerns to multiply in church-related higher education with our acceptance of it. Yet, ultimately a prudent synergy can occur

---

[10] See for example the recent editorial by U. S. News and World Report's John Leo, "We Need New, Undamaged Colleges," Universal Press Syndicate, reported in The Spokesman-Review (April 15, 1999), B6.

when a conscientious, holy tension constantly pervades the ongoing deliberations at Christian colleges and universities regarding everything from curriculum and student life to sports and admissions. There can be no simplistic solution while church-related higher educators hold two such contentious epistemologies as concurrently foundational. There will be no ultimate resolution unless one or the other is jettisoned for the sake of peace, because the human experience of the divine and of the mundane continues to unwind, and with each unwinding come new challenges and fresh opportunities for engagement. But if comfortable stability and once-and-future resolution take precedence over prophetic living and proclamation, perhaps it would be helpful if we remembered that neither Athens nor Jerusalem is our destination, merely our points of origin. The journey lies always ahead and in between.[11]

A third concern regarding the type of holistic education evident in the essays of this volume is the fear of offending those with other religious preferences or none at all. While I am sympathetic to those who find overtly Christian language problematic in church-related institutions that have become progressively more diverse over the past two generations, I find this objection flawed for a number of reasons. First, it assumes that raising issues connecting Christian faith to disciplinary matters in the classroom equals proselytizing, which is clearly not what either I or any of the essayists advocate. Collectively we are simply arguing that we must allow for legitimate discussion of faith issues in our church-related colleges and universities as they impinge upon the disciplines we teach. A second observation I would like to make regarding this concern is that I have never heard anyone hold the same scruples about challenging a stu-

---

[11] There are some significant, hopeful signs that sustained and difficult conversations regarding the prudent synergy of theistic authority and critical rationalism are occurring with greater regularity both in scholarly literature and in academic conferences, as noted in the introduction and in the concluding bibliography. See also the discussion initiated at Georgetown University by the internal document "Centered Pluralism: A Report of a Faculty Seminar on the Jesuit and Catholic Identity of Georgetown University" (November 1996) and the recent issue of *Christian Scholar's Review* 26, no. 2 (winter 1996) committed to a discussion of postmodernity, including Christian–non-Christian dialogue.

ARLIN C. MIGLIAZZO

dent's politics, gender or ethnic sensitivities, or personal study habits. After all, is it not one of our cardinal beliefs about the education of university students that they learn best when confronted with a belief or value different from their own? It is compassionate confrontation in a supportive environment that maximizes learning. I would note that Christians and non-Christians alike will learn more about why they believe what they believe if we do not shirk these most important issues for fear of offending. Our charge as Christian educators should be to venture forth in sensitivity and compassion, allowing our classrooms to be what they should be—venues for examining the tough questions confronting us as individuals and as members of the human community from a holistic perspective, giving credence to the rightful place of both critical rationalism and theistic authority.

Often we are so busy protecting those whom we think might be offended if we address directly issues of faith in our classrooms that we fail to challenge those Christian students and searchers who are struggling to see the big picture. Our times saturate us with the conviction that even to raise issues related to religious faith or values grounded in faith assumptions (aside from the values currently also cherished by the culture) must be offensive to those who do not share similar beliefs and values. If we really subscribe to this conviction, what we are in effect saying is that anything approaching religious, ethical, or moral pedagogy is inappropriate in the classroom because someone may not agree with the topics of conversation.[12] The inconsistency in this position becomes apparent when we try to recall any professor of our acquaintance who ever halted a lecture or discussion on a political, social, or creative theory because it might offend someone in the classroom.

I believe that there are two additional, more personal, and therefore more difficult concerns to address regarding holistic education as advocated in this book. Some Christian professors are reticent to link beliefs, values, and disciplinary content be-

---

[12] The character-education movement has been debating this issue for quite some time. For one of the more recent and synthetic treatments of the subject see Robert J. Nash, *Answering the Virtuecrats: A Moral Conversation on Character Education* (New York: Teachers College Press, 1997).

cause these professors come out of a faith tradition or family background in which deeply held religious convictions and their implications for life and thought, no matter what the context, have been deemed too ineffable or holy to express before others. This indeed is a delicate issue and one on which I would hope we could think collectively toward resolution. Since such communal dialogue is not an option here, I would like to advance two queries that might help clarify my concern without calling into question the very real convictions of our colleagues who feel this hesitancy. I would ask first: What is it, after all, that draws us to a career in the church-related college or university in the first place? If our answers have more to do with the desire for a comfortable insularity or a heightened sense of professional safety rather than a commitment to challenge compassionately our students at a whole host of levels, I wonder if the Christian nature of church-related college teaching is more for our nurture and education than it is for our students' growth and development. While none would discount the desire for a pleasant work environment, if this is our basic rationale for taking a position in a church-related institution, then I would suggest that we have reversed the role of professor and student. Such a role reversal does an injustice to the cause of Christian higher education because of our unwillingness or inability to push ourselves in the same ways we push our students to go as far as we can and then just a little farther.

A second question cuts to the heart of faith itself: What is it about Christianity that is unique and equips us for life in this world? If we professors have come to some tentative conclusions on the subject that have been central to our lives (and it seems perfectly logical to assume that we have because of our affiliation with the Church and with Christian higher education), then I believe that we do a disservice to our students not to raise them for consideration, when appropriate, in (and out) of the classroom. We need to risk being vulnerable to each other—and this is a deep risk. To encourage mutual vulnerability, Christian institutions might encourage departmental retreats or implement supportive interdisciplinary colloquia or college-wide administration/staff/faculty workshops where integration issues could be explored from a variety of perspectives and led by senior administrative and faculty colleagues. At Whitworth College, our administration sets aside a specific session at the new faculty orientation retreat each September for mutual discussion of integration issues across the curriculum. In this way, our entering professors are freed to think and teach integratively from their own particular Christian faith tradition from the beginning of their appointments. Church-related institutions with a more religiously diverse faculty could offer such programs for Christian faculty as well as for faculty from other faith traditions.

Another legitimate concern surfaces when we contemplate connecting faith and values to disciplinary content in the classroom. For not only does such an undertaking go against all our graduate training, it also threatens us because we are not trained to know how to do it. Kenneth Gangel perhaps made it worse when he argued that each professor should be an amateur theologian or should not be allowed to teach in a Christian college or university.[13] However disconcerting Gangel's contention, his point is well taken, for some theological awareness is necessary. And it will be hard work, for the acquisition of such knowledge will have to come in addition to our more traditional academic duties. Thankfully, there are those who are attempting to make it easier for us.[14] This is not an easy or quick process, however. It will take some hits and misses, but I am convinced that if we are going to fulfill the mission of the church-related college and university, we must struggle toward educational wholeness in our pedagogical efforts. It would be a tragic mistake to institute campus-wide policies as to how this should happen. However, significant faculty development opportunities, supported by the administration and located anywhere from the departmental and divisional levels to the entire faculty, could provide time for significant individual and collective reflection on points of contact between Christian faith and the various disciplines. The look of integrative teaching will vary from discipline to discipline, from professor to professor, from faith tradition to faith

---

[13] Kenneth O. Gangel, "Integrating Faith and Learning: Principles and Process," *Bibliotheca Sacra* 135, no. 538 (April–June 1978): 106–7.

[14] For example see Ward Gasque, "Must Ordinary People Know Theology?" *Christianity Today* 29 (February 1, 1985): 32–34 and Harold Heie, "Bursting Educational Wineskins," *Faculty Dialogue* no. 11 (spring 1989): 127–29.

tradition, and from institution to institution. But to be about the business of linking beliefs, values, and academic disciplines is to move toward the goal of equipping the next generation for a life of significance in this world.

Church-Related Higher Education in the Twenty-First Century: From the Cities of Our Heritage to a Common Destination

The next generation of scholars is maturing in an intellectual and cultural environment very different than the one most of the currently practicing professoriate knew in its formative years. For those of us at or beyond the midpoint of our careers, the boundaries between legitimate inquiry (read empirical objectivism) and academic dilettantism (read any a priori values or assumptions) were clearly drawn in graduate school. But the contemporary cultural battle raging between modernists and postmodernists in a host of venues from popular culture to race relations at least cracks a door open to alternative possibilities and more holistic approaches to higher education.

Ultimately, those possibilities will be limited only by our inability as Christian educators to continue the pursuit of an epistemological equilibrium in our church-related institutions, which we know from the outset will always be tentative, provisional, and open to reinterpretation. But the alternatives to a prudent synergy of critical rationalism and theistic authority— submission to rigid fideism, modernist empirical objectivism, or postmodern critical relativism—will signal the demise of a viable Christian educational voice in U.S. academic culture.

The last decade of the twentieth century, like its two immediate predecessors, was replete with conferences, debates, and books profiling, pontificating, and predicting the place of Christian higher education in the third millennium. Among the most instructive perspectives introduced were two significant pronouncements from the Roman Catholic Church, which bracketed the discourse on Christian higher education in the 1990s. Taken together, *Ex Corde Ecclesiae* (August 1990) and *Fides et Ratio* (October 1998) refocused problematic issues regarding the relationship between the Academy and the Church. *Ex Corde Ecclesiae* has generated intensive discourse proceeding from concerns that the document paves the way for more theistic authority than most U.S. Catholic colleges and universities are willing to concede.[15] On the other hand, *Fides et Ratio* reiterated the Church's support for the role of reason in the life of the communicant based on the Thomistic syllabus.[16] As enlightening discussions regarding the practical ramifications of these papal documents continue among Roman Catholic scholars, it could be reasonably hoped that the intensity of these conversations will spark similar discourse among Protestant academic communities and will clarify that the true point of tension was, is, and always will be an epistemological one.

I offer no palliation of the struggle for ongoing definition and epistemological balance, no magic bullet that will eliminate the opposition to Christian ways of doing higher education. History seems to warn us against advocating any final resolution of the tension between critical rationalism and theistic authority as our goal. If the past is any indication, humans are notorious for lock-stepped rigidity whenever resolution beckons. I would, however, like to conclude with a few observations on how I believe church-related institutions and those who love them might face the Sisyphusian task of reaching epistemic equipoise.

---

[15] The 1990s have been filled with interpretations and warnings regarding the potential impact on U.S. Catholic institutions of higher learning of *Ex Corde Ecclesiae*, subsequent Church deliberations on it, and related documents. In addition to titles cited in the Selected Bibliography, numerous popular analyses have also appeared. See, for example, Hanna Rosin, "Papal Decree Means Church Can Discipline Dissenters," *Washington Post*, reported in *The Spokesman-Review* (July 2, 1998): A8; Grayden Jones, "Church May Have Stronger Voice at Gonzaga," *The Spokesman-Review* (January 11, 1999): A5–A6; Roberto Sanchez, "Vatican Edict Could Be Risky for U.S. Colleges," *Seattle Times*, reported in *The Spokesman-Review* (July 15, 1999): A1, A8. More recently, the Cardinal Newman Society for the Preservation of Catholic Higher Education has weighed in on the need for an even more conservative stance. See Linda Borg, "Catholic Group Calls on Colleges to Tighten Their Religious Identity," *Providence Journal*, reported in *The Spokesman-Review* (December 17, 2000): A18 and Virginia de Leon, "GU Professor Discounts Newman Guidelines," *The Spokesman-Review* (December 17, 2000): A18–A19.

[16] Like *Ex Corde Ecclesiae*, *Fides et Ratio* has been the subject of extended debate. For a more accessible brief account of the issues highlighted in it, see Richard N. Ostling, "'Faith and Reason,'" *The Spokesman-Review* (October 17, 1998): E3.

First, Christian educators and the church-related colleges and universities we serve must be in regular, pointed conversation regarding the theological presuppositions that ground our labors. We must forge explicit linkages between those presuppositions and what happens in the day-to-day life of our institutions. If one goal of the mission statement is to achieve a "caring community" or to "educate the whole person," special attention must be paid to flesh out the mandate for that goal on the basis of theistic authority. This does not mean that critical rationalism cannot also be appropriated to generate more political or social reasons for the college's goals. It does mean, however, that the time for presenting *only* rationalistic justification for such goals must end. In presenting both a distinctly Christian case for the goals of the college centered in theistic authority *and* the humanistic apologetic for them, a prudent synergy of both epistemologies can be operationalized even at this most basic level.

Second, these theological and humanistic presuppositions should permeate all sectors of the campus community. Creative approaches to implement them have the potential to be deeply transformational, but mission statements can only energize the life of the college if they truly reflect what happens there. This is, of course, the core issue at our Christian institutions of higher learning. We will never be able to embrace fully the grand promise of church-related higher education if all we do is accept uncritically the norms of the elite educational establishment or submit unequivocally to fideistic Christian traditionalism. Neither of these options will provide an education characterized by a prudent epistemic synergy that prepares graduates to live authentic lives. If the only possibilities we can imagine in church-related colleges and universities are the ones already imagined for us by the secular academy or by theistic ideologues, we are either devoid of creativity or deficient in courage.[17]

---

[17] David L. Wolfe and Harold Heie have offered a quite remarkable alternative program of study. See their *Slogans or Distinctives: Reforming Christian Higher Education* (Lanham, Md.: University Press of America, 1993). While not quite as innovative as Heie and Wolfe's proposal, the recent creation of the Graduate School at Trinity International University and the announcement of a fifty-million-dollar gift by Domino's Pizza founder Tom Monaghan to create a law school stressing Catholic values demonstrate the same creative spirit.

Third, let us recognize the possibility that there are dangerous ideas—not in the sense that they are dangerous to consider but in the sense that they are considered dangerous to question. The naivete of some Christian educators would be amusing if it did not perpetuate such destructive consequences for church-related institutions. For example, in the name of disciplinary loyalty, one might initially tend to agree with Waldo Beach when he writes that "To require the teacher of psychology or sociology to conform his subject matter to the Lordship of Christ is to violate the integrity of his discipline and to subject universality of truth to parochial dogma."[18] But Beach, in true modernist fashion, seems to take what the disciplines say about themselves at face value and would appear to castigate Christian educators such as Professors Van Leeuwen and Clark for daring to encourage their students to question the underlying assumptions of the disciplines they study. By the same token, academic freedom is a cornerstone of higher education orthodoxy and has been since the nineteenth century. But if church-related colleges and universities operate under the auspices of theistic authority as well as critical rationalism, might this in some way constrain the ways such freedom is exercised? To some educators, simply to raise the question is not only dangerous, it is a sign of oppression.[19] Even the inductive method can be examined for its own presuppositions and limitations as a mode of investigation, but how many Christian educators are willing to open this line of inquiry with their students?[20] If Socrates correctly observed that the unexamined life is not worth living, could not a possible corollary be that the unexamined idea is not worth entertaining? Christian educators should be at the forefront of this questioning of the bedrock assumptions of our culture. Yet in reality we seem much

[18] Waldo Beach, "Christian Ethical Community As a Norm," pp. 169–85 in Averill and Jellema, *Colleges and Commitments*, 176.

[19] It is intriguing to note that the idea of academic freedom, born in the German universities of the early nineteenth century, was substantially limited by political and social restraints and conditioned by German nationalism. See Burton J. Bledstein, *The Culture of Professionalism: The Middle Class and the Development of Higher Education in America* (New York: W. W. Norton & Co., 1976), 317–18.

[20] Arthur F. Holmes, *All Truth is God's Truth* (Grand Rapids, Mich.: William B. Eerdmans Publishing Co., 1977), 99–100.

more ready to critique knowledge gained through theistic authority via critical rationalism than the obverse. We are called into a relationship with both epistemologies that is synergistic *and* prudently cautious in both directions.

Finally, we have every reason to be cautious with truth claims gleaned from either theistic authority or critical rationalism. The liabilities of each have been clearly established historically. In the postmodern climate, those failures have allowed claims to propositional truth as well as personal truth to be demeaned as idiosyncratic and so relative to time, place, and person. Yet some postmodernists would have us believe that because critical rationalism has led us in some destructive ways, it cannot guide us to any beneficent universal constructions. And because theistic authority has often been co-opted by agents of oppression, it cannot point us toward justice and grace. Contemporary critics of a more modernist bent cringe at the thought of theistic authority as a pathway to truth because it relies on a source beyond human ken.

It is important for those of us committed to the synergy of theistic authority and critical rationalism to recognize these as appropriate concerns that should not be taken lightly. Knowledge gained through the avenue of theistic authority is both personal and propositional,[21] the subject of insight and also its object. Critical rationalism was not viewed in the same manner until the dawn of our postmodern age, but given the predilections of this present era, if church-related colleges and universities are to be agents of holistic education, Christian educators must stand for the truths of both epistemologies as we best see them.

The problem with affirming any prescriptive truth is that whenever Christians have promulgated what they believe to be the truth, dangerous ossification has followed close behind. Time and again we have been found deficient and, if not completely truthless, at least not full of truth. All truth may be God's truth, but unfortunately, a great deal of it seems to get rather muddled at this end. We may struggle to know God's mind, but we never truly will. What do we do when errors creep into our

---

[21] Holmes, *All Truth*, 77.

critical reasoning about God? How ought theistic authority to inform our disciplines and our teaching? How might we even know that we are in error in the first place?

We do the same thing that we were taught to do in graduate school as practitioners in our respective disciplines. We review the evidence, rethink our conclusions, reimagine other possibilities, and renew our relationships with other seekers after truth. We do not dismiss out of hand our conclusions because they are not shared by others knowledgeable in our fields, but we do remain open to alternatives. In our desire to take seriously a prudent synergy of theistic authority and critical rationalism, we speak and teach with integrity what we believe to be true, drawing on both epistemologies. But we are always ready to listen for the voice of the other and so remain open to God's Spirit, who grants us a refreshed vision for our institutions, our students, and God's kingdom. Remember that open hands sustain all that is contained in them but also allow others to participate in the perception of their contents. To aspire to such a simultaneously provisional and confident view of our goal as teachers in church-related institutions means that resolution of the tensions inherent in epistemic duality is as distant as the cities of our intellectual and spiritual heritage often seem to be. Perhaps the deepest encouragement is to remember daily those twin points of origin on this journey of Christian higher education and to realize how far we have come, not how far we have yet to go.

APPENDIX A

Christianity and Higher Education: A Selected Bibliography

THE LITERATURE ON Christian higher education has expanded exponentially over the past five decades. The bibliography that appears below does not presume to be exhaustive, but it does claim to be representative of the types of studies available to the interested reader (excluding institutional histories—the number of which is astronomical). A reader desiring a more detailed bibliography can go to www.iupui.edu/~raac/html/bibliographies.html, Web site for the Center for the Study of Religion and American Culture directed by Conrad Cherry, which maintains a well-annotated set of bibliographies.

The first section of the present bibliography lists significant works from the formative period of modern writing on church-related higher education (1940–1980). The second section provides an extensive listing of the most important studies of the past twenty-two years broken down into general and confessional categories. While a number of the studies cited below are authored or edited by scholars within one of the five traditions surveyed in this present anthology, unless the particular volume has a strong confessional theme, such studies will be found in the general category for the contemporary period.

This bibliography is intended as a complement to the disciplinary bibliographies provided by each of the contributors to this volume. For additional print sources from disciplinary perspectives visit the Council for Christian Colleges and Universities' website at http://cccu.org/ and click on the Resource Center button to browse categories. For links to a wide variety of Christian academic organizations committed to bringing faith perspectives to bear on the enterprise of higher education, visit the Weyerhaeuser Center for Christian Faith and Learning site at www.whitworth.edu/FaithCenter/Links.htm.

Since the following bibliography is concerned primarily with the broad issues affecting Christian higher education since 1940, references to concerns such as the general state of Christian intellectual life, worldview analyses, and Christian engagement of culture beyond higher education are cited, with a few notable exceptions. Book titles predominate, but some important articles culled from the vast literature are also included.

The Formative Period (1940–1980)

Ahlstrom, Sydney. "What's Lutheran About Higher Education?—A Critique." Paper presented at the Sixtieth Annual Convention, Lutheran Educational Conference of North America. February 1974.

Averill, Lloyd J. and William W. Jellema, eds. *Colleges and Commitments*. Philadelphia: Westminster Press, 1971.

Baepler, Richard, et al. *The Church-Related College in an Age of Pluralism: The Quest for a Viable Saga*. Valparaiso, Ind.: Published for the Association of Lutheran College Faculty, 1977.

Baker, James C. *The First Wesley Foundation: An Adventure in Christian Higher Education*. Nashville, Tenn.: Parthenon, 1960.

"The Basis for Partnership Between Church and College." *A Statement of the Lutheran Church in America* (Adopted by the Eighth Biennial Convention, Boston, Mass., July 21–28, 1976). New York: Lutheran Church in America, 1976.

Bender, Richard N., ed. *The Church-Related College Today: Anachronism or Opportunity?* Nashville, Tenn.: Division of Higher Education of the United Methodist Church, 1971.

Brown, Robert McAfee. "The Reformed Tradition and Higher Education." *The Christian Scholar* 41, no. 1 (March 1958): 21–40.

Bruning, Charles R. *Relationships Between Church-Related Colleges and Their Constituencies*. New York: Division for Mission in North America, Lutheran Church of America, 1975.

Brushaber, George K. *Foundation of Christian Higher Education*. Christian College Consortium, 1979.

Calvin College, *Christian Liberal Arts Education: Report of the Cal-*

vin *College Curriculum Study Committee*. Grand Rapids, Mich.: Calvin College and William B. Eerdmans Publishing Co., 1970.

Campanelle, Thomas. "A Critique on Catholic Higher Education." *Catholic Educational Review* 61, no. 5 (1963): 313–21.

Carlson, Edgar M. *Church-Sponsored Education and the Lutheran Church in America*. New York: Board of College Education and Church Vocations, Lutheran Church in America, 1967.

——. *The Future of Church-Related Higher Education*. Minneapolis: Augsburg Publishing House, 1977.

Clark, Gordon H. *A Christian Philosophy of Education*. Grand Rapids, Mich.: William B. Eerdmans Publishing Co., 1946.

Coleman, A. John. *The Task of the Christian in the University*. New York: Association Press, 1947.

A College-Related Church: United Methodist Perspectives. Nashville, Tenn.: The National Commission on United Methodist Higher Education, 1976.

Contemporary Thoughts on Christian Higher Education: The University Year, 1960–61. Tacoma, Wash.: Pacific Lutheran University, 1961.

Cully, Kendig Brubaker, ed. *The Episcopal Church and Education*. New York: Morehouse-Barlow Co., 1966.

Cuninggim, Merrimon. *The Protestant Stake in Higher Education*. Washington, D.C.: Council of Protestant Colleges and Universities, 1961.

Dayton, Donald W. *Discovering an Evangelical Heritage*. New York: Harper & Row, 1976.

Defferrari, Roy J., ed. Series of volumes resulting from summer workshops on integration held at the Catholic University of America and published by CUA Press: *The Philosophy of Catholic Higher Education* (1948), *Integration in Catholic Colleges and Universities* (1950), *Discipline and Integration in the Catholic College* (1951), *The Curriculum of the Catholic College: Integration and Concentration* (1952), *Theology, Philosophy and History as Integrating Disciplines* (1953).

Ditmanson, Harold H., Howard V. Hong, and Warren A. Quanbeck, eds. *Christian Faith and the Liberal Arts*. Minneapolis: Augsburg Publishing House, 1960.

Doescher, Waldemar O. *The Church College in Today's Culture*. Minneapolis: Augsburg Publishing House, 1963.

Donovan, Charles F. "The Challenge of the Future in Catholic Education." *Catholic Educational Review* 62, no. 2 (1964): 73–80.

Donovan, John D. *The Academic Man in the Catholic College*. New York: Sheed and Ward, 1964.

Ellis, John Tracy. *American Catholics and the Intellectual Life*. Chicago: The Heritage Foundation, Inc., 1956.

Ferré, Nels F. S. *Christian Faith and Higher Education*. New York: Harper & Brothers, 1954.

———. *A Theology for Christian Education*. Philadelphia: Westminster Press, 1967.

Gamelin, Francis C. *Church-Related Identity of Lutheran Colleges*. Washington, D.C.: Lutheran Educational Conference of North America, 1975.

Gangel, Kenneth O. "Integrating Faith and Learning: Principles and Process." *Bibliotheca Sacra* 135, no. 538 (April–June 1978): 99–108.

Ganss, George E., S.J., *St. Ignatius' Idea of a Jesuit University*, 2d ed. Milwaukee, Wisc.: Marquette University Press, 1956.

Greeley, Andrew M. *From Backwater to Mainstream: A Profile of Catholic Higher Education*. New York: McGraw-Hill, 1969.

———, William C. McCready, and Kathleen McCourt. *Catholic Schools in a Declining Church*. Kansas City, Mo.: Sheed and Ward, 1976.

Grollmes, Eugene E. "A Blueprint for Catholic Colleges." *Catholic Educational Review* 63, no. 3 (1965): 164–72.

Hart, Charles A., ed. *Aspects of the New Scholastic Philosophy*. New York: Benziger Brothers, 1932. Though published before 1940, Hart provides the intellectual context for Catholic thought at midcentury.

Hassenger, Robert, ed. *The Shape of Catholic Higher Education*. Chicago: The University of Chicago Press, 1967.

Holmes, Arthur F. *All Truth is God's Truth*. Grand Rapids, Mich.: William B. Eerdmans Publishing Co., 1977.

Holmes, Robert Merrill. *The Academic Mysteryhouse: The Man, the Campus, and Their New Search for Meaning*. Nashville, Tenn.: Abingdon Press, 1970.

Hong, Howard, V. ed. *Integration in the Christian Liberal Arts College*. Northfield, Minn.: St. Olaf College Press, 1956.

Hotchkiss, Wesley A. *Meeting the Crisis in Church-Related Higher Education*. Philadelphia: Pilgrim Press, 1968.

Institutional Mission and Identity in Lutheran Higher Education. Papers and proceedings from the Lutheran Educational Conference of North America, 1979.

Jahsmann, Allan Hart. *What's Lutheran in Education?: Explorations Into Principles and Practices*. St. Louis, Mo.: Concordia Publishing House, 1960.

Kaiser, Robert Blair. "The Remaking of the Jesuit Colleges." *World* (November 21, 1972): 30–35.

Kelly, George A., ed. *Why Should the Catholic University Survive?: A Study of the Character and Commitments of Catholic Higher Education*. New York: St. John's University Press, 1974.

Kohlbrenner, Bernard J. "Whither Catholic Education?" *Catholic Educational Review* 61, no. 9 (1963): 593–600.

Kraybill, Donald B. *Mennonite Education: Issues, Facts, and Changes*. Scottdale, Pa.: Herald Press, 1978.

Lawler, Justus George. *The Catholic Dimension in Higher Education*. Westminster, Md.: The Newman Press, 1959.

Lonergan, Bernard. *Topics in Education: The Cincinnati Lectures of 1959 on the Philosophy of Education*. Vol. 10 in *The Collected Works of Bernard Lonergan* edited by Robert M. Doran and Frederick E. Crowe. Toronto: University of Toronto Press, 1993.

Lowry, Howard Foster. *The Mind's Adventure: Religion and Higher Education*. Philadelphia: Westminster Press, 1950.

Lucey, Gregory F. "The Meaning and Maintenance of Catholic as a Distinctive Characteristic of American Catholic Higher Education: A Case Study." Unpublished Ph.D. dissertation, University of Wisconsin, Madison, 1978.

McCluskey, Neil G., S.J. *Catholic Education in America: A Documentary History*. New York: Teachers College Press, Columbia University, 1964.

———, ed. *The Catholic University: A Modern Appraisal*. Notre Dame, Ind.: University of Notre Dame Press, 1970.

———. *Catholic Viewpoint on Education*. Garden City, N.Y.: Doubleday, 1959.

McCoy, Charles S. *The Responsible Campus: Toward a New Identity for the Church-Related College*. Nashville, Tenn.: Division of

Higher Education, Board of Education, the United Methodist Church, 1972.

McGrath, Earl J. *Study of Southern Baptist Colleges and Universities.* Nashville, Tenn.: The Education Commission of the Southern Baptist Convention, 1977.

Maloney, Edward F. "A Study of the Religious Orientation of the Catholic Colleges and Universities in New York State from 1962–1972." Unpublished Ph.D. dissertation, New York University, 1973.

Manier, Edward, and John W. Houck, eds. *Academic Freedom and the Catholic University.* Notre Dame, Ind.: University of Notre Dame Press, 1967.

Meyer, Albert J. "Getting It All Together." *Gospel Herald,* 11 April 1972, 326.

———. "Needed: A Mennonite Philosophy of Higher Education." *Mennonite Life* (January 1962): 3–4.

———. "Peoplehood Education." *Mennonite Educator* 1, no. 1 (January 1974): 1–6.

———. "Schools—Among the Vital Organs." *Gospel Herald,* 11 January 1977: 18.

———. "Two Models: Some Theological and Policy Perspectives." Presentation at the Princeton Consultation, Department of Higher Education, National Council of Churches, September 1972.

———. "What Manner of Measuring Stick for Our Church Schools?" *Gospel Herald,* 27 May 1975: 400–401.

Miller, Alexander. *Faith and Learning: Christian Faith and Higher Education in Twentieth Century America.* New York: Association Press, 1960.

Miller, Randolph Crump. *The Clue to Christian Education.* New York: Charles Scribner's Sons, 1950.

Miller, R. C., and Henry H. Shires, eds. *Christianity and the Contemporary Scene.* New York: Morehouse-Gorham, 1943.

"The Mission of LCA Colleges and Universities." New York: Board of College Education and Church Vocations, Lutheran Church in America, 1969.

Moroney, Rev. Joseph P. "Background of Catholic Higher Education." *Duquesne Review* 9, no. 2 (1964): 137–47.

Newman, John Henry Cardinal. *Discourses on the Scope and Na-*

ture of University Education. Dubuque, Iowa: William C. Brown Reprint Library, 1967.

Occasional Papers on Catholic Higher Education, 1975–78. Published by the National Catholic Educational Association, College and University Department, Washington, D.C.

Pace, C. Robert. *Education and Evangelism: A Profile of Protestant Colleges*, (Carnegie Commission on Higher Education Study). New York: McGraw-Hill, 1972.

Parsonage, Robert Rue, ed. *Church-Related Higher Education: Perceptions and Perspectives*. Valley Forge, Pa.: Judson Press, 1978.

Pattillo, Manning M., Jr., and Donald M. Mackenzie. *Church-Sponsored Higher Education in the United States: Report of the Danforth Commission*. Washington, D.C.: American Council on Education, 1966.

Power, Edward J. *A History of Catholic Higher Education in the United States*. Milwaukee, Wisc.: Bruce Publishing Co., 1958; 1977.

―――― and Walter Bernard Kolesnik, eds. *Catholic Education: A Book of Readings*. New York: McGraw-Hill, 1965.

Ramm, Bernard. *The Christian College in the Twentieth Century*. Grand Rapids, Mich.: William B. Eerdmans Publishing Co., 1963.

Redden, John D., and Francis A. Ryan. *A Catholic Philosophy of Education*. Milwaukee, Wisc.: Bruce Publishing Co., 1942.

Ryan, Mary Perkins. *Are Parochial Schools the Answer?: Catholic Education in Light of the Council*. New York: Holt, Rinehart, & Winston, 1963.

Snavely, Guy. *The Church and the Four Year College: An Appraisal of the Relation*. New York: Harper & Brothers, 1955.

Strommen, Merton P. "Images and Expectations of LCA Colleges." In *Papers and Proceedings of the Lutheran Educational Conference of North America*. Washington, D.C.: Lutheran Educational Conference, 1977.

Trueblood, Elton. *The Idea of a College*. New York: Harper & Brothers, 1959.

Von Grueningen, J. P., ed. *Toward a Christian Philosophy of Higher Education*. Philadelphia: Westminster Press, 1957.

Wakin, Edward. *The Catholic Campus*. New York: Macmillan, 1963.

Ward, Leo R. *Blueprint for a Catholic University.* St. Louis, Mo.: B. Herder Book Co., 1949.

Wicke, Myron F. *The Church-Related College.* Washington, D.C.: The Center for Applied Research in Education, Inc., 1964.

Wickey, Gould. *The Lutheran Venture in Higher Education.* Philadelphia: Muhlenberg Press for The Board of Publication of the United Lutheran Church in America, 1962.

Williams, George H. *The Theological Idea of the University.* Revised from an article entitled "An Excursus: Church, Commonwealth and College: The Religious Sources of the Idea of the University," in *The Harvard Divinity School.* Boston: Beacon Press, 1954.

Young, M. Norvel. *A History of the Colleges Established and Controlled by Members of the Churches of Christ.* Kansas City, Mo.: Old Paths Book Club, 1949.

The Contemporary Period (1980–2002)

General, Comparative, Anthological, and Ecumenical Sources

Academe 82, no. 6 (November–December 1996). Six essays on the relationship between religion and higher education.

Beaty, Michael D., J. Todd Buras, and Larry Lyon. "Christian Higher Education: An Historical and Philosophical Perspective." *Perspectives in Religious Studies* 24, no. 2 (summer 1997): 145–65.

———— and Larry Lyon. "Integration, Secularization, and the Two-Spheres View at Religious Colleges: Comparing Baylor University with the University of Notre Dame and Georgetown College." *Christian Scholar's Review* 29, no. 1 (fall 1999): 73–112.

Beck, David W., ed. *Opening the American Mind: The Integration of Biblical Truth in the Curriculum of the University.* Grand Rapids, Mich.: Baker Book House, 1991.

Benne, Robert. *Quality with Soul: How Six Premier Colleges and Universities Keep Faith with Their Religious Traditions.* Grand Rapids, Mich.: William B. Eerdmans Publishing Co., 2001.

Buford, Thomas O. *In Search of a Calling: The College's Role in Shaping Identity.* Macon, Ga.: Mercer University Press, 1994.

Burtchaell, James Tunstead, C.S.C. "The Decline and Fall of the Christian College." *First Things* no. 12 (April 1991): 16–29.

———. "The Decline and Fall of the Christian College II." *First Things* no. 13 (May 1991): 30–38.

———. *The Dying of the Light: The Disengagement of Colleges and Universities from Their Christian Churches.* Grand Rapids, Mich.: William B. Eerdmans Publishing Co., 1998.

Carpenter, Joel A., and Kenneth W. Shipps, eds. *Making Higher Education Christian: The History and Mission of Evangelical Colleges in America.* Grand Rapids, Mich.: Christian University Press and William B. Eerdmans Publishing Co., 1987.

Christian Scholar's Review. Theme issues on "Christian Higher Education—1990s," 21, no. 3 (March 1992) and "Christian Scholarship in the Twenty-First Century: Prospects and Projects," 30, no. 4 (summer 2001).

The Cresset: A Review of Literature, Arts, and Public Affairs. (Note especially the spring special issues on the Lilly Fellows Program in Humanities and the Arts.) Published by Valparaiso University, Valparaiso, Indiana.

Cuninggim, Merrimon. *Uneasy Partners: The College and the Church.* Nashville, Tenn.: Abingdon Press, 1994.

De Jong, Arthur J. *Reclaiming a Mission: New Directions for the Church-Related College.* Grand Rapids, Mich.: William B. Eerdmans Publishing Co., 1990.

Diekema, Anthony J. *Academic Freedom and Christian Scholarship.* Grand Rapids, Mich.: William B. Eerdmans Publishing Co., 2000.

Dockery, David S., and David P. Gushee. *The Future of Christian Higher Education.* Nashville, Tenn.: Broadman & Holman, 1999.

Dykstra, Craig. *Vision and Character: A Christian Educator's Alternative to Kohlberg.* New York: Paulist Press, 1981.

Edwards, Mark U. "Christian Colleges: A Dying of the Light or a Different Refraction." *Christian Century* 116, no. 13 (April 21–28, 1999): 459–63.

Elliott, Daniel C., ed. *Nurturing Reflective Christians to Teach: A Valiant Role for the Nation's Christian Colleges and Universities.* Lanham, Md.: University Press of America, 1995.

Faculty Dialogue, 1984–95. Published by the Institute for Christian Leadership, Tigard, Oregon.

Fisher, Ben C. *The Idea of a Christian University in Today's World.* Macon, Ga.: Mercer University Press, 1989.

Hasker, William. "Faith-Learning Integration: An Overview." *Christian Scholar's Review* 21, no. 3 (March 1992): 234–48.

Hauerwas, Stanley, and John H. Westerhoff, eds. *Schooling Christians: "Holy Experiments" in American Education.* Grand Rapids, Mich.: William B. Eerdmans Publishing Co., 1992.

Heie, Harold, and David L. Wolfe, eds. *The Reality of Christian Learning: Strategies for Faith-Learning Integration.* Grand Rapids, Mich.: Christian University Press and William B. Eerdmans Publishing Co., 1987.

Holmes, Arthur F. *Building the Christian Academy.* Grand Rapids, Mich.: Willliam B. Eerdmans Publishing Co., 2001.

———. *The Idea of a Christian College,* revised ed. Grand Rapids, Mich.: William B. Eerdmans Publishing Co., 1987.

———, ed. *The Making of a Christian Mind: A Christian World View and the Academic Enterprise.* Downers Grove, Ill.: InterVarsity Press, 1985.

———. *Shaping Character: Moral Education in the Christian College.* Grand Rapids, Mich.: William B. Eerdmans Publishing Co., 1991.

Hughes, Richard T. *How Christian Faith Can Sustain the Life of the Mind.* Grand Rapids, Mich.: William B. Eerdmans Publishing Co., 2001.

———, and William B. Adrian, eds. *Models for Christian Higher Education: Strategies for Success in the Twenty-First Century.* Grand Rapids, Mich.: William B. Eerdmans Publishing Co., 1997. This anthology contains thoughtful essays on each of the faith traditions represented in this volume and their linkages to higher education. It also includes others significant to the broader Christian family tree.

Hunt, Thomas C., and James C. Carper, eds. *Religious Higher Education in the United States: A Source Book.* New York: Garland Publishing, Inc., 1996.

Larsen, David. "Evangelical Christian Higher Education, Culture, and Social Conflict: A Niebuhrian Analysis of Three Colleges in the 1960s." Unpublished Ph.D. dissertation, Loyola University, 1992.

Lee, John D., Alvaro L. Nieves, and Henry L. Allen, eds. *Ethnic Minorities and Evangelical Christian Colleges.* Lanham, Md.: University Press of America, 1991.

Malloy, Edward A., C.S.C. *Culture and Commitment: The Challenges of Today's University.* Notre Dame, Ind.: University of Notre Dame Press, 1992.

Mannoia, V. James, Jr. *Christian Liberal Arts: An Education that Goes Beyond.* Lanham, Md.: Rowman and Littlefield, 2000.

Marsden, George M. *The Soul of the American University: From Protestant Establishment to Established Nonbelief.* New York: Oxford University Press, 1994.

———, and Bradley J. Longfield, eds. *The Secularization of the Academy.* New York: Oxford University Press, 1992.

Miller, Randolph Crump. *The Theory of Christian Education Practice: How Theology Affects Christian Education.* Birmingham, Ala.: Religious Education Press, 1980.

Moore, Steve, ed., with Tim Beuthin, consulting ed. *The University Through the Eyes of Faith.* Indianapolis, Ind.: Light and Life Communications, 1998.

Newman, John Henry Cardinal. *The Idea of a University,* edited by Frank M. Turner. New Haven, Conn.: Yale University Press, 1996.

O'Reilley, Mary Rose. *The Peaceable Classroom.* Portsmouth, N.H.: Heinemann, 1993.

Palmer, Parker J. *The Courage To Teach: Exploring the Inner Landscape of a Teacher's Life.* San Francisco: Jossey-Bass, 1998.

———. *Let Your Life Speak: Listening for the Voice of Vocation.* San Francisco: Jossey-Bass, 2000.

———. *To Know As We Are Known: A Spirituality of Education.* San Francisco: Harper & Row, 1983.

Pelikan, Jaroslav. *The Idea of the University: A Reexamination.* New Haven, Conn.: Yale University Press, 1992.

Research on Christian Higher Education, 1994–. Published by the Council for Christian Colleges and Universities, Washington, D.C.

Ringenberg, William C. *The Christian College: A History of Protestant Higher Education in America.* Grand Rapids, Mich.: Christian University Press and William B. Eerdmans Publishing Co., 1984.

Roberts, Jon H., and James Turner. *The Sacred and the Secular University*. Princeton, N.J.: Princeton University Press, 2000.

Schwehn, Mark R. *Exiles From Eden: Religion and the Academic Vocation in America*. New York: Oxford University Press, 1993.

Scriven, Charles. "Schooling for the Tournament of Narratives: Postmodernism and the Idea of the Christian College." In *Theology Without Foundations: Religious Practice and the Future of Theological Truth*, 273–88. Ed. by Stanley Hauerwas, Nancey C. Murphy, and Mark Nation. Nashville, Tenn.: Abingdon Press, 1994.

Sloan, Douglas. *Faith and Knowledge: Mainline Protestantism and American Higher Education*. Louisville, Ky.: Westminster/John Knox Press, 1994.

Springsted, Eric O. *Who Will Make Us Wise: How the Churches Are Failing Higher Education*. Cambridge, Mass.: Cowley Publications, 1988.

Sterk, Andrea, ed. *Religion, Scholarship, and Higher Education: Perspectives, Models, and Future Prospects*. Notre Dame, Ind.: University of Notre Dame Press, 2002.

Stoltzfus, Victor. *Church-Affiliated Higher Education: Exploratory Case Studies of Presbyterian, Roman Catholic, and Wesleyan Colleges*. Goshen, Ind.: Pinchpenny Press, 1992.

Various Denominations and Black Higher Education. *Black Issues in Higher Education* 9 (14 January 1993).

Wolfe, David L., and Harold Heie. *Slogans or Distinctives: Reforming Christian Higher Education*. Lanham, Md.: University Press of America, 1993.

Wolterstorff, Nicholas. "The Christian College and Christian Learning." *Seattle Pacific University Review* (autumn 1987).

———. "The Mission of the Christian College at the End of the Twentieth Century." *The Reformed Journal* 33 (June 1983): 14–18.

Higher Education and the Anabaptist Tradition

Beaty, Michael D., J. Todd Buras, and Larry Lyon. "Baptist Higher Education: A Conflict in Terms?" *The Baylor Line* 59, no. 1 (winter 1997): 43–51.

————, and Stephanie Littizette. "Challenges and Prospects for Baptist Higher Education." *The Southern Baptist Educator* 61, no. 4 (April–June 1997): 3–6.

Draper, James T., Jr. "A Vision for a Christian Baptist University." In *The Future of Christian Higher Education*, David S. Dockery and David P. Gushee, eds. Nashville, Tenn.: Broadman & Holman, 1997.

Hawkley, Ken, ed. *Mennonite Higher Education: Experience and Vision*. Newton, Kans.: Higher Education Council, General Conference Mennonite Church, 1992.

Mennonite Board of Education. "How Should We As a Mennonite Church Engage in Liberal Arts Education?" Unpublished report, 1984.

Meyer, Albert J. *Education with a Difference: An Approach to Church Involvement in Higher Education with New Intentionality in a Postmodern Era*, forthcoming.

————. "Factors in Churches' Formation and Maintenance of Value-Distinctive Higher Educational Institutions: An Open Systems Inquiry." Paper presented at the conference "The Church-Related College's Postmodern Opportunity," Rhodes College, 2–4 May 1997.

————. "The Importance of Overeducation," *Gospel Herald*, 28 September 1982, 653.

————. "Mennonite Identity and Main Currents in American Higher Education." Address presented at the centennial conference on "The Church and College in Partnership: A Vision for the Future," Goshen College, March 23–26, 1995.

Rawlyk, G. A., ed. *Canadian Baptists and Christian Higher Education*. Kingston and Montreal: McGill-Queen's University, 1988.

Williams, D. Newell, ed. *A Case Study of Mainstream Protestantism: The Disciples' Relation to American Culture, 1880–1989*. Grand Rapids, Mich.: William B. Eerdmans Publishing Co., 1991.

Higher Education and the Lutheran Tradition

Benne, Robert. "A Lutheran Vision/Version of Christian Humanism." *Lutheran Forum* 31 (fall 1997): 40–46.

————. "Recovering a Christian College: From Suspicious Tension, Toward Christian Presence." *Lutheran Forum* 27 (May 1993): 58–61.

Bunge, Wilfred F. *Success, Wealth, and Happiness: The Goals of Lutheran Higher Education*. Moorhead, Minn.: s. n., 1986. Part of the series *Occasional Papers on the Christian Faith and the Liberal Arts*. Moorhead, Minn.: Division for College and University Services of the American Lutheran Church, Christian Faith and Liberal Arts Study Group, 1982–.

Contino, Paul J., and David Morgan, eds. *The Lutheran Reader*. Valparaiso, Ind.: Valparaiso University, 1999.

Dovre, Paul. "The Vocation of a Lutheran College: Context." Paper presented at the ELCA Conference, August 1995.

Gengenbach, Connie, ed. *Faith, Learning and the Church College: Addresses by Joseph Sittler*. Northfield, Minn.: St. Olaf College, 1989.

Intersections: Faith + Life + Learning, 1996–. Published by the Division for Higher Education and Schools, The Evangelical Lutheran Church in America, Columbus, Ohio.

Johnson, K. Glen. "The Lutheran University: Mission, Task and Focus." In *Proceedings: Lutheran Educational Conference of North America*, 1994.

Lagerquist, DeAne. "Incarnating a Tradition: Personal and Institutional Reflections." Lecture given at Gustavus Adolphus College, September 1998.

Meilaender, Gilbert. "Forming Heart and Mind: Lutheran Thoughts About Higher Education." *Lutheran Education* 134 (January–February 1999): 152–65.

The Mission of the ELCA Colleges and Universities: The Joseph Sittler Symposium. Chicago: ELCA, 1989.

Nordquist, Philip. "From Pietism to Paradox: The Development of a Lutheran Philosophy of Education." *Intersections* 8 (winter 2000).

Simmons, Ernest L. "A Lutheran View of Christian Vocation in the Liberal Arts—I: Martin Luther on the Calling of the Christian." *The Cresset* 52, no. 2 (December 1988): 13–17.

———. "A Lutheran View of Christian Vocation in the Liberal Arts—II: Education and Scholarship in Theonomous Perspective." *The Cresset* 52, no. 3 (January 1989): 11–15.

——. *Lutheran Higher Education: An Introduction for Faculty.* Minneapolis, Minn.: Augsburg Fortress, 1998.

Solberg, Richard W. *Lutheran Higher Education in North America.* Minneapolis, Minn.: Augsburg Publishing House, 1985.

—— and Merton P. Strommen. *How Church-Related Are Church-Related Colleges?: Answers Based on a Comprehensive Survey of Supporting Constituencies of Eighteen LCA Colleges.* Philadelphia: Board of Publication, Lutheran Church in America, 1980.

Higher Education and the Reformed Tradition

Bratt, James D. " 'Big Ideas, Little People': Theological Education in the Dutch New-Calvinist Tradition." Unpublished paper prepared for the ISAE "Theological Education in the Evangelical Tradition" Conference, Wheaton College, 2–4 December 1994.

——. "Reformed Tradition and the Mission of Reformed Colleges." Unpublished paper presented at the RUNA Conference, Grand Rapids, Michigan, 11 March 1993.

Coalter, Milton J., John M. Mulder, and Louis B. Weeks. *The Pluralistic Vision: Presbyterians and Mainstream Protestant Education and Leadership.* Louisville, KY: Westminster/John Knox Press, 1992.

Hodgson, Peter C. *God's Wisdom: Toward a Theology of Education.* Louisville, Ky.: Westminster/John Knox Press, 1999.

Loving God With Our Minds. Louisville, Ky: The Committee on Higher Education, Presbyterian Church (U.S.A.), 1991.

A Point of View, 1990–. Published by the Association of Presbyterian Colleges and Universities (P.C.U.S.A.), Louisville, Kentucky.

On Being Faithful: The Continuing Mission of the Presbyterian Church (U.S.A.) in Higher Education. Louisville, Ky.: Higher Education Program Team, 1995.

Plantinga, Alvin. *The Twin Pillars of Christian Scholarship.* Grand Rapids, Mich.: Calvin College, 1990.

Presbyterians and Black Higher Education, various articles. *Black Issues in Higher Education* 9 (31 December 1992).

Smith, Harry E. "Theological Principles Which Shape Presbyterian-Related Colleges," *Presbyterian Outlook* 175, no. 37 (25 October 1993): 8–9.

Task Force on the Church and Higher Education. "The Church's Mission in Higher Education." *Journal of Presbyterian History* 59, no. 3 (1981): 440–65.

Wells, Ronald A., ed. *Keeping Faith: Embracing the Tensions in Christian Higher Education*. Grand Rapids, Mich.: William B. Eerdmans Publishing Co., 1996.

Weston, William, and Duncan S. Ferguson, eds. *The Vocation of the Presbyterian Teacher: The Calling to Teach from a Reformed Perspective*. Louisville, Ky.: Geneva Press, forthcoming.

Wolterstorff, Nicholas. *Educating for Responsible Action*. Grand Rapids, Mich.: CSI Publications and William B. Eerdmans Publishing Co., 1980.

———. *Reason Within the Bounds of Religion*. Grand Rapids, Mich.: William B. Eerdmans Publishing Co., 1984.

———. *Until Justice and Peace Embrace: The Kuyper Lectures for 1981 Delivered at the Free University of Amsterdam*. Grand Rapids, Mich.: William B. Eerdmans Publishing Co., 1983.

Higher Education and the Roman Catholic Tradition

ACCU Update. Bimonthly newsletter published by the Association of Catholic Colleges and Universities, Washington, D.C. highlighting higher education issues of import.

Annarelli, James John. *Academic Freedom and Catholic Higher Education*. New York: Greenwood Press, 1987.

Apczynski, John, ed. *Theology and the University*. Lanham, Md.: University Press of America, 1990.

Boys, Mary C. *Educating in Faith: Maps and Visions*. Kansas City, Mo.: Sheed and Ward, 1989.

Buckley, Michael J., S.J. "Jeusit, Catholic Higher Education: Some Tentative Theses." *Review for Religious* 47, no. 3 (May–June 1983): 338–49.

Byron, William J., S.J. *Quadrangle Considerations*. Chicago: Loyola University Press, 1989.

Carlin, David R. "What Future for Catholic Higher Education?" *America* 174, no. 6 (24 February 1996): 15–17.

Carmody, Denise Lardner. *Organizing a Christian Mind: A Theol-*

ogy of Higher Education. Valley Forge, Pa.: Trinity Press International, 1996.

Catholics and Black Higher Education, various articles. *Black Issues in Higher Education* 9 (19 November 1992).

CCICA Annual. Published by the Catholic Commission on Intellectual and Cultural Affairs.

Conversations on Jesuit Higher Education, 1987–. Published by the National Seminar on Jesuit Higher Education, Baltimore, Maryland.

Curran, Charles E. *Catholic Higher Education, Theology, and Academic Freedom*. Notre Dame, Ind.: University of Notre Dame Press, 1990.

———. "The Elusive Idea of a Catholic University." *National Catholic Reporter*, 7 October 1994, 12–15.

Current Issues in Catholic Higher Education, 1980–. Published by the Association of Catholic Colleges and Universities, Washington, D.C.

Feeney, Joseph J., S.J. "Can Jesuit College Education Survive in a New Century?: A Historic Initiative." *America* 170, no. 19 (28 May 1994): 14–19.

Gallin, Alice, O.S.U., ed. *American Catholic Higher Education: Essential Documents, 1967–1990*. Notre Dame, Ind.: University of Notre Dame Press, 1992.

———. *Independence and a New Partnership in Catholic Higher Education*. Notre Dame, Ind.: University of Notre Dame Press, 1996.

———. *Negotiating Identity: Catholic Higher Education Since 1960*. Notre Dame, Ind.: University of Notre Dame Press, 2000.

Gleason, Philip. *Contending With Modernity: Catholic Higher Education in the Twentieth Century*. New York: Oxford University Press, 1995.

———. *Keeping Faith: American Catholicism Past and Present*. Notre Dame, Ind.: University of Notre Dame Press, 1987.

Hassel, David J., S.J. *City of Wisdom: A Christian Vision of the American University*. Chicago: Loyola University Press, 1983.

Hesburgh, Theodore M., C.S.C., ed. *The Challenge and Promise of a Catholic University*. Notre Dame, Ind.: University of Notre Dame Press, 1994.

Landy, Thomas M., ed. *As Leaven in the World: Catholic Perspec-*

tives on Faith, Vocation, and the Intellectual Life. Franklin, Wisc.: Sheed and Ward, 2001.

Langan, John P., S.J., ed. *Catholic Universities in Church and Society: A Dialogue on* Ex Corde Ecclesiae. Washington, D.C.: Georgetown University Press, 1993.

Lazarus, Francis M., ed. *Faith, Discovery, Service: Perspectives on Jesuit Education.* Milwaukee, Wisc.: Marquette University Press, 1992.

Leahy, William P., S.J. *Adapting to America: Catholics, Jesuits and Higher Education in the Twentieth Century.* Washington, D.C.: Georgetown University Press, 1991.

Murphy, J. Patrick, C.M. *Visions and Values in Catholic Higher Education.* Kansas City, Mo.: Sheed and Ward, 1991.

O'Brien, David J. *From the Heart of the American Church: Catholic Higher Education and American Culture.* Maryknoll, N.Y.: Orbis Books, 1994.

————. *Minding the Time 1492–1992: Jesuit Education and Issues in American Culture.* Washington, D.C.: Georgetown University Press, 1992.

Poorman, Mark L., C.S.C. *Labors from the Heart: Mission and Ministry in a Catholic University.* Notre Dame, Ind.: University of Notre Dame Press, 1996.

Readings in Ignatian Higher Education 1989–. Published by the Jesuit Conference of the Society of Jesus in the United States.

Reiser, William, S.J., ed. *Love of Learning, Desire for Justice: Undergraduate Education and the Option for the Poor.* Scranton, Pa.: University of Scranton Press, 1995.

Rowntree, Stephen C., S.J. "Ten Theses on Jesuit Higher Education." *America* 170, no. 19 (28 May 1994): 6–12.

Salvaterra, David L. *American Catholicism and the Intellectual Life, 1880–1950.* New York: Garland Publishing, 1988.

Turner, James. "The Catholic University in Modern Academe: Challenge and Dilemma." Paper presented at the conference "Storm Over the University," University of Notre Dame, October 13, 1992.

Woodward, Kenneth L. "Catholic Higher Education: What Happened?" *Commonweal* 120, no. 7 (9 April 1993): 13–18.

Higher Education and the Wesleyan Tradition

Cole, Charles E., ed. *Something More Than Human: Biographies of Leaders in American Methodist Higher Education.* Nashville, Tenn.: United Methodist Board of Higher Education and Ministry, 1986.

Conn, Robert H., ed. *Loving God with One's Mind: Selected Writings by F. Thomas Trotter.* Nashville, Tenn.: The Board of Higher Education and Ministry of the United Methodist Church, 1987.

Gyertson, David John. "The Church-Related College: Higher Education in the Free Methodist Church During the Decade of the Seventies: Implications for the Eighties." Unpublished Ph.D. dissertation, Michigan State University, 1981.

Johnson, Terrell E. "A History of Methodist Education and Its Influence on American Public Education." Unpublished Ph.D. dissertation, Southern Illinois University at Carbondale, 1989.

Methodists and Black Higher Education, various articles. *Black Issues in Higher Education* 9 (3 December 1992).

Moore, James R. "The Christian Mission in Higher Education: A Wesleyan Perspective." *Faculty Dialogue* no. 23 (winter 1995): 115–22.

APPENDIX B

Ecumenical Christian Professional Associations

SINCE IT IS OFTEN HELPFUL to remain in contact with Christians who share your disciplinary and scholarly interests, the following list of ecumenical professional societies is provided for those who might like to pursue those connections. There has been an explosion in the number of these professional societies over the past decade or so, and they can provide needed support and encouragement as you seek to learn and teach from a Christian worldview in the Academy. The organizations listed here are a sampling of those available to Christian professionals from a variety of faith traditions. Membership information is available from the contact persons and addresses cited below. In addition to these ecumenical associations, specific traditions may also maintain their own organizations, the Roman Catholic tradition having the most comprehensive set.

Affiliation of Christian Biologists: Dr. Gerald Hess, President, Messiah College, College Avenue, Grantham, PA 17027

Affiliation of Christian Geologists: Paul Ribbe, President, Dept. of Geological Sciences, Virginia Tech, 4044 Derring Hall, Blacksburg, VA 24061

American Association of Christian Counselors: Dawn Emeigh, P.O. Box 739, Forest Grove, VA 24551

American Political Science Association, Section on Religion and Politics: Professor Clarke Cochran, Chair, Dept. of Political Science, Texas Tech University, P.O. Box 4290, Lubbock, TX 79409

American Scientific Affiliation: Dr. Donald William Monro, Jr., Executive Director, PO Box 668, Ipswich, MA 01938

American Society of Missiology: George Hunsberger, Secretary/Treasurer, Western Theological Seminary, 101 E. 13th, Holland, MI 49423–3622

American Theological Society—Midwest: Dr. John Weborg, North Park Theological Seminary, 3225 W. Foster Ave., Chicago, IL 60625

Association for Public Justice: 321 8th Street NE, Washington, D.C. 20002

Association of Business Administrators of Christian Colleges: Jim Olsen, Executive Director, 8686 SE Alabama Pl., Hobe Sound, FL 33455

Association of Christian Collegiate Media: 1000 Regent Drive, Virginia Beach, VA 23464–9840

Association of Christian Economists: Dr. John Mason, Executive Secretary, Gordon College, Wenham, MA 01984

Association of Christian Engineers and Scientists: Orvin and Carol Olson, 479 Rose Avenue, Vernonia, OR 97064

Association of Christian Librarians: Nancy Olson, Executive Director, P.O. Box 4, Cedarville, OH 45314

Association of Christians in Mathematical Sciences: Dr. Robert Brabenec, Dept. of Mathematics, Wheaton College, Wheaton, IL 60187

Association of Christians Teaching Sociology: Dr. Russell Heddendorf, Dept. of Sociology, Covenant College, Lookout Mountain, GA 30750

Christian Association for Psychological Studies: Dr. Randolph Sanders, Executive Secretary, P.O. Box 310400, New Braunfels, TX 78131

Christian Business Faculty Association: Dr. Lisa Klein Surdyk, Seattle Pacific University, Seattle WA 98119–1997

Christian Career Women: Mary Reynolds Williams, Executive Director, P.O. Box 531152, Indianapolis, IN 46253–1552

Christian Educator's Association: Forrest L. Turpen, PO Box 50025, Pasadena, CA 91115

Christian Legal Society: Steven T. McFarland, Director, Center for Law and Religious Freedom, 4028 Evergreen Lane, Suite 222, Annandale, VA 22003

Christian Medical and Dental Society: Dr. David Stevens, Executive Director, 501 5th Street, PO Box 5, Bristol, TN 37621–0005

Christian Nuclear Fellowship (Nuclear Science & Technology): V. O. Uotinen, 9102 Oakland Circle, Lynchburg, VA 24502

Christian Sociological Society: Dr. Ronald Akers, Dept. of Sociology, University of Florida, Gainesville, FL 32611

Christian Veterinary Mission: Dr. Kit Flowers, 19303 Fremont Ave. N., Seattle, WA 98133

Christians in the Arts Networking: Phillip Charles Griffith II, Executive Director, 21 Harlow Street, Arlington, MA 02174–0003

Christians in Political Science: Dr. Corwin Smidt, Secretary/Treasurer, Dept. of Political Science, Calvin College, 3201 Burton St. SE, Grand Rapids, MI 49546

Christians in Theatre Arts: Dale Savidge, PO Box 26471, Greenville, SC 29616

Christians in Visual Arts: Sandra Bowden, PO Box 18117, Minneapolis, MN 55418–0117

Christianity and Communication: Dr. Robert Fortner, Calvin College, 3201 Burton St. SE, Grand Rapids, MI 49546

Conference on Christianity and Literature: Dr. Robert Snyder, Dept. of English, State University of Georgia, Carrollton, GA 30118–2200

Conference on Faith and History: Dr. Richard Pierard, Dept. of History, Indiana State University, Terre Haute, IN 47809

The Evangelical Missiological Society: Dr. Michael Pocock, Dallas Theological Seminary, 3909 Swiss Ave., Dallas, TX 75204

Evangelical Philosophical Society: Dr. David Clark, Secretary/Treasurer, Bethel Theological Seminary, 3949 Bethel Drive, St. Paul, MN 55112

Evangelical Theological Society: James A. Borland, Secretary/Treasurer, 112 Russell Woods Drive, Lynchburg, VA 24502–3530

Fellowship of Artists for Cultural Evangelism: Eugene and Mary Lou Totten, 1605 E. Elizabeth Street, Pasadena, CA 91104

Fellowship of Christian Foresters: Professor Dennis Lynch, Dept. of Forest Sciences, Colorado State University, Ft. Collins, CO 80523

Fellowship of Christian Librarians and Information Services: Dr. Paul Smezek, Wheaton College, Wheaton, IL 60187

Fellowship of Christian Musicians: Bill Anderson, Director, Dept. of Instrumental Music, Ponca City High School, Fifth and Overbrook, Ponca City, OK 74601

Health Physics Society Christian Fellowship: Dr. Steve Sims, 1002 Northview Dr., Lenior City, TN 37771

International Christian Visual Media Association: Paul Marks, Administrator, 4533 East Peakview Ave., Littleton, CO 80121–3231

National Association of Christians in Social Work: Dr. Ed Kuhlmann, Executive Director, PO Box 7090, St. Davids, PA 19087–7090

National Association of Professors of Christian Education: Ms. Carrie Salstrom, (Dr. Dennis Williams, Executive Administrator), 850 North Grove Avenue, Suite C, Elgin, IL 60120

NeuroScience Christian Fellowship: Dr. Kenneth J. Dormer, University of Oklahoma, Health Science Center, PO Box 26901, Oklahoma City, OK 73190

North American Association of Christian Foreign Language and Literature Faculty: Dr. Barbara Carvill, Calvin College, 3201 Burton St. SE, Grand Rapids, MI 49546

North American Association of Christians in Social Work: Rick Chamiec-Case, MSW, MAR, P.O. Box 121 Botsford, CT 06404–0121

Nurses Christian Fellowship: P.O. Box 7895, Madison, WI 53707–7895

Religion and Politics, Professor Hubert Morken: Dept. of Political Science, Oral Roberts University, Tulsa, OK 74171

Religious Speech Communication Association: Dr. Roxane Lulofs, Executive Secretary, Azusa Pacific University, 901 E. Alosta Ave., Azusa, CA 91702

Society of Christian Philosophers: Dr. Kelly J. Clark, Secretary/Treasurer, Dept. of Philosophy, Calvin College, 3201 Burton St. SE, Grand Rapids, MI 49546

NOTES ON CONTRIBUTORS

Lee Anne Chaney has taught biology for twenty-two years at Whitworth College in Spokane, Washington, where she is an associate professor. She trained in plant genetics at the University of New Hampshire and in botany and microbiology at the University of Arkansas. She worked as a clinical chemist after college and came of age during the Vietnam War. As an undergraduate she studied at Southwest Baptist College in Missouri and Beloit College in Wisconsin. Her research interests include ethnobotany as well as genetic control of reproduction in flowering plants. She especially enjoys collaborative and interdisciplinary teaching.

Robert A. Clark is professor of sociology at Whitworth College in Spokane, Washington. He has also taught at Gordon College in Wenham, Massachusetts, and at a state university. He has graduate degrees in sociology from the University of Oregon and Washington State University. His teaching and scholarly interests include marriage and family, sociological theory, and the relationship between Christianity and sociology. He has published in the areas of family life, Christianity and the sociology of knowledge, and faith and culture. He serves on the board of an ecumenical community service agency and is an elder in a Presbyterian church.

Harold Heie is director of the Center for Christian Studies at Gordon College and senior fellow at the Council for Christian Colleges and Universities. He previously served as vice president for academic affairs at Messiah College (Pa.) and Northwestern College (Iowa), after teaching mathematics at Gordon College and The King's College (N.Y.). He holds a Ph.D. in mechanical and aerospace engineering from Princeton University. He is coauthor, with David Wolfe, of *The Reality of Christian*

Learning: Strategies for Faith-Discipline Integration and *Slogans or Distinctives: Reforming Christian Higher Education.* He is a member of the Evangelical Covenant Church.

Michael T. Ingram is chair and associate professor of communications studies at Whitworth College in Spokane, Washington. For nine years he was also the director of forensics at Whitworth, coaching both individual events and parliamentary debate. He is a life-long Southern Baptist and is a licensed Southern Baptist minister. He is married and father of three children.

Lois Kieffaber has taught in both public and private institutions over the past twenty-five years, beginning with the Malayan Teachers College in Penang, Malaysia, as a Peace Corps volunteer. She currently teaches in the physics department at Whitworth College and also serves as team leader for an interdisciplinary course called The Scientific Tradition, which is a required course for all graduating students. Her research area is in atmospheric physics; she and her students observe the nighttime airglow to detect the presence of internal atmospheric gravity waves. Her research is supported by the National Science Foundation and has resulted in twenty-seven published papers and abstracts. Her other interests include mentoring young women pursuing scientific careers and improving science education for pre-service teachers. She grew up in the Church of the Brethren and now makes her church home with the Quakers. For recreation she enjoys reading and playing the piano.

Ron Kirkemo teaches international relations at Point Loma Nazarene University. Dr. Kirkemo received his B.A. in history from Pasadena College and his M.A and Ph.D. in international relations from American University. He is author of *An Introduction to International Law* (1974), *Between the Eagle and the Dove: The Christian and American Foreign Policy* (1976), and *For Zion's Sake: A History of Pasadena/Point Loma College* (1992). He also contributed "Renouncing the Use of Nuclear Weapons: Strategic Implications" to *Evangelicals and the Bishop's Letter* (1984), edited by Dean Curry, and "Point Loma Nazarene College: Modernization in Christian Higher Education" to *Models for Christian Higher Ed-*

ucation (1997), edited by Richard Hughes and William Adrian. Dr. Kirkemo is a member of the First Church of the Nazarene in San Diego and of the Christian Action Committee of the Southern California District of that denomination. He ran for the California state legislature in 1976 and served two terms on the Historical Site Board of the City of San Diego.

Edward Knippers holds a B.A. degree in art from Asbury College and an M.F.A. degree in painting from the University of Tennessee. He studied in the studios of Zao Wou-ki (1970) and Otto Eglau (1976) at the International Summer Academy of Fine Arts in Salzburg where he took the Prize of Salzburg in printmaking in 1976. He was also a fellow at S. W. Hayter's Atelier 17 in Paris (1980) and has studied at the Sorbonne and the Pennsylvania Academy of Fine Arts in Philadelphia. Mr. Knippers estimates that he has more than 150 awards and exhibitions (of which more than half are one-man shows and invitationals). Exhibition venues abroad include Canada, England, Greece, Italy, and Austria. Domestically he has exhibited at universities (Oklahoma, Kentucky, and numerous others), museums (Los Angeles County Museum of Art, the Virginia Museum, the Roanoke Museum, J. B. Speed Museum), and art centers (Biblical Arts Center, Dallas; Tennessee Fine Arts Center, Nashville; Southeast Center for Contemporary Art, Winston-Salem). His work is in numerous public and private collections including the Vatican, the Armand Hammer Museum, the Billy Graham Museum, Vanderbilt University, and the University of Oklahoma. Knippers has taught painting, drawing, printmaking, design, and art history at the University of Tennessee, Transylvania University, Asbury College, and Messiah College and has lectured and participated as a panelist at numerous other colleges and museums. Knippers is a founding member and serves on the board of directors of Christians in Visual Arts. He lives with his wife Diane in Arlington, Virginia. They attend Truro Episcopal Church in Fairfax where he sings in the choir.

Charlotte Y. Kroeker is interim vice president for advancement at Goshen College in Indiana, where she holds a concurrent title of visiting professor of music. She has been involved in church-related higher education for twenty-five years as a music professor, administrator, and development officer. Most recently she has served as a consultant in higher education, developing the Center for Church Music at Goshen College while continuing her work in church music and piano performance. She has a Ph.D. from Kansas State University, a M.M. in piano performance from Oklahoma City University, and a B.A. from Wheaton College in Illinois.

Arlin G. Meyer was raised on a farm in a Dutch Christian Reformed community in northwest Iowa. He attended Dordt College for two years and then received his B.A. in English from Calvin College. After teaching English for four years at Holland Christian High School, Meyer earned his M.A. in English at the University of Michigan and a Ph.D. from Ohio University. Since 1967, Meyer has been a member of the faculty at Valparaiso University, teaching in the department of English and holding a number of administrative positions. He was director of the Valparaiso University Study Center in Cambridge, England, for two years, chair of the department of English for three years, and dean of Christ College (the honors college) for twelve years. For the past eleven years, Meyer has served as program director of the Lilly Fellows Program in Humanities and the Arts. Raised and catechized in the Christian Reformed denomination, Meyer has been a member of Immanuel Lutheran Church since he moved to Valparaiso with his family.

Arlin C. Migliazzo, a native of Southern California, has taught history at both private and public colleges and universities including Biola University, Pacific Lutheran University, Washington State University, Judson Baptist College, Spokane Community College, and Keimyung University in Daegu, Republic of Korea. He is currently professor of history and director of faculty development at Whitworth College and teaches primarily in modern world history, contemporary U.S. history and culture, and the philosophy of history. He received his B.A. from Biola University (1974), the M.A. from Northern Arizona University (1975), and the Ph.D. from Washington State University (1982). Dr. Migliazzo has published in ethnic studies, Pacific

Northwest history, comparative democratic development, and the history and culture of higher education. His book *Lands of True and Certain Bounty* is the first comprehensive compilation of the writings of the eighteenth-century Swiss explorer and colonial enthusiast Jean Pierre Purry. He has received a number of research grants and was Fulbright/Hays Scholar of American Studies at Keimyung University in 1990. Since the founding of the Lilly Fellows Program in Humanities and the Arts in 1991, Professor Migliazzo has served as the faculty representative from Whitworth College to the program. He was elected to the Lilly Network Board in 2001. The faculty of Whitworth selected him as the recipient of the college's 1996–97 Teaching Excellence Award. He is currently deep into his sixth year of piano study. His West Coast Presbyterian proclivities remain strong, although he and his family currently attend and serve at an independent church in Spokane.

Elizabeth Murray Morelli is a professor in the philosophy department at Loyola Marymount University. She attended Santa Clara University and did her graduate work at the University of Toronto. Her research is into the thought of Lonergan, Kierkegaard, and Sartre. She teaches in areas of existential phenomenology and ancient Greek philosophy. She is the author of *Anxiety: A Study of the Affectivity of Moral Consciousness* (1985) and is coeditor with her husband, Mark D. Morelli, of Bernard Lonergan's *Understanding and Being* (1980/1990) and *The Lonergan Reader* (1997). She is founder and current president of the Lonergan Philosophical Society. She has been the Loyola Marymount faculty representative to the Lilly Fellows Program in Humanities and the Arts since its founding in 1991, and she enjoyed a term on its national Network Board. She also formerly served a term on the Executive Council of the American Catholic Philosophical Society. Currently, she is a member of the National Seminar on Jesuit Higher Education. She lives in Los Angeles with her husband and two sons, and she enjoys rock climbing in the desert and the High Sierras. She is a board member of the Southern California Mountaineering Association.

Shirley A. Mullen teaches modern British and European history at Westmont College in Santa Barbara, California. She grew up in a small holiness denomination in eastern Canada. Shirley attended Houghton College and did her graduate work at the University of Toronto, the University of Minnesota, and the University of Wales. She holds doctorates in the fields of both history and philosophy. Except for her two years in residence-life work at Bethel College in St. Paul, Minnesota, Shirley has spent her working life in the department of history at Westmont. Her primary area of scholarly interest is the legacy of the Enlightenment, particularly in Britain. In addition to studying history, Shirley enjoys reading theology and ethics, and traveling—especially in Europe. She has taken eight student groups to Europe on a study-travel course entitled Art and Ideas of the Western Tradition.

John Steven Paul chairs the department of theatre and television arts at Valparaiso University, Valparaiso, Indiana, where he teaches dramatic literature, play directing, and play writing. He also directs plays for the Valparaiso University Theatre. Dr. Paul received the Ph.D. from the University of Wisconsin-Madison. He is also the director of Soul Purpose, the liturgical drama troupe of the Valparaiso University Theatre. The Valparaiso University Alumni Association selected Professor Paul to receive its Distinguished Teaching Award for 1999. He was inducted into the Dickmeyer Professorship of Christian Education in August 2001.

Mary Stewart Van Leeuwen is a social and cross-cultural psychologist who is resident scholar at Eastern University's Center for Christian Women in Leadership. Her research interests include philosophy of social science, human sexuality, and the interaction of gender with theology and church history. She has done fieldwork in Central and West Africa and has had previous academic appointments at York University in Toronto and Calvin College in Michigan. Her most recent book, coedited with Anne Carr, is *Religion, Feminism and the Family* (Westminster/ John Knox Press, 1996).

Charles K. Wilber received his bachelor's (1957) and master's (1960) degrees from the University of Portland and the Ph.D.

from the University of Maryland (1966). He worked in public accounting and received his CPA certificate from the state of Oregon in 1959. He has taught at Multnomah College, Catholic University of Ponce, Puerto Rico, Trinity College (Washington, D.C.), and The American University. Since 1975 he has been at the University of Notre Dame as professor of economics. He chaired the economics department from 1975 to 1984 and has served as a consultant to the Peace Corps, Interamerican Development Bank, George Meany Center for Labor Studies, The United States Bishops' Committee on Catholic Social Thought and the U.S. Economy, and the Oblates of Mary Immaculate North/South Dialogue in Washington, D.C., and Lima, Peru. His major research areas are economic development, economic ethics, and the relation between faith and economic practice. Dr. Wilber has published in excess of one hundred articles and has authored *The Soviet Model and Underdeveloped Countries* (1969), coauthored with Kenneth Jameson *An Inquiry into the Poverty of Economics* (1983) and *Beyond Reaganomics: A Further Inquiry into the Poverty of Economics* (1990), and coedited *Directions in Economic Development* (1979), *Religious Values and Development* (1980), *Socialist Models of Development* (1982), and *The Political Economy of Development and Underdevelopment*, 6th ed., with Kenneth Jameson. He also coedited *Growth with Equity: Essays on Economic Development* (1979) with Mary Evelyn Jegan, and *Capitalism and Democracy: Schumpeter Revisited* (1985) with Richard D. Coe. His most recently completed research includes "The Ethics of Consumption: A Roman Catholic View," in *The Ethics of Consumption and Global Stewardship* (1997), edited by David Crocker, and *Economics, Ethics and Public Policy* (1998).

INDEX